MEDIA, FEMINISM, CULTURAL STUDIES

Stepping Forward: Essays, Lectures and Interviews
by Wolfgang Iser

Wild Zones: Pornography, Art and Feminism
by Kelly Ives

Global Media Warning: Explorations of Radio, Television and the Press
by Oliver Whitehorne

'Cosmo Woman': The World of Women's Magazines
by Oliver Whitehorne

Andrea Dworkin
by Jeremy Mark Robinson

Cixous, Irigaray, Kristeva: The Jouissance of French Feminism
by Kelly Ives

Sex in Art: Pornography and Pleasure in Painting and Sculpture
by Cassidy Hughes

The Erotic Object: Sexuality in Sculpture
From Prehistory to the Present Day
by Susan Quinnell

Women in Pop Music
by Helen Challis

Detonation Britain: Nuclear War In the UK
by Jeremy Mark Robinson

Julia Kristeva: Art, Love, Melancholy, Philosophy, Semiotics
by Kelly Ives

Luce Irigaray: Lips, Kissing, and the Politics of Sexual Difference
by Kelly Ives

Helene Cixous I Love You: The Jouissance of Writing
by Kelly Ives

The Poetry of Cinema
by John Madden

The Sacred Cinema of Andrei Tarkovsky
by Jeremy Mark Robinson

Feminism and Shakespeare
by B.D. Barnacle

The Cinema of Richard Linklater
by Thomas A. Christie

Walerian Borowczyk
by Jeremy Mark Robinson

The Cinema of Hayao Miyazaki
Jeremy Mark Robinson

Liv Tyler
by Thomas A. Christie

EROTIC ART
In the Renaissance

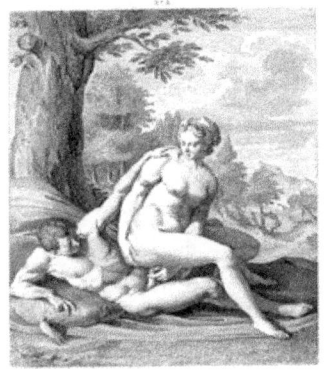

ANGÉLIQUE ET MÉDOR

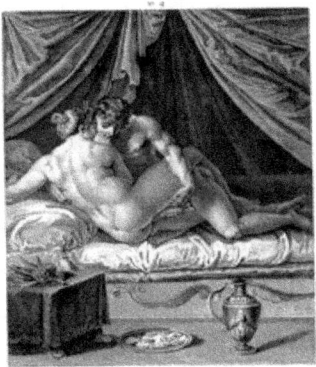

ANTOINE ET CLÉOPATRE

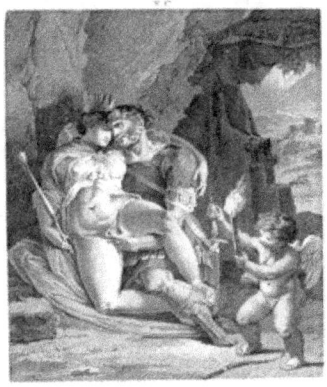

ÉNÉE ET DIDON

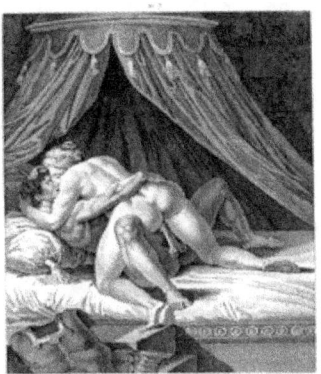

MARS ET VÉNUS

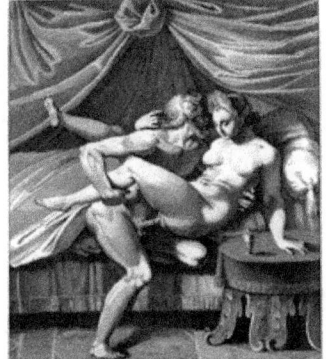

JUPITER ET JUNON

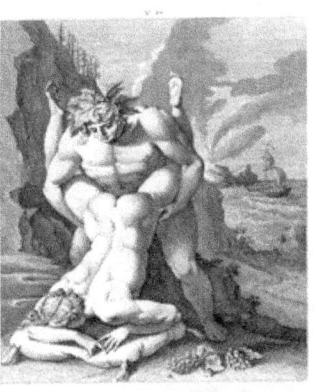

BACHUS ET ARIANE

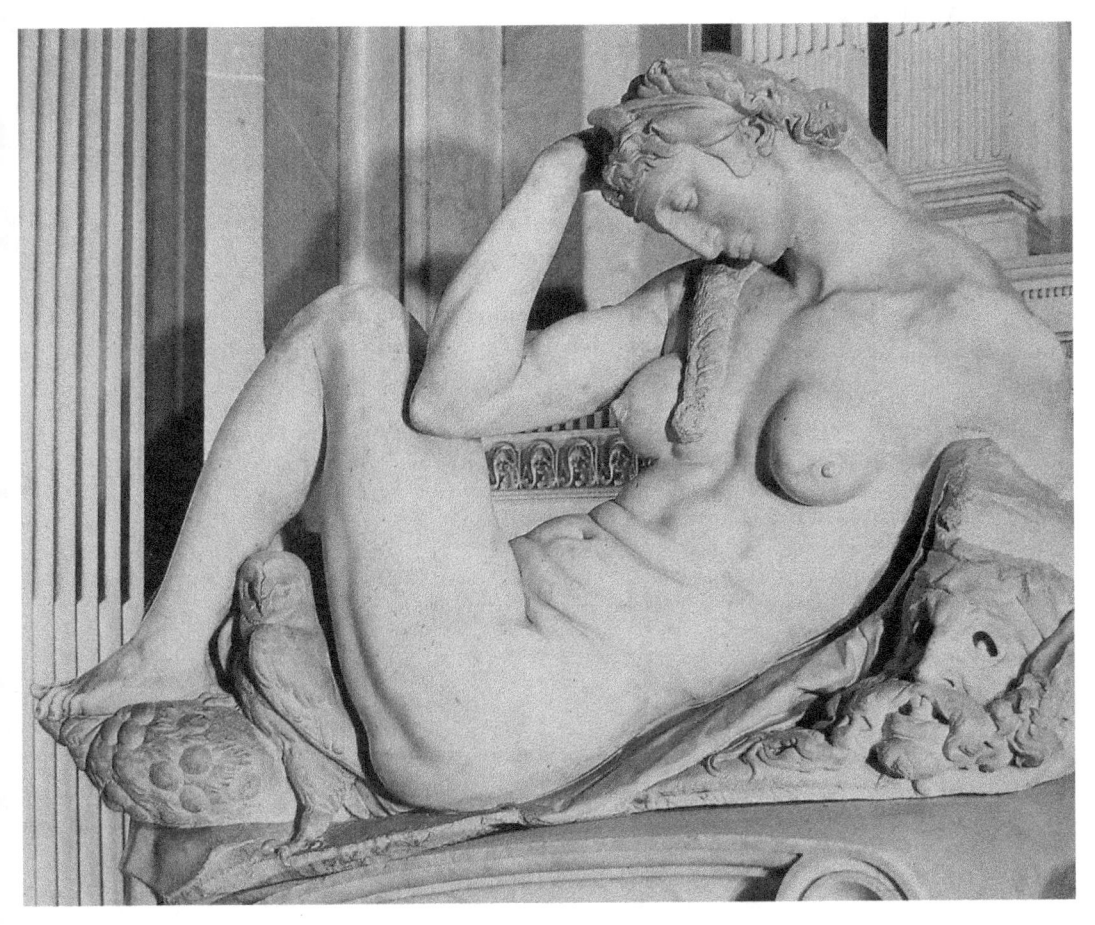

EROTIC ART
In the Renaissance

Cassidy Hughes

Crescent Moon

First published 2015.
© Cassidy Hughes 1998, 2015.

Printed and bound in the U.S.A.
Set in Book Antiqua 10 on 14pt.
Designed by Radiance Graphics.

British Library Cataloguing in Publication data

Hughes, Cassidy
Erotic Art In the Renaissance
I. Title
704.9

ISBN-13 9781861715036 (Hbk)
ISBN-13 9781861715128 (Pbk)

CRESCENT MOON PUBLISHING
P.O. Box 1312, Maidstone, Kent, ME14 5XU
Great Britain, www.crmoon.com

CONTENTS

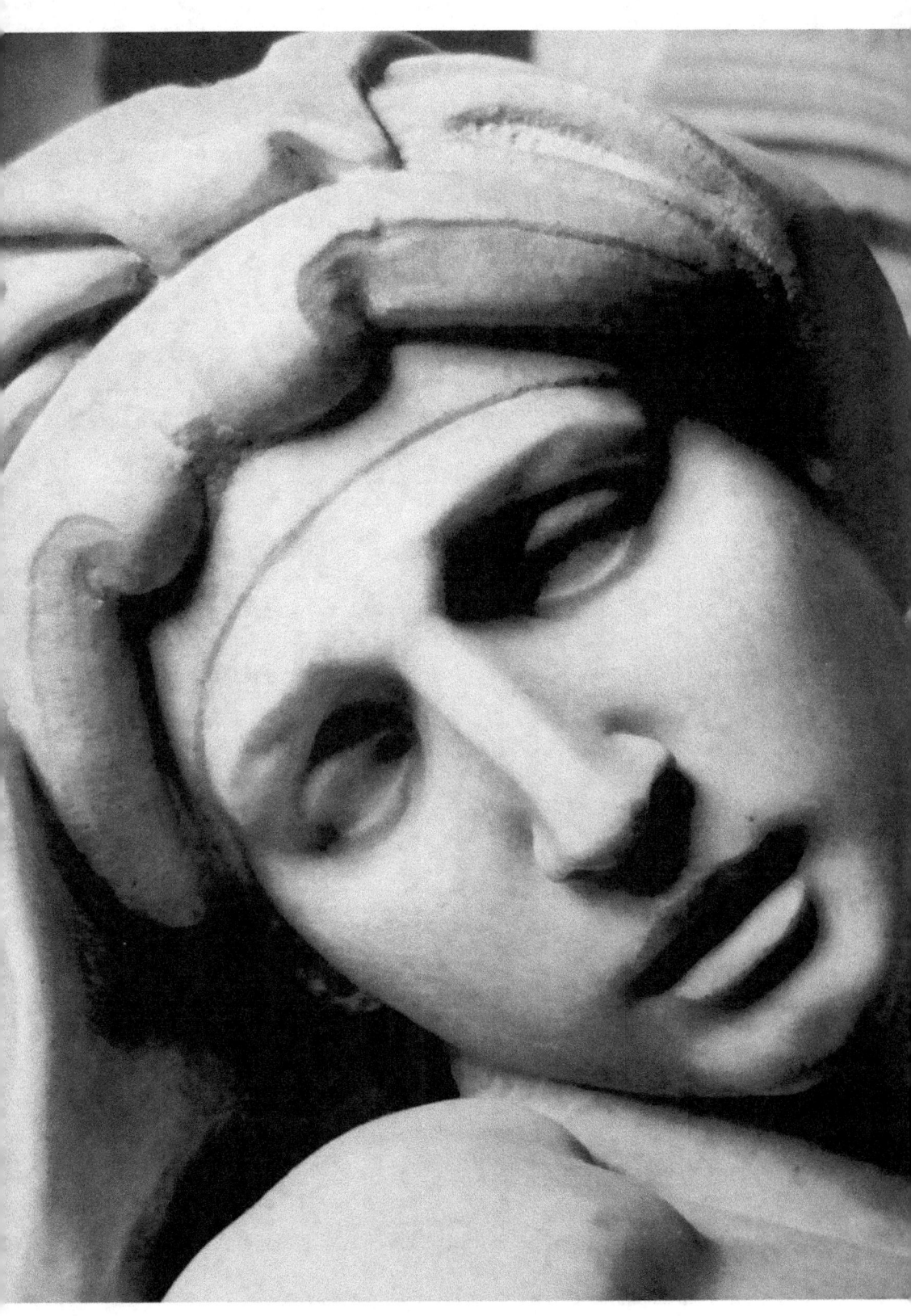

Michelangelo, Dawn, detail, Medici Chapel, Florence

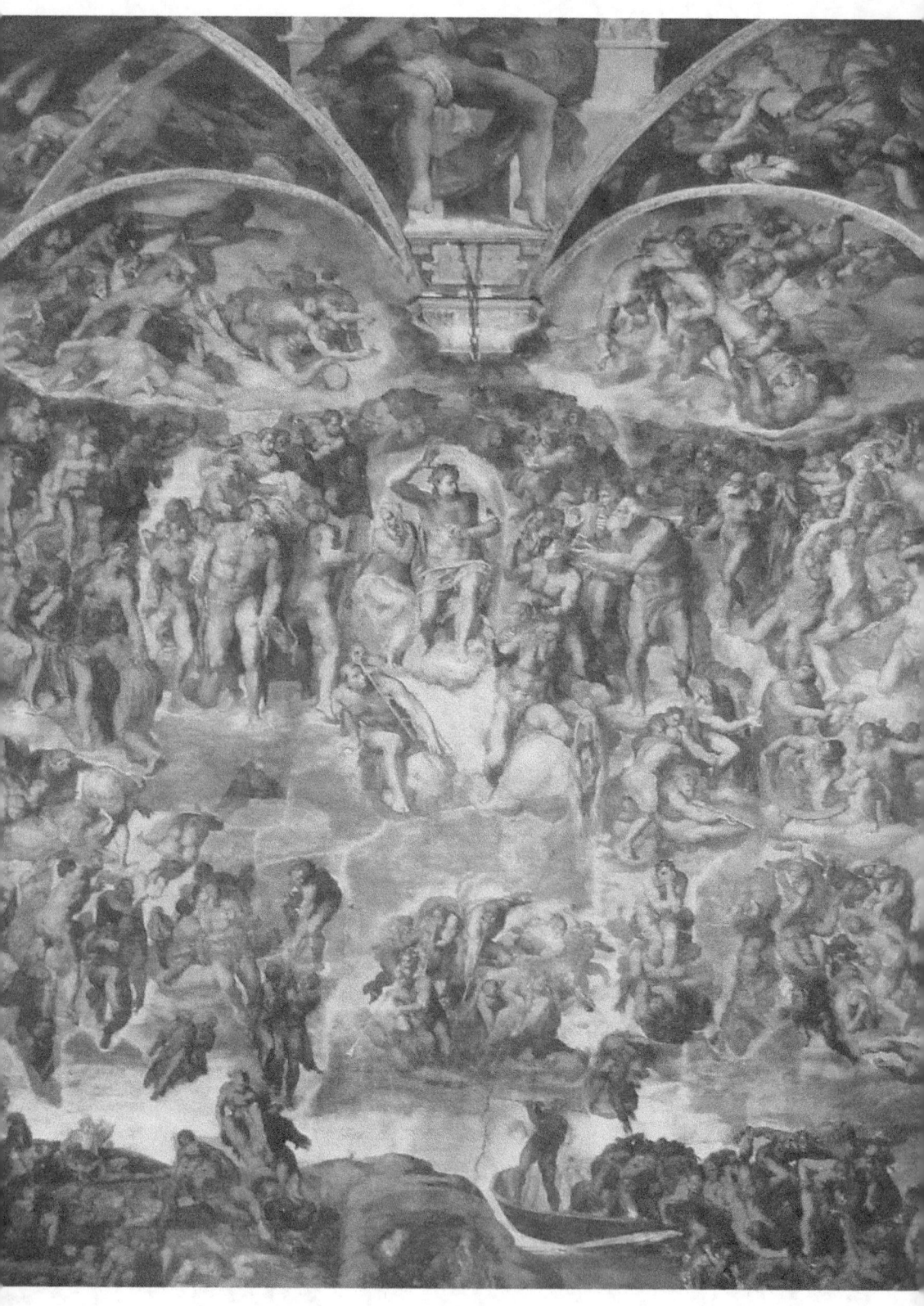

Michelangelo, The Last Judgement, Vatican, Rome

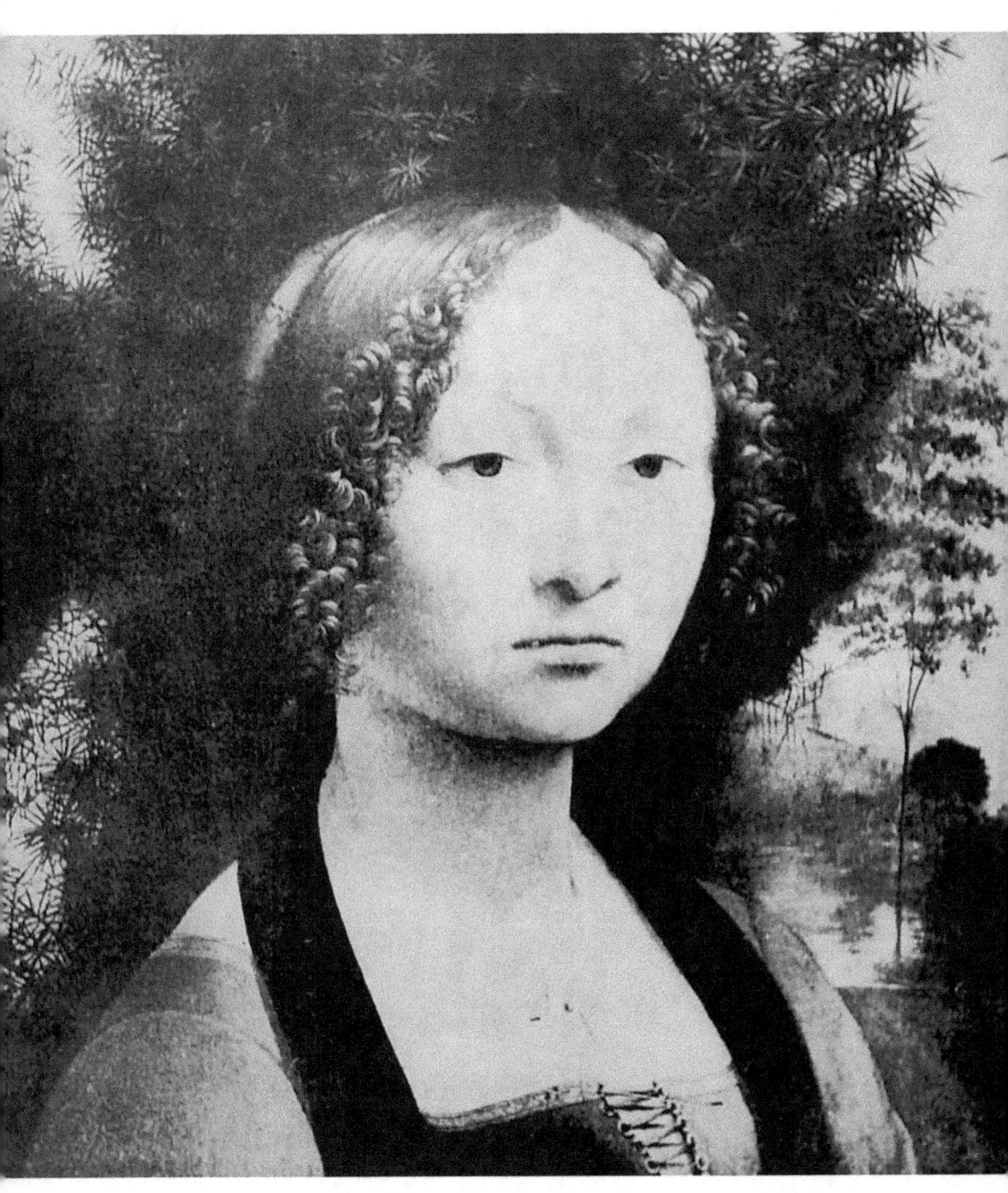

Leonardo da Vinci, Portrait of a Woman (Ginerva Benci?), c. 1474-76, National
Gallery of Art, Washington

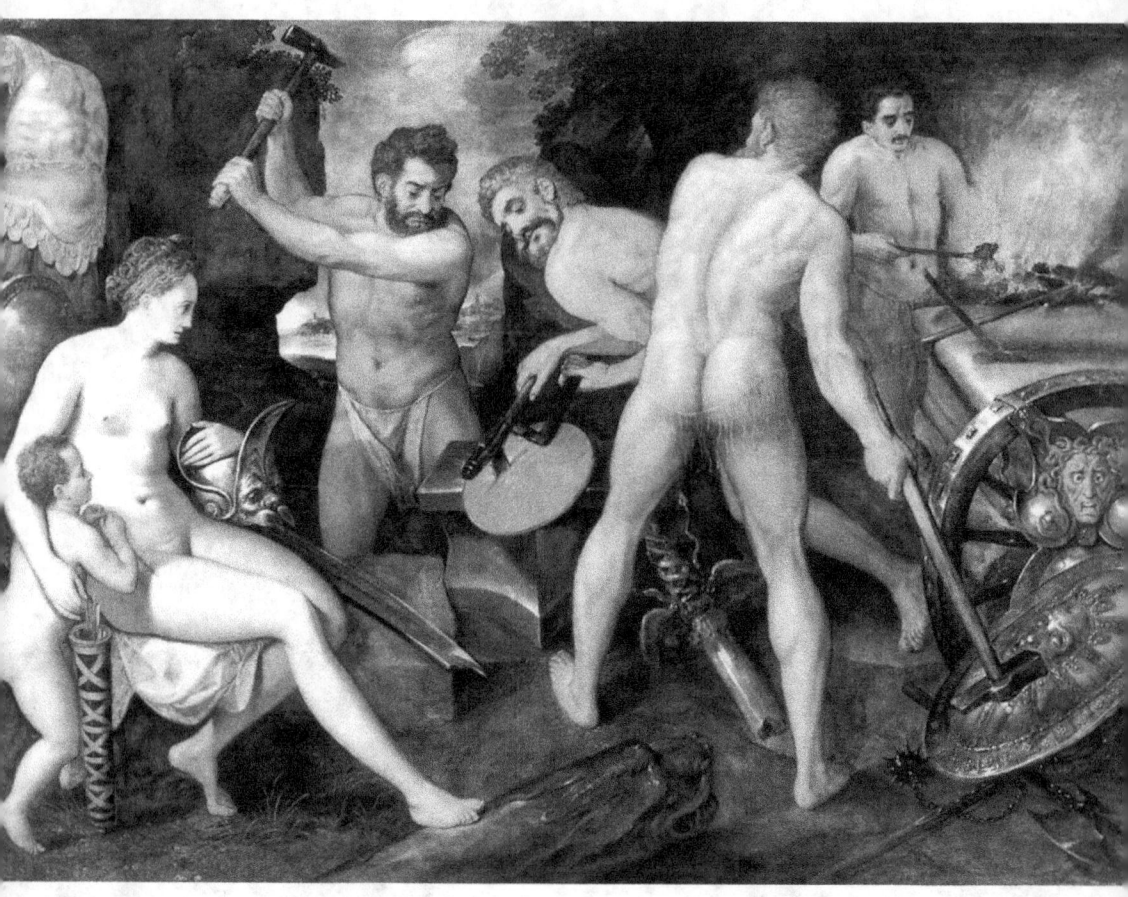

Frans Floris, Venus in the Forge of Vulcan, c. 1560-64

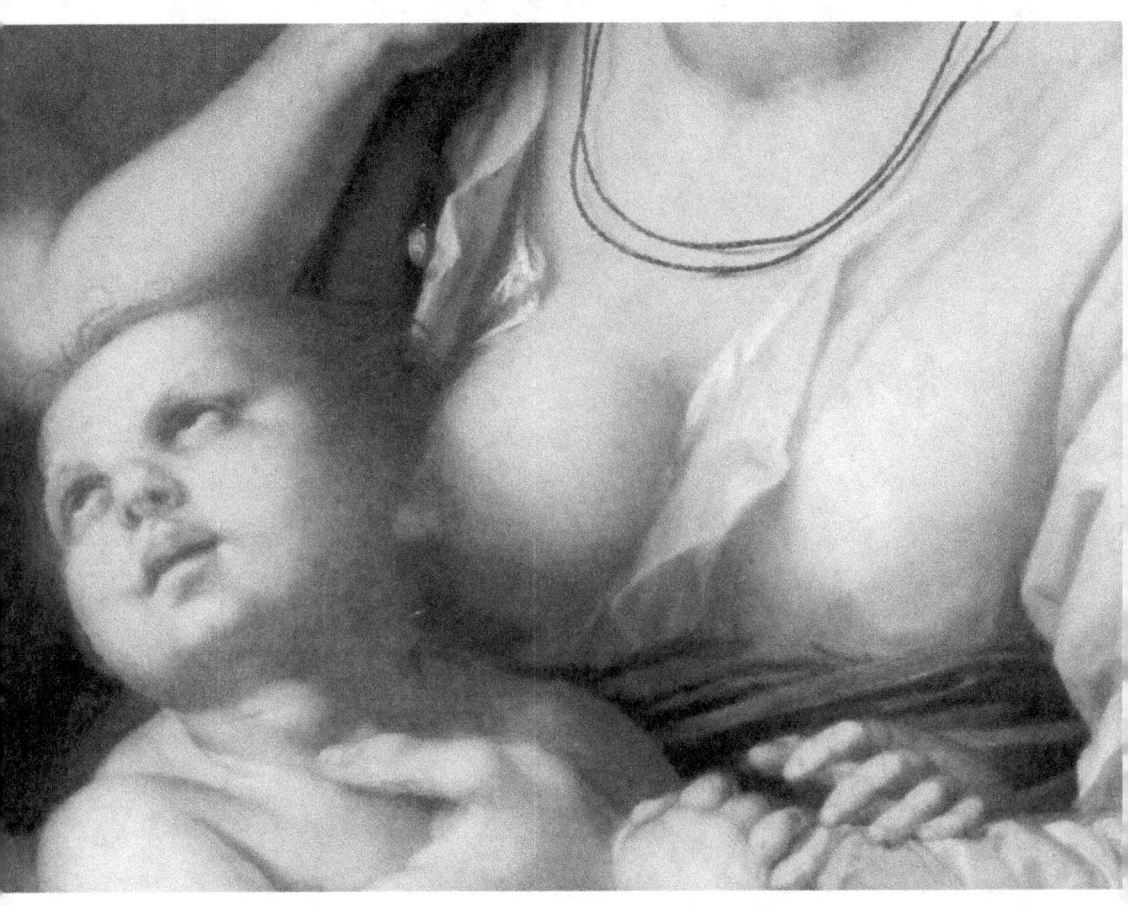

Andrea del Sarto, Madonna and Child, detail

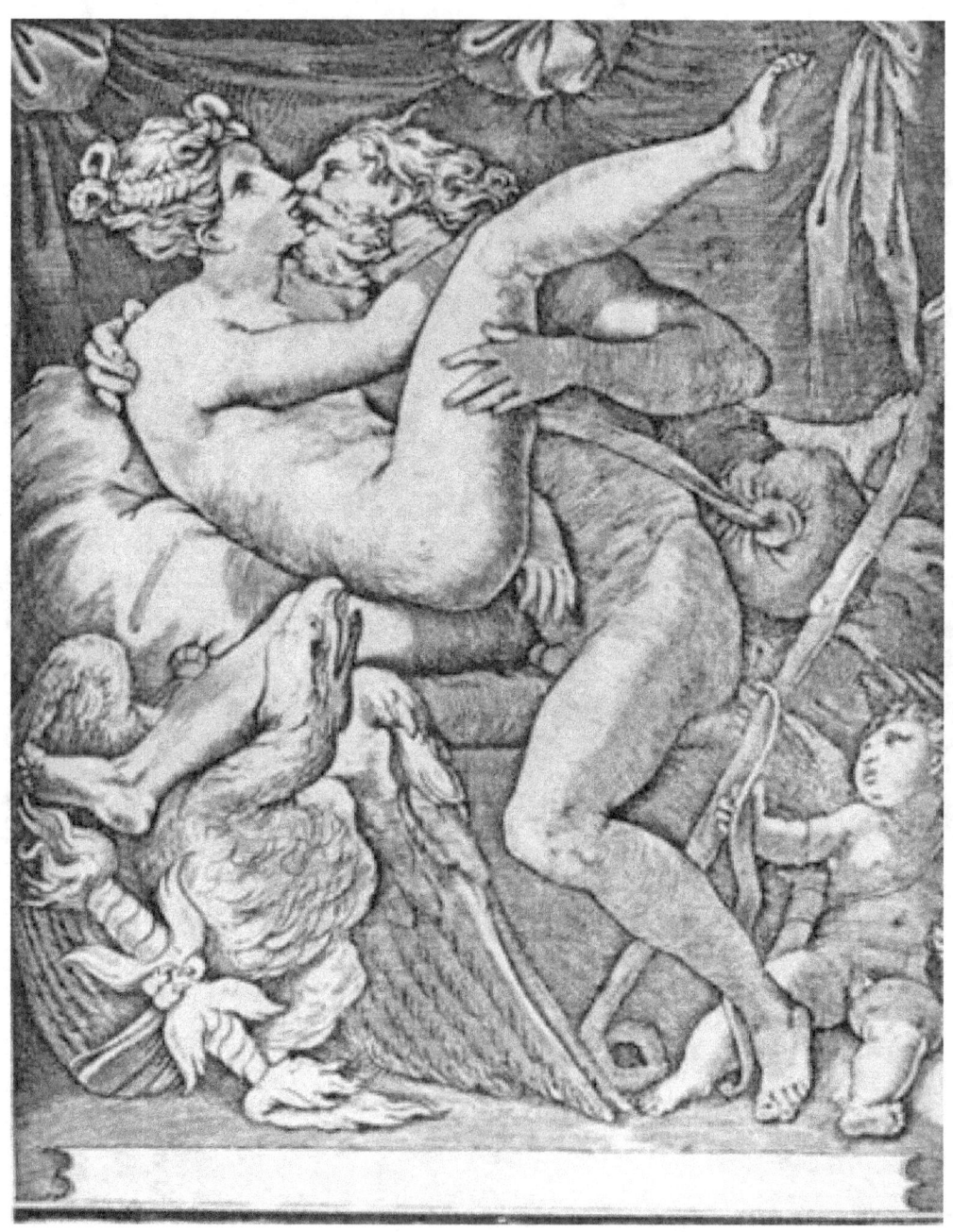

Perino de Vaga

The first part of this book on Renaissance erotic art uses short entries about aspects of erotic art (with examples from the whole history of erotic art).

The bulk of the second part of the book focusses on the celebrated artists of the Renaissance whose work is considered erotic, as well as many anonymous works.

Part One

Issues In Erotic Art

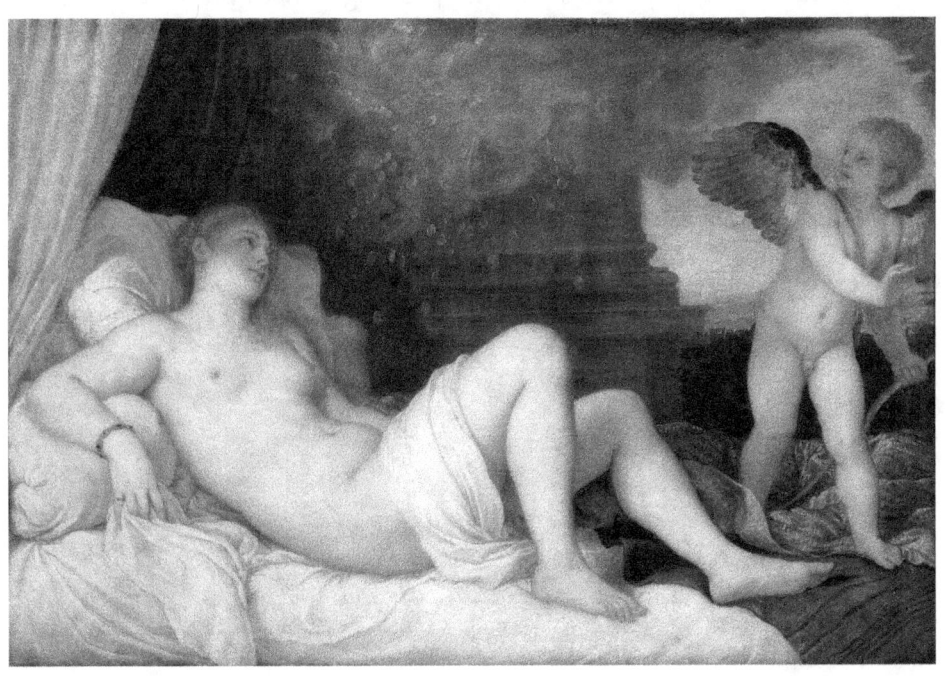

EROTIC ART AND PORNOGRAPHY

The establishment art historical view of erotic art and pornography is that true erotic or high art engenders quiet contemplation, a detached ravishing of the senses, a meditation on Platonic, Aristotlean and Kantian ideas of 'beauty' and æsthetics. 'High art', which is legitimate art, art which justifies itself by its 'genius' or obvious 'greatness', is about distance and disinterested pleasure. The high art nude, in painting or sculpture, in the patriarchal view, justifies its existence by the brilliance of its production, the sumptuousness of its colour and form, the marvel of its human touches, the grandeur of its design, the loftiness of its ambition, the dynamism of its structures, and so on. As that producer of exquisite bodies, French Neo-Classical artist J.A.D. Ingres, wrote:

> There are not two arts, there is only one: it is the one which has as its foundation the beautiful, which is eternal and natural.[1]

---

1 J.A.D. Ingres, quoted in R. Goldwater, 216

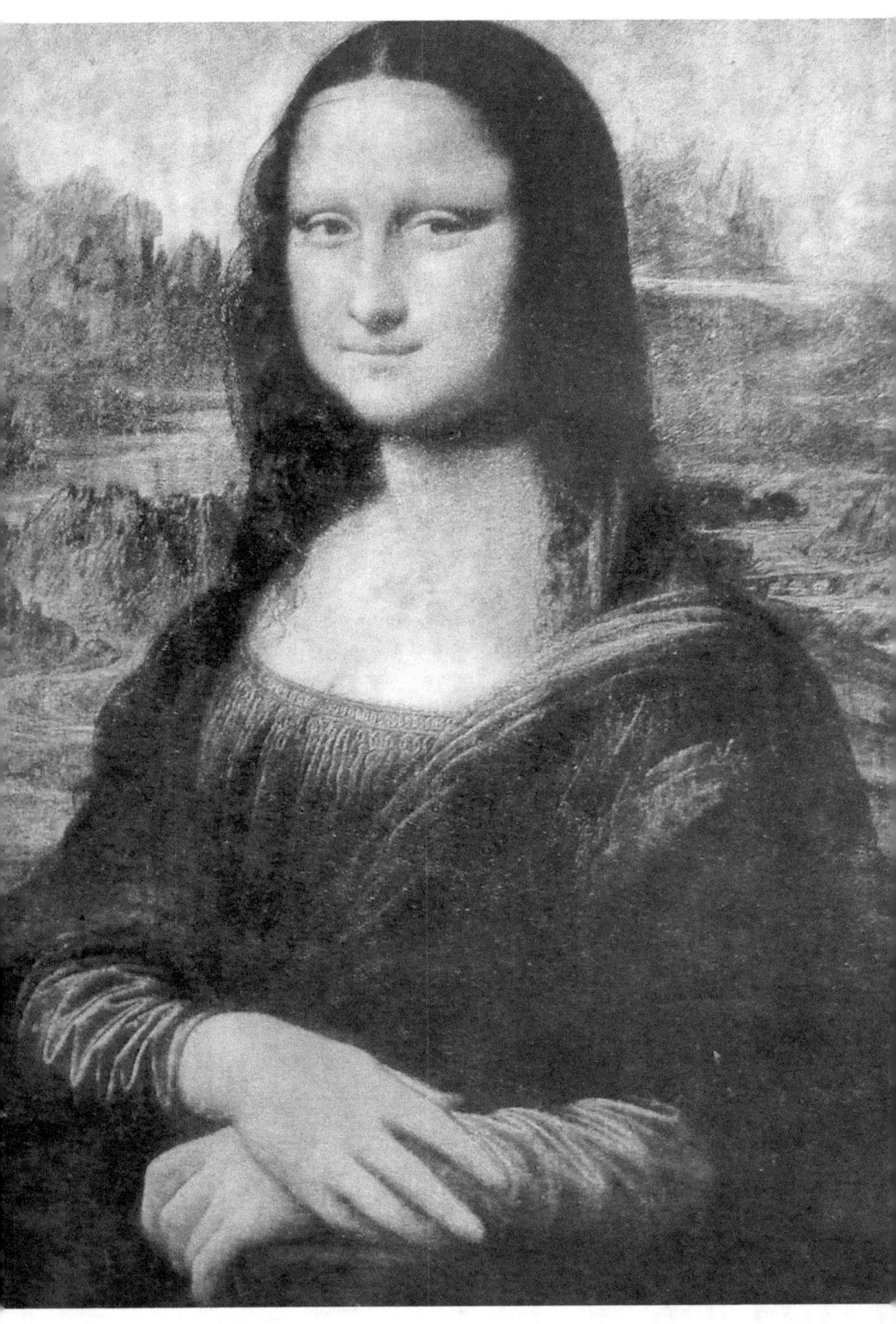

EROTIC ART VERSUS PORNOGRAPHY

We know the male/ patriarchal view of the art versus pornography debate. Eroticism is justified and good because it is 'high art', it is superbly crafted, it is a 'work of art'. Thus the Kronhausens, the organizers of a major exhibition of 'erotic art' (of 1968),[1] write:

> one can perhaps distinguish between pornography and art. The criterion would be that the more a picture contains evidence of interpretative, creative elaboration, the closer it is to art.[2]

For the Kronhausens, as for so many artists and philosophers and intellectuals, erotic art is art because it is done well. Pornography is simply bad art.

Many guardians of æsthetics, many professors of art history and dons of 'the beautiful' go along with this view. Kenneth Clark is a typical establishment critic who puts forward the patriarchal view: nudes are OK provided they are æsthetically pleasing, provided they remain 'in the realm of contemplation' as he put it.[3]

1 The 'first international exhibition of erotic art' was at the Museum of Art, Lund, Sweden, and Aarhus, Denmark, in 1968
2 Phyllis & Eberhard Kronhausen: *Erotic Art: A survey of erotic fact and fancy in the fine arts*, W.H. Allen, 1971, 3
3 Quoted in Lord Longford: *Pornography: The Longford Report*, Coronet, 1972, 99f

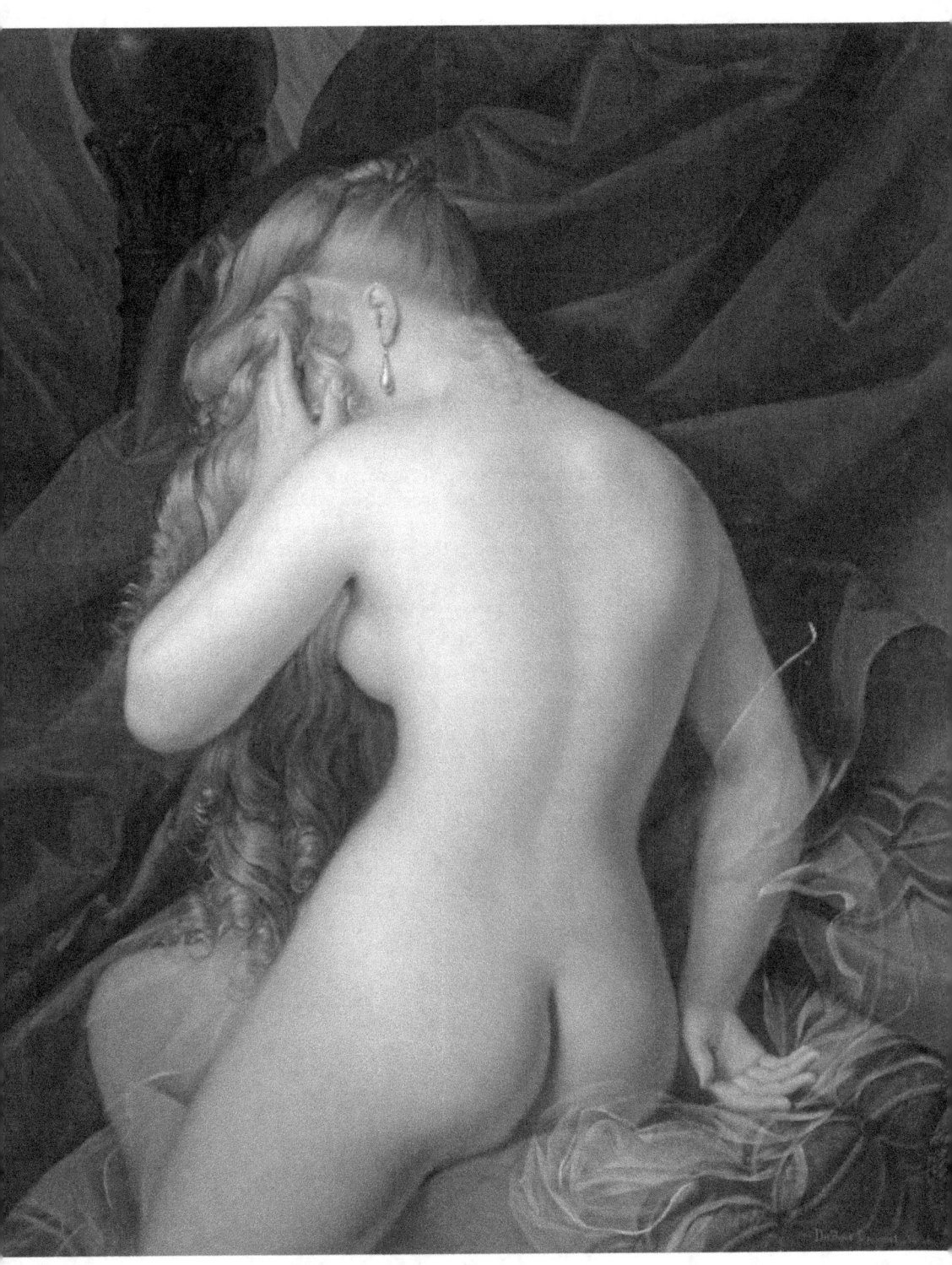

Alexandre-Jean Dubois-Drahonet,
Female Nude, 19th century

THE FEMALE NUDE

The 'sublime' qualities of high art, to use one popular adjective of art criticism, are crucial to its success, as Carol M. Armstrong notes in her essay on Edgar Degas:

> One of the things any painted object does is to resist signification at some level because of its very objecthood. And the female nude – because of *its* objecthood may be seen as almost emblematic of that level of resistance. In fact, the female nude has been linked to that stratum of painting most in tension with the work of signification – the stratum we connect to what we call, inadequately, "abstraction"; facture, the handling of paint per se, foregrounded as an obvious fact of the painting. Femaleness and facture, facture and the female nude, they go together somehow. One need only think of Titian, the first great painter of the female nude in the Western tradition.[1]

Much as worshippers properly gaze at an icon or an image of a deity with wonder, the art critic and historian kneels before 'great art' and worships it.[2] The female nude is the highest form of non-religious art, and it confers a religious awe in its æsthete consumers. The emphasis is on Neoplatonic terms such as 'purity', 'beauty', 'form' and 'symmetry'. As Aristotle puts it: '[t]he chief forms of beauty are order and symmetry and definiteness.'[3]

---

1 Carol M. Armstrong; "Edgar Degas and the Representation of the Female Body", in S. Suleiman, 223
2 See Pierre Bourdieu: *Distinction: A Social Critique of the Judgment of Taste*, tr Richard Nice, Routledge & Kegan Paul, New York 1984
3 Aristotle: *Metaphysics*, book XIII, in Albert Hofstadter & Richard Kuhns, eds: *Philosophies of Art and Beauty: Selected Readings in Aesthetics From Plato to Heidegger*, Random House, New York 1964, 96

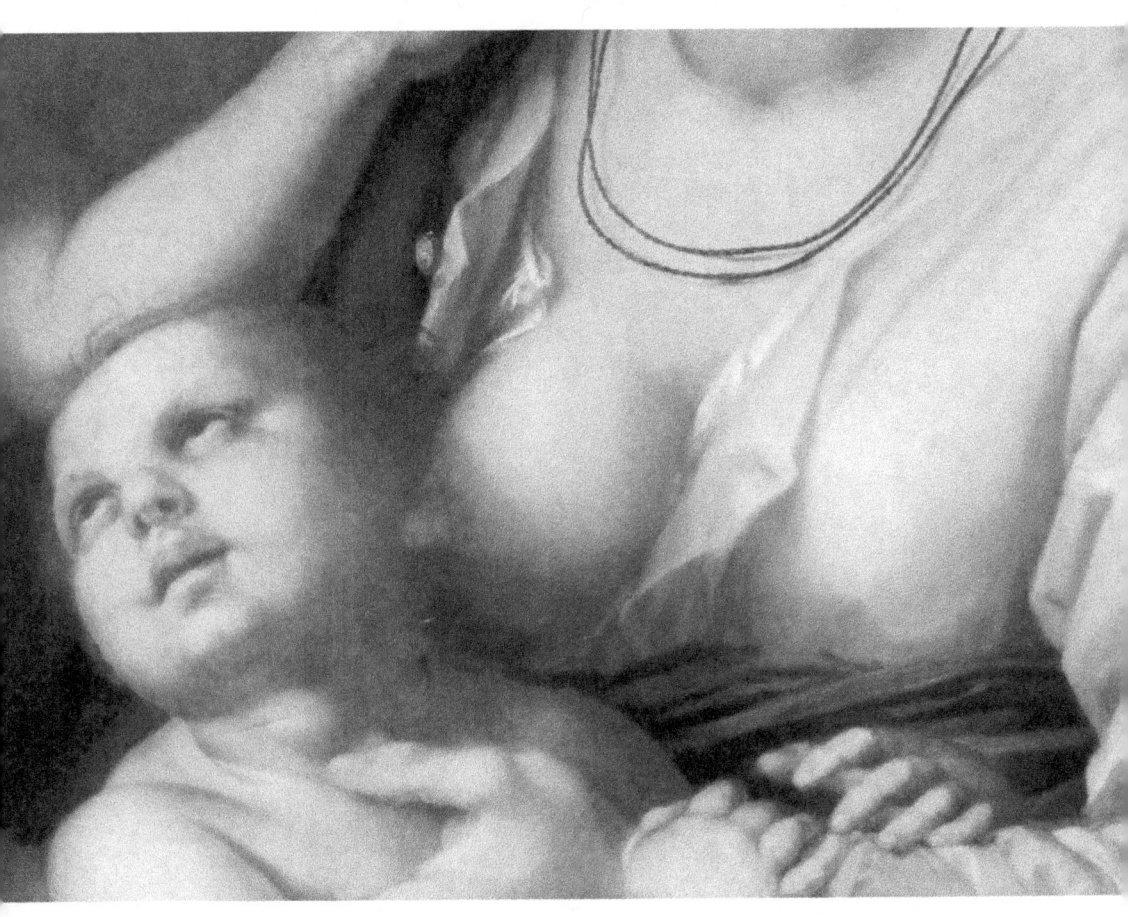

Andrea del Sarto, Madonna and Child, detail

THE FEMALE NUDE

Depictions of the female nude and of erotic gestures or acts can be problematic. The female body, for instance, is already 'objectified' even before it is painted or represented. Once painted, it becomes a cultural artifact, a mass of codes, meanings, signs and values, none of them fixed, all of them dependent on the context of consumption, dependent on the socio-political make-up of the viewer, and so on. None of this, however, has prevented erotic nudes and female nudes from being produced.

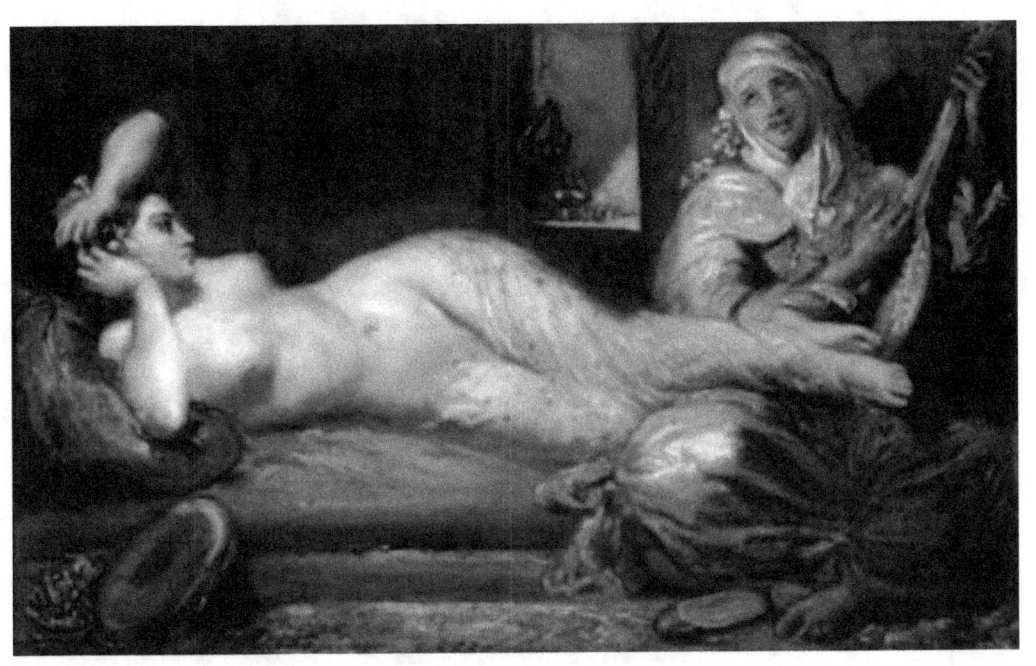

Théodore Chasséreau (1819-56)

William Bouguereau,
The Birth of Venus,
above

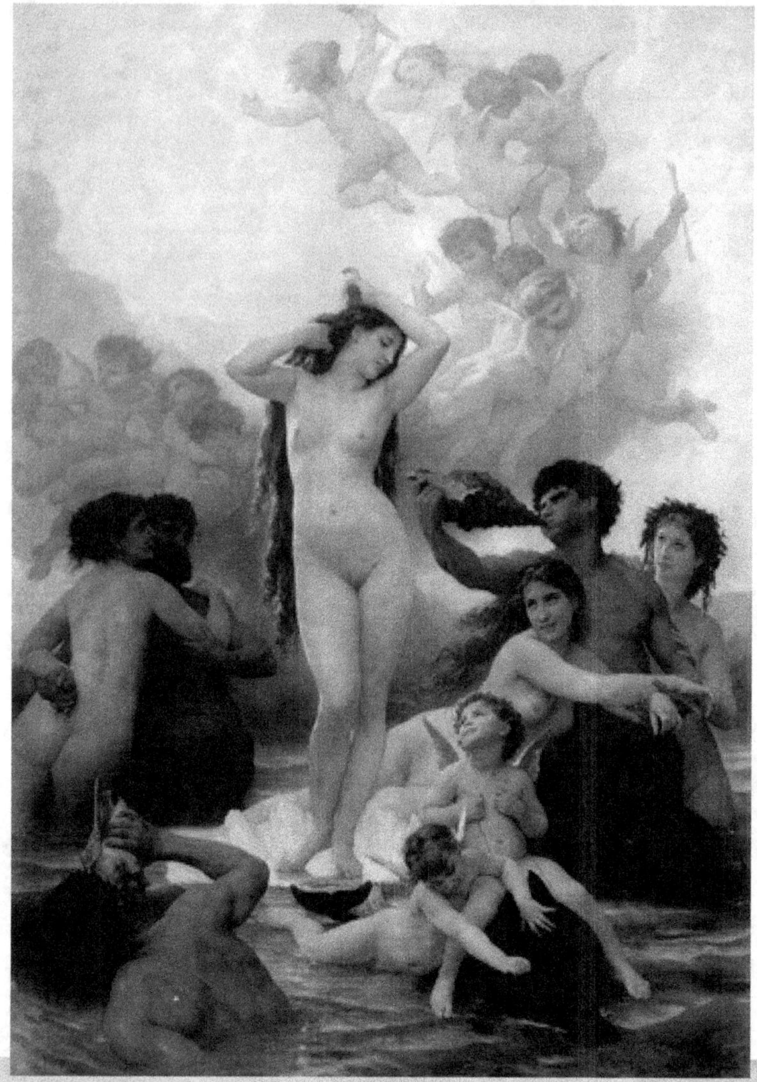

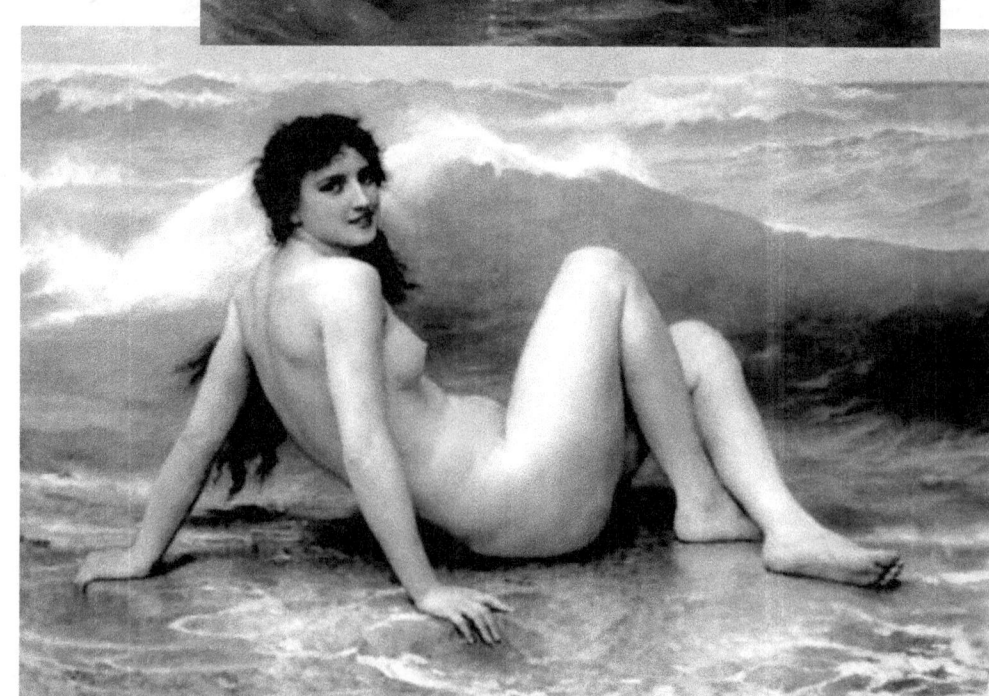

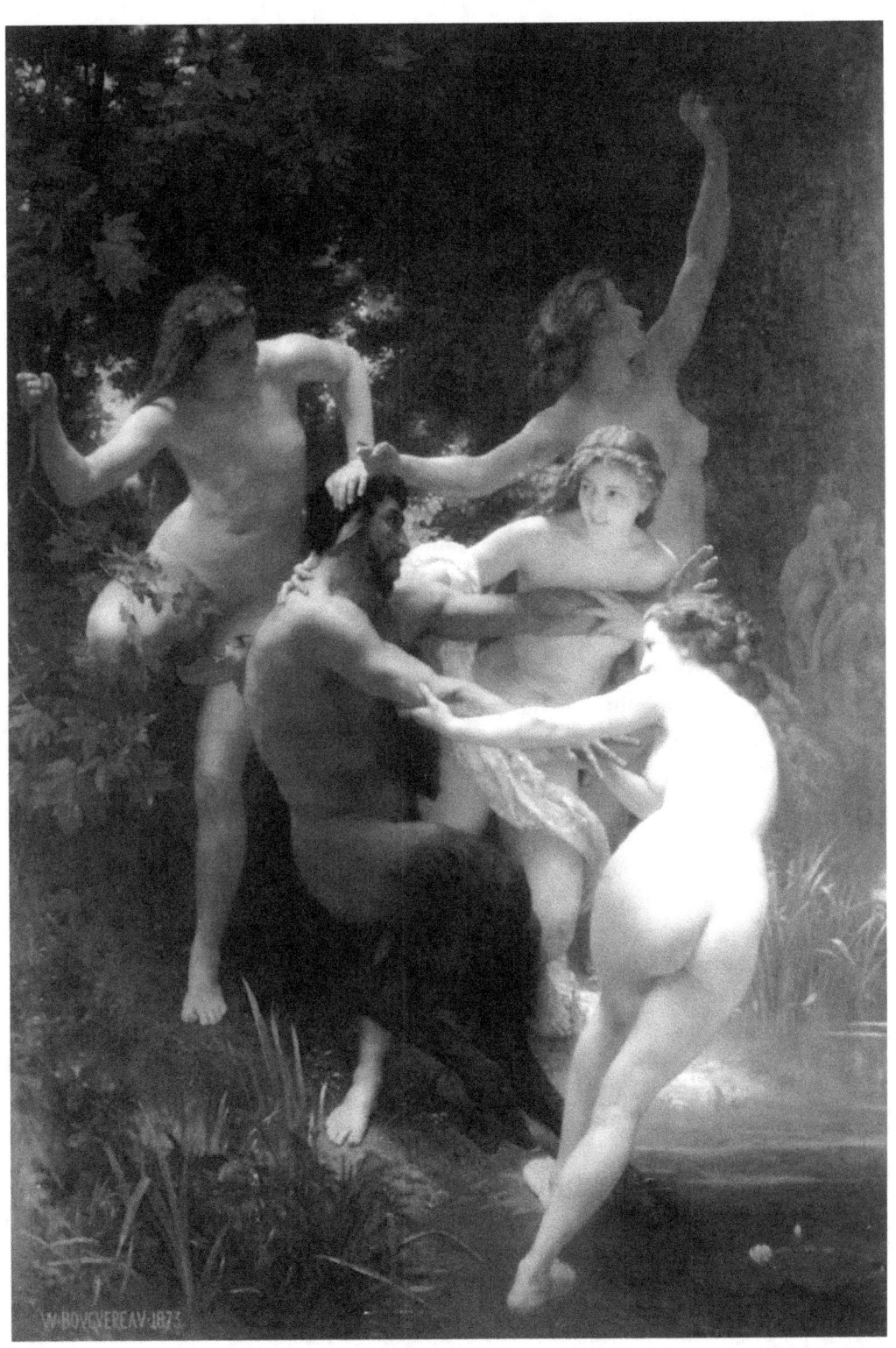

William Bouguereau, Nymphs and Satyr

THE FEMALE NUDE

Context is crucial in matters of eroticism. An image that is seen as 'erotic' in one context can easily be seen as 'pornographic' in another context. Take an image out of context, and soon a new, often ironic set of meanings are set in motion. Jacques Derrida has shown that a text may have many contexts, and is not fixed in one context forever.[1] Feminist artists have explored meanings and contexts, by placing traditional images in new contexts. Meanings are constantly in a state of flux. Nothing is fixed anymore. As Catherine Belsey writes: 'meanings circulate between text, ideology and reader' (144). Roland Barthes wrote that '[a]ll images are polysemous...they imply, underlying their signifiers, a floating chain of signifieds'. The consumer has the ability to 'choose some and ignore others'.[2] The cultural environment, socialization, economy, power relations, education, any number of factors can influence the meanings drawn from an image. With the female nude, in painting or erotica, the meanings are contextualized as erotic. As Anne Hollander notes, the nude always has a sexual dimension to it.

For instance, men can 'possess' and yet never 'possess' a female nude painting. It remains an image. The 'possession' or consumption is of a cerebral order, which is why critics and professors such as Kenneth Clark, Bernard Berenson, Jacob Burckhardt, Walter Pater, John Ruskin, Aby Warburg, Roger Fry, Ernst Gombrich and other art critics emphasize the *intellectual* nature of enjoying art. Art for the head, not the body, art for the eyes, not the full five senses.

---

1 Jacques Derrida: *Eperons. Les styles de Nietzsche*, Flammarion, Paris 1978, 103f
2 Roland Barthes: *Image-Music-Text*, Hill & Wang, New York 1977, 39

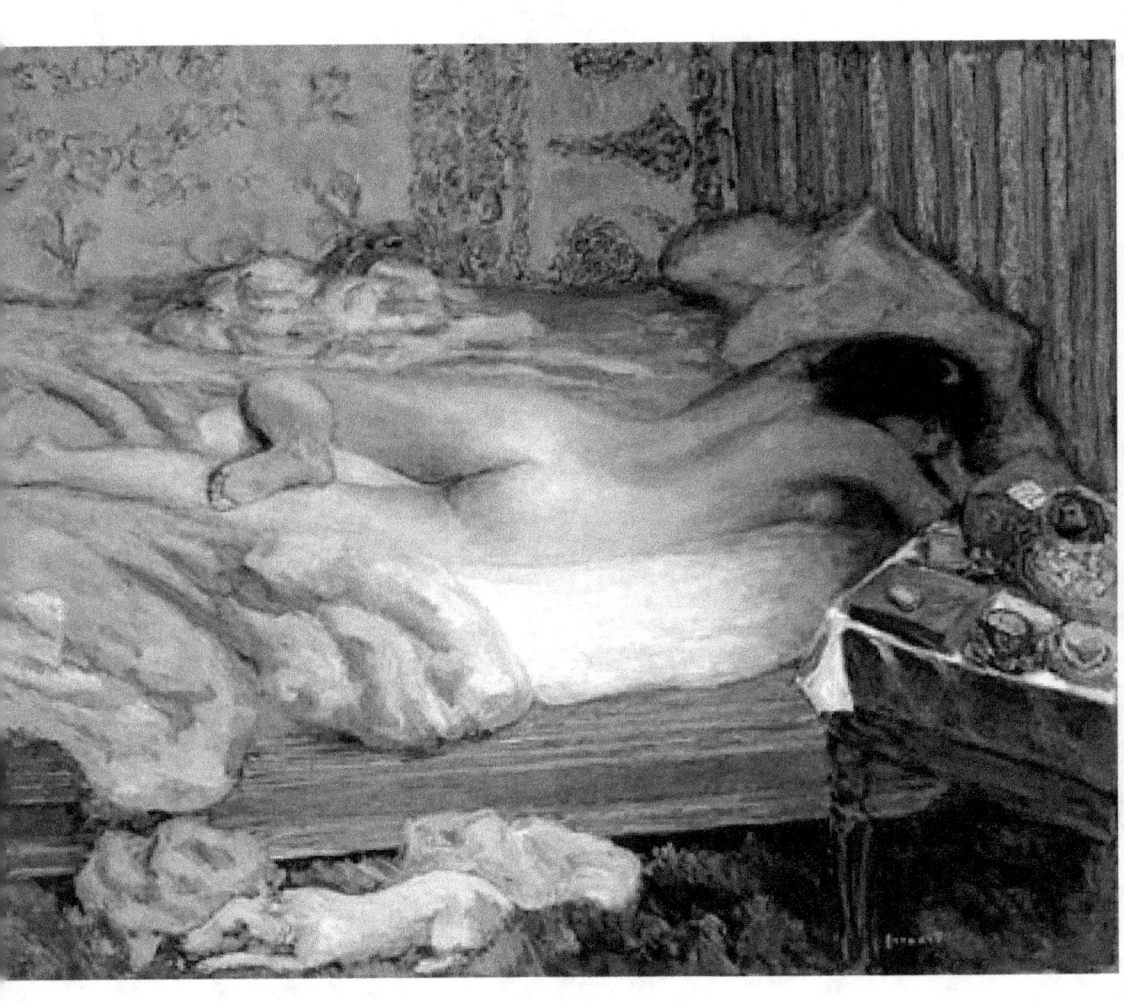

Pierre Bonnard

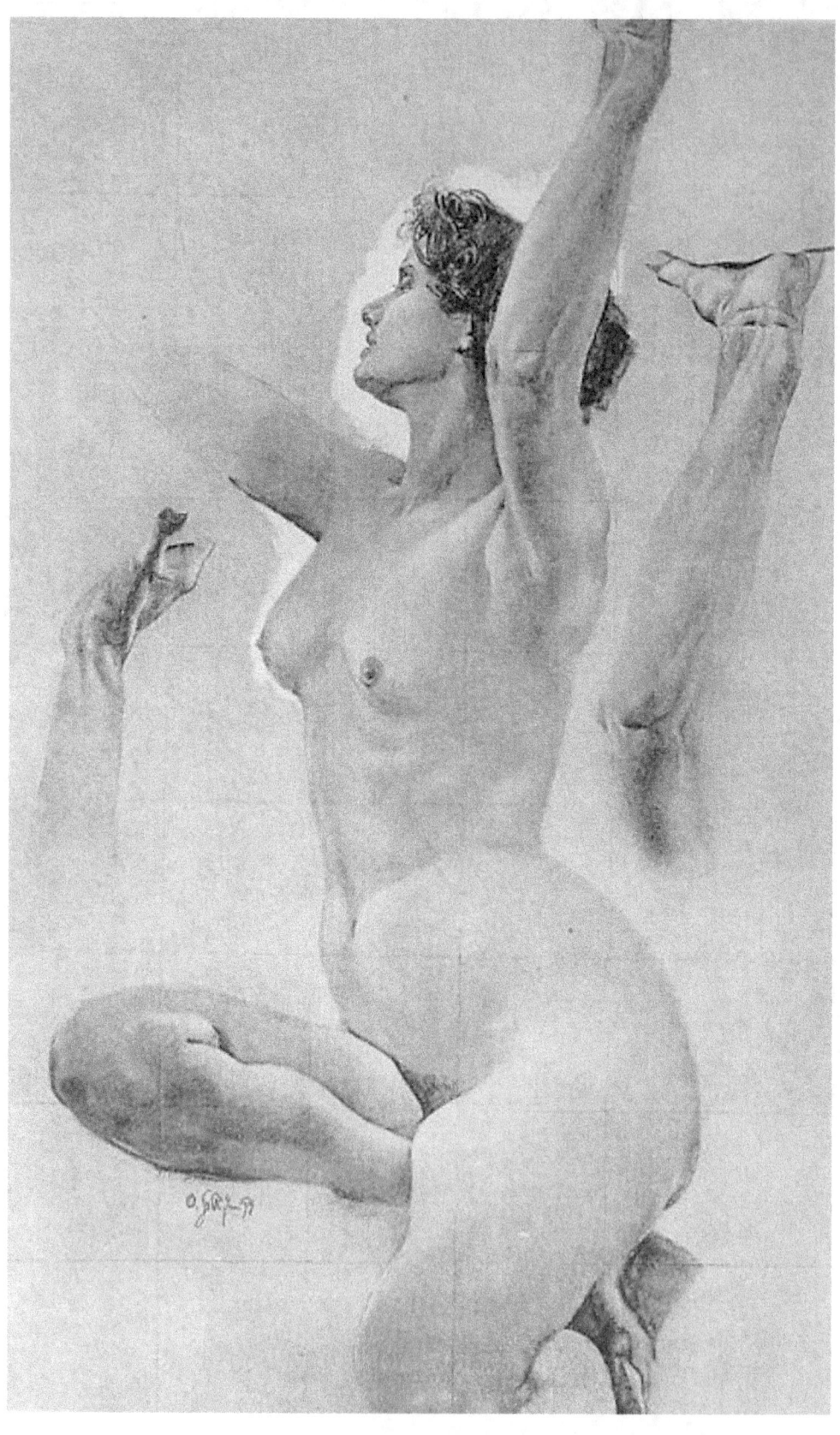

Otto Grenier, Study For Odysseus, 1912-33

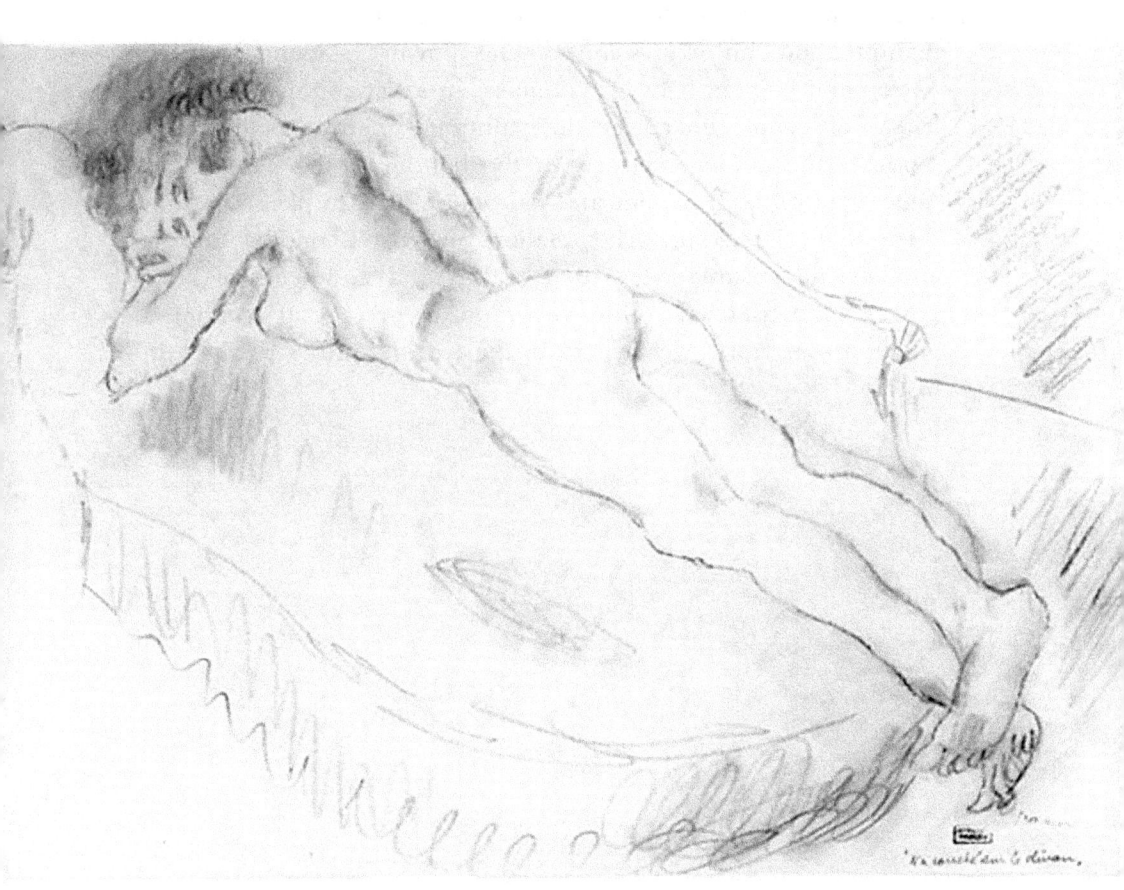

Jules Pascin

THE FEMALE NUDE

The high art nude, then, is a site of political and economic manipulation, an expression of the power relations between patron and painter, between connoisseur, artist and model. In the trinity of people linked by the painting – patron, painter and model – the model is clearly at the bottom of the pile. She is dependent on both painter and patron. She has to please both of them to be successful. The relation of artist to model thus is another manifestation, like that of husband and wife, of male power, of patriarchal culture in action, of the sexual economics which are at work everywhere in the world, and everywhere in history.

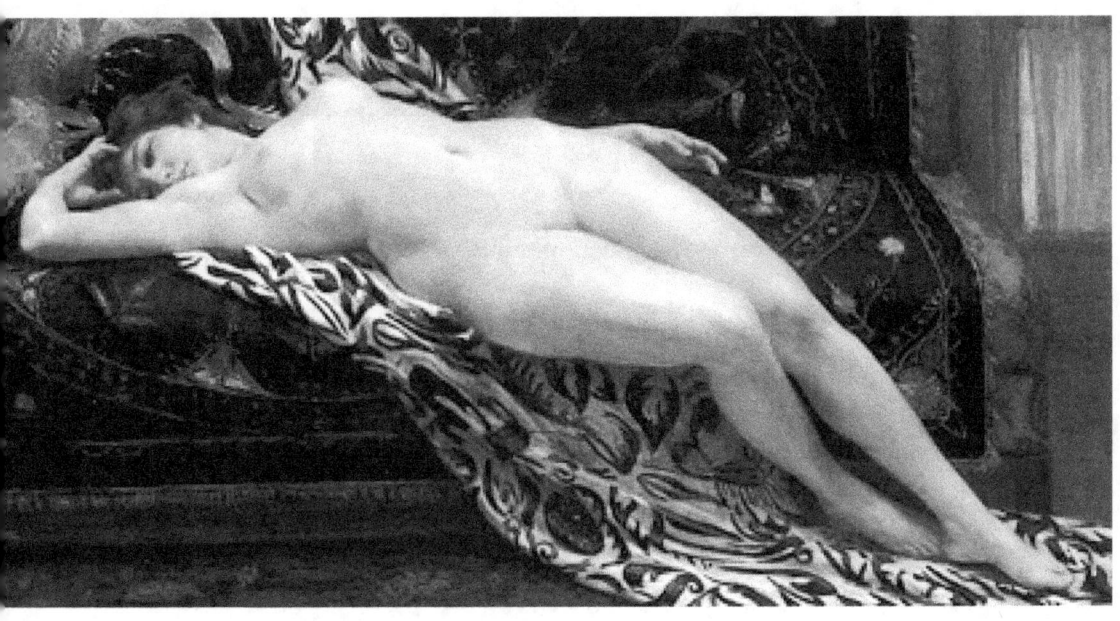

Guillaume Seignac, L'Abandon (above).
The Wave (below).

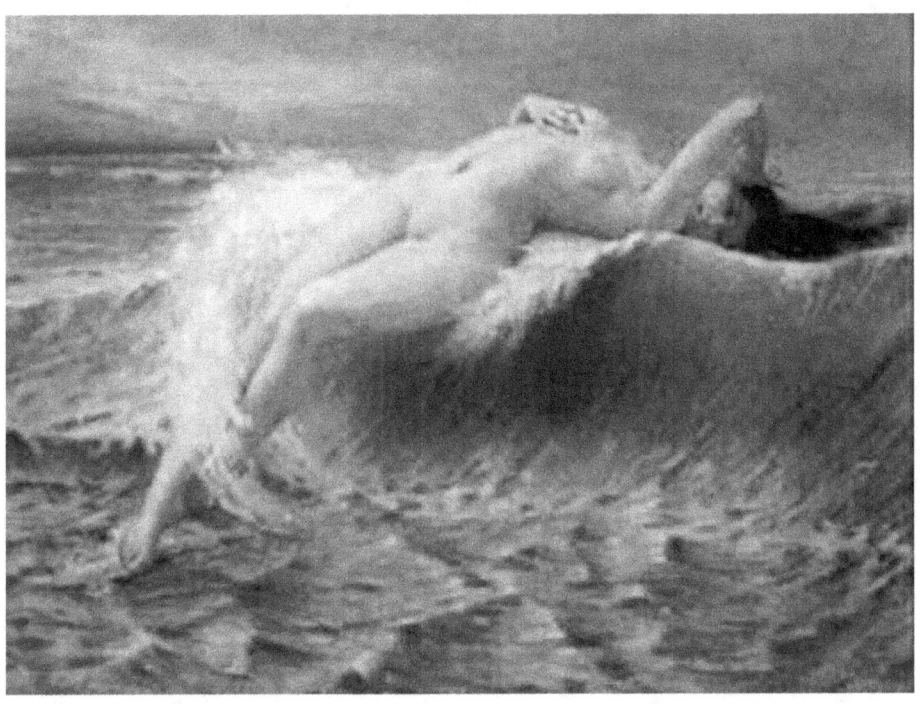

MALE NUDES

The male nude can be seen as a phallus, as Gill Saunders pointed out:

> The male body, while not constructed as the site of sexual pleasure, is often symbolic of phallic power. The whole body, muscular, potent, active, may come to represent the phallus.[1]

The penis isn't a phallus, so, to make up for the disappointing insufficiency of the penis, macho masculinity is demonstrated by bulging muscles, clenched fists, sturdy poses. The male nude poses with a body of 'rippling muscles', bizarrely exaggerated, or gripping a gun, or standing next to a motorcycle, a car, a machine, something that can connote phallic power.

---

1 G. Saunders: *The Nude*, 26.

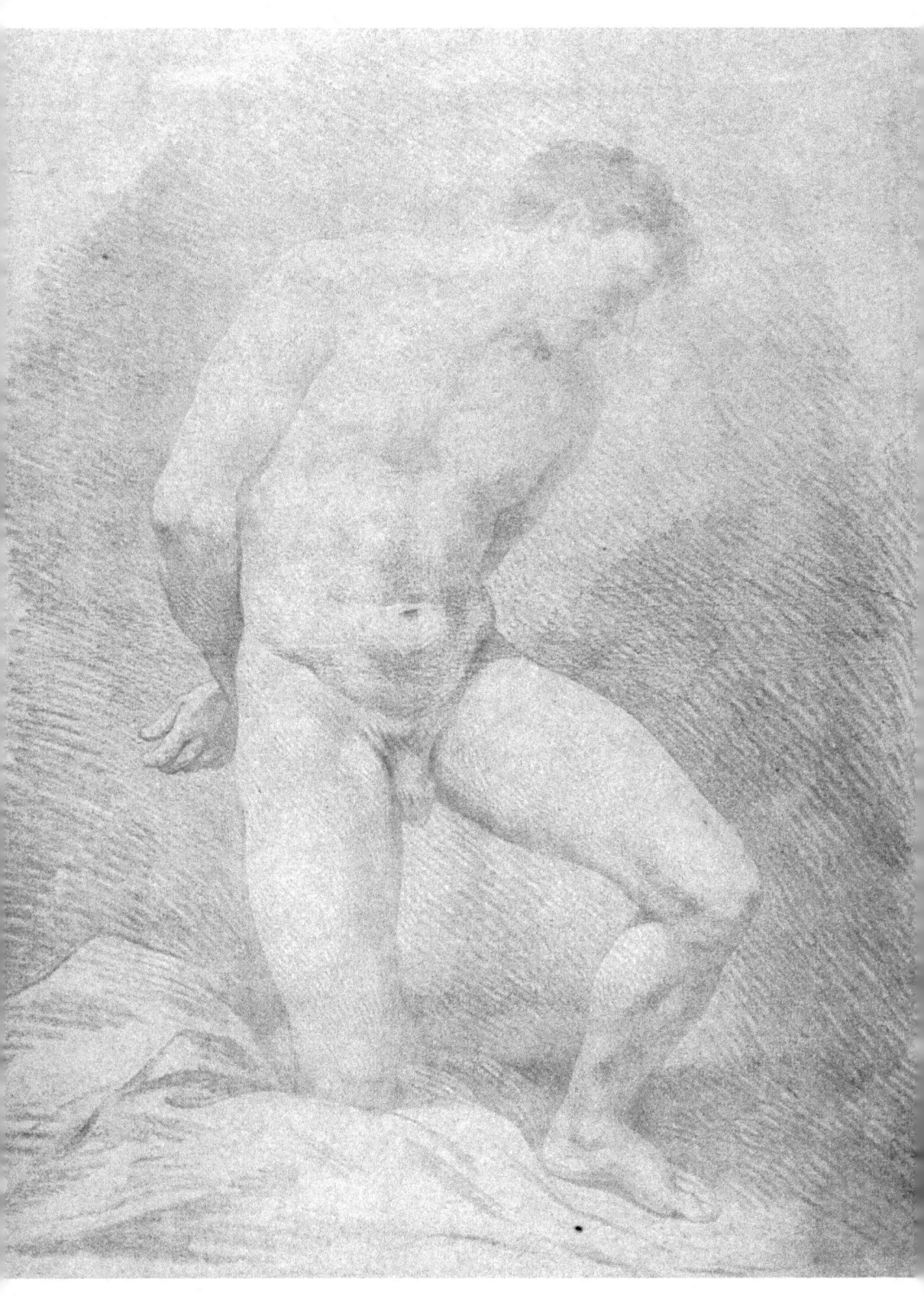

Male Nude, 19th century

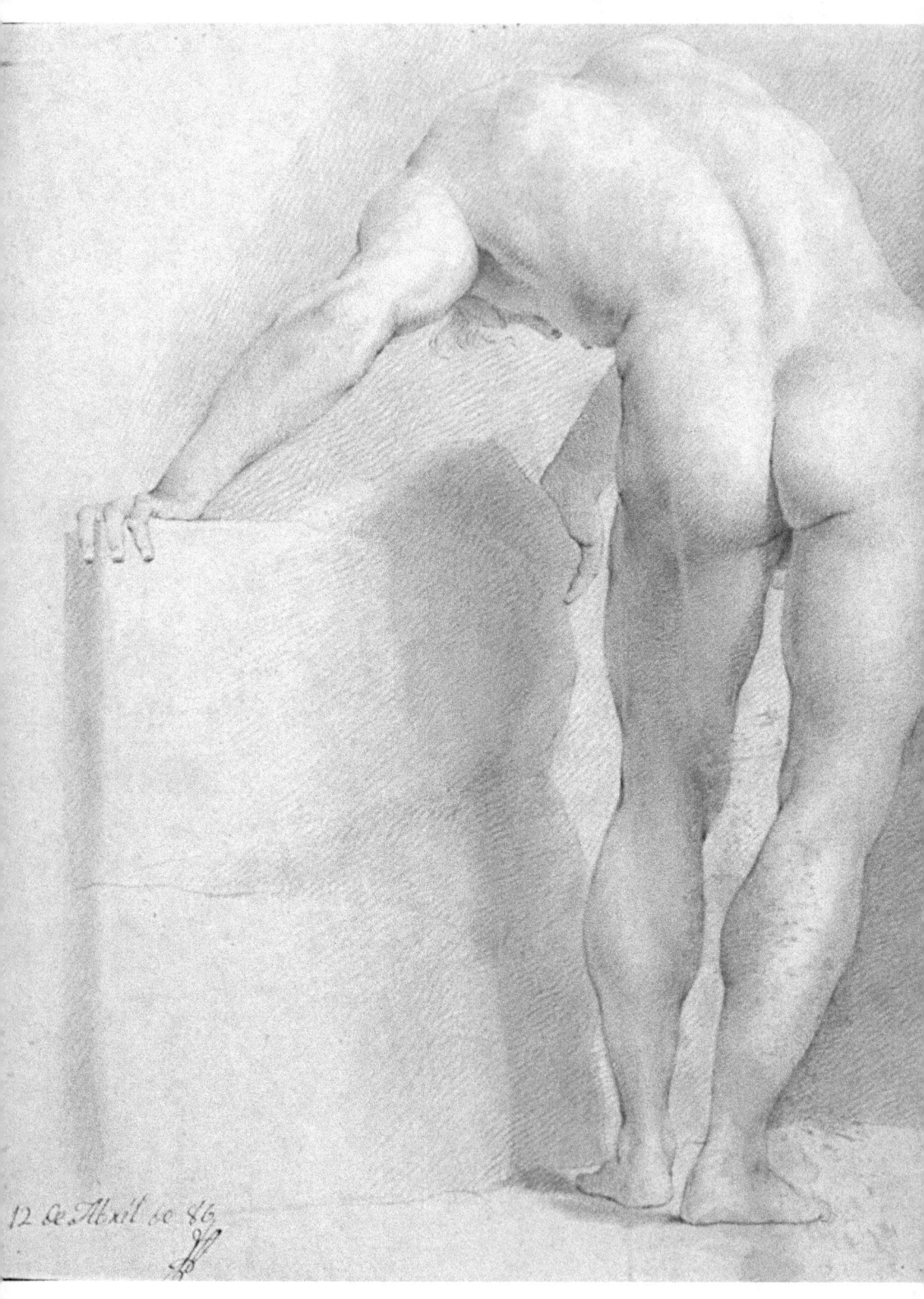

12 de Abril de 86

Mariano Amare, Male Nude, 1786.

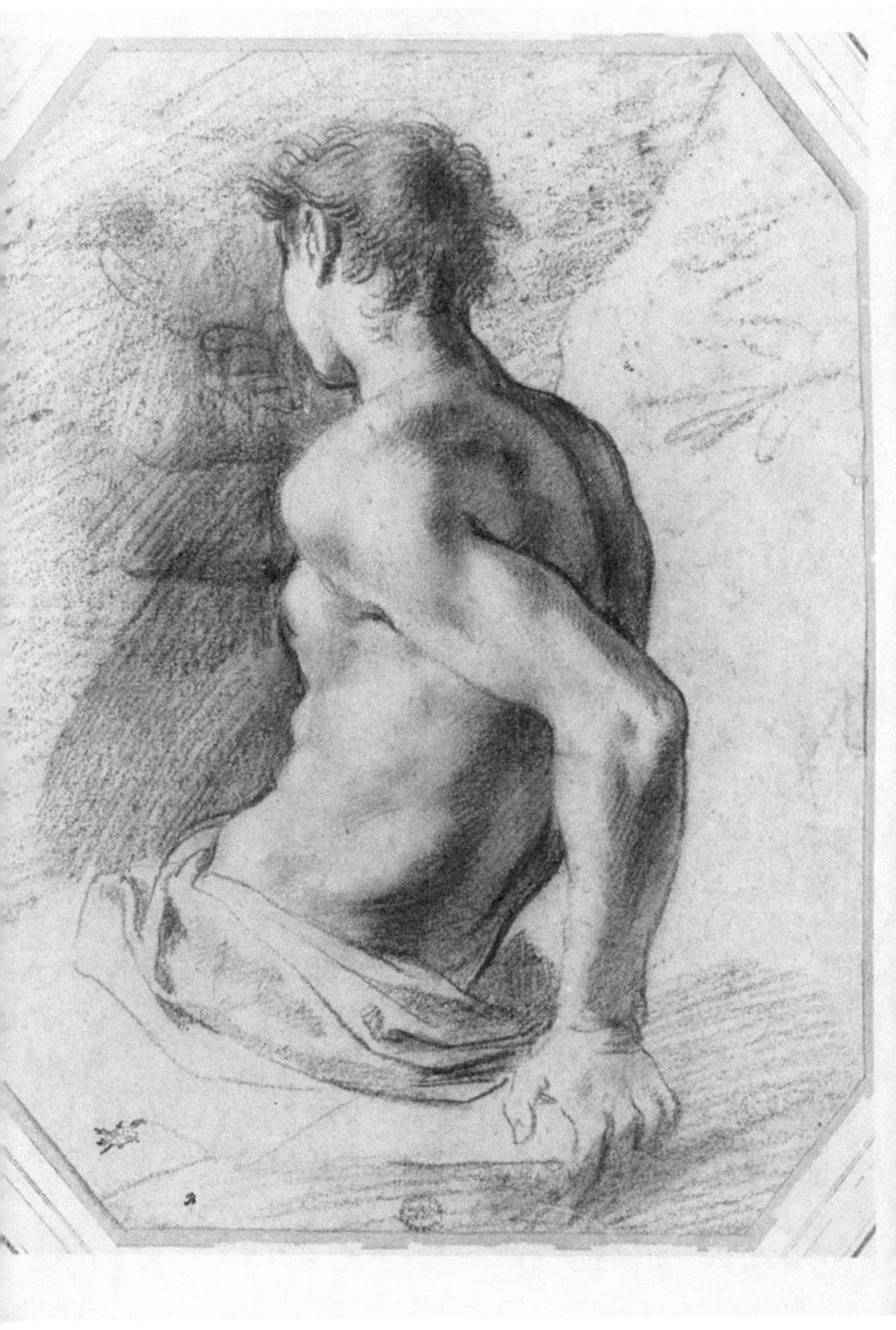

Annibale Carracci, Male Nude, Half-Figure, 16th century

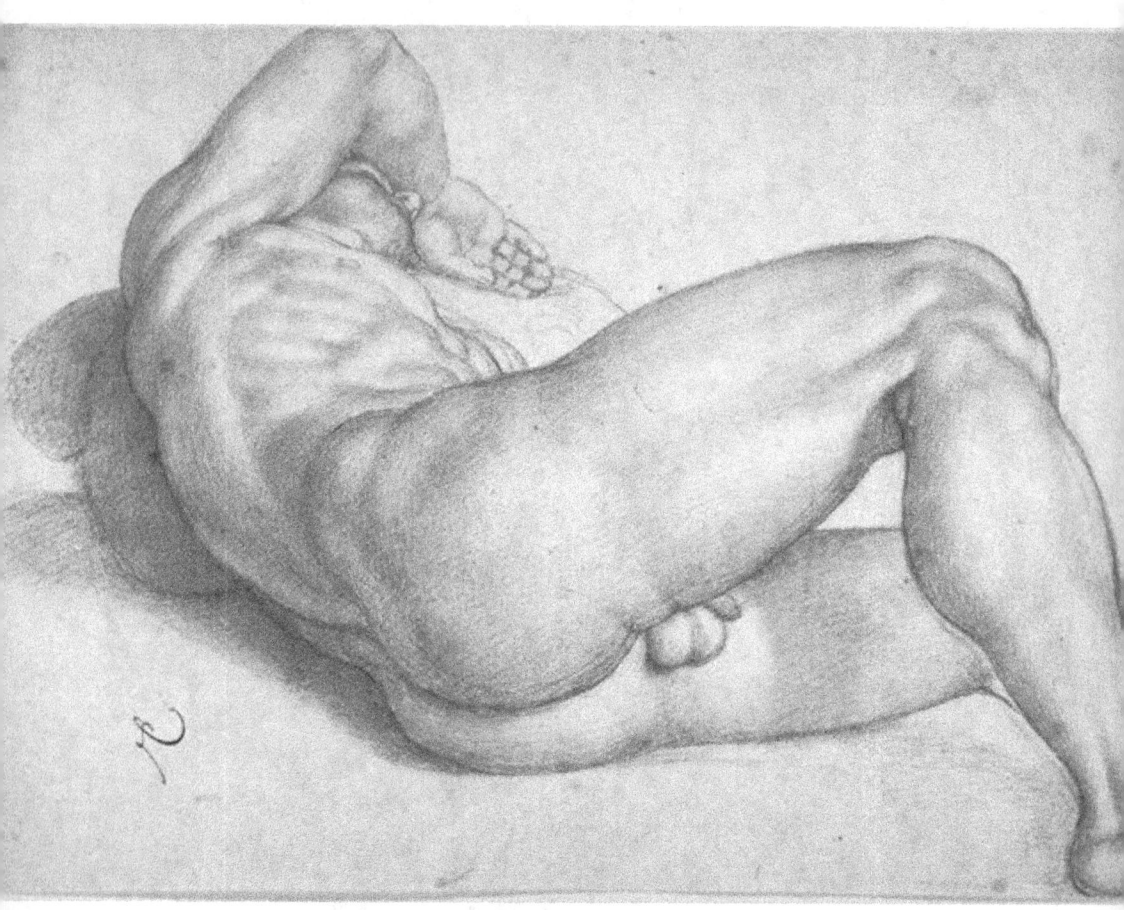

Agnolo di Cosimo (Il Bronzino),
Naked Man Lying On His Back, 16th century

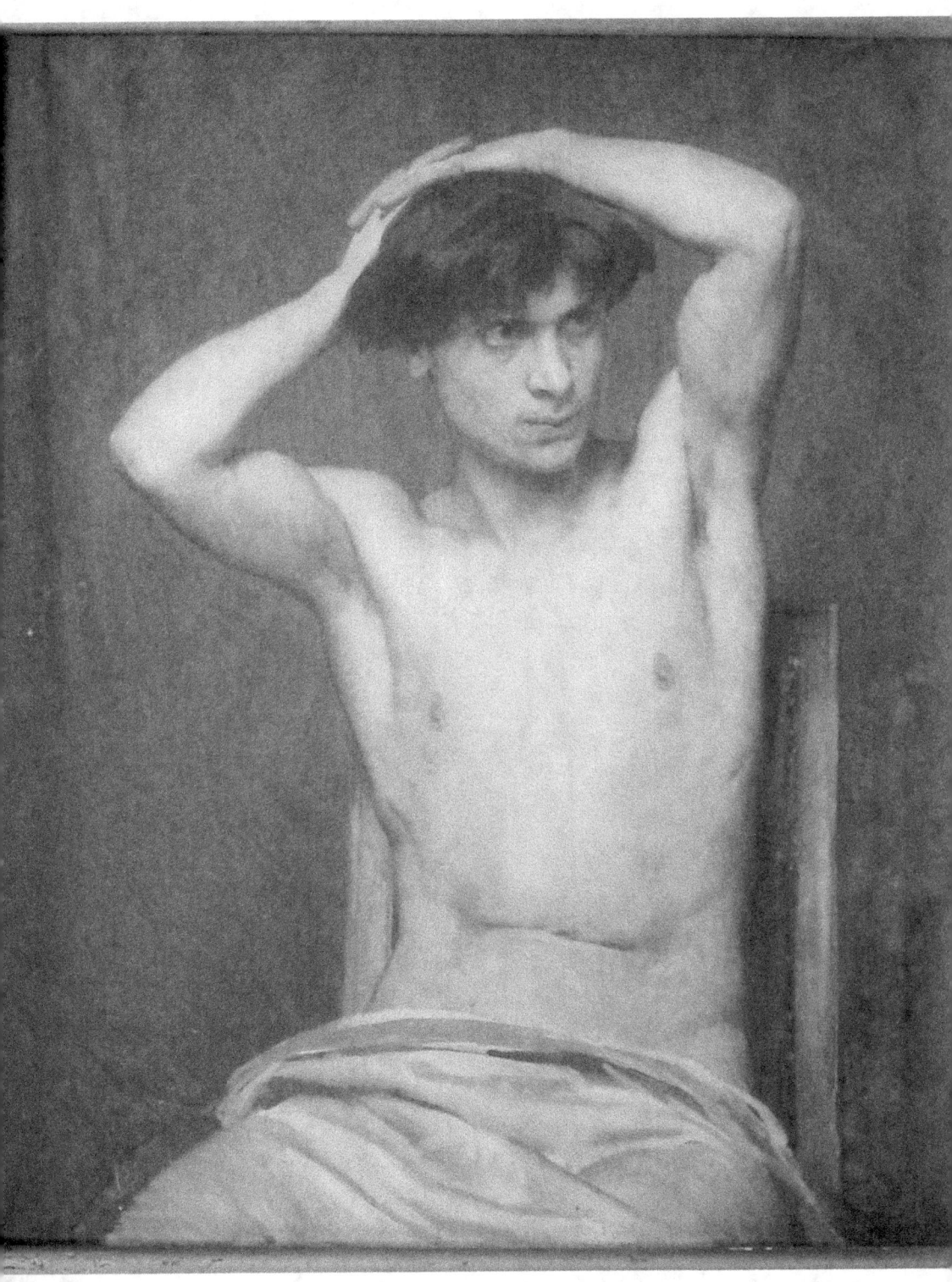

Henri-Lucien Doucet, Half-Nude Figure, 1879

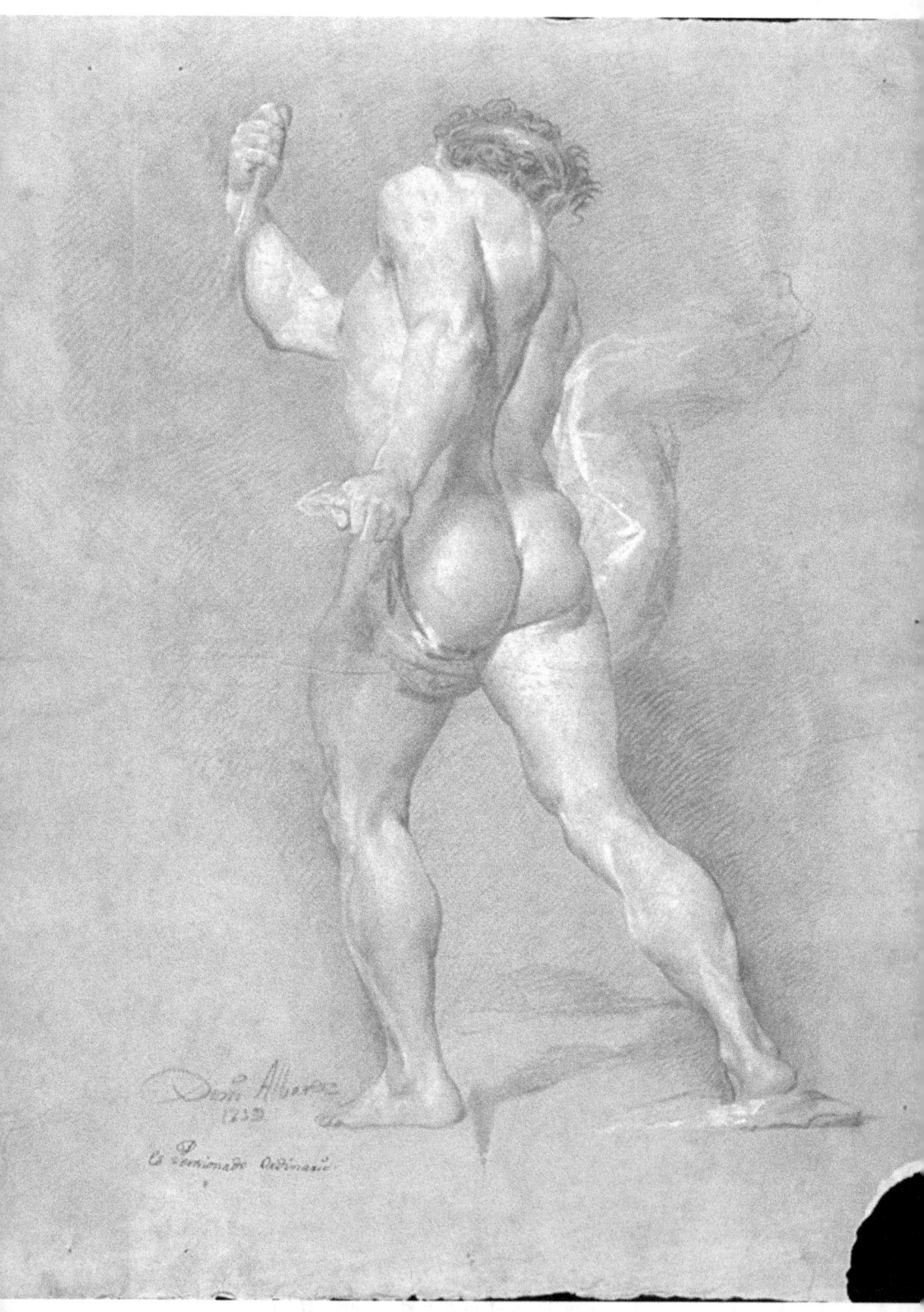

Domingo Alvarez Enciso, Male Nude, 1759

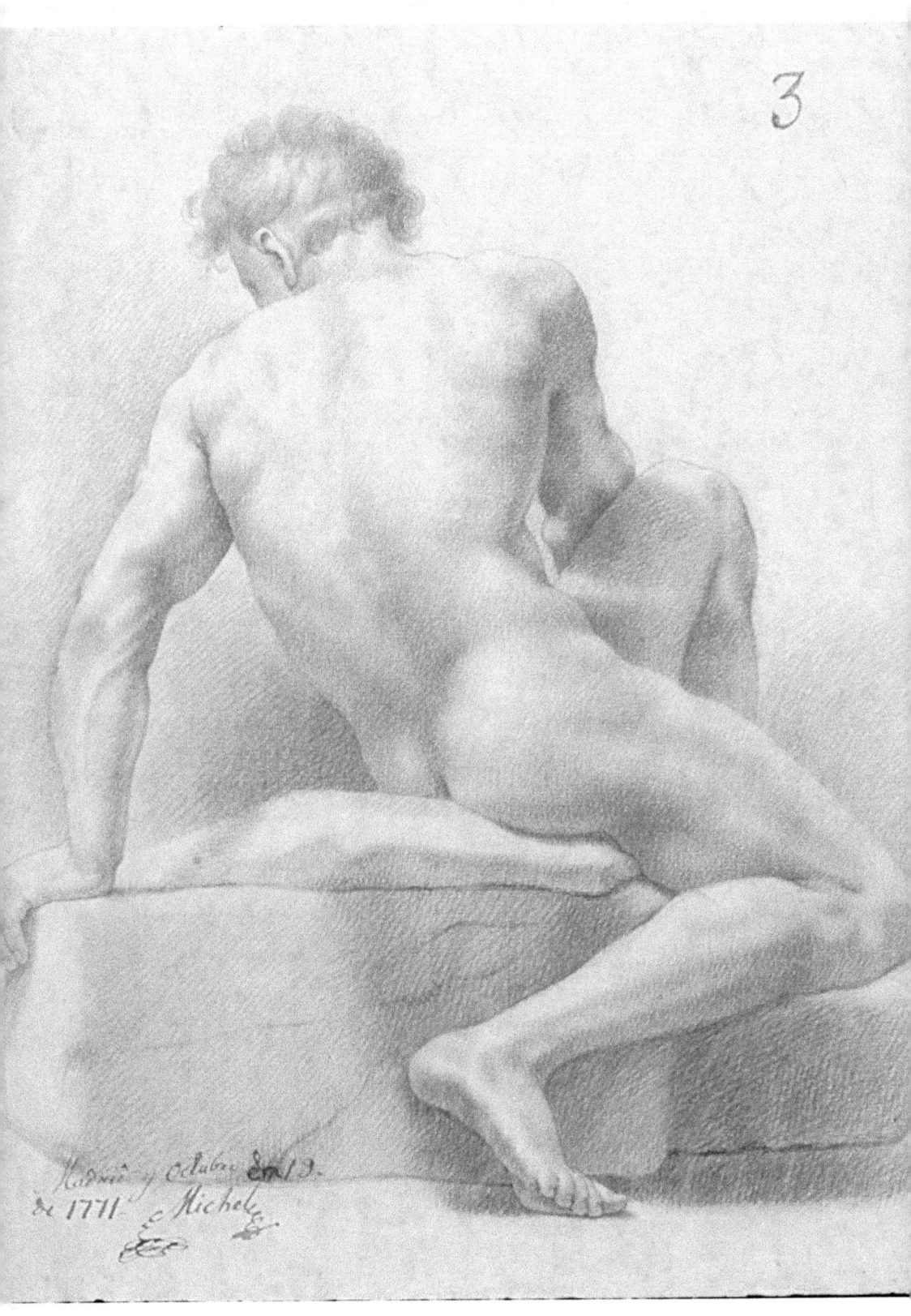

Pedro Pascual Munoz, Seated Male Nude, 1771

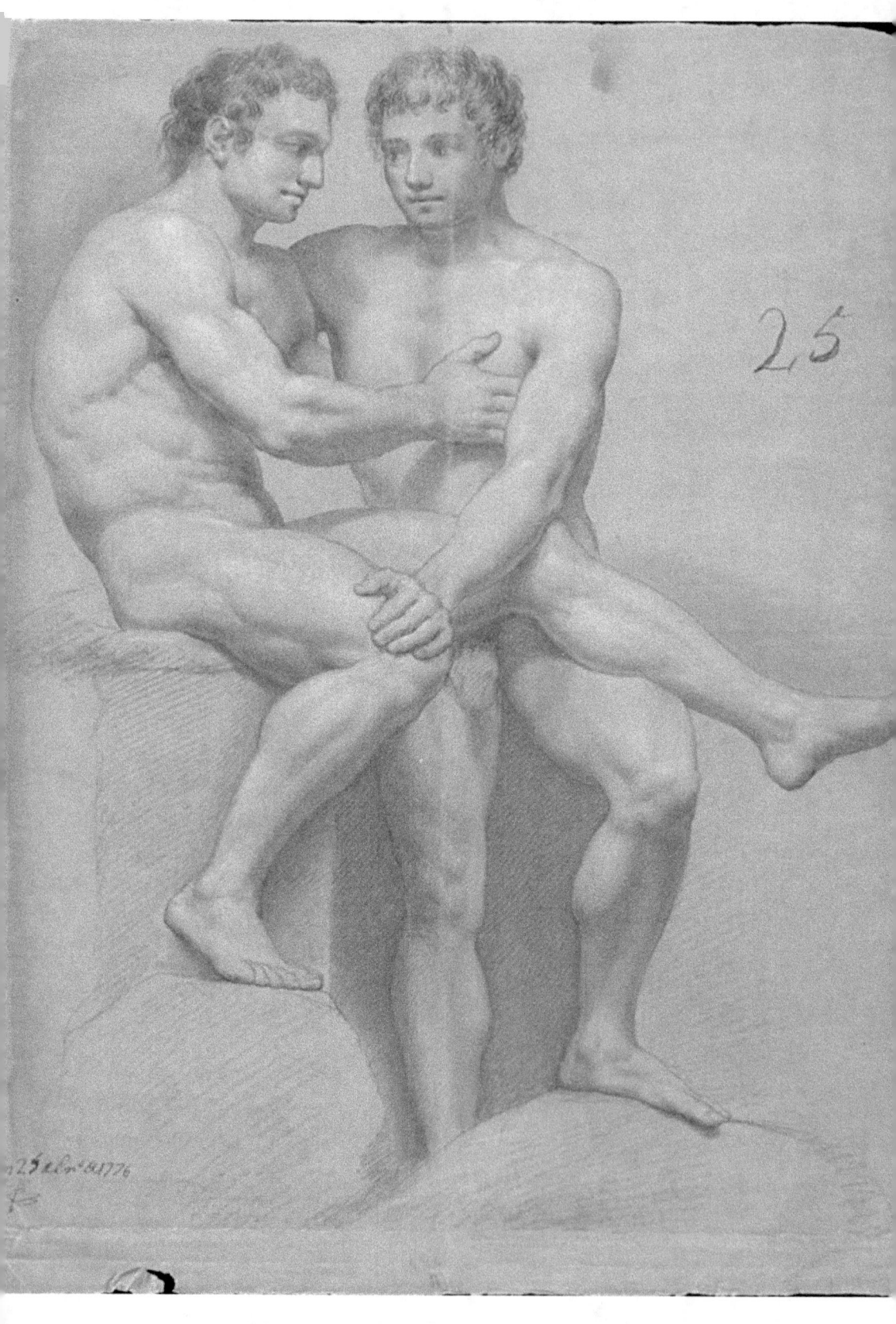

Gustin Esteve Marques, Two Male Nudes, 1776

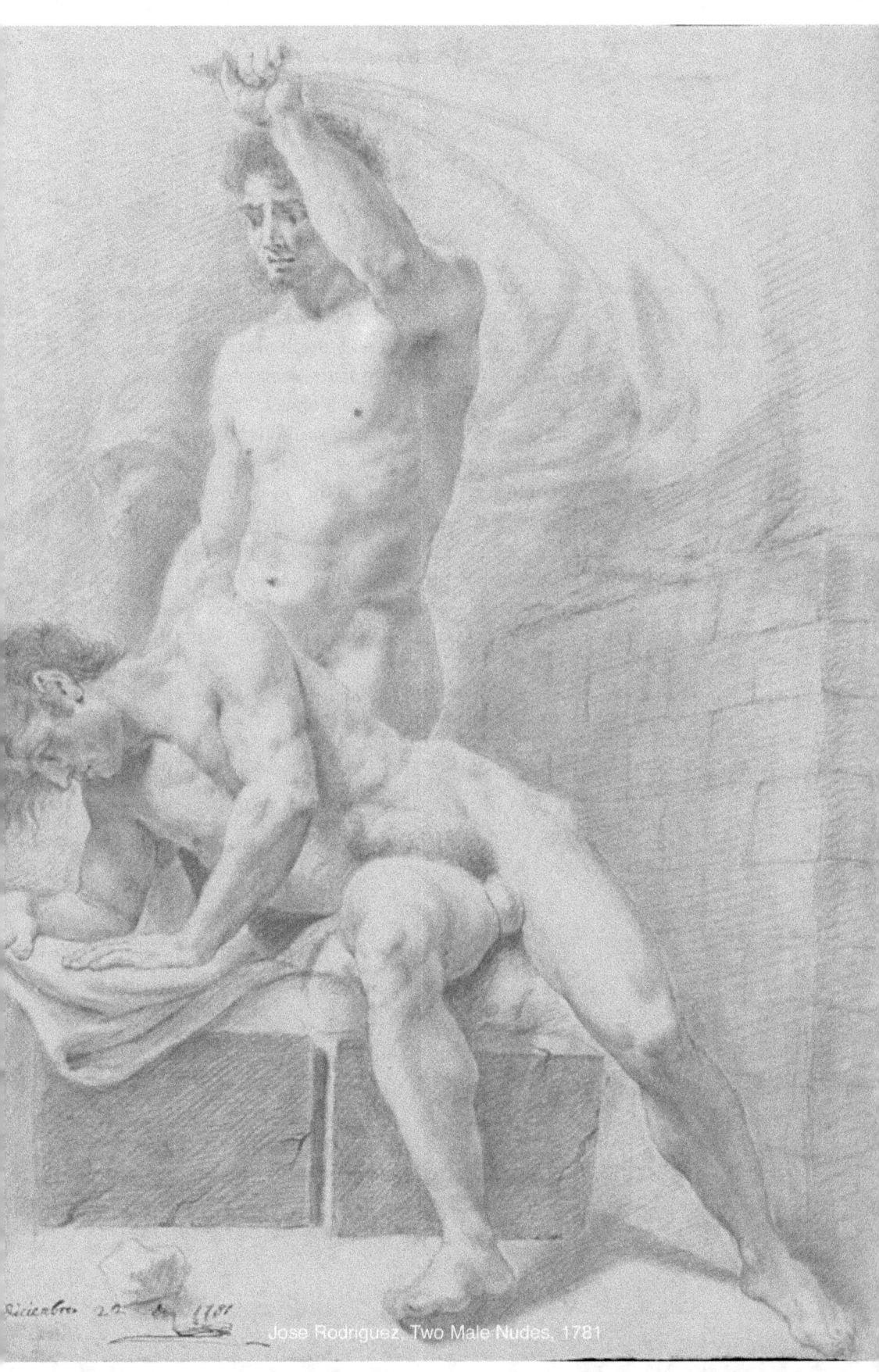

Jose Rodriguez, Two Male Nudes, 1781

MALE NUDES

The male nude can be appear uncomfortable. He doesn't like his photograph or painting or sculpture to be looked at like female nudes. He is used to being the one doing the looking. When the roles are reversed, ambiguity and confusion seeps in. The male nude is set up as spectacle, and as a passive object. To counter the awkwardness of this passivity, the male nude is shown *doing* something. Running, throwing a spear, fighting, etc. It tries to engage a position of activity, because to be the 'looked-at' one, the passive sex object, is very disquieting. Further, the activity of the male nude, which's seen everywhere – in photographs by Eadweard Muybridge,[1] in sculptures by Michelangelo Buonarroti, in movies, in gay porn – aims at portraying phallic power. 'Even in an apparently relaxed, supine pose,' Richard Dyer in 1983,

> the model tightens and tautens his body so that the muscles are emphasized, hence drawing attention to the body's potential for action. More often, the male pin-up is not supine anyhow, but standing taut ready for action.[2]

1 See L. Williams: "Film Body, an implantation of perversions", *Cinétracts*, vol. 3, no.4, Winter 1981, 19-25.
2 Richard Dyer: 'Don't Look Now", *Screen*, vol. 23, 3/ 4, 1983, 20, and in Angela McRobbie, 206

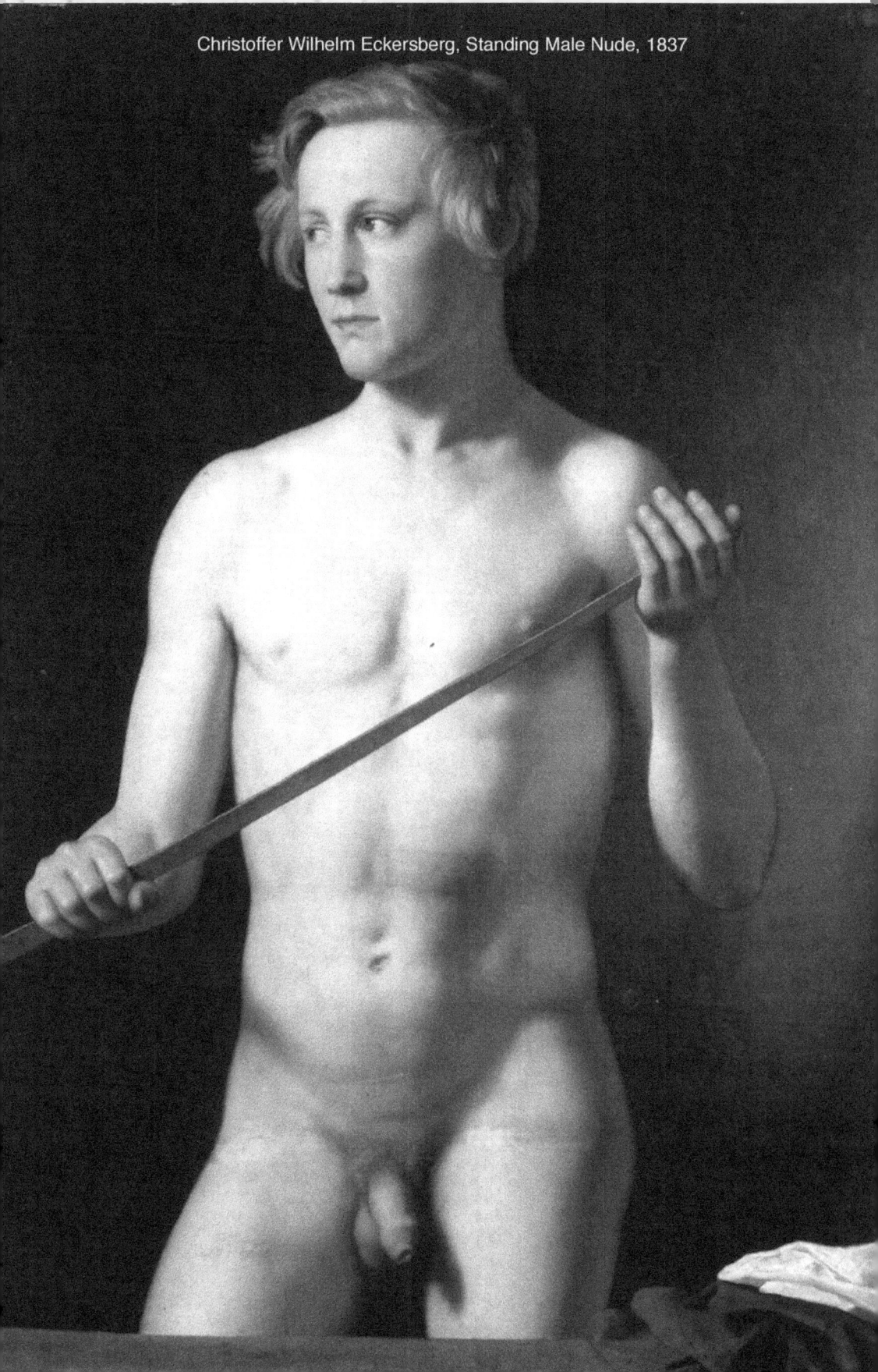
Christoffer Wilhelm Eckersberg, Standing Male Nude, 1837

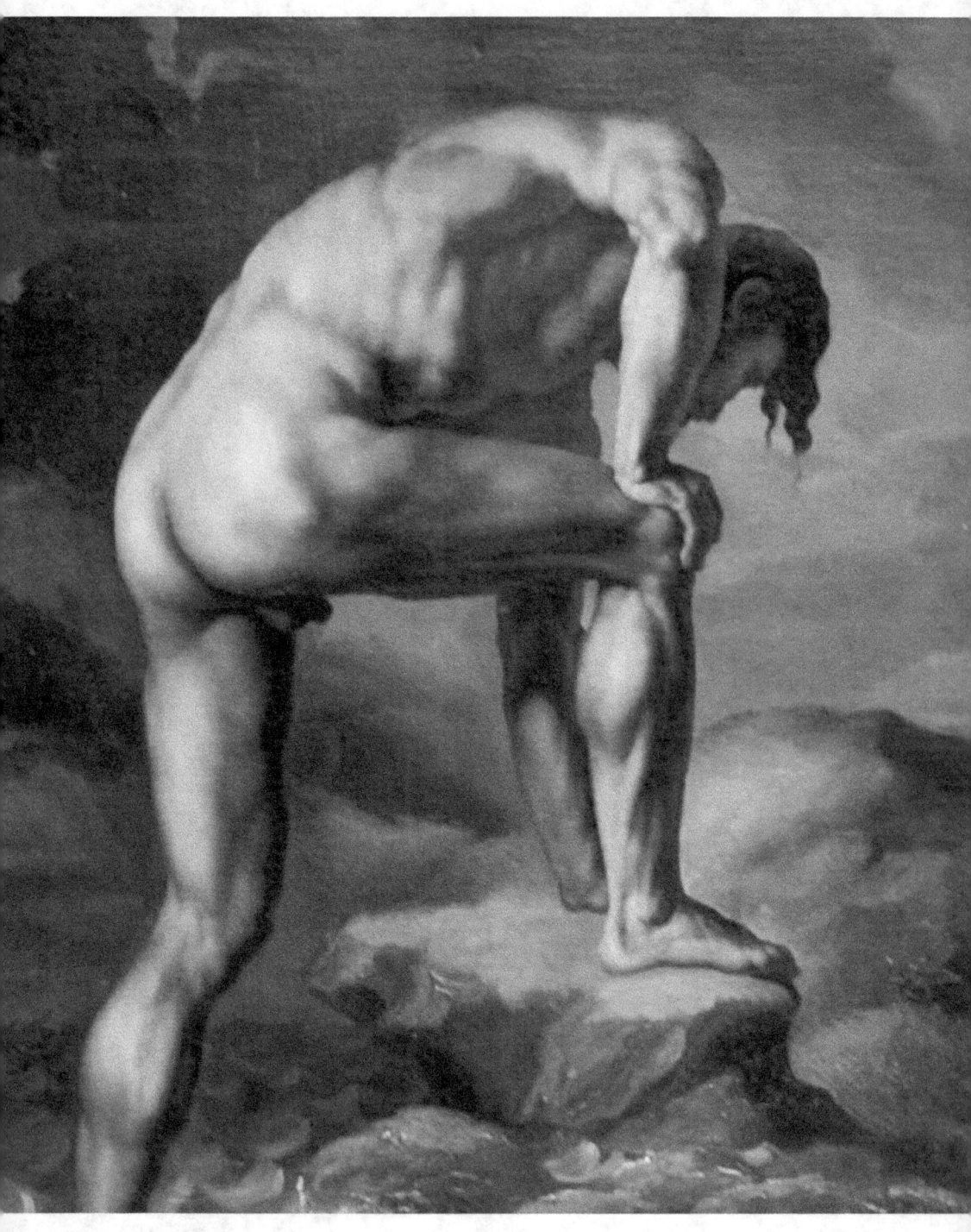

Jean-Louis Andre Theodore Géricault, A Shipwreck, c. 1819

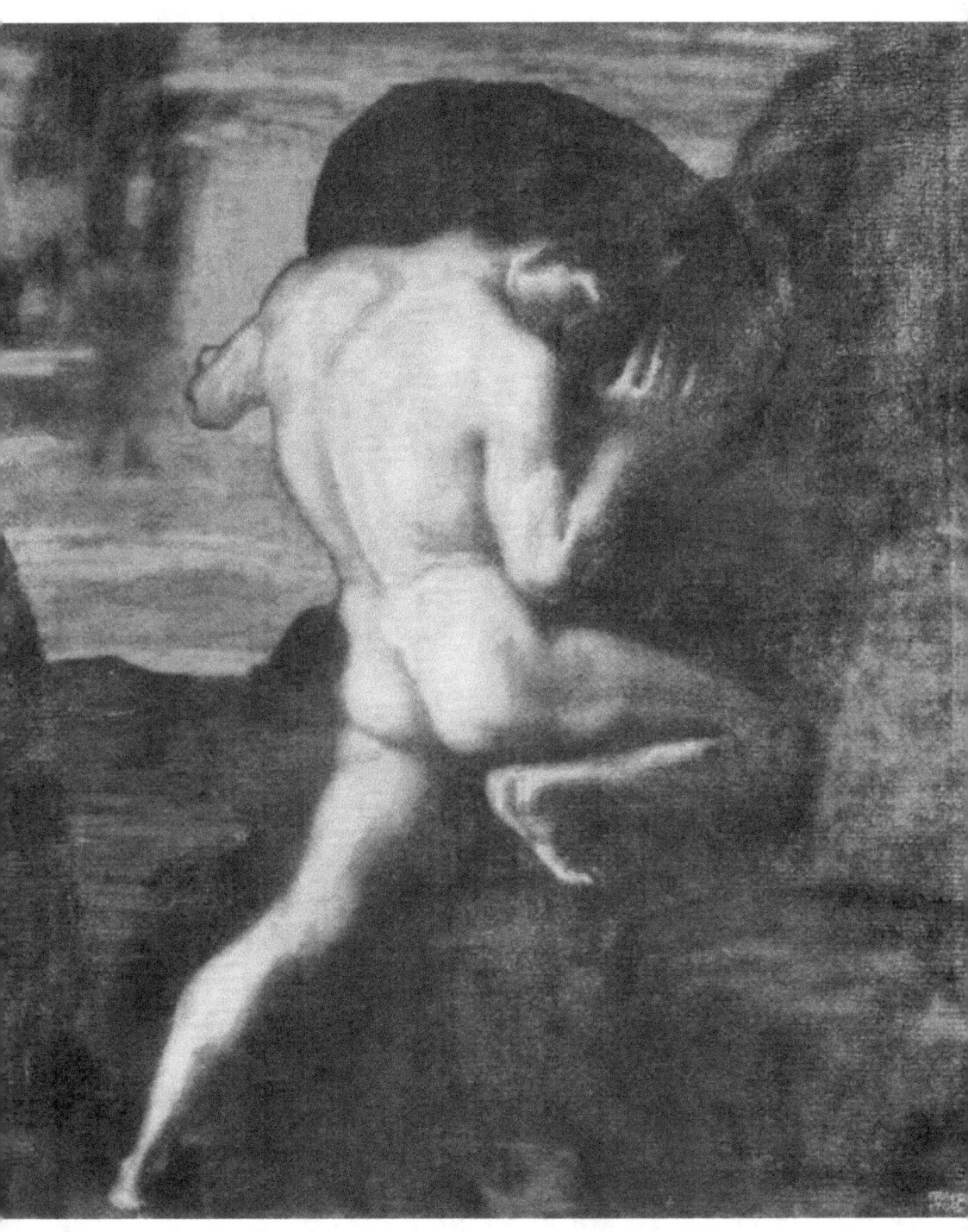

Franz von Stuck, Sisyphus

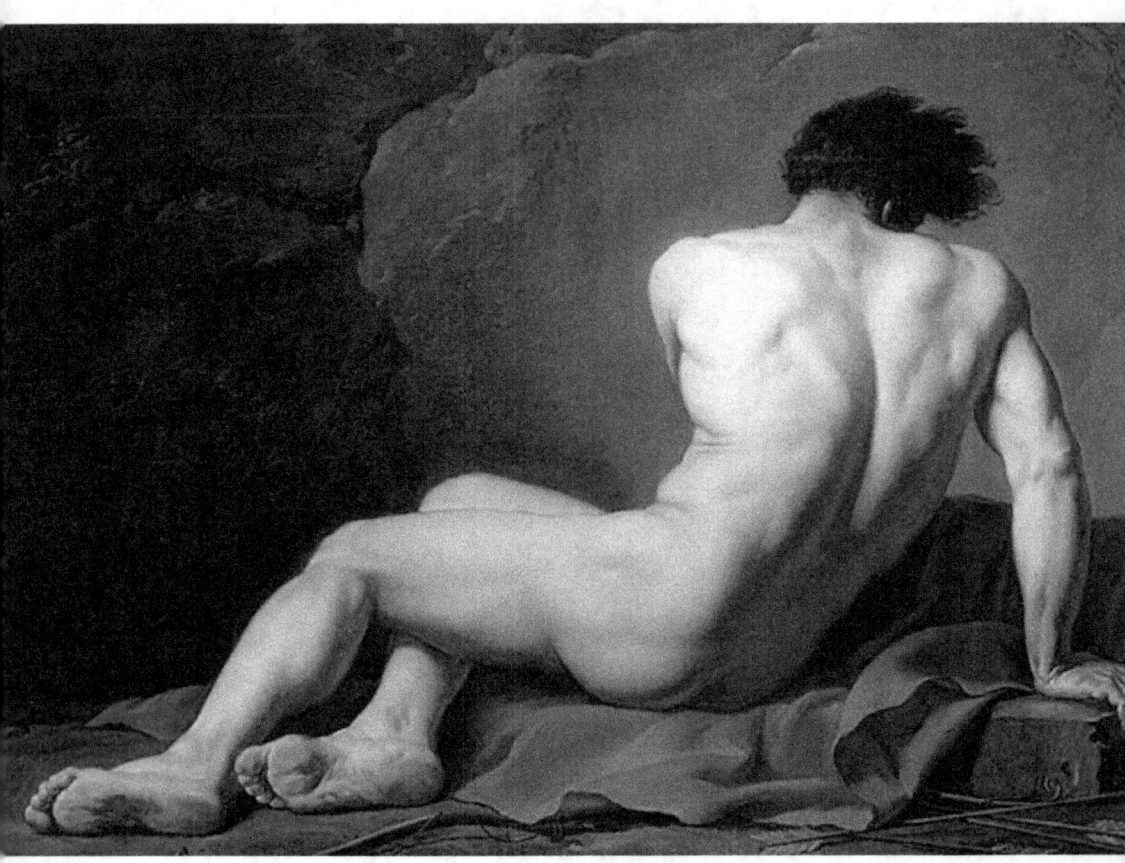

A classical French male nude painting
by Jacques-Louis David (known as Patrocles)

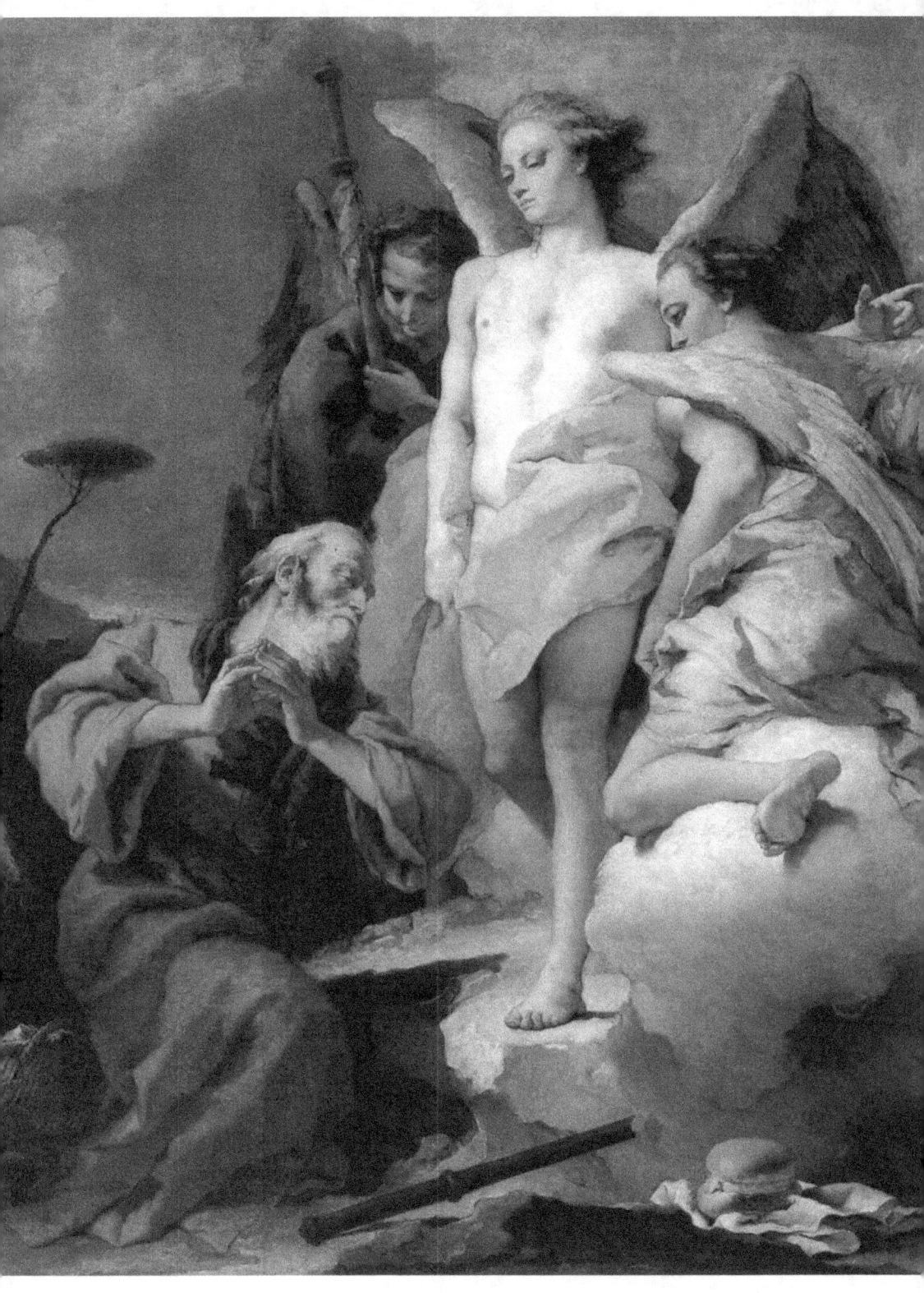

Giovanni Battista Tiepolo, Abraham and Three Angels, c. 1770

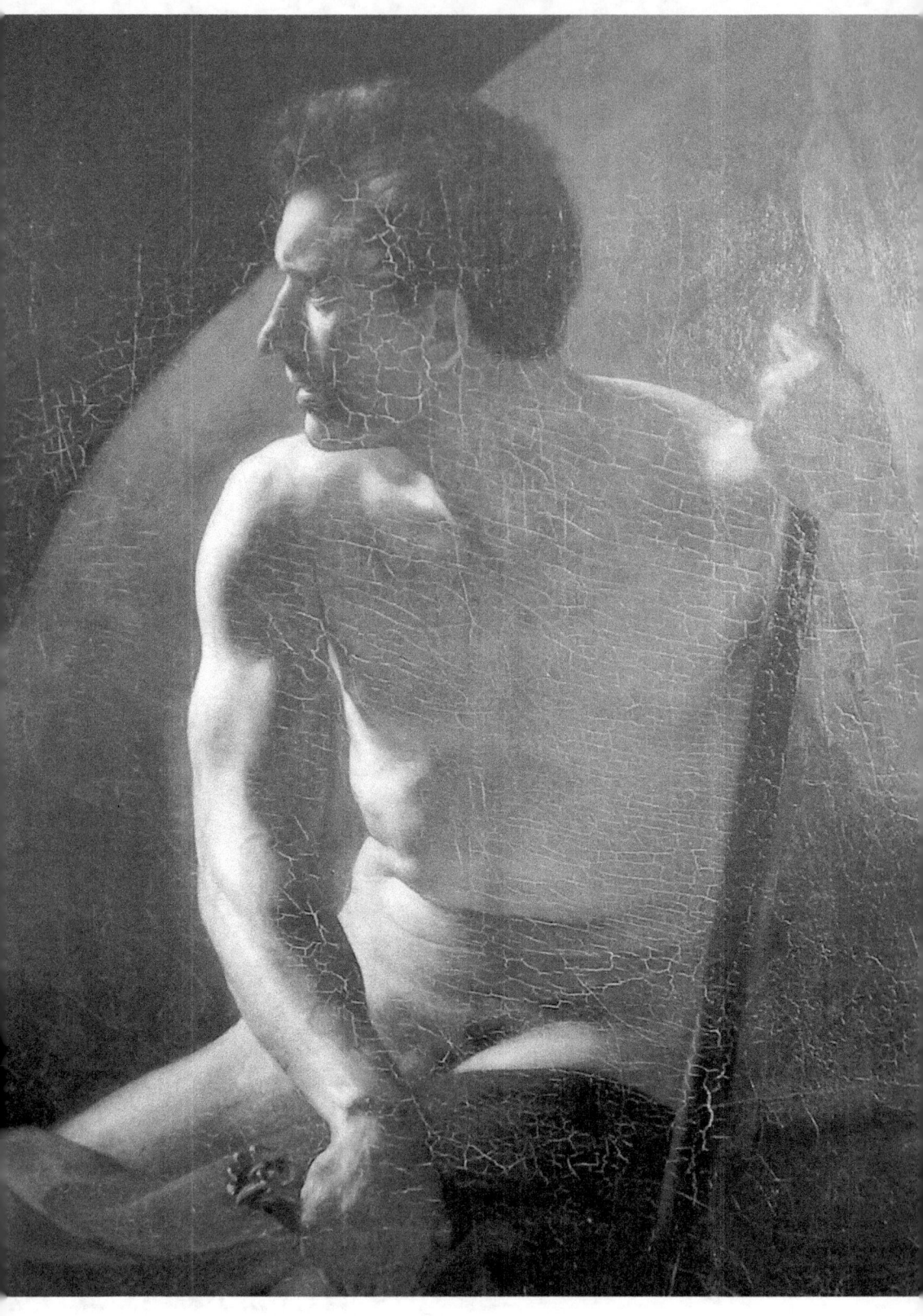

Hippolyte Dominique Holfeld, Half-Nude Figure, 1831

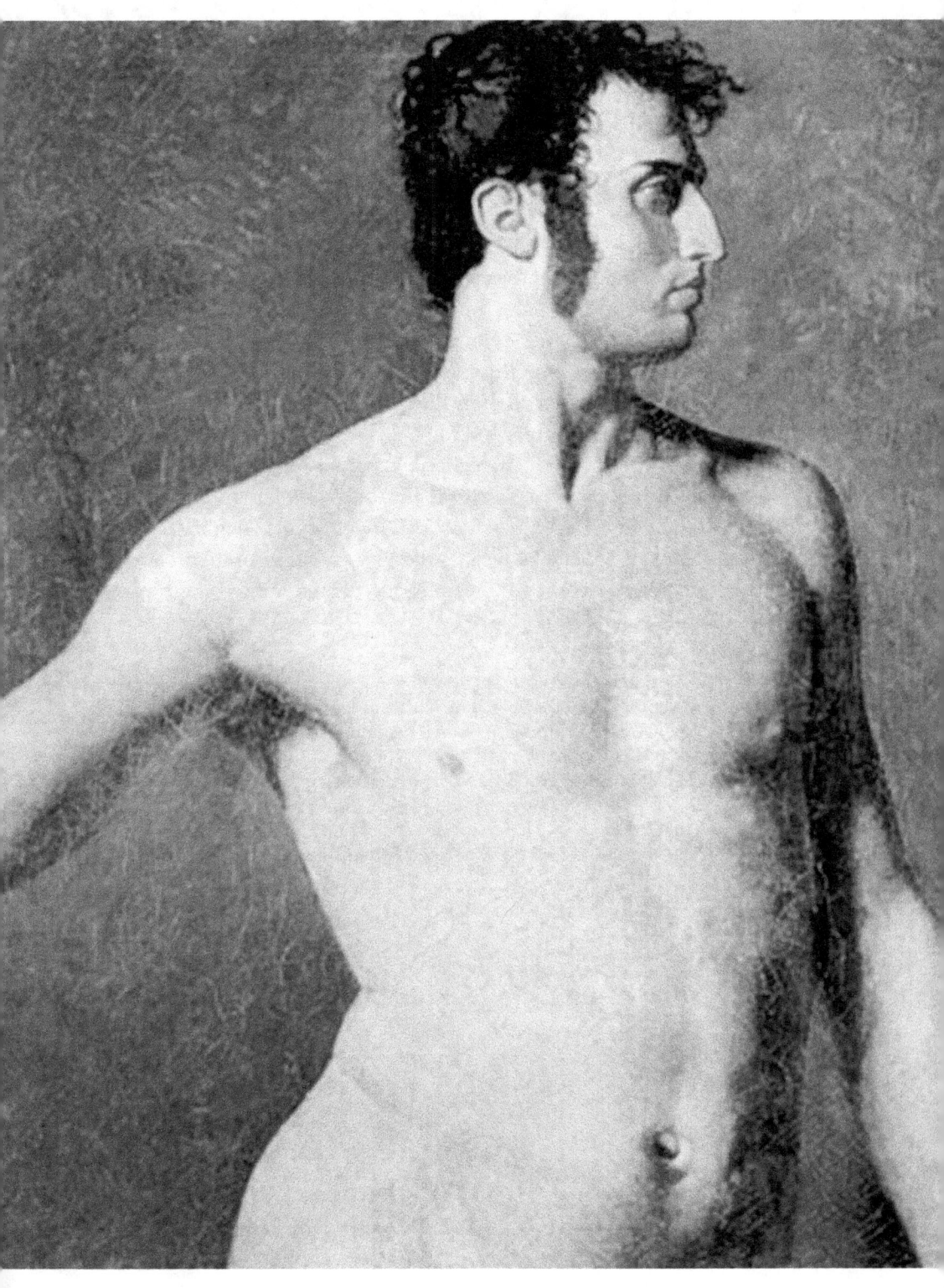

J.A.D. Ingres, Male Torso, 1801, Musée Ingres

MALE NUDES

The male nude image is subject to the same changes in culture as anything else: if you look at the nudes included here, you'll see the changes in fashion and style, at the superficial level, as well as the developments in the politics and society of the time, reflected in the nude images. Even though the body is nude, there are still numerous marks of culture upon it.

In the advanced capitalist, technological world, the body is not a 'natural' form any more, as Elizabeth Grosz explains in *Volatile Bodies*: clothing, exercise, jewellery, lifestyle, habits, negotiations of the cultural and social as well as the physical environment, and all sorts of activities alter it, inscribe it, turn it into something definitely not 'natural':

> Makeup, stilettos, bras, hair sprays, clothing, underclothing mark women's bodies, whether black or white, in ways in which hair styles, professional training, personal grooming, gait, posture, body building, and sports may mark men's. There is nothing natural or ahistorical about these modes of corporeal inscriptions. Through then, bodies are made amenable to the prevailing exigencies of power. They make the flesh into a particular type of body – pagan, primitive, medieval, capitalist, Italian, American, Australian. (142)

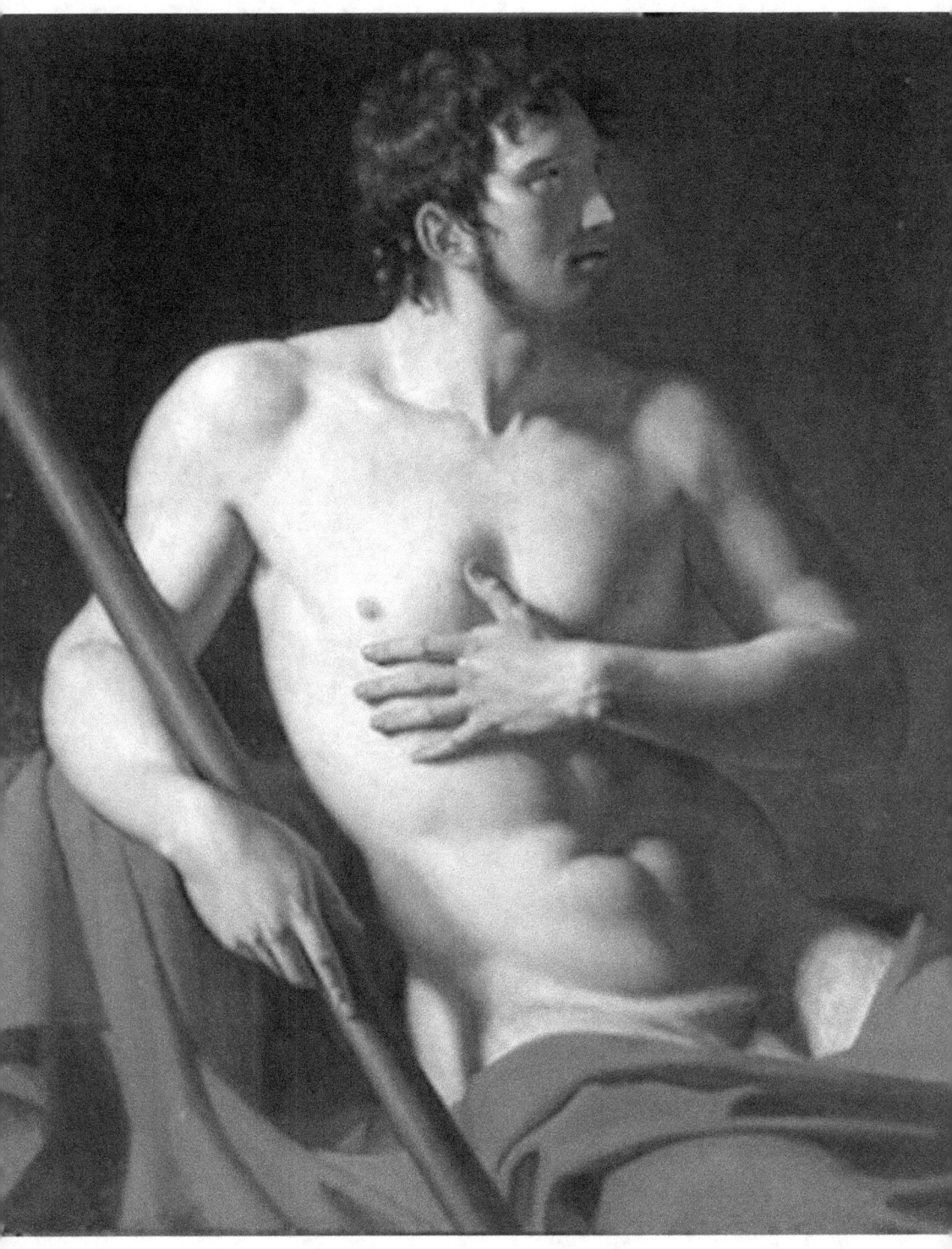

Auguste-Alphonse Gaudar de la Verdine, Male Nude, 1799

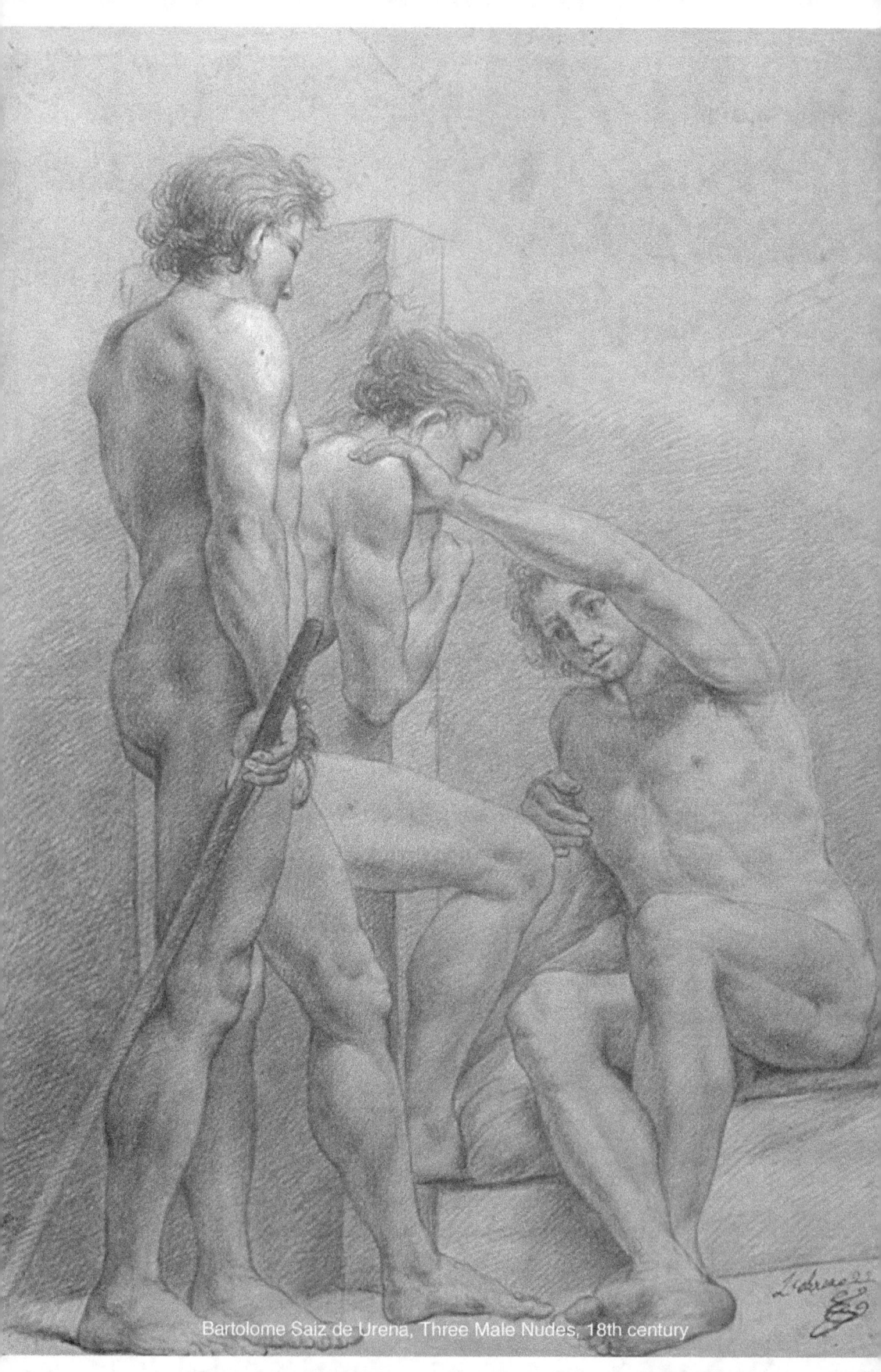

Bartolome Saiz de Urena, Three Male Nudes, 18th century

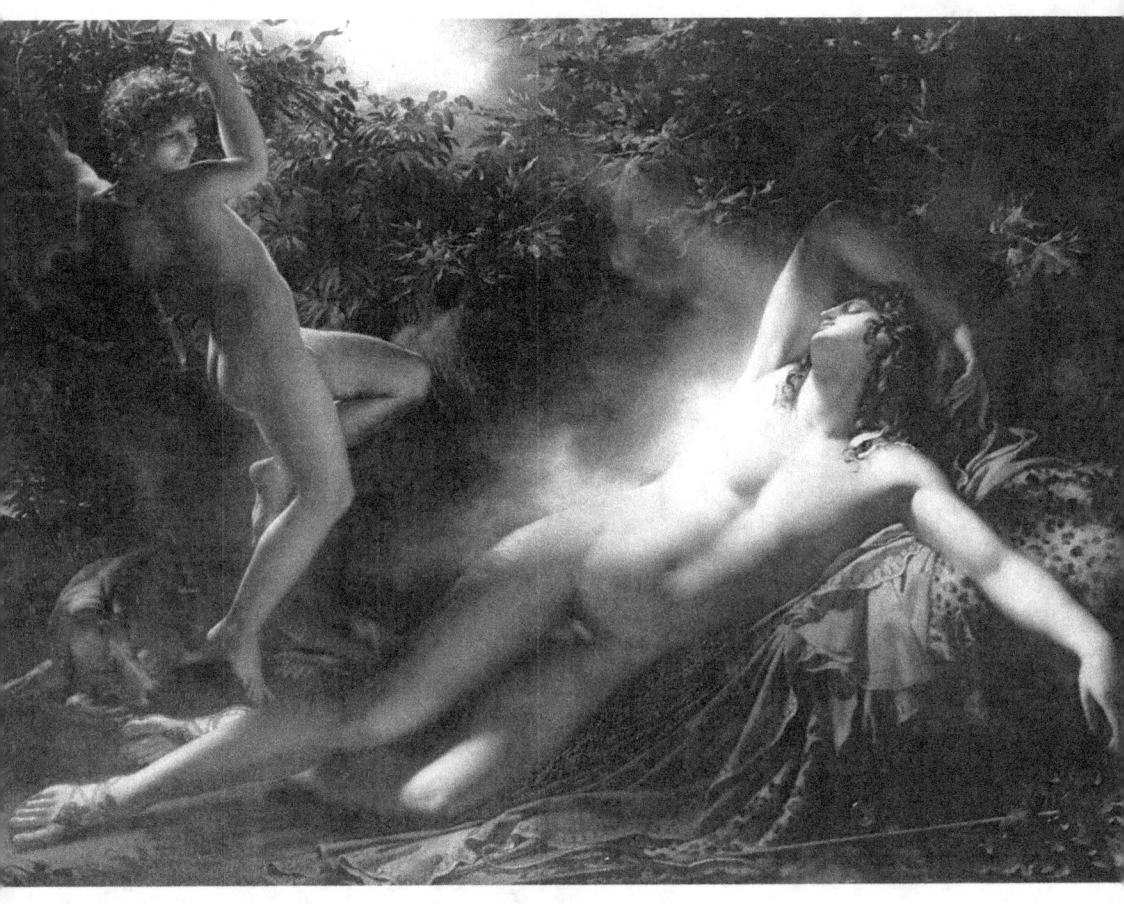

Anne-Louis Girodet-Trioson, Endymion, 1793

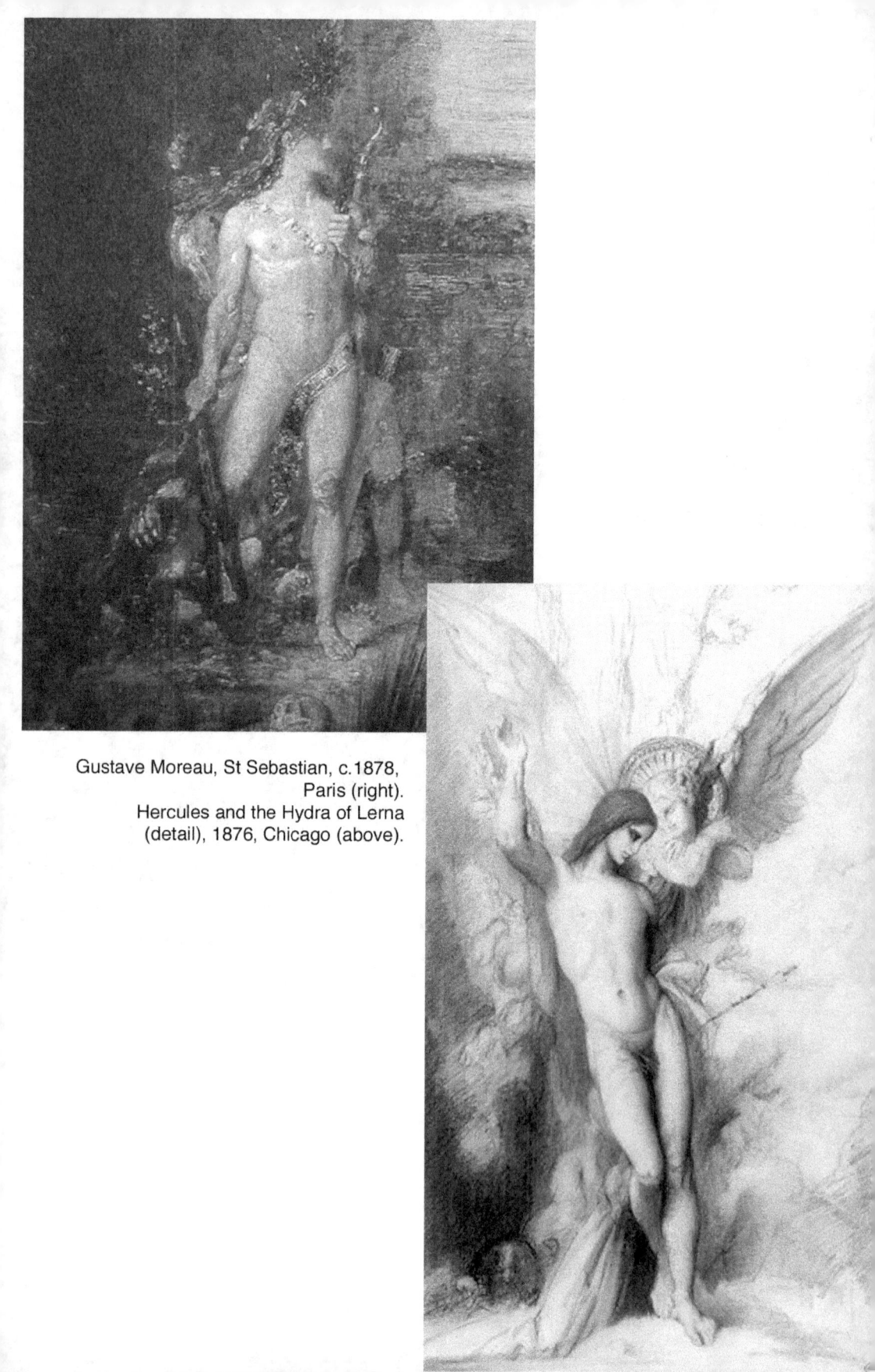

Gustave Moreau, St Sebastian, c.1878,
Paris (right).
Hercules and the Hydra of Lerna
(detail), 1876, Chicago (above).

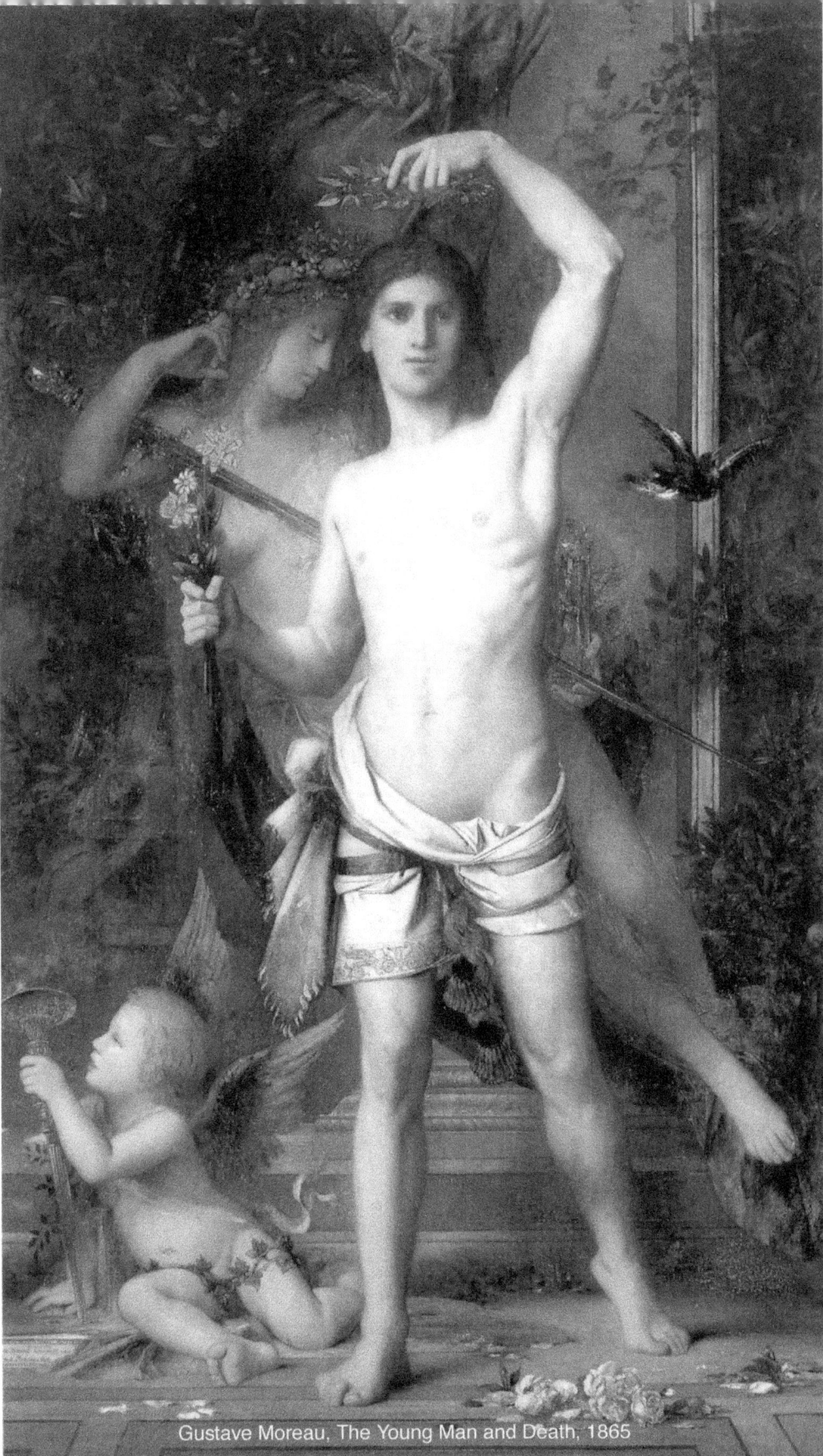

Gustave Moreau, The Young Man and Death, 1865

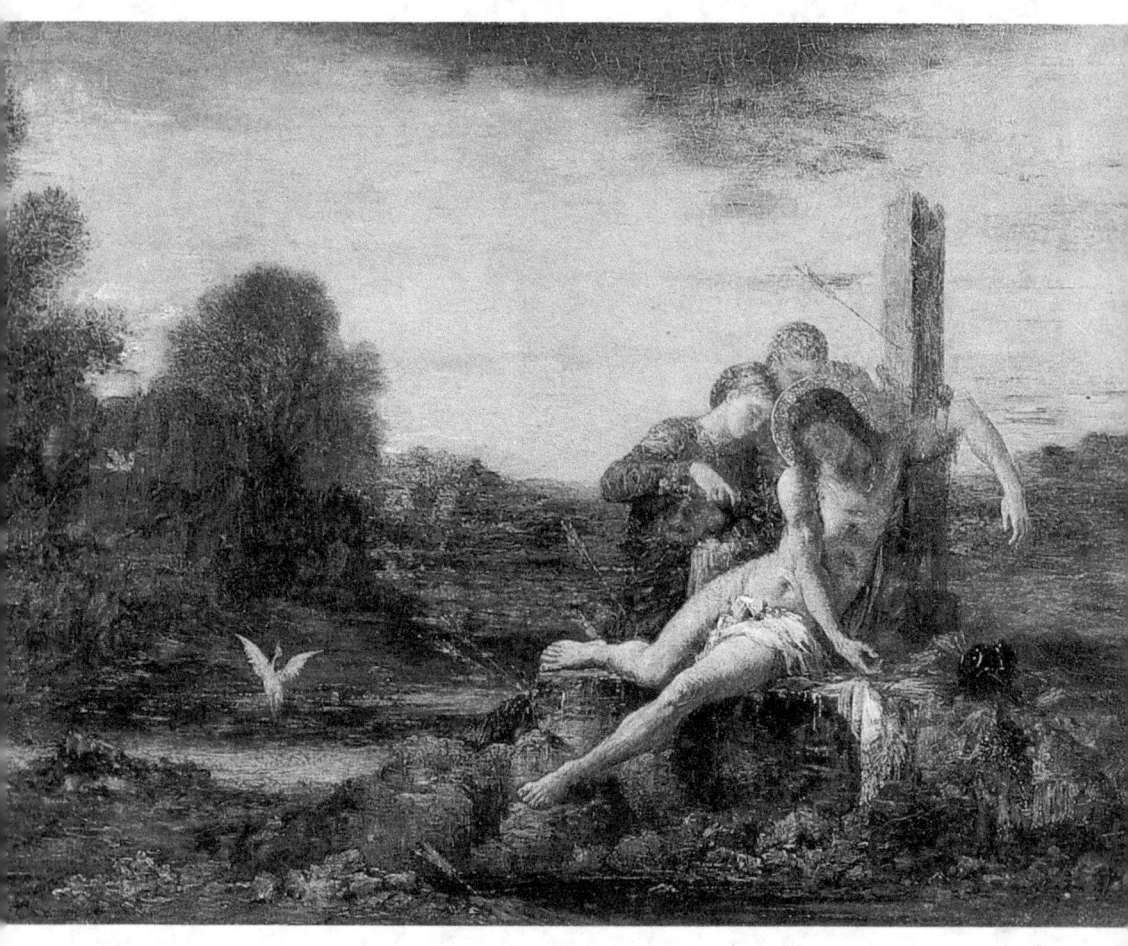

Gustave Moreau, St Sebastian, 1869

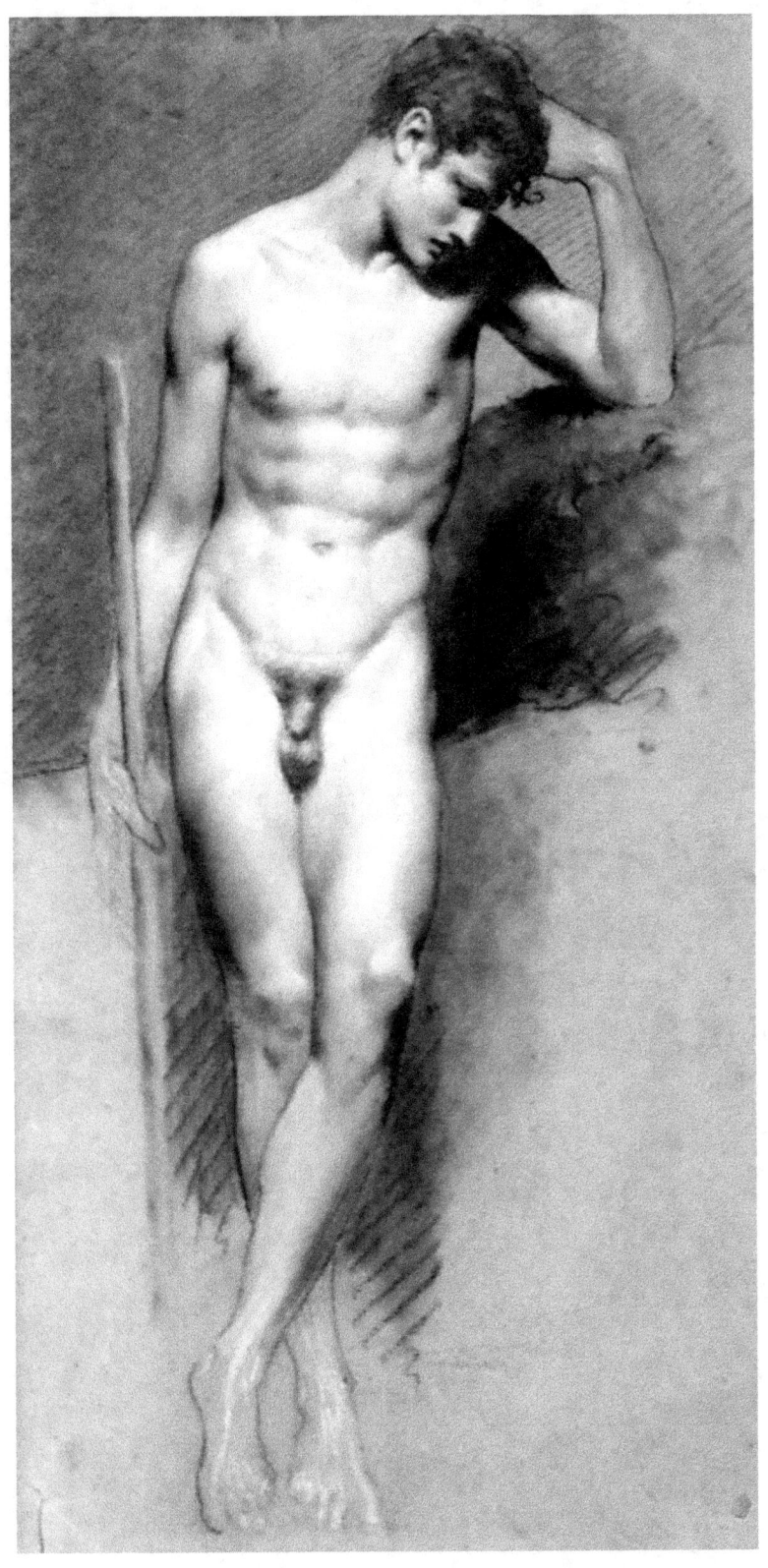

Pierre-Paul Prud'hon (1758-1823), Male Nude Standing

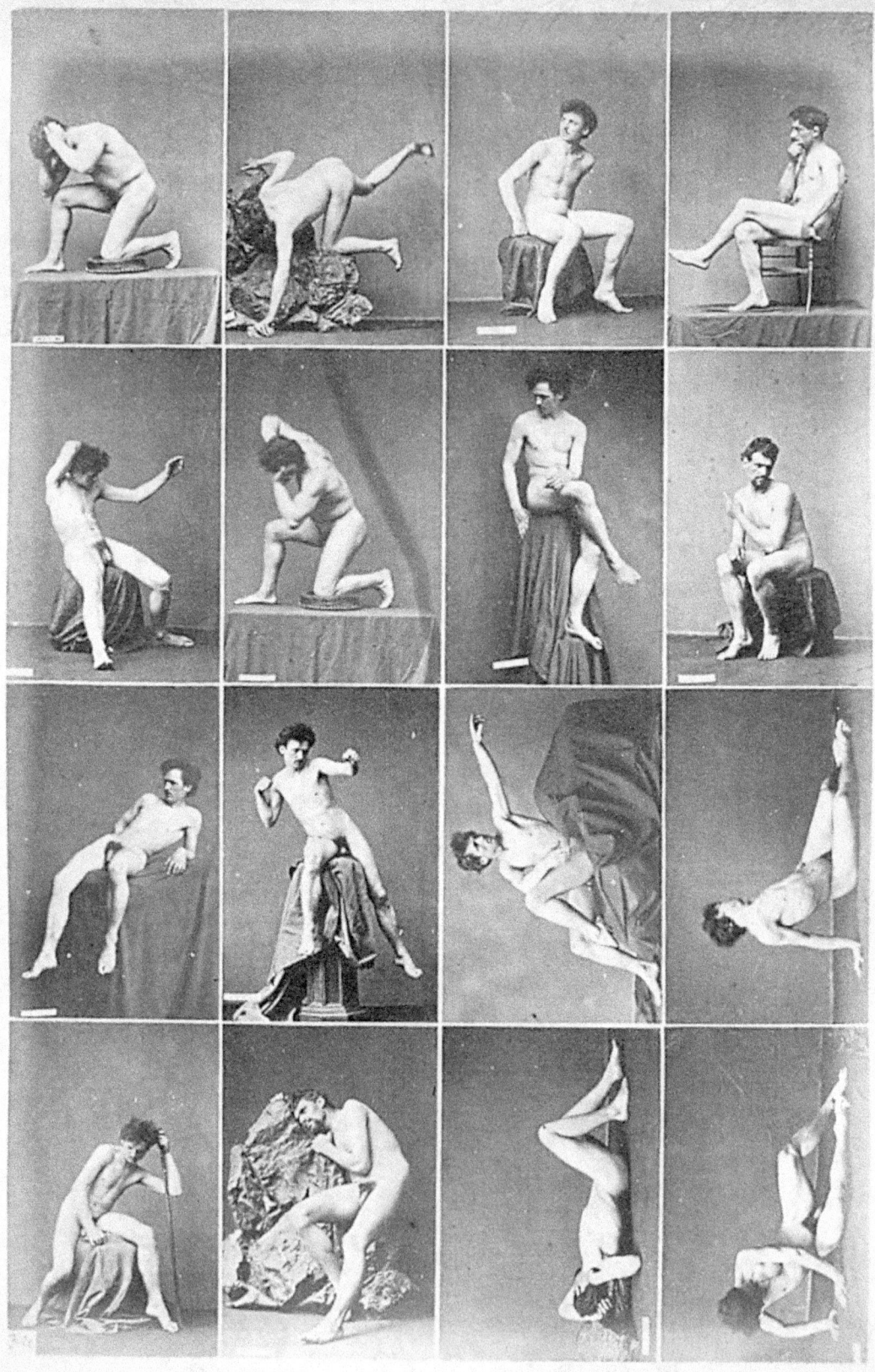

Ignout, Male Nude Studies, 1875

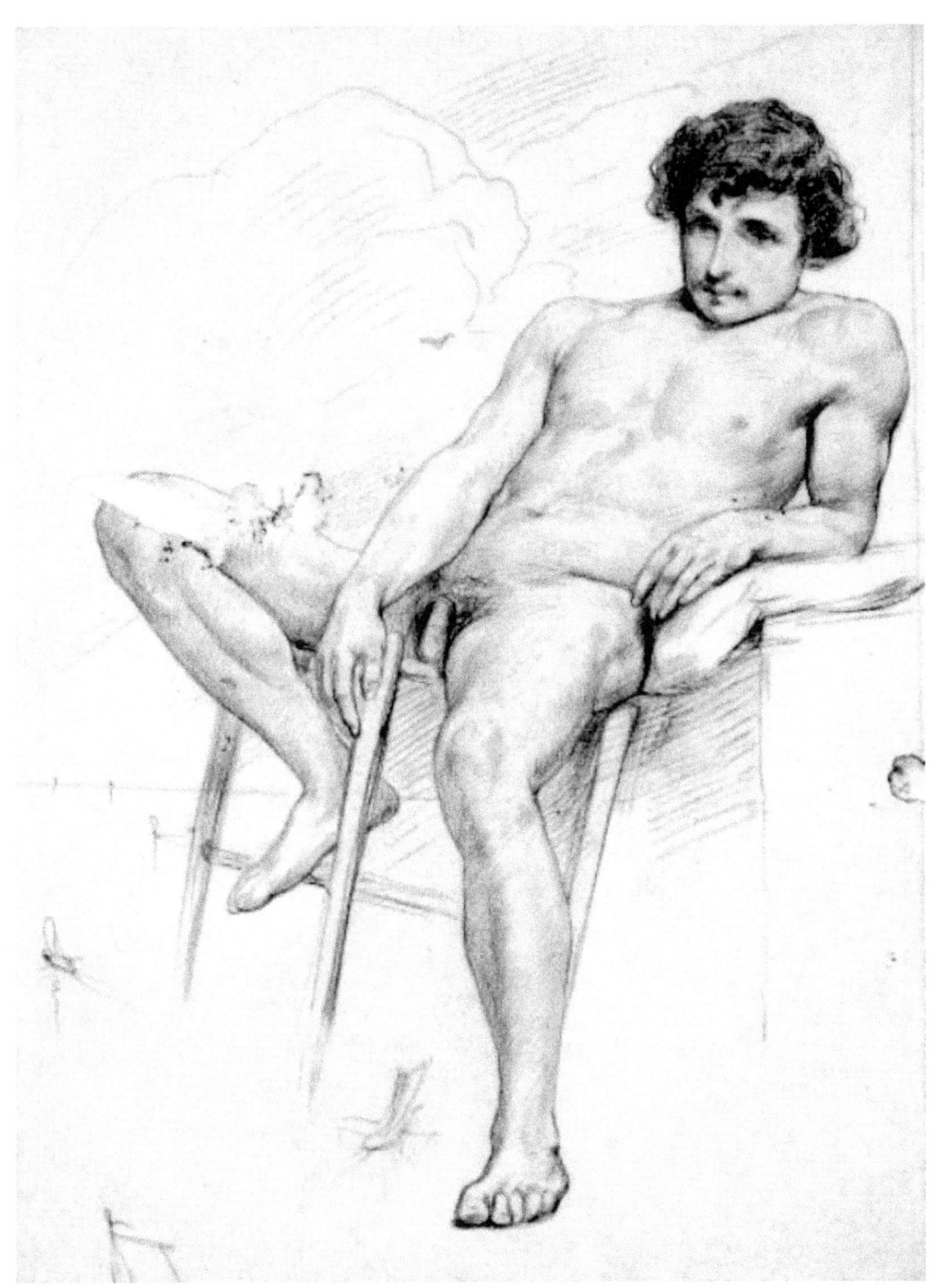

Lord Leighton, life drawing

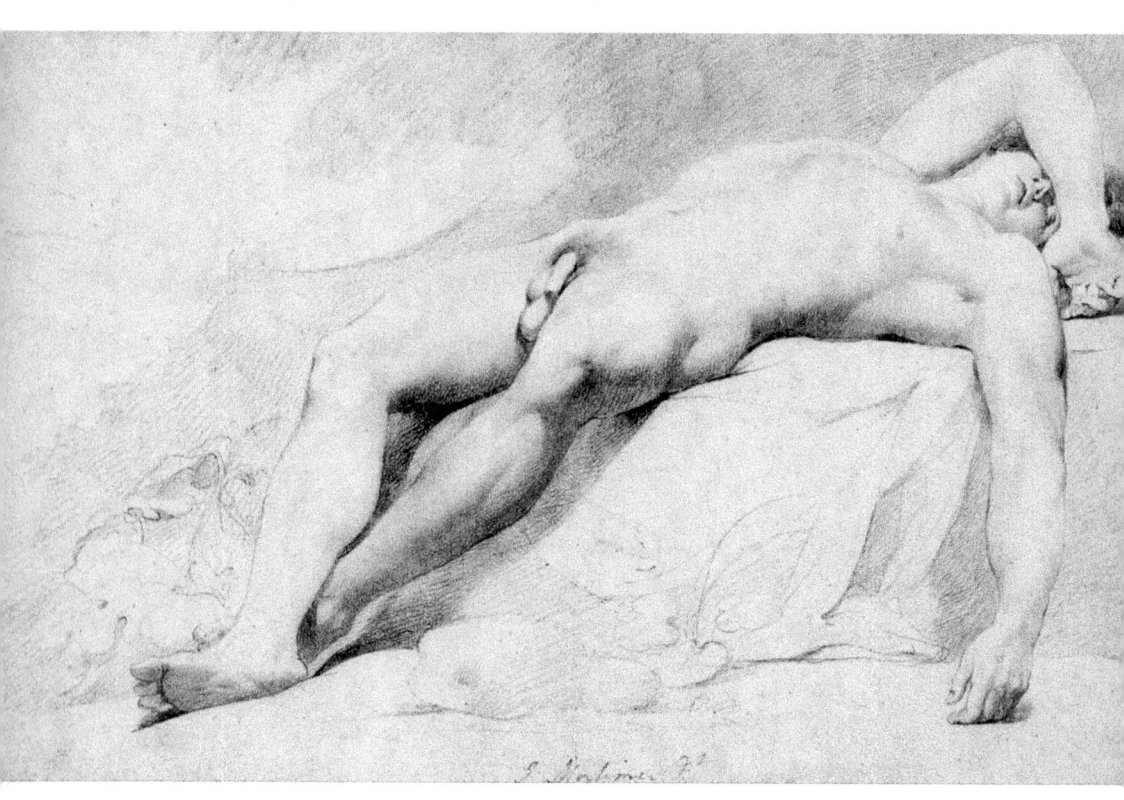

John Hamilton Mortimer, Recumbent Male Nude, c. 1773

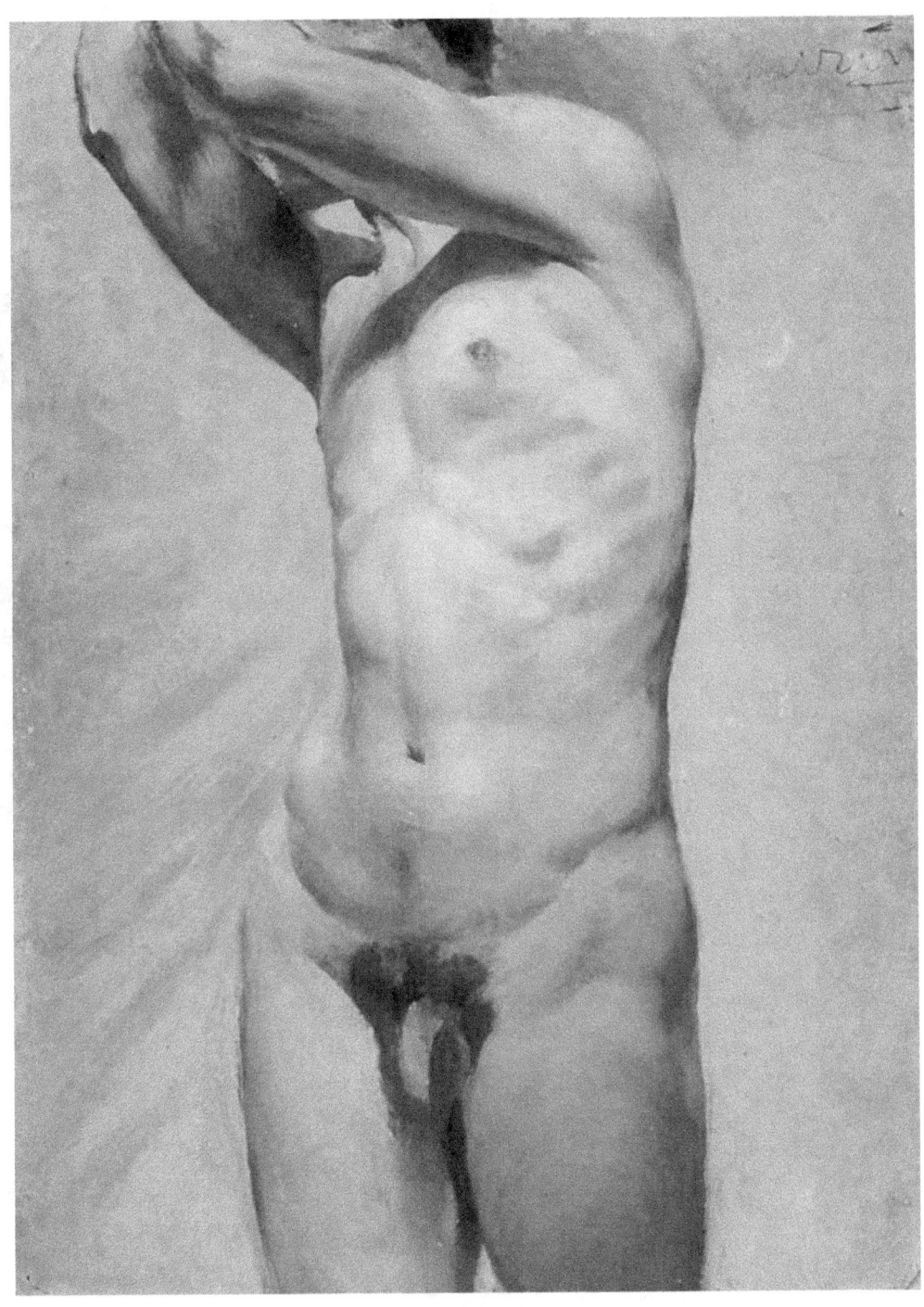

French school, c. 1890

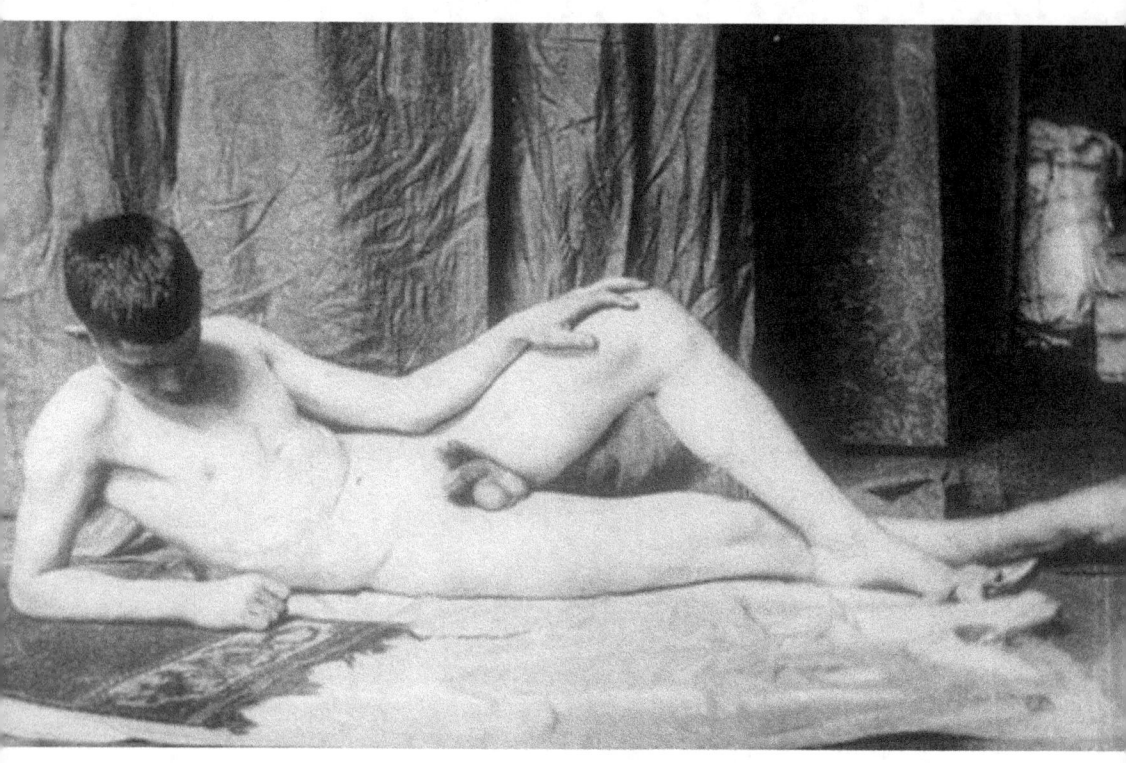

Reclining Male Nude, 1887–92,
Thomas Eakins, platinum print

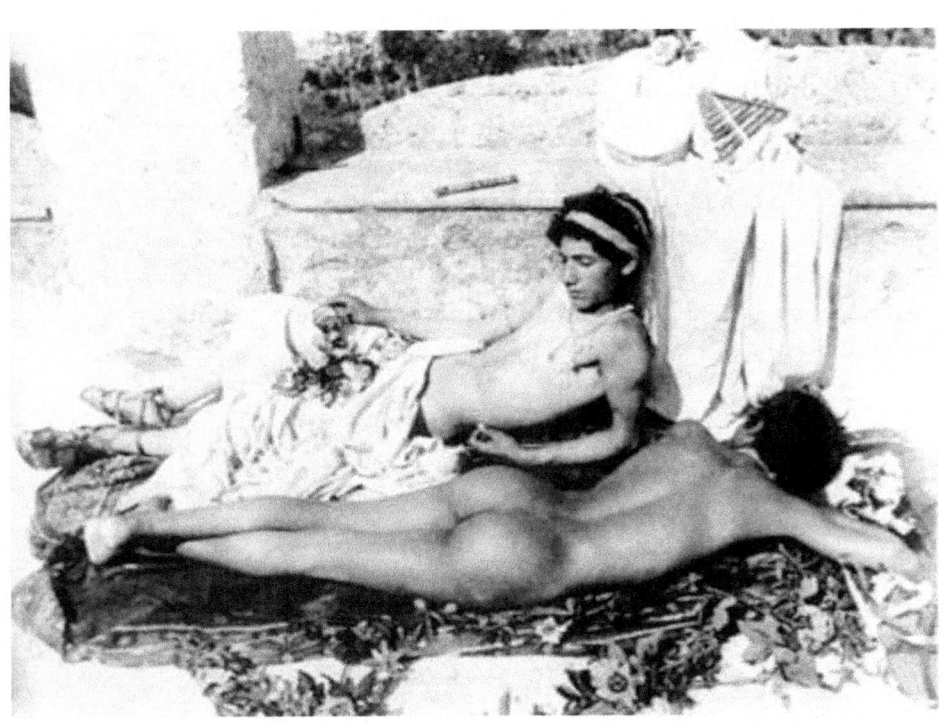

Wilhelm von Gloeden, c. 1900

PORNOGRAPHY

There are many different kinds of pornography, as there are many different kinds of art or feminism. Seen through cultural or postmodern or deconstructionist or semiological theory, pornography can be viewed as a realm of codes, meanings, contexts, signifiers, values, experiences and attitudes, which are politically controlled, manufactured by social, economic and political needs and demands. Pornography is thus the *representation* of... something; maybe certain kinds of sexuality, maybe somebody's thoughts on certain kinds of sexuality. Pornography is not *sexuality in itself*, it is mediation, representation, communication, a relic, a trace.

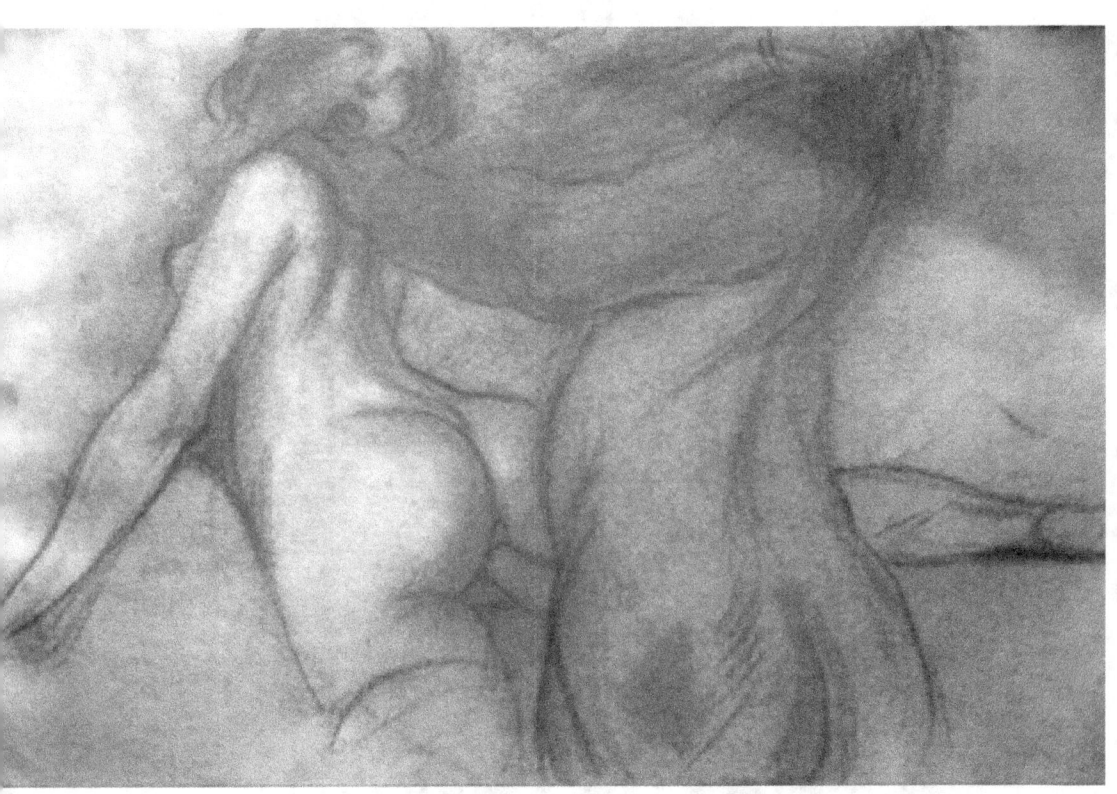

Aroldo Bonzagni

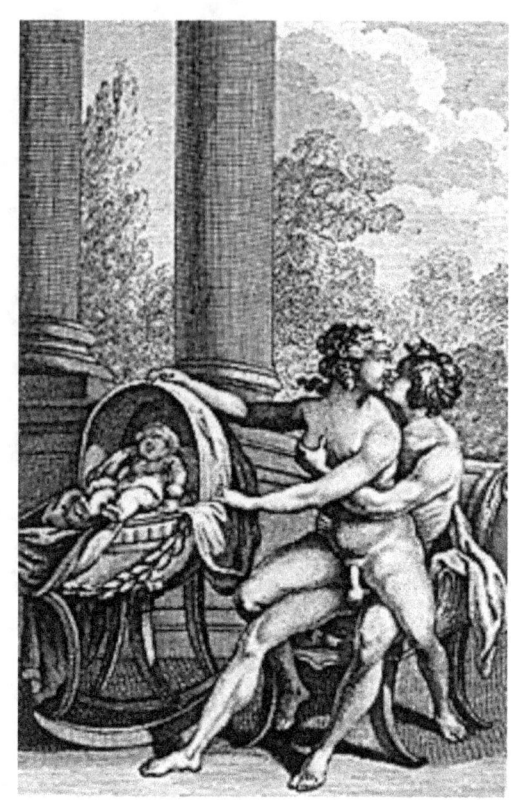

Anonymous, illustrations to
the Sonnets by Pietro Aretino

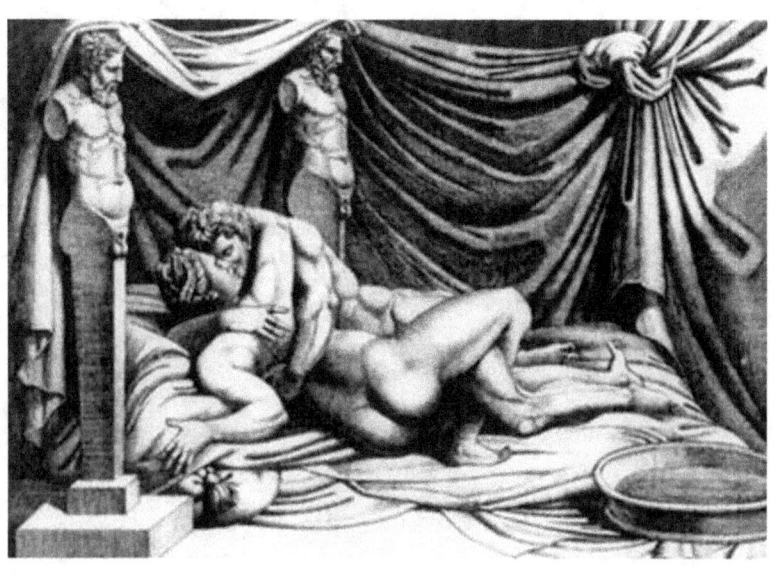

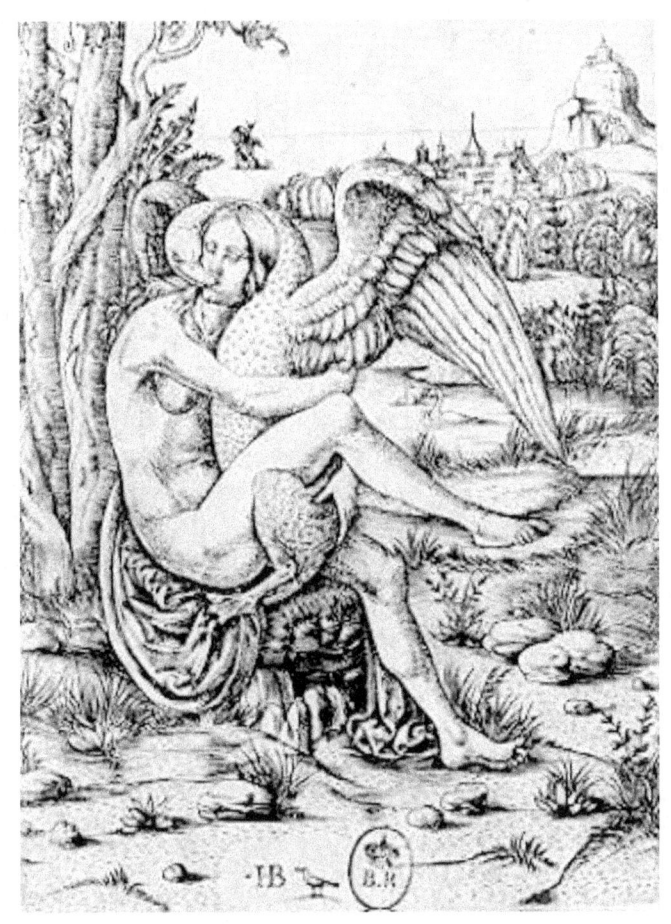

Hans Baldung (1484-1545), this page and over

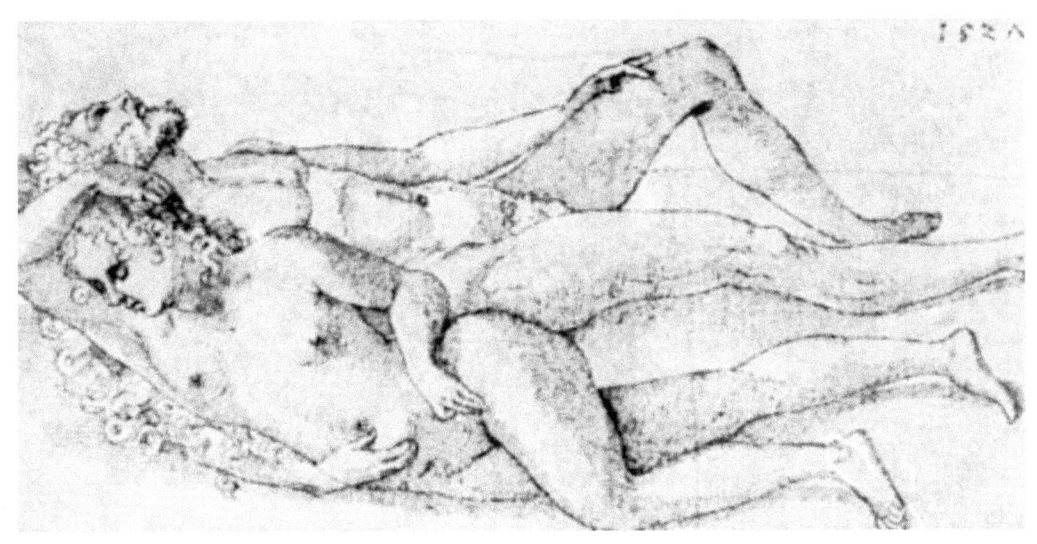

Pornography has its own 'genres' of sub-categories: there is S/M, hardcore, lesbian, gay porn, soft core, and pornography geared to any number of fetishes; rubber, leather, boots, large breasts, bondage, etc.[1] What's your fetish? Porn will have something for you!

The history of art too has its categories and forms of erotic art, with the reclining (female) nude as perhaps the most well-known, and the most celebrated in art criticism. Other forms include humans and deities, humans and animals (often gods in beast-form), sexual positions, religious subjects, mythological subjects, Venus and Cupid, etc.

---

1 These sub-genres are institutions in themselves, with their own codes and structures, but their institutionalized sexual images do not express the real eroticism that people experience (they suggest it, perhaps, or reflect parts of it).

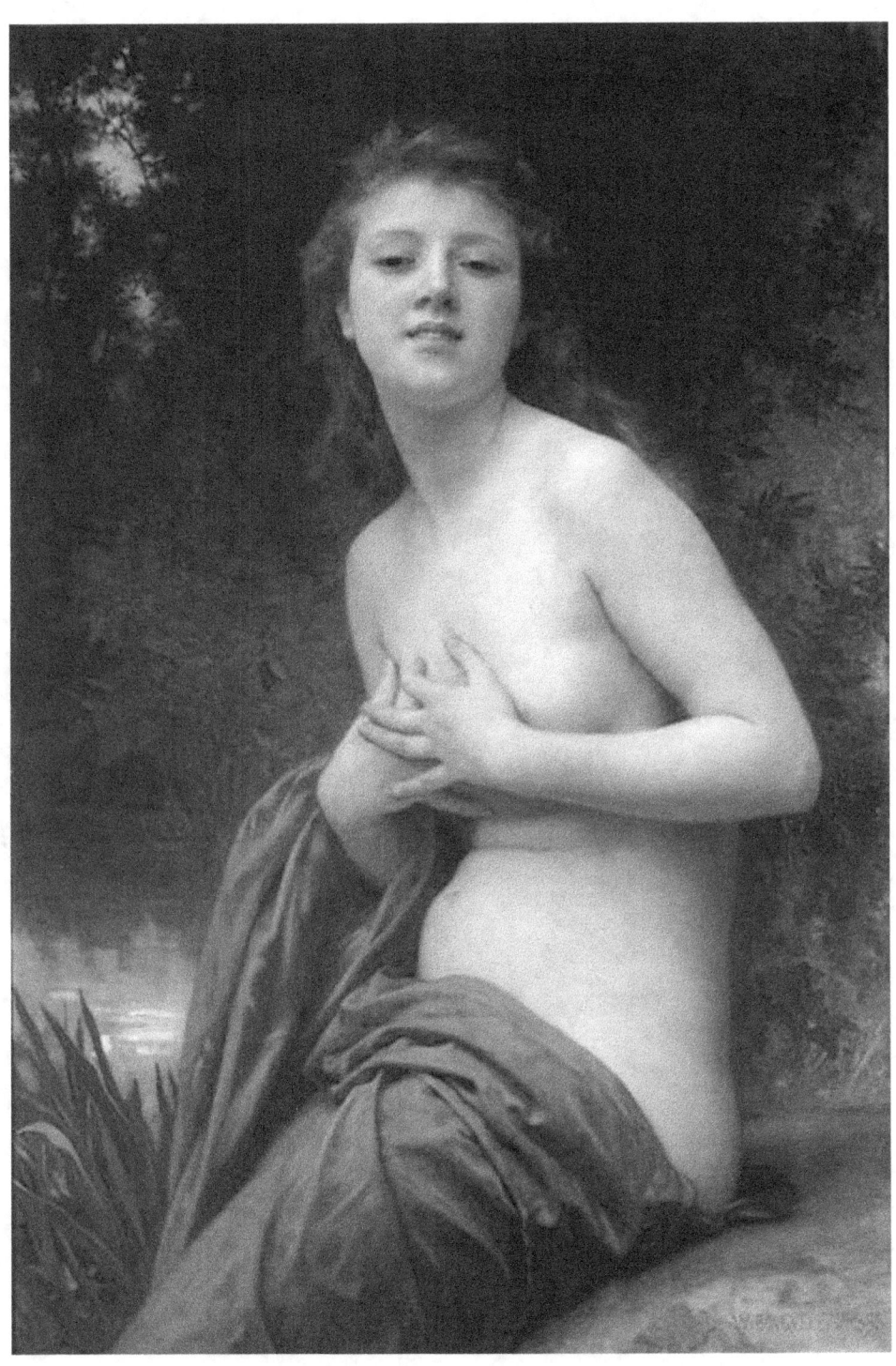

William Bouguereau, Spring Breeze, 1895

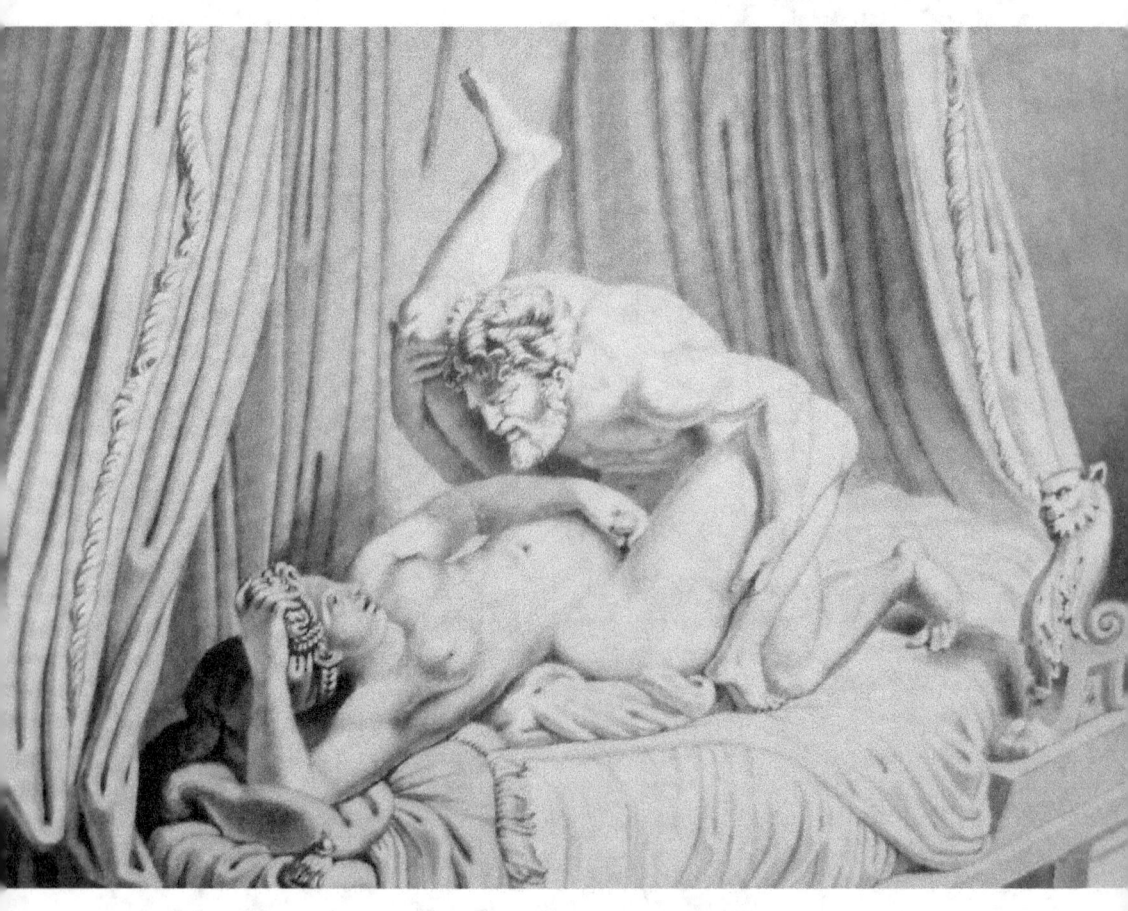

Friedrich von Waldeck, from Postures, c. 1858
(This page and following pages)

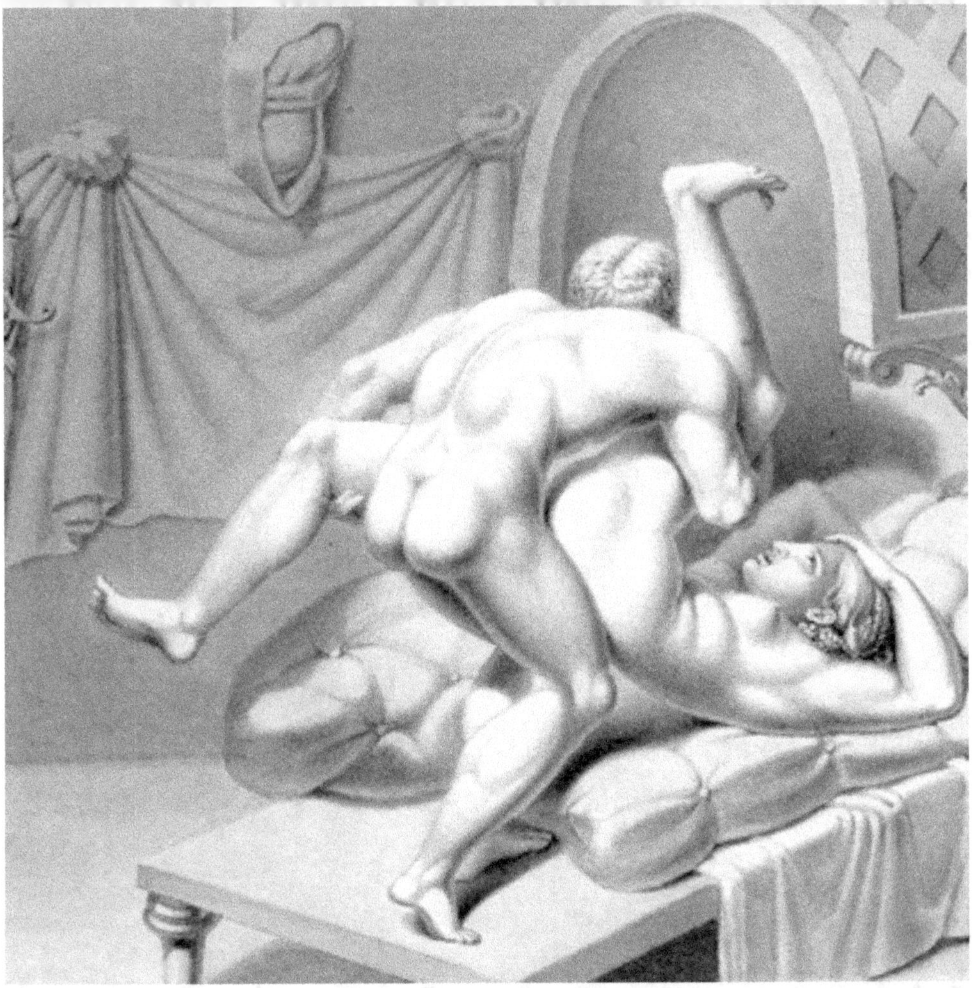

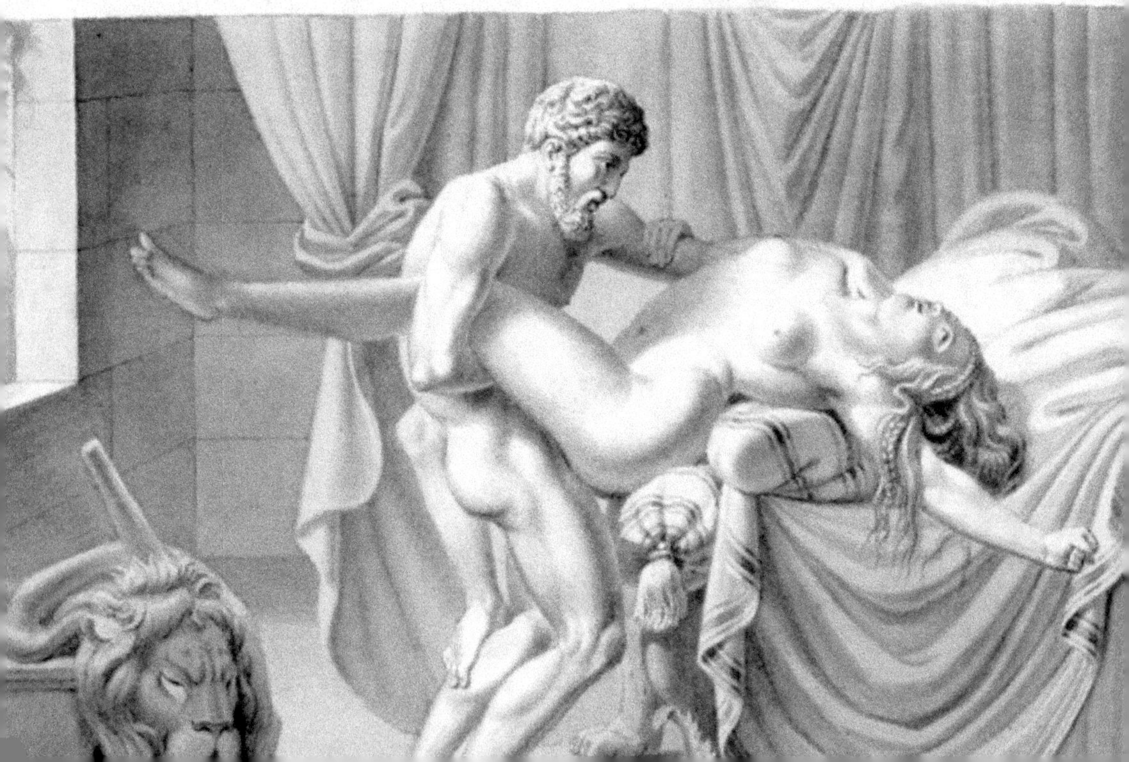

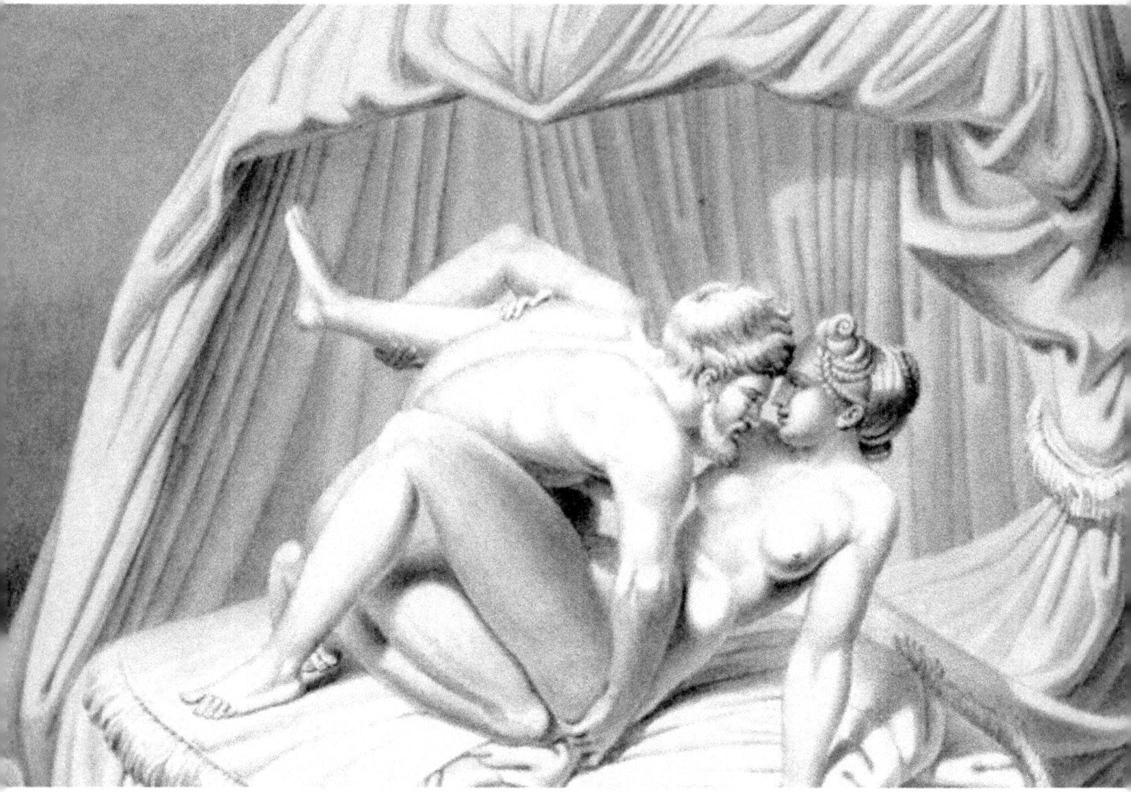

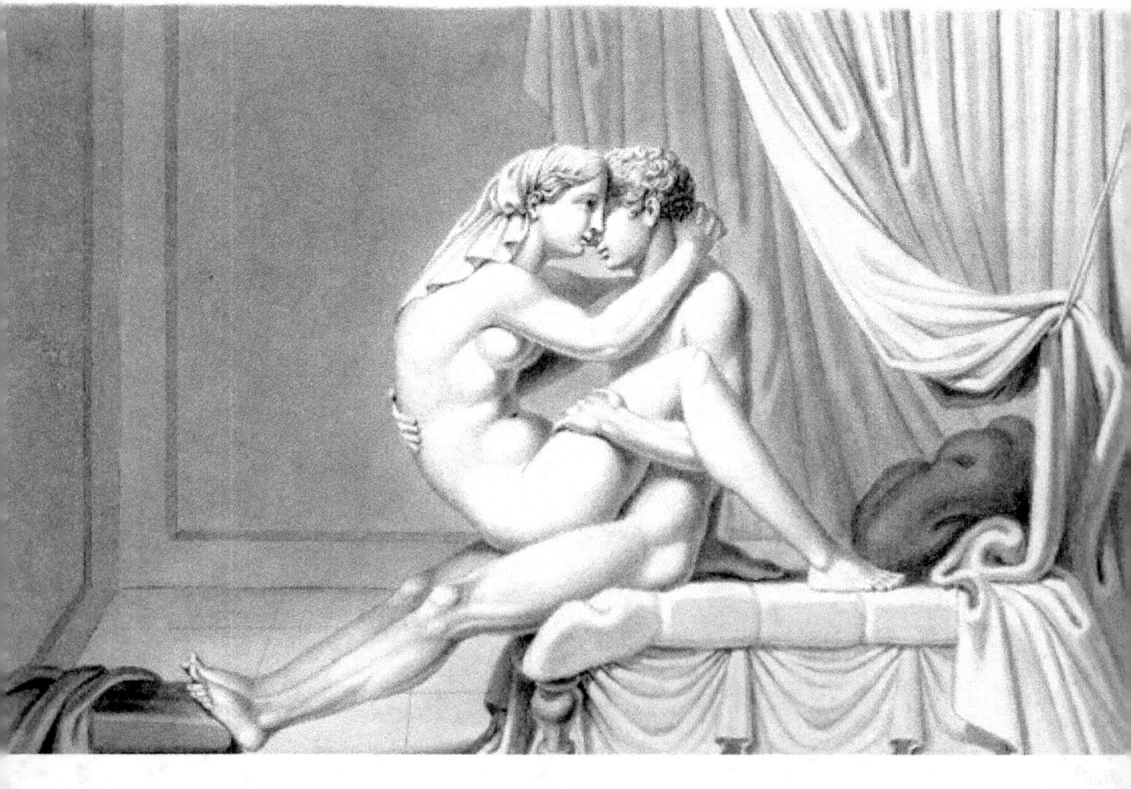

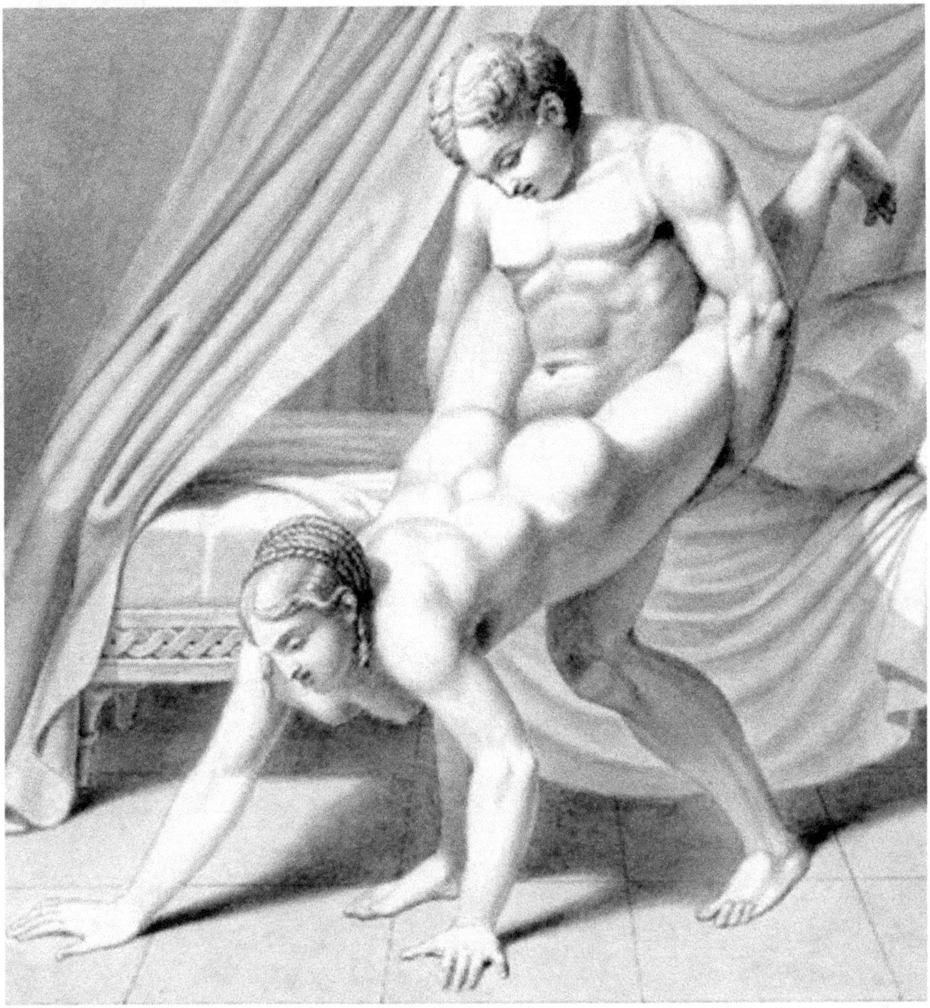

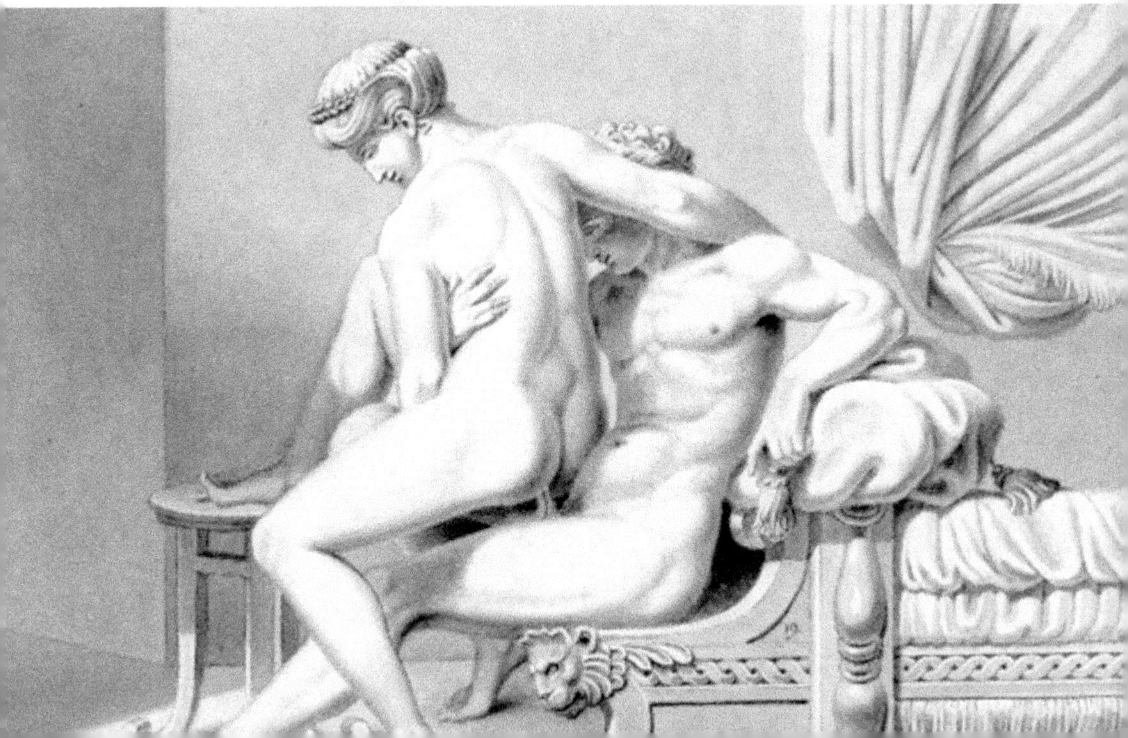

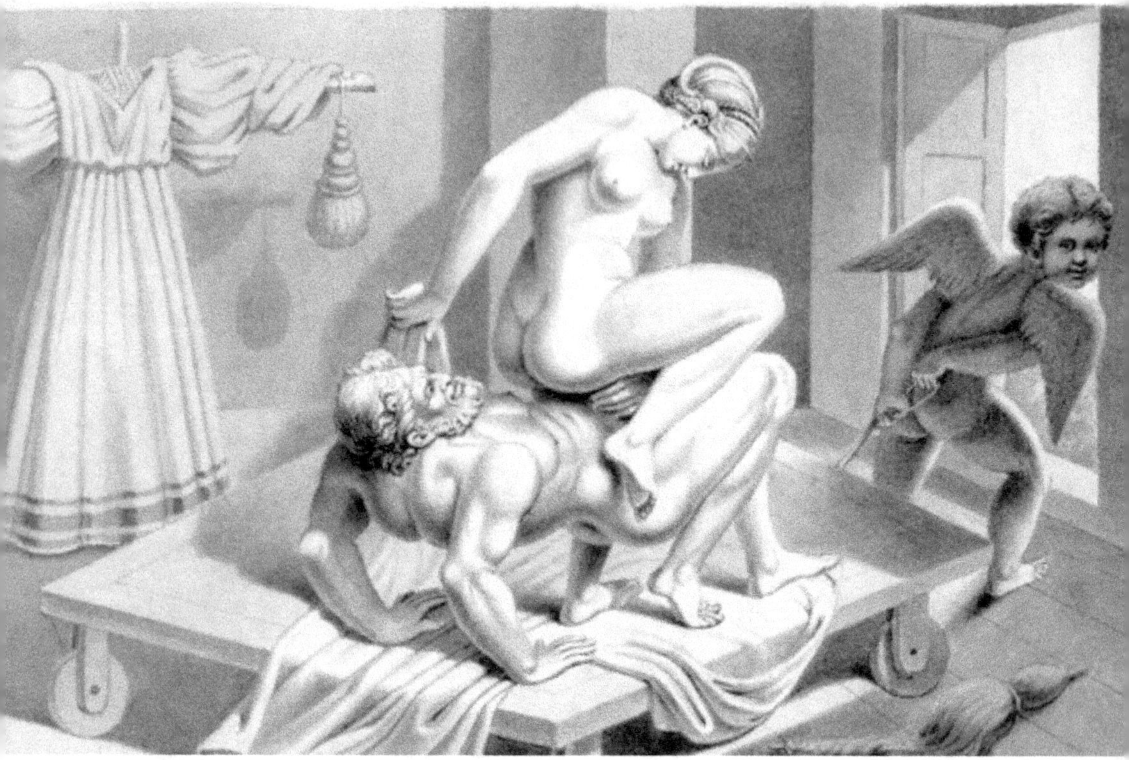

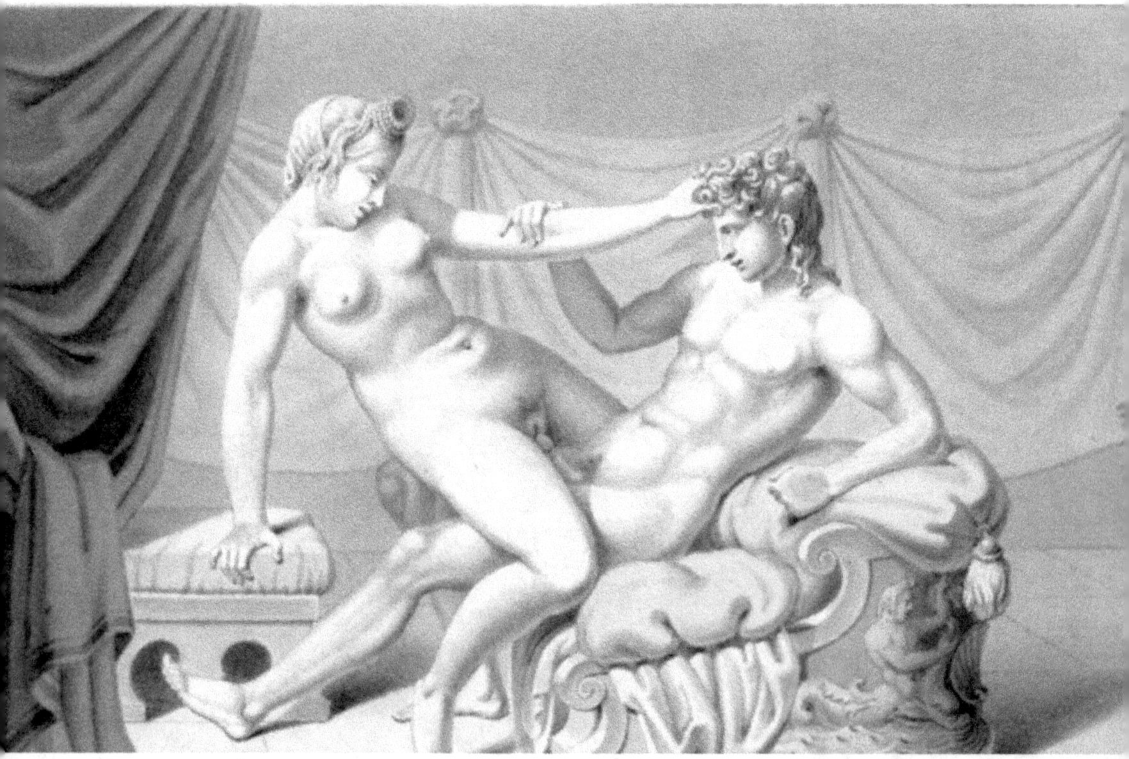

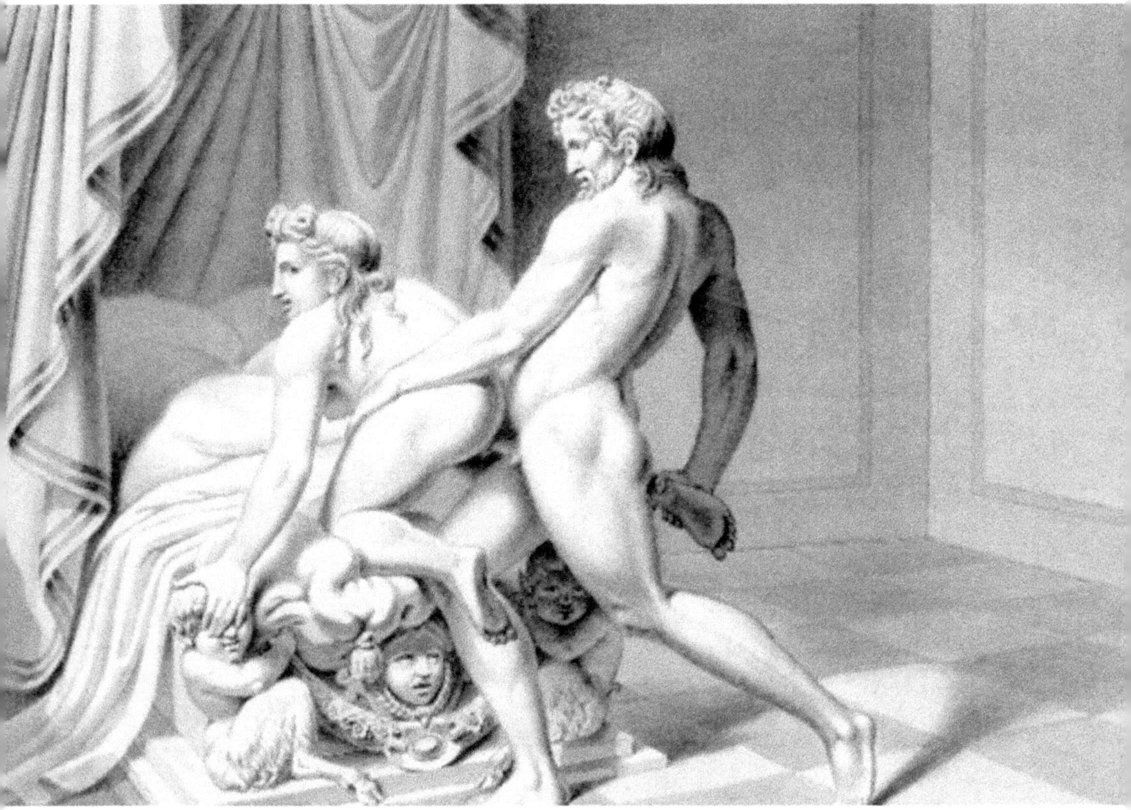

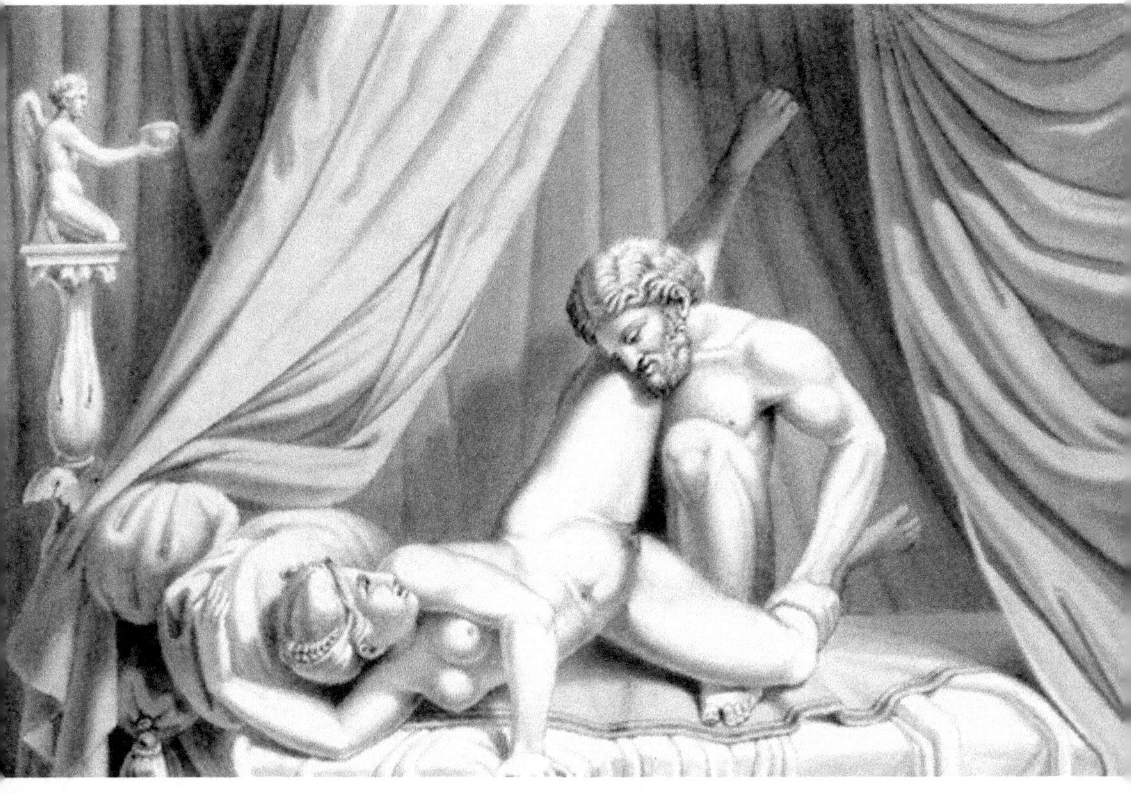

What occurs in most Western art, from Greek and Roman sculpture through the glories of the Renaissance to the latest pornography are male representations of female eroticism. Feminists say that there are no real depictions of female *jouissance* in art or literature. 'In my opinion,' wrote Marguerite Duras, 'women have never expressed themselves.'[1] What she means, perhaps, is that women have expressed themselves thus far in the terms and means and social structures defined by men. There is no 'feminine' or 'women's' writing, according to some feminists. Hélène Cixous reckons she's found only three 'inscriptions of femininity' this century: Colette, Marguerite Duras and Jean Genet.[2] In art, there are many women artists who have tackled erotic issues, but in the history of art, going back to, say, the Renaissance, the number of women artists who have survived are far fewer.

---

1 Duras, interview in *Signs*, Winter 1975, in E. Marks, 175.
2 H. Cixous: "The Laugh of the Medusa", *Signs*, summer 1976, in E. E. Marks, 249.

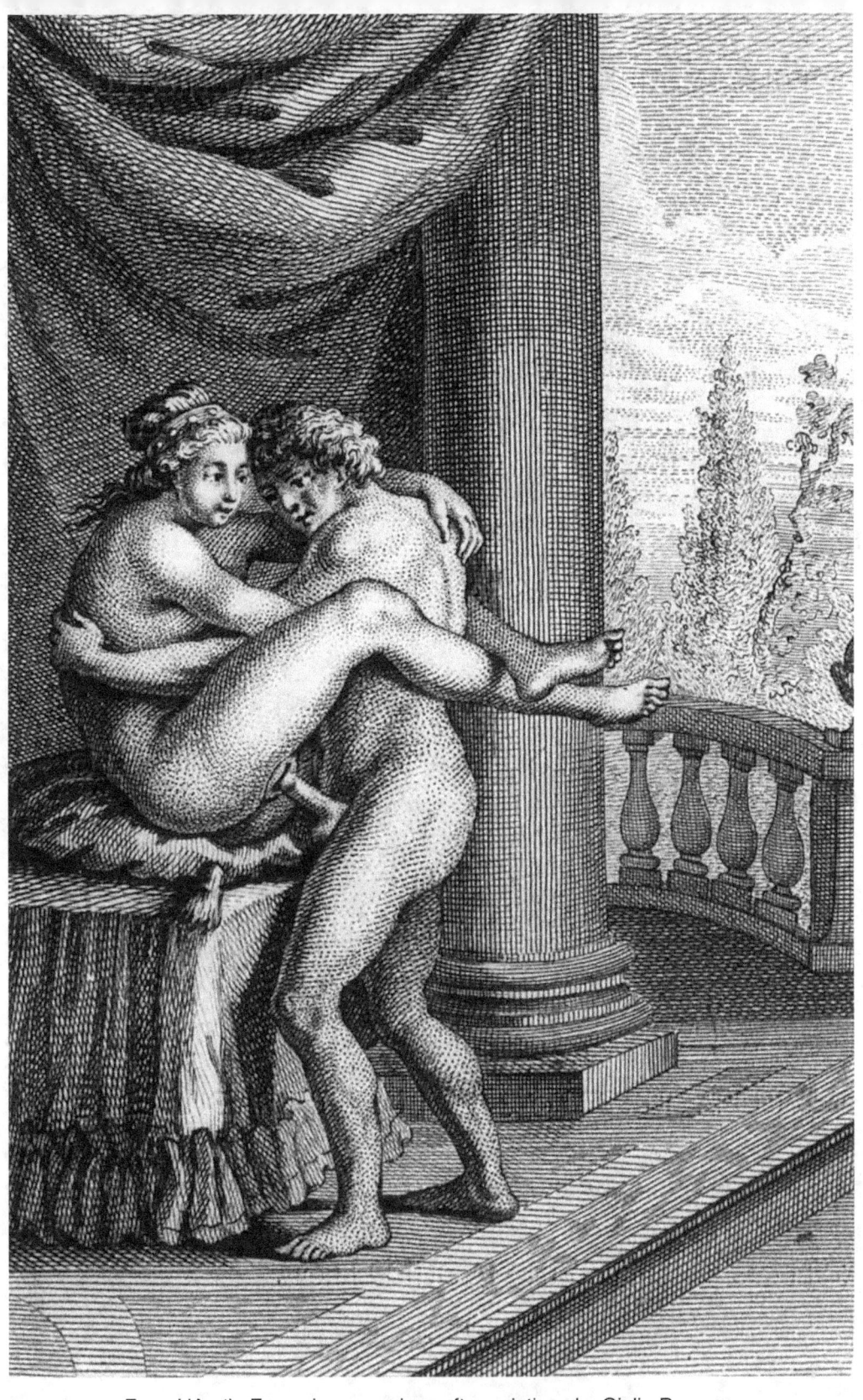

From L'Aretin Francais, engravings after paintings by Giulio Romano,
illustrating the Sonnets of Pietro Aretino
(this page and following pages)

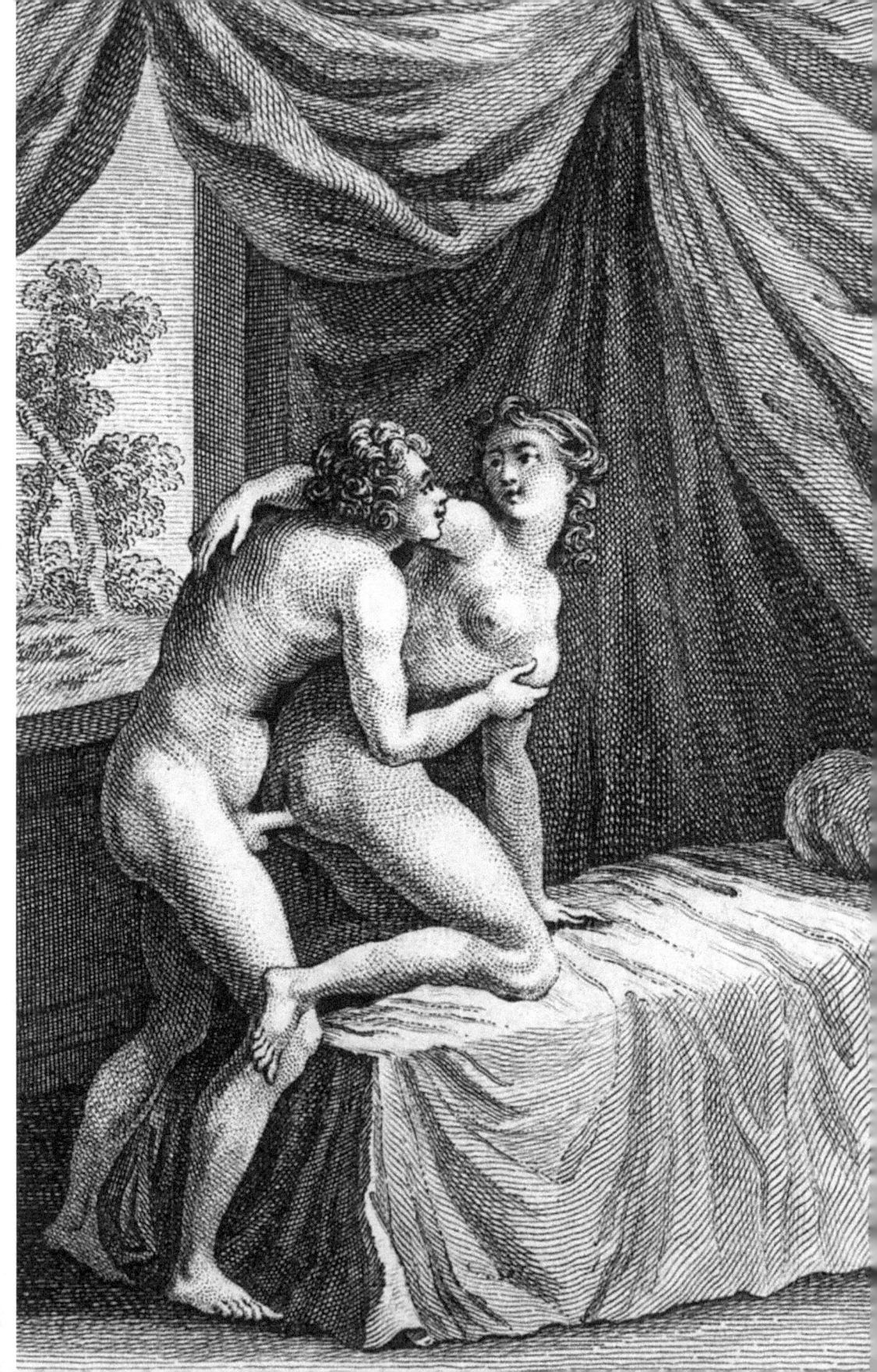

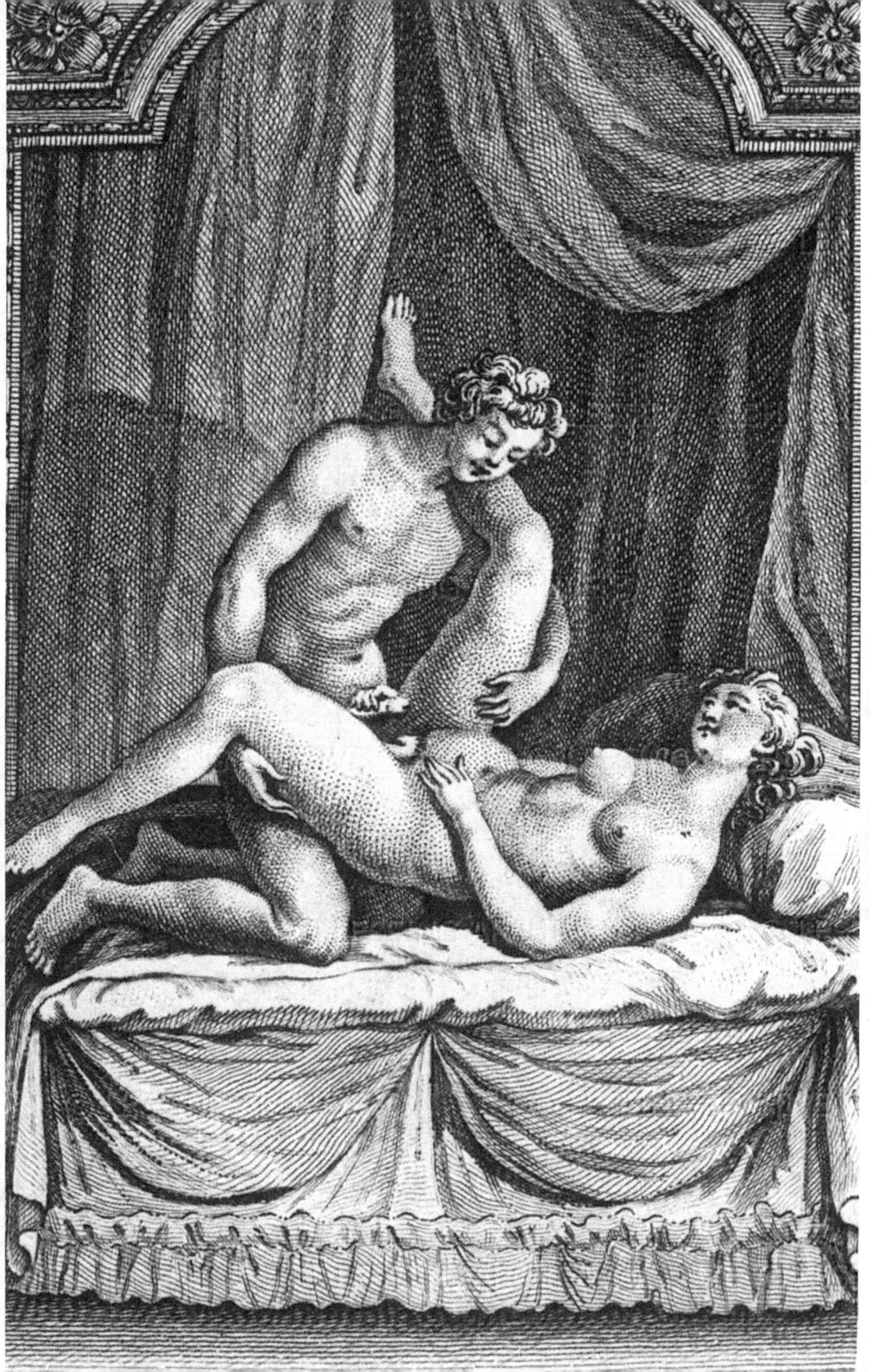

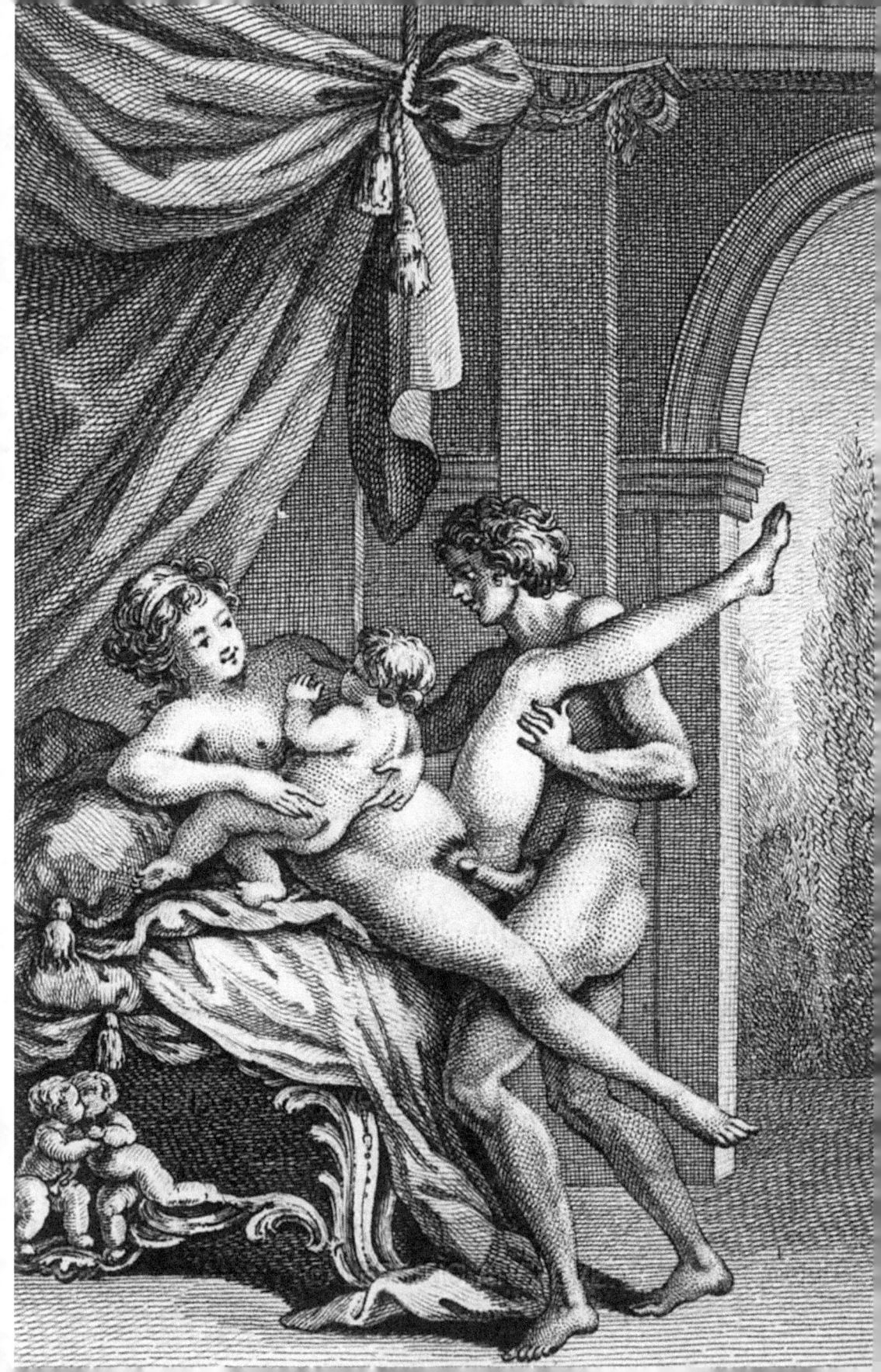

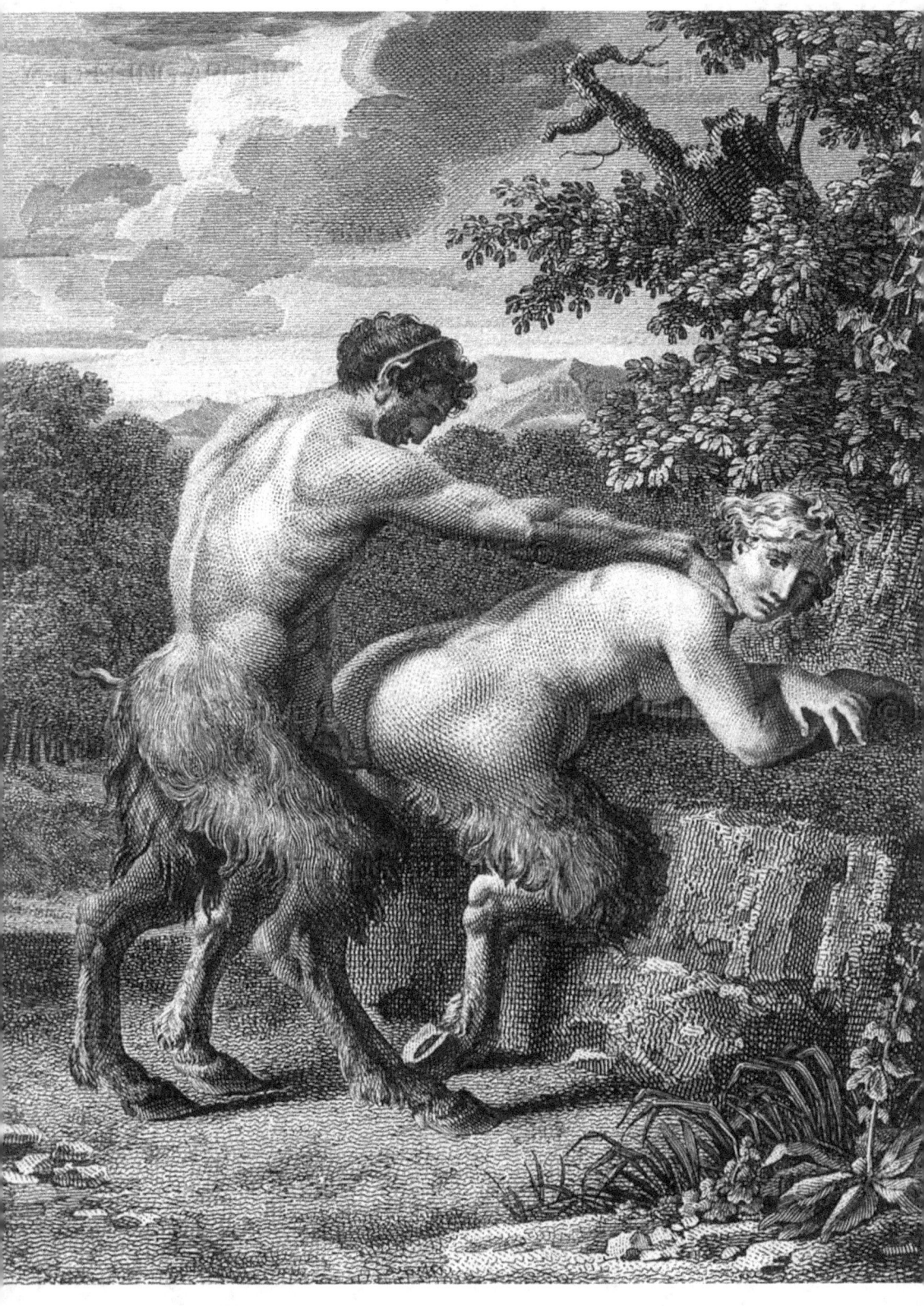

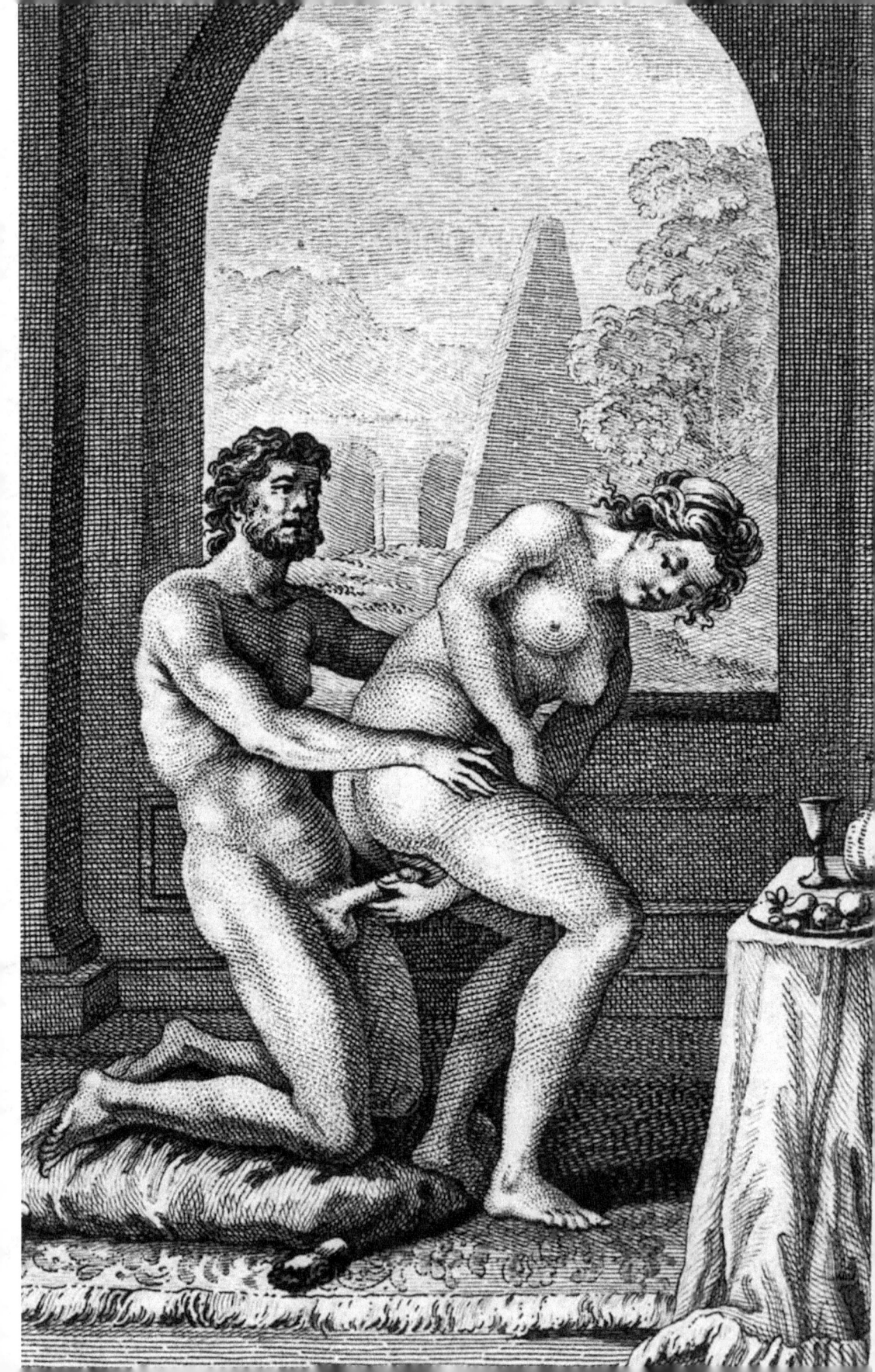

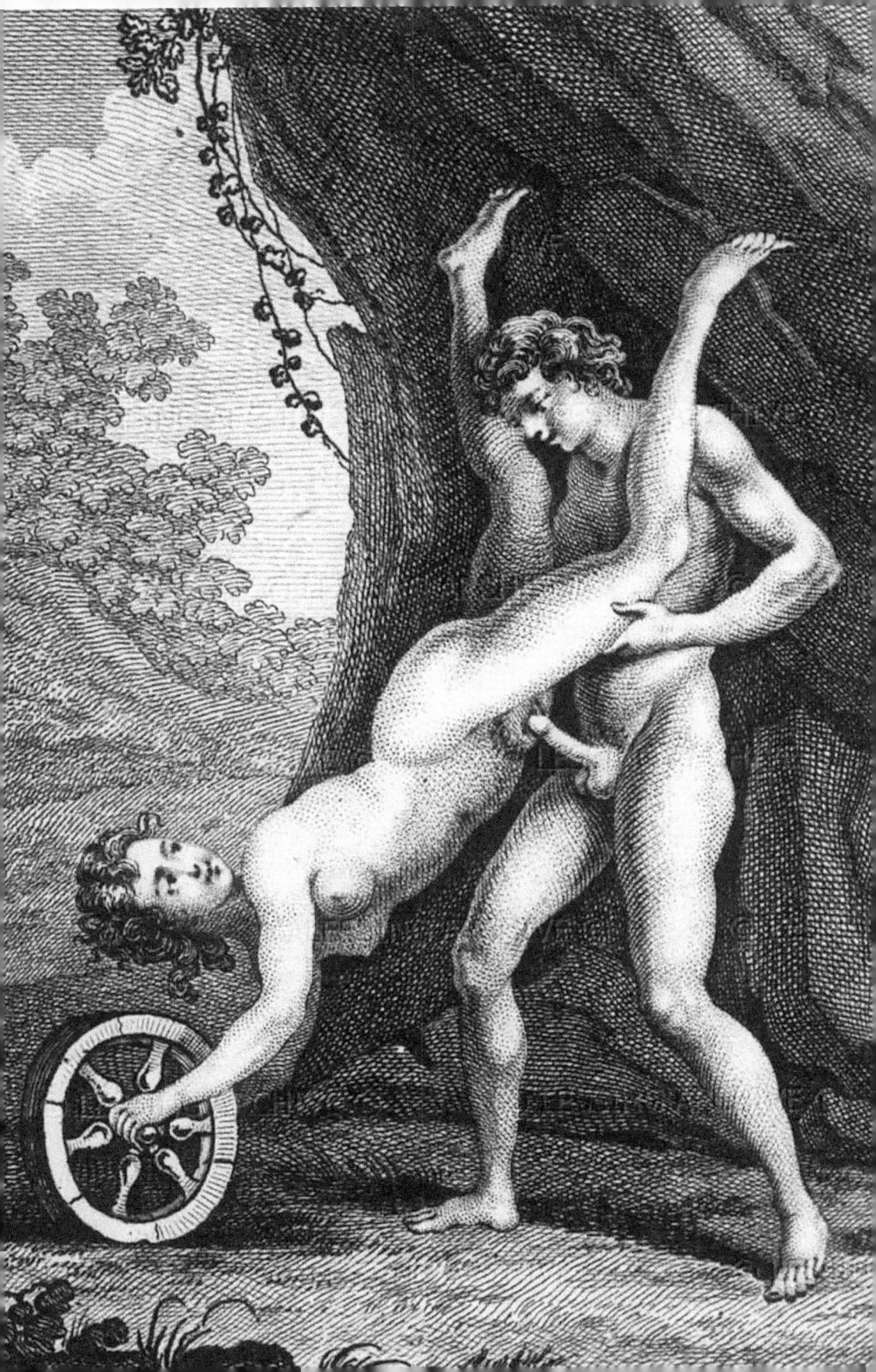

For law-abiding citizens, it seems, the 'line' has to be drawn somewhere. Somewhere between public and private, between sex and love, between visible and invisible, between freedom and control, between secrecy and publicity, between availability and censorship. Indeed, Walter Kendrick said the only definition of pornography is in terms of its forbidden or secret nature.[1]

Pornography brings the secret life of people out into the open. What the Western world holds most dear – the primacy and holiness of the individual, and the primacy and holiness of (heterosexual) love, of marriage, of the family – is cast into doubt by pornography.

Hardcore pornography, in particular, tries to make everything as clear and as visible as possible, and is thus disruptive and unsettling for the establishment. There are, thus, many close-ups of genitals in hard core pornography. Sex is ecstatic, so hard core pornography has to show this ecstasy. It does this by focussing on the genitals.

---

1 W. Kendrick: *The Secret Museum: Pornography in Modern Culture*, Viking, New York, NY, 1987.

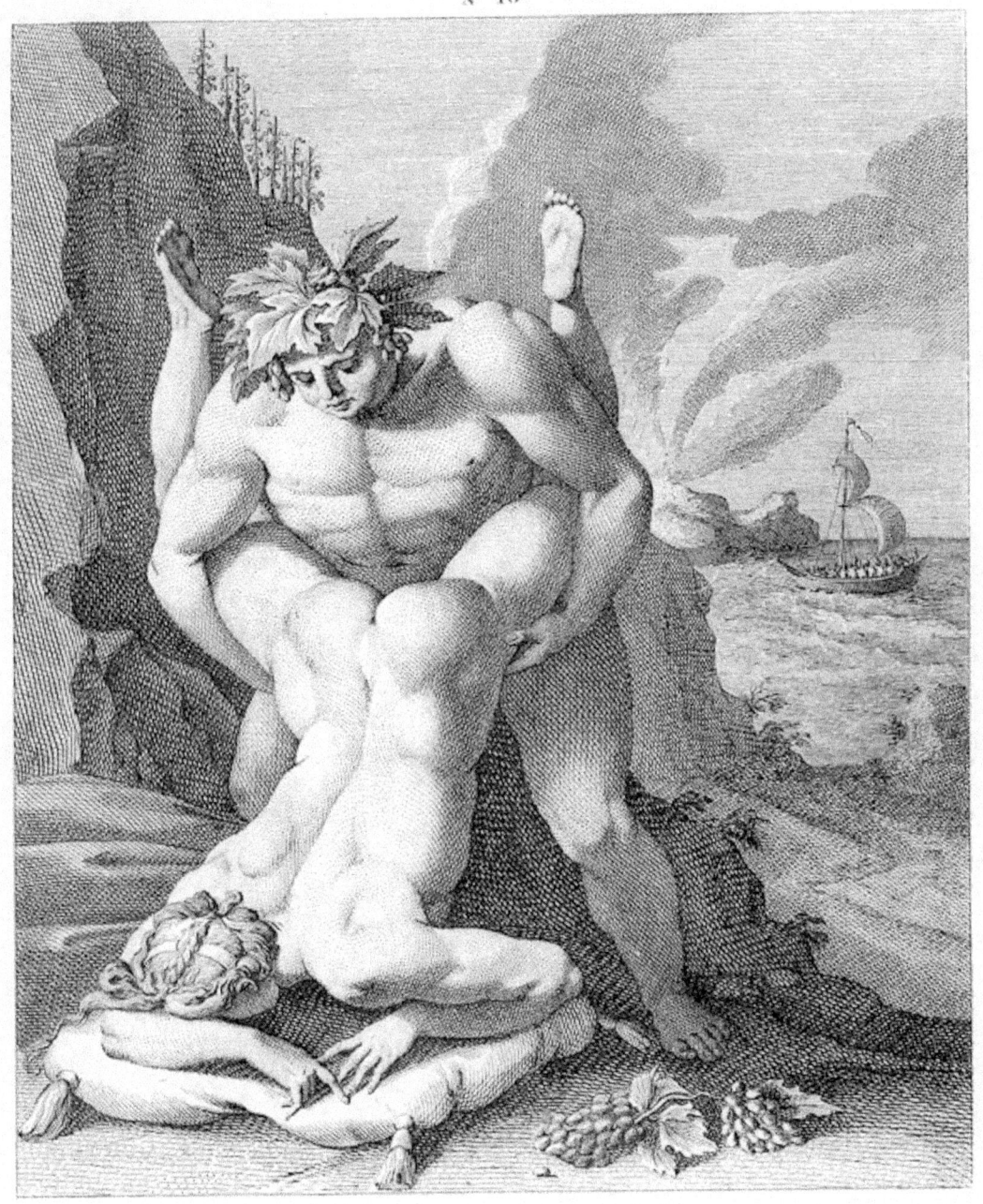

BACHUS ET ARIANE.

After Agostino Caracci, from I Modi

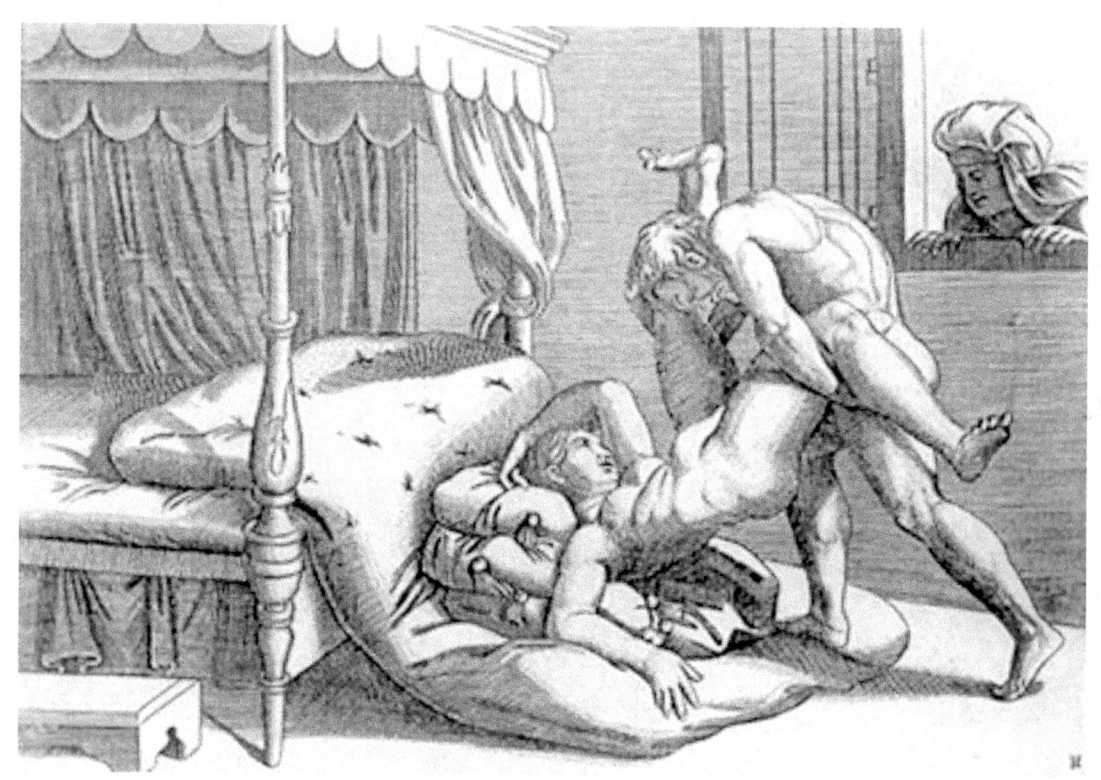

I Modi, by Pietro Aretino, illustrated by Giulio
Romano, 16th century

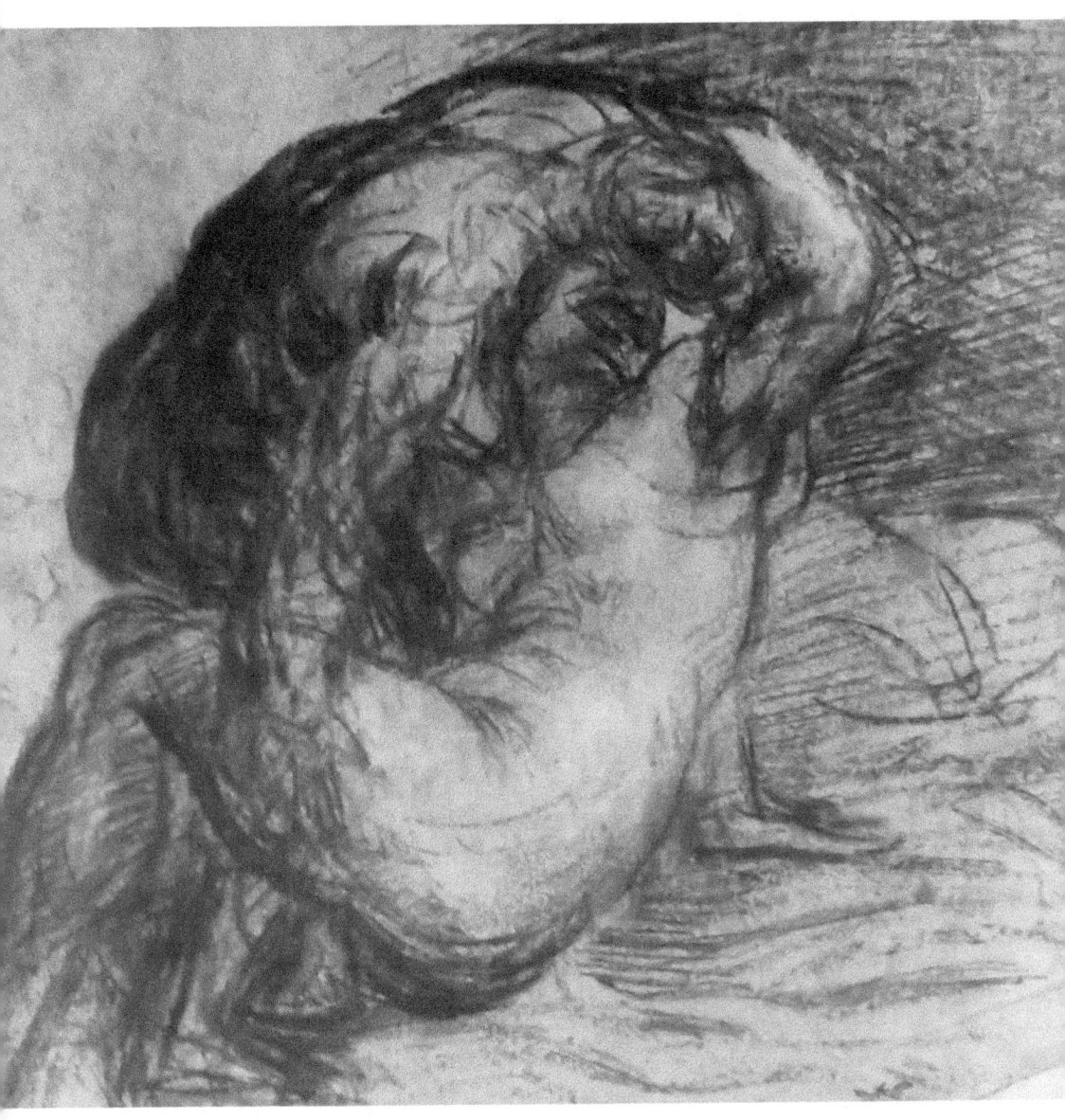

Titian, A Couple, c. 1570, Cambridge

Pornography is the culture of eroticism in the West. There is sex on TV, in fiction, in blockbuster films, in theatre, in pop music, but it is in pornography that erotic feelings are most frequently communicated. Yet pornography is commodified sex, materialist sex, sex manufactured into particular types, genres, roles and modes. There are standard pornographic encounters, standard pornographic camera angles, standard pornographic orgasms. Eroticism, as Freud knew, is powerful, whether emotionally, psychologically, culturally or politically. Pornography, then, deals with really wild eroticism by categorizing it, putting into particular genres or narratives. The visual aspect of pornography helps to deal with the wildness and passion of erotic feeling. Pornography produces images and representations, which are easier to deal with than the real thing. Jane Gallop wrote that the 'visual mode produces representations as a way of mastering what is otherwise too intense'.[1] Experiences such as orgasm and erotic desire can be too overwhelming to be communicated in words. Putting these experiences into visual representations enables them to be controlled, packaged, commodified.

1 J. Gallop: *The Daughter's Seduction: Feminism and Psychoanalysis*, Cornell University Press, New York, NY, 1982, 35.

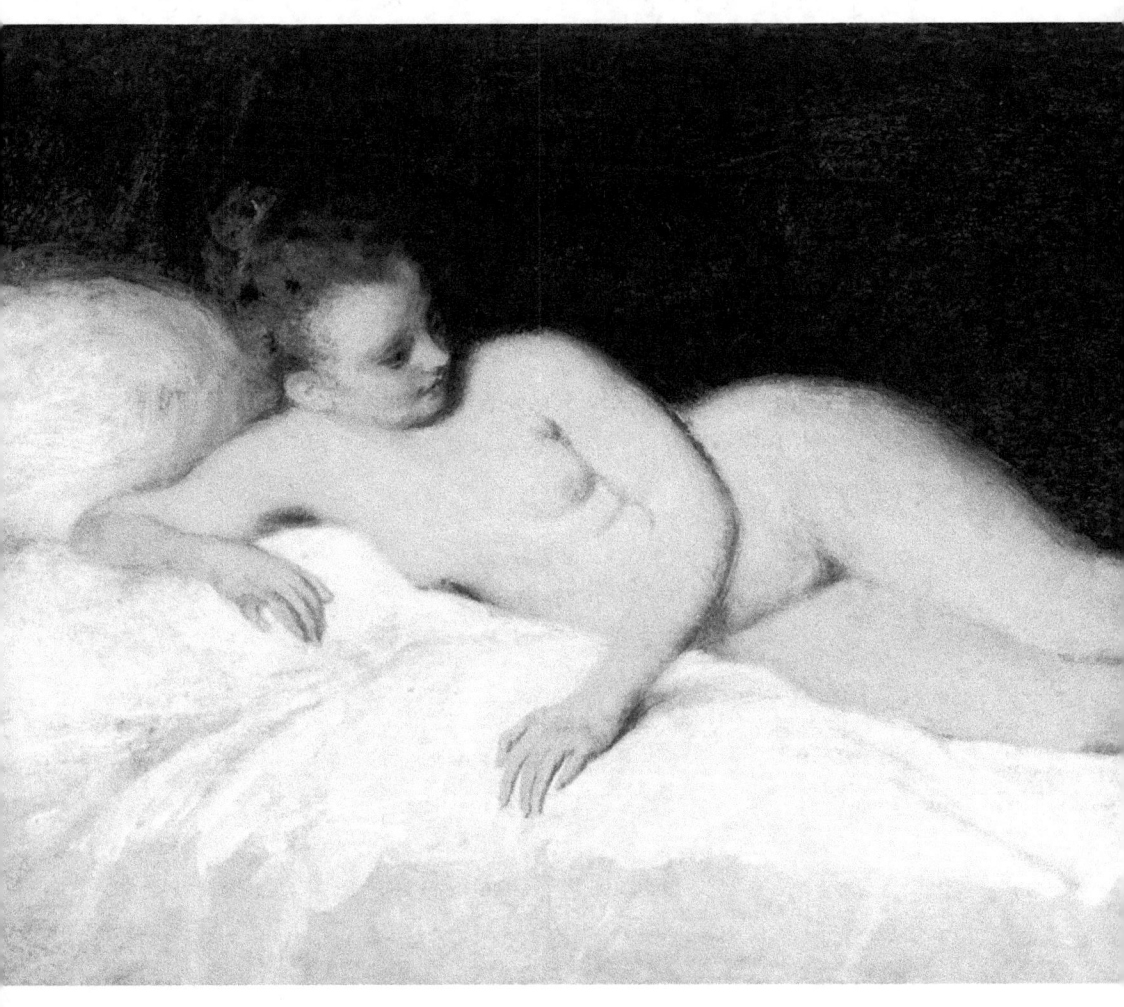

Antoine Watteau, Reclining Woman, 1713-17

Pornography is *fantasy*, as well as genre, product, system, and materialism. Pornography does not offer the consumer real people, but images, narratives, ideas, suggestions. The visual dimension of pornography helps to create certain kinds of representations of erotic feelings which the consumer can deal with, because they are communicated in recognizable forms. So now we're in an S/M narrative – masters, mistresses and slaves Or, over here we're in the narrative where a sexually frustrated male picks up a female hitchhiker. Or, here we are in the 'bored housewife' scenario: sex-starved, she humps the plumber over the washing machine. The consumer always knows where she or he is with pornography.

Pornography delivers the goods.

It delivers the goods: which's why it's bigger than the movie or pop music industries.

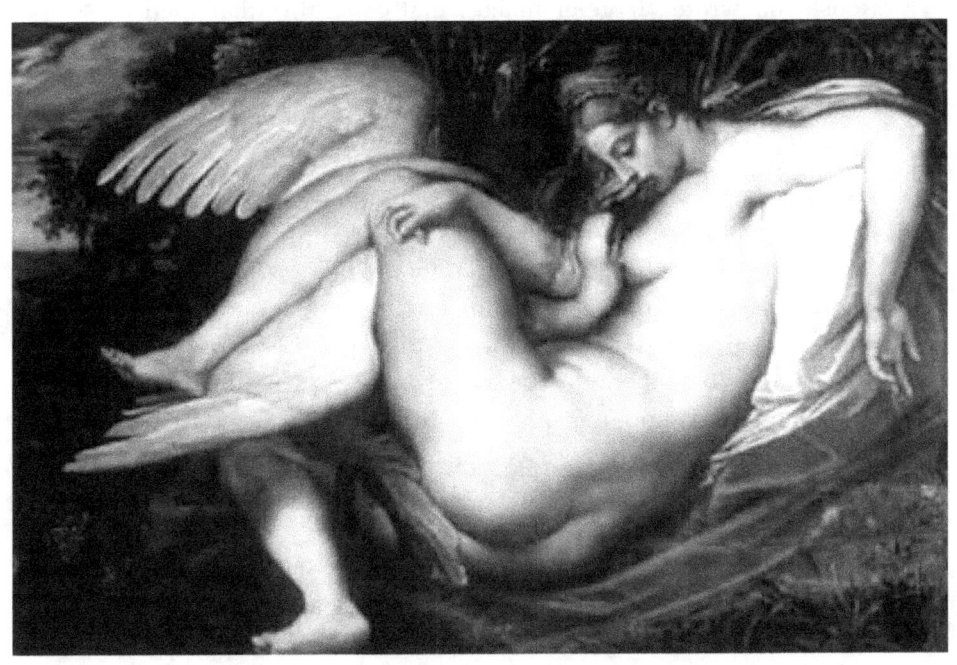

Peter Paul Rubens, Leda and the Swan

If some work is erotic – a scene on TV, a photo, a sculpture, a dance – it's because, in the opinion of some people, you don't 'see' everything. Something is hidden. The 'erotic' in art is about anticipation, waiting, yearning. It's about potential and possibility, hidden but not hidden, partially clothed. As the photographer Grace Lau, who has made many pictures of fetishism, wrote: 'I prefer images that conceal, rather than those that reveal all.'[1]

Pornography, meanwhile, has people doing it now. They undress, and start attacking each other immediately. There's nothing to get in the way, not contraception, not fear, not aversions, not menstruation, not impotence, not interruptions, not anything. In short: it's *fantasy*.

Pornography turns 'what if?' into a reality. What if somebody took their clothes off in this train carriage and started having sex? is a typical question that erotic art suggests but pornography answers. What if this woman at home turns out to be a nymphomaniac and this plumber turns out to be a superstud? What if the wedding guest who just smiled at you turns out to be the fuck of a lifetime? In pornography, people *do* rip their clothes and start mashing each other up.

Pornography presents as a normal, everyday occurrence what is hidden away, what is desired but unspoken. Pornography is the ultimate in fantasy, for in the fairy tale world of pornography, every dream comes true. And it is not only 'true', it is 'real'.

---

1 Grace Lau: "Confessions of a Complete Scopophiliac", in Gibbons, 195

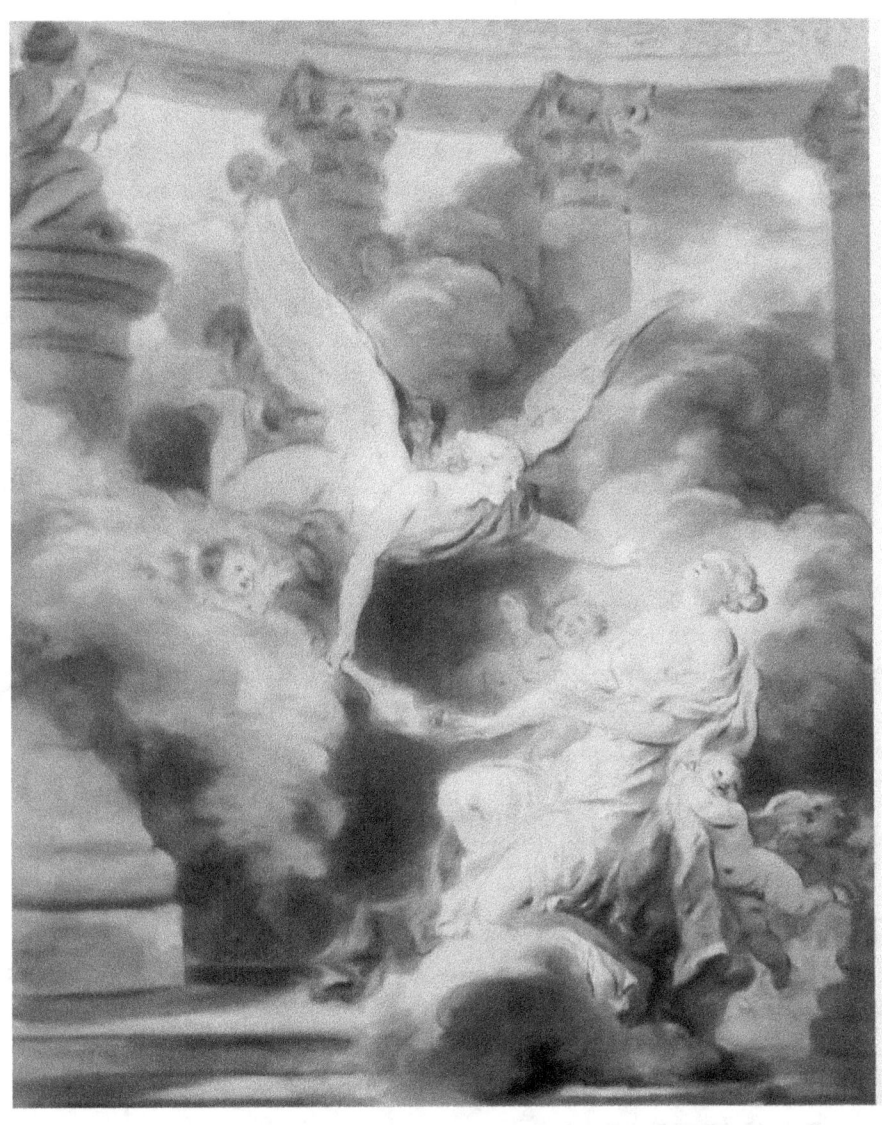

Jean-Honoré Fragonard, The Sacrifice of the Rose, c. 1780,
private collection

CENSORSHIP

One of the most contentious and fiercely debated aspects of erotic art and pornography is the issue of obscenity, taste and censorship. Throughout the history of art and pornography, different individuals or groups of people have sought to defend certain territories, whether moral, psychological, emotional, spiritual, religious, philosophical, political or ideological. There is always some line between the 'acceptable' and the 'obscene'.

The history of censorship is long and complex. In the 20th century there were many confrontations between artists and the establishment: with D.H. Lawrence's *Lady Chatterley's Lover*, with *Ulysses*, with films such as *Last Tango in Paris, Kids, Natural Born Killers, The Killing of Sister George, Performance, Trash, A Clockwork Orange* and countless others, with the *Oz* trials, with Senator Jesse Helms trying to stop NEA tax payers' money funding 'obscene' work, with reference to the photographer Robert Mapplethorpe (whose photos have created much 'controversy'),[1] with internet porn, with punk rock and gangsta rap, and so on.[2]

---

1 See M. Schoofs: "Robert Mapplethorpe: Exquisite Subversions", *Windy City Times*, 16 Mch, 1989; H. Kramer: "Mapplethorpe Show at the Whitney: A Big, Glossy, Offensive Exhibit", *The New York Observer*, 22 Aug, 1988; A.C. Danto: *Encounters & Reflections*, Farrar Straus Giroux, New York 1990; E. Kastor & Carla Hall: "Mapplethorpe Aftermath", *Washington Post*, 23 June 1989; T.A. Yasui: "The Mapplethorpe Bonanza", *Washington Post*, 21 Aug, 1989; P. Schjeldhal: "The Mainstreaming of Mapplethorpe: Taste and Hunger", *7 Days*, 10 Aug, 1988; R. Rooney: "The unambiguous stare of Mapplethorpe's lens", *Australian*, 25 Feb, 1986.
2 More Mapplethorpe articles: D. Dominick: "Robert Mapplethorpe's Proud Finale", *Vanity Fair*, Feb, 1989; "Robert Mapplethorpe: Aestheticizing the Perverse", *Artscribe International*, Nov/Dec 1988; J. Ribalta: "Decorative Heroism, The death of Mapplethorpe", *Lapiz*, Apl, 1989.

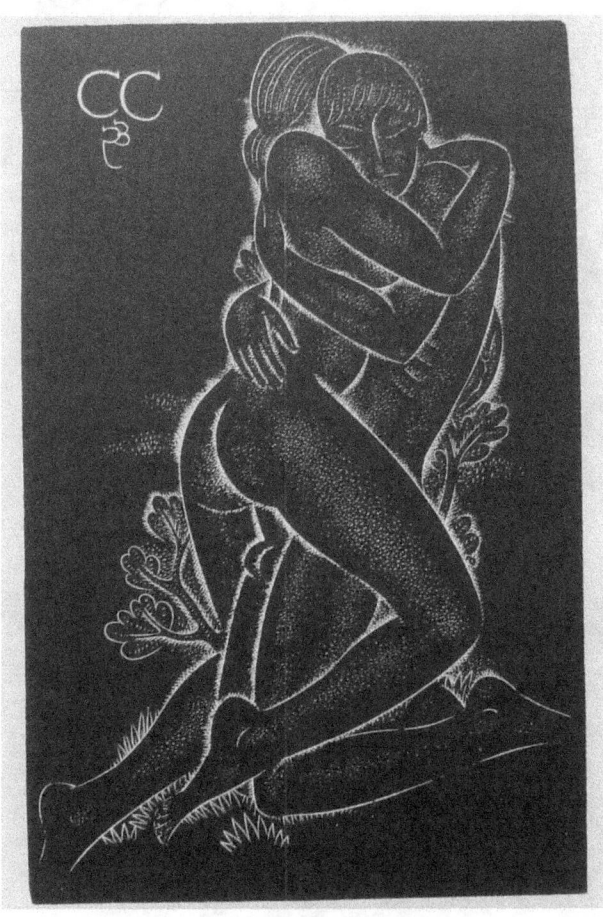

Fucking a flame into being: one of
Eric Gill's illustrations for D.H. Lawrence's book

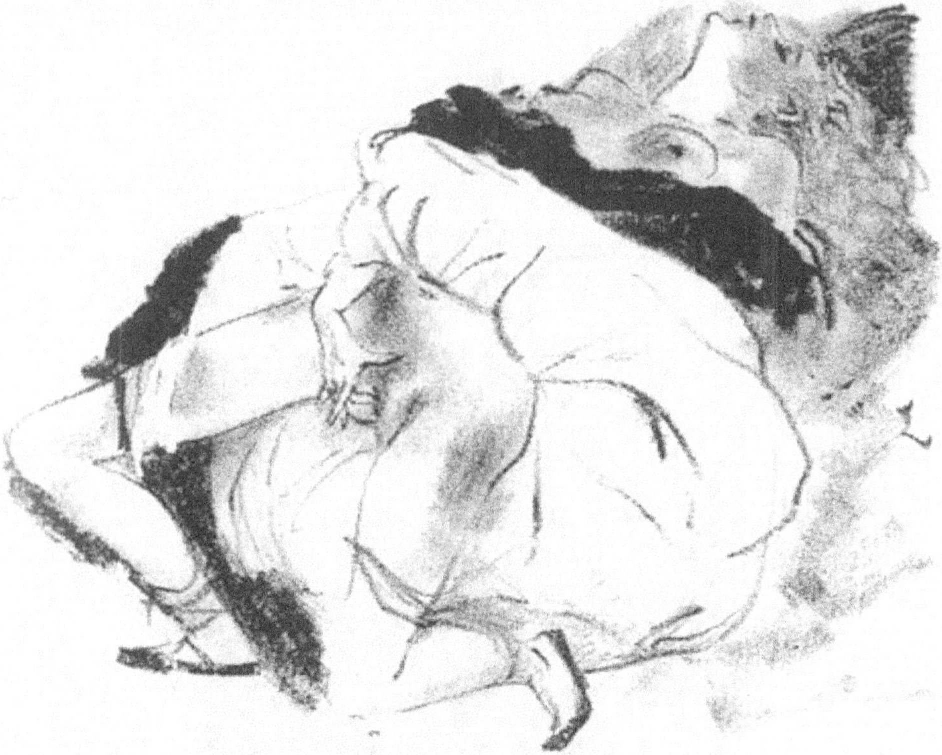

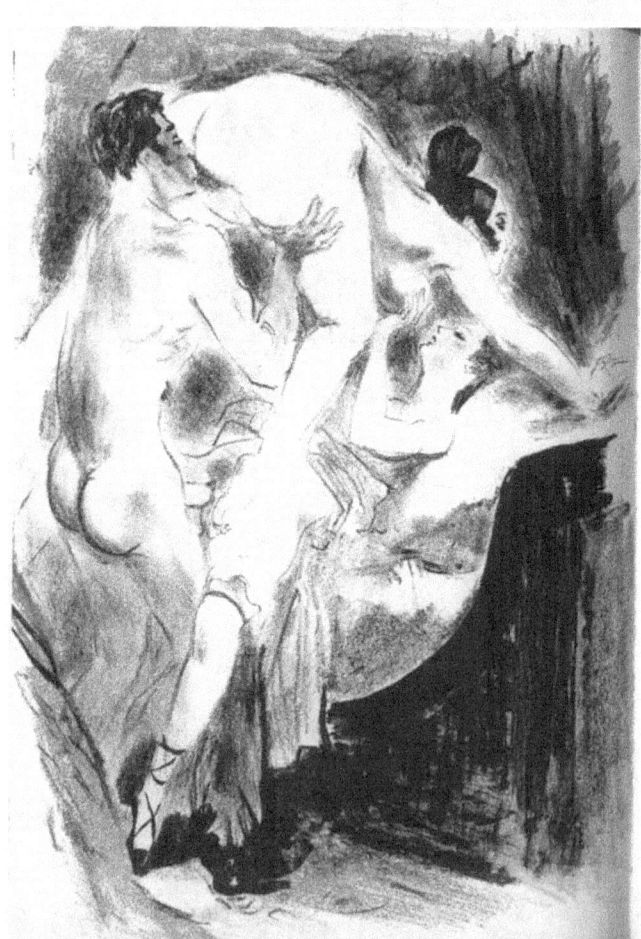

Louis-André Berthomme
Saint-André, Gamiani ou Deux Nuits
d'Excés, by Alfred de Musset

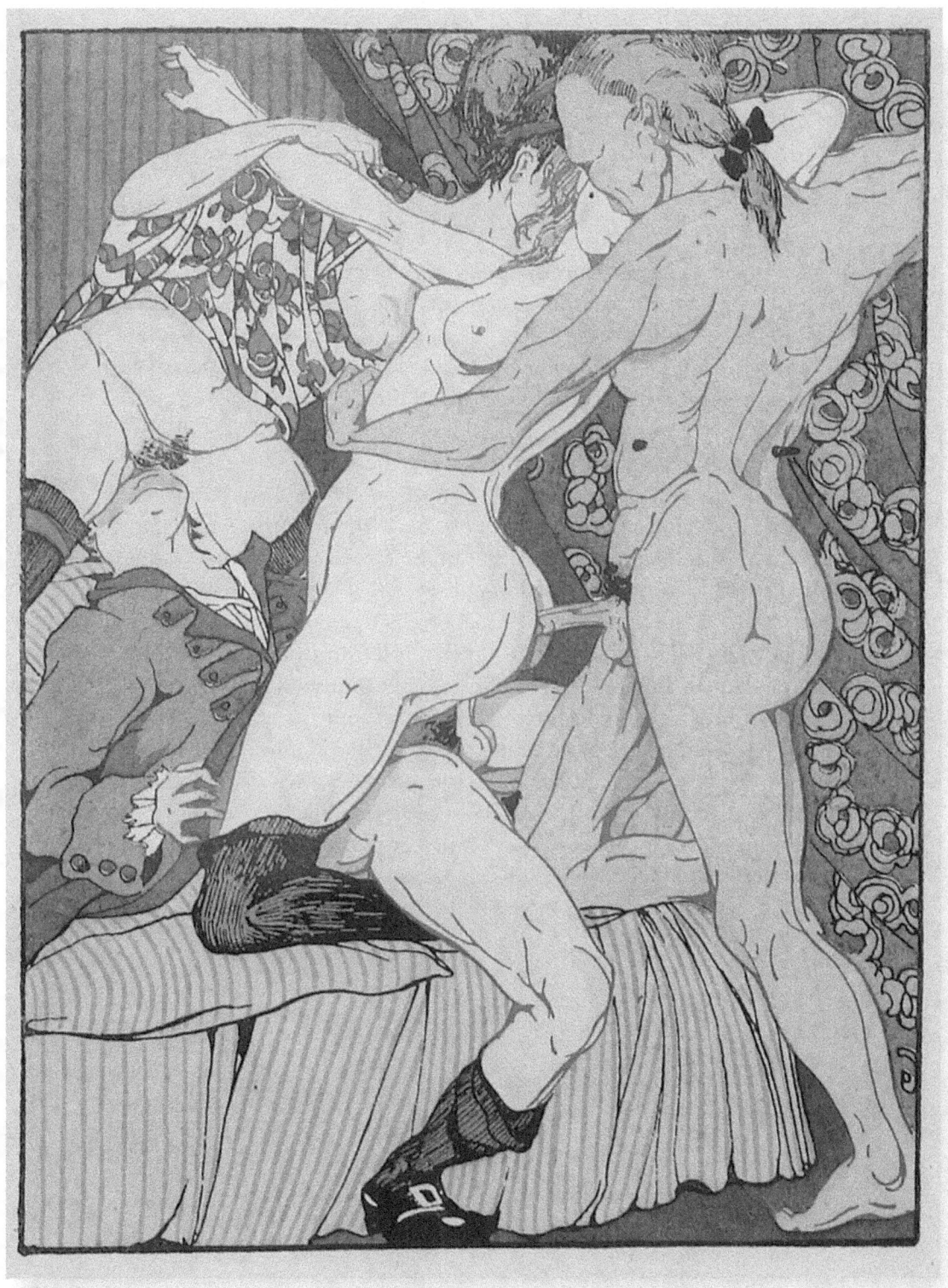

Illustration for the Marquis de Sade,
Le Bordel de Venise, 1921,
by Couperyn (a.k.a. George A. Drains), Paris

CENSORSHIP

The many debates concerning several Obscene Publications Acts and bills, the First Amendment of the American constitution, different regulatory groups, pressure groups, media organizations, publishers, and all manner of intellectuals and artists, have been intense, complex, protracted, and often a shambles. The confusions and ambiguities are at the centre of Western society. Pornography debates produce, very quickly, all manner of confusions and hypocrisies, of a moral, religious, psychological, social and ideological nature.[1] For some, though, the censorship debate is 'in fact, a little internal quibble between sections of the bourgeois community' (according to Suzanne Kappeler).

Pornography goes to the heart of what people hold dear: their identities, their feelings, their philosophical, spiritual and political views, their view of the 'quality of life'. Pornography unsettles these notions and structures. The fervour and uncertainty of the many attempts at legislation and policing show how problematic pornography is. In a case of recent years, five 'homosexual sadomasochists' were convicted in 1990 of inflicting 'injuries on each another's genitals during ritual sex' which involved 'cutting each other's genitals with surgical scalpels, sandpapering scrotums and pushing hooks into penises'. Their appeal was rejected by the courts.[2]

---

1 See *Art in America*, May 1990; C.H. Rolph: *The Trial of Lady Chatterley*, Penguin, London, 1961; G. Robertson: *Obscenity: an Account of Censorship Laws and Their Enforcements in England and Wales*, Weidenfeld & Nicolson, London, 1979; *The Attorney General's Commission on Pornography – the Meese Commission – Final Report*, US Government Printing Office, Washington DC, 1986; L. Lederer, ed, op. cit.
2 I. MacKinnon: "Lords reject appeals by sado-masochists", *The Independent*, 12 Mch, 1993.

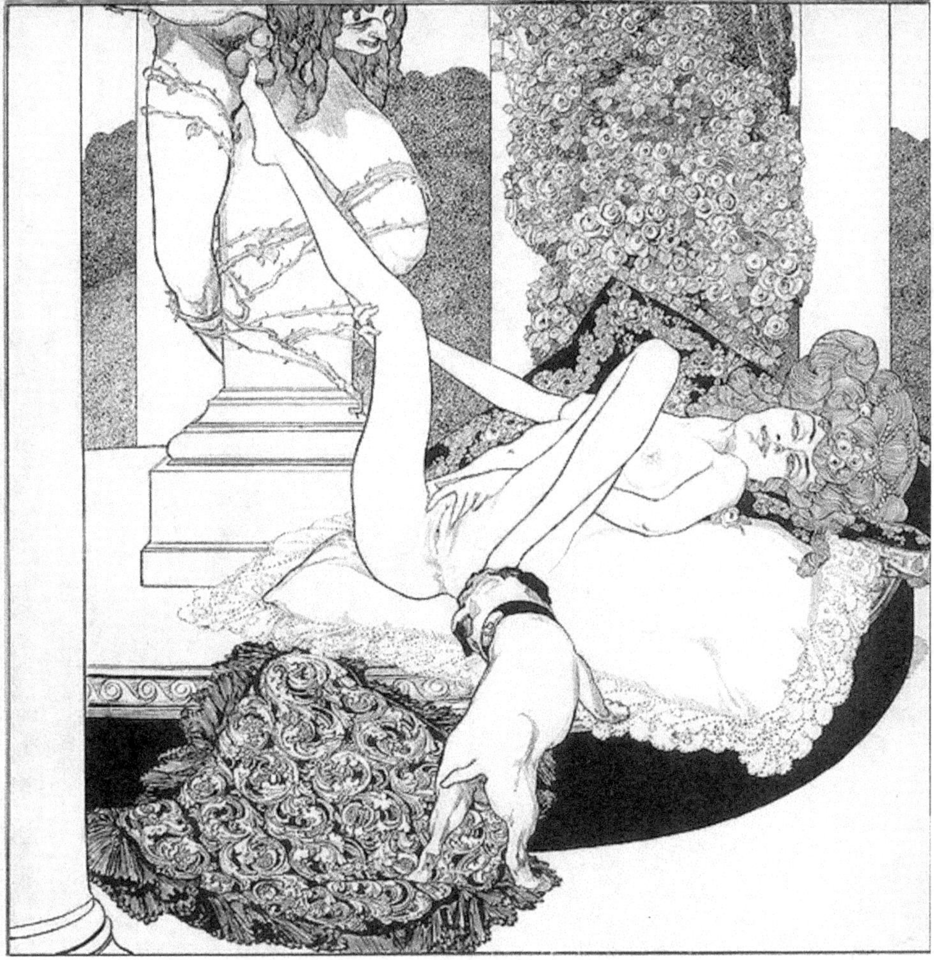

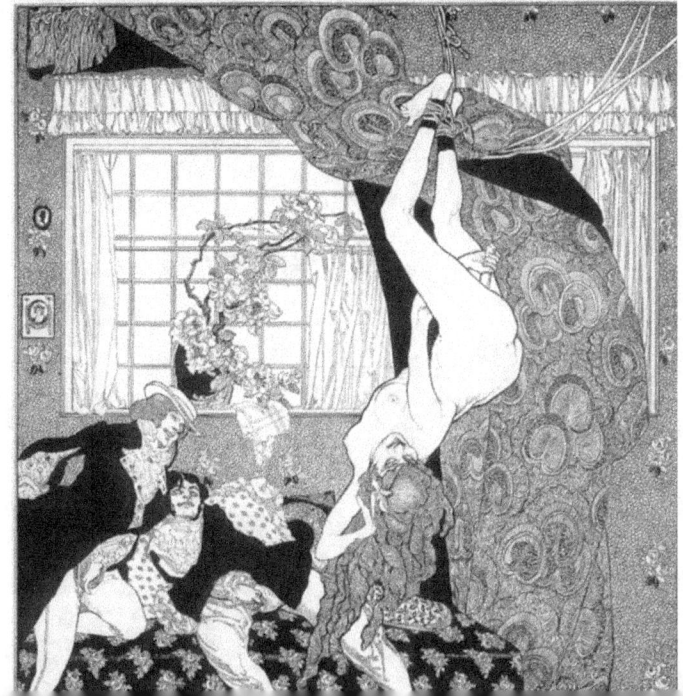

Franz von Bayros (1866-1924),
Der Toilettentisch, Tantalus, 1908

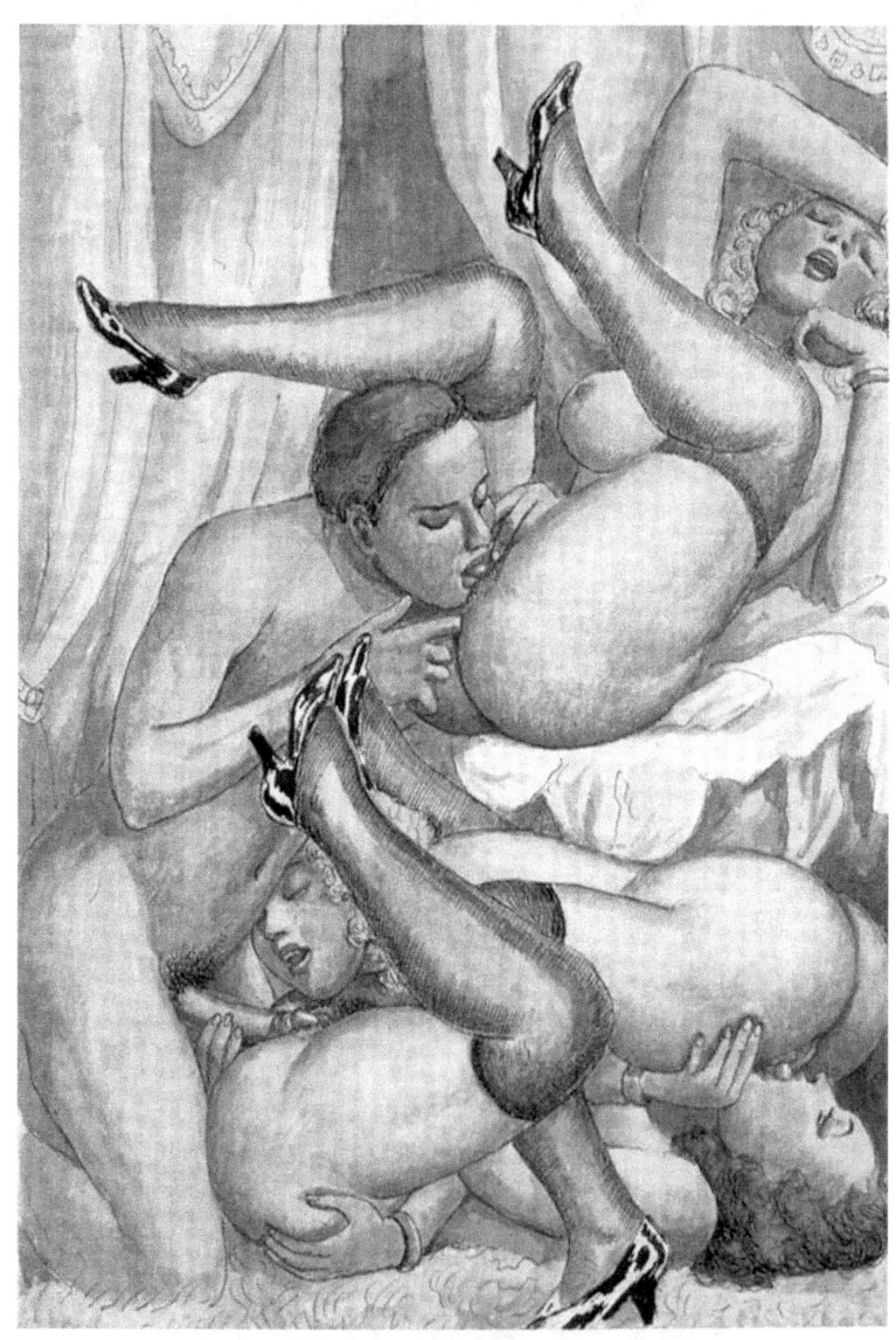

Anonymous, early 20th century

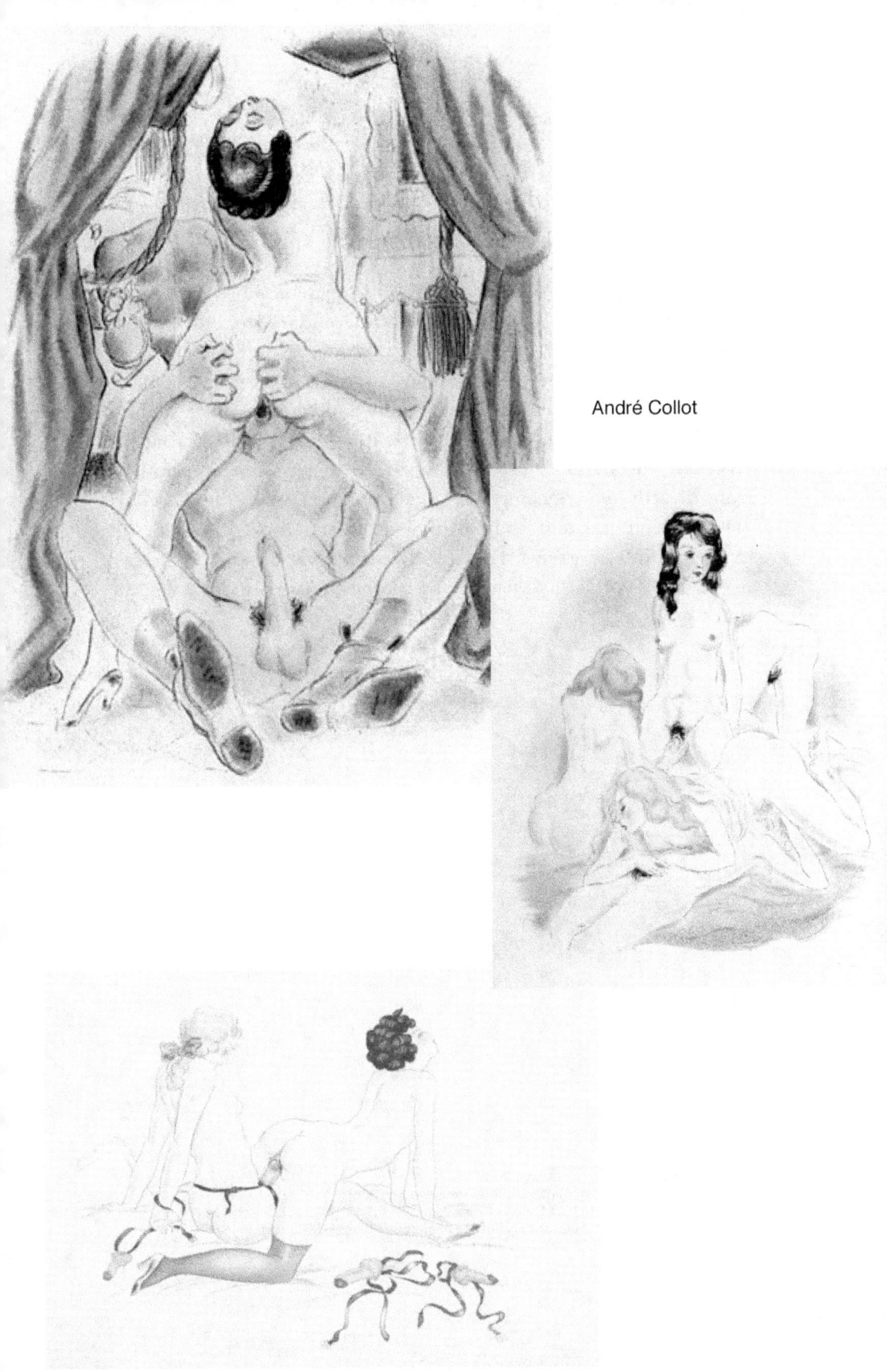

André Collot

FEMALE ORGASM

The female orgasm is 'anatomically invisible', as far as erotica is concerned. So the history of erotica and porn, for some commentators, 'is the history of visual strategies to overcome the anatomical invisibility of the female orgasm'.[1] In erotica, female orgasm is regarded with confusion and ambivalence. What actually is it? eroticists ask, what does it feel like? (Note that most eroticists throughout history have been men, forever excluded from directly experiencing the female orgasm). Thus the controversy over clitoral and vaginal orgasm, over female 'ejaculation', over 'multiple' orgasms. Female 'ejaculation' is 'visible evidence' of orgasm, yet it is censored by pornographers themselves at times.[2]

1 L. Nead, 98; see also L. Williams, 1990.
2 See S. Bell: "Feminist Ejaculations", in Arthur and Marilouise Kroker, eds: *The Hysterical Male: New Feminist Theory*, St Martin's Press, New York, 155-169; also C. Straayer: "The Seduction of Boundaries: Feminist Fluidity in Annie Sprinkle's Art/Education/Sex", in P. Gibson, ed, 168f

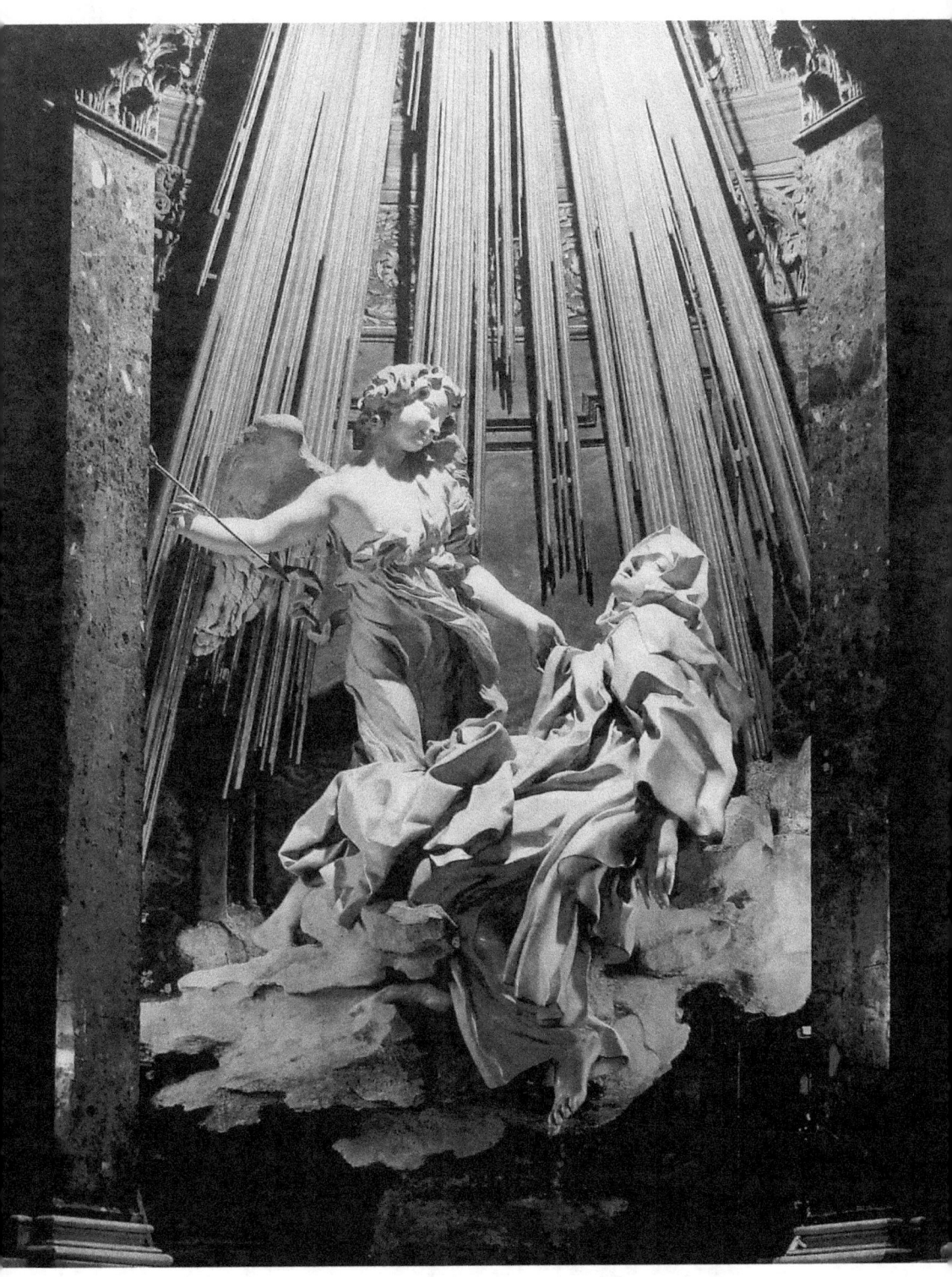

Gianlorenzo Bernini, The Ecstasy of St Theresa, 1652, Rome

ORGASM

Sexuality is not what you *are*, but what you *do*. It is not *who* is fucking *whom*, but *how*.[1] The question is *how is this fucking being done?* Never *why*, always *how*.

For patriarchal people, of either or any sex, it seems it is essential to know *who* is speaking about sex. Is the author male or female (or some other gender)? What is her/ his sexual identity? Patriarchal people are disturbed when their expectations of gender are disrupted. When, say, a male author writes of lesbian sexuality as if from the 'inside', as if in the 'character' of a lesbian. For example, who is the speaker and who is the subject of this poem:

> First, I want to make
> > kiss you...
> I want to make you come
> in my mouth like a storm.[2]

It seems the speaker (Marilyn Hacker) is female and she is describing lesbian sex. But the words could just as apply hetero-sexual or homosexual eroticism. Only when parts of the body are mentioned – clitoris, nipples, penis, breasts – is it possible to decipher the gender of speaker, text or subject, and sometimes not even then.

1 see Valerie Traub, in V. Wayne, 83
2 Marilyn Hacker: 'Noces', from *Love, Death and the Changing of the Seasons*, Arbor House 1986

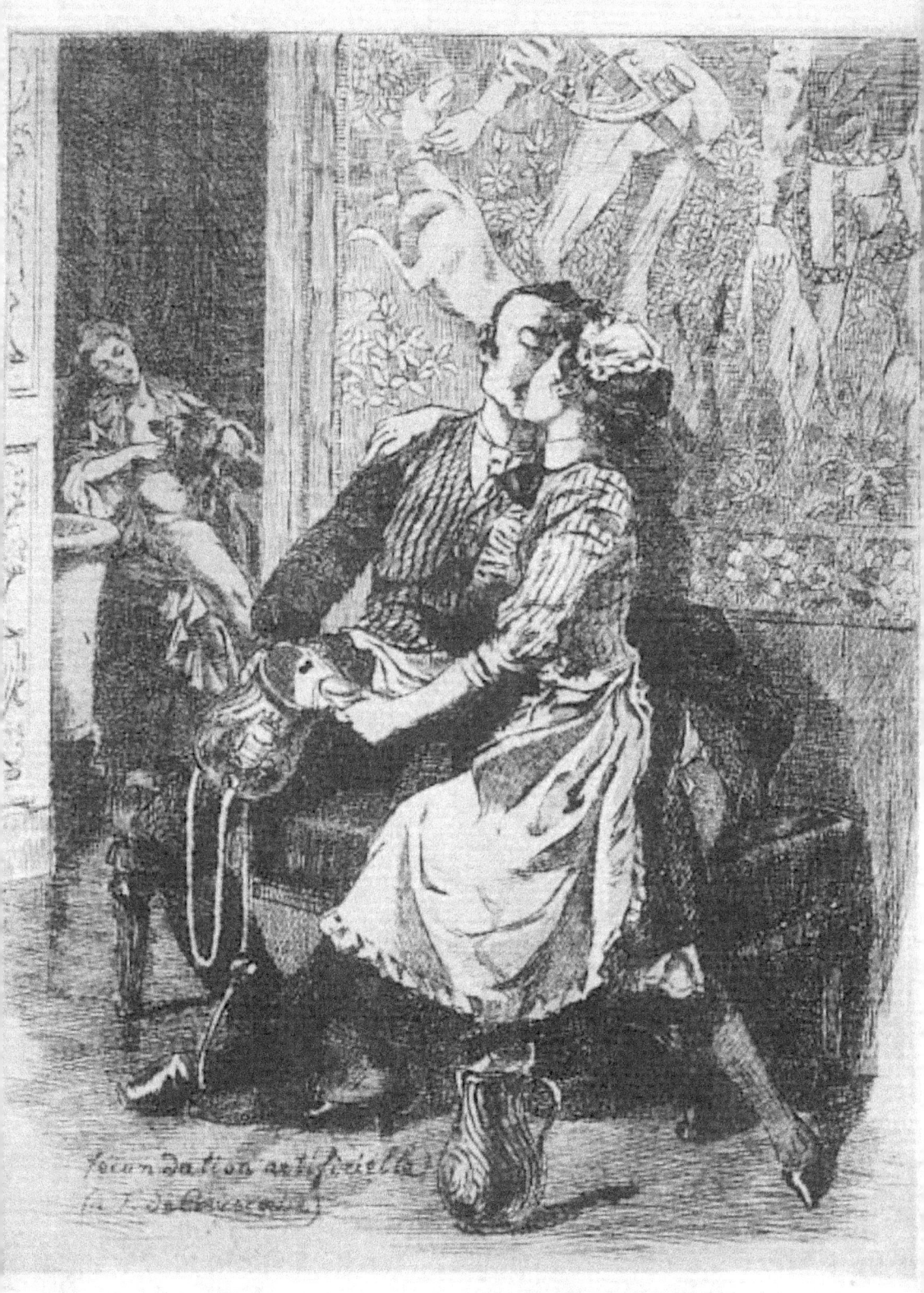

Martin van Maele

THE PHALLUS

In pornography, the great signifier is the phallus, while the site of pleasure is the woman's body. Reclining on a million couches in artists' studios, the female nude offers itself up as a country to be colonized. It is both a pleasure machine and a fantasy. The orchestrator of pleasure in this pornographic scenario is that little slip of flesh, the penis. The phallus is good, whole, true, unifying, as opposed to the bad, fragmented, impure, chaotic vagina.[1] The phallus is the emblem of male power, as many commentators, not only feminists, note: '[t]he supreme power is the power that prevails over mortality', and this power is 'reasonably equated with the phallus'.[2] For feminists, the West is a phallic/ phallocentric/ phallogocentric society, where the phallus, the sublime signifier, the most censored image in the West, is the beginning and the end of sexual pleasure. For Madeleine Gagnon, the phallus is an emblem of male narcissism:

> The phallus... represents repressive capitalist ownership, the exploiting bourgeois... The phallus means everything sets itself up as a mirror. Everything that erects itself as perfection.[3]

1 See T. Moi: *Sexual/ Textual Politics*, 66f; S.M. Gilbert & S. Gubar: *The Madwoman in the Attic: The Woman Writer and the Nineteenth Century Literary Imagination*, Yale University Press, New Haven, CT, 1979.
2 L. Steinberg: *The Sexuality of Christ in Renaissance Art and in Modern Oblivion*, Pantheon, New York, 1984, 90.
3 M. Gagnon: "Corps I", *La venue à l'écriture*, UGE, 10/18, Paris 1977; in E. Marks, 180.

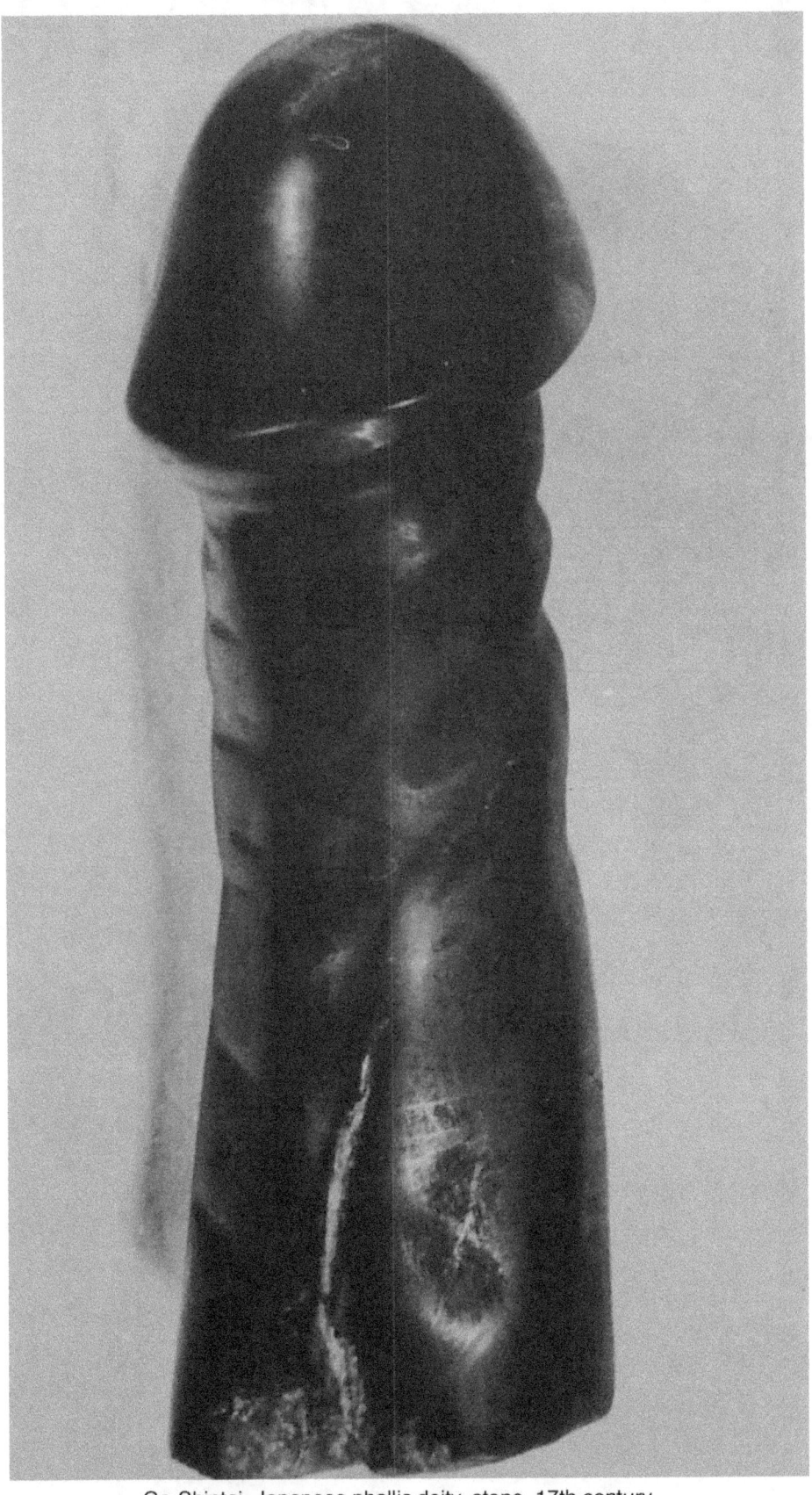

Go-Shintai, Japanese phallic deity, stone, 17th century

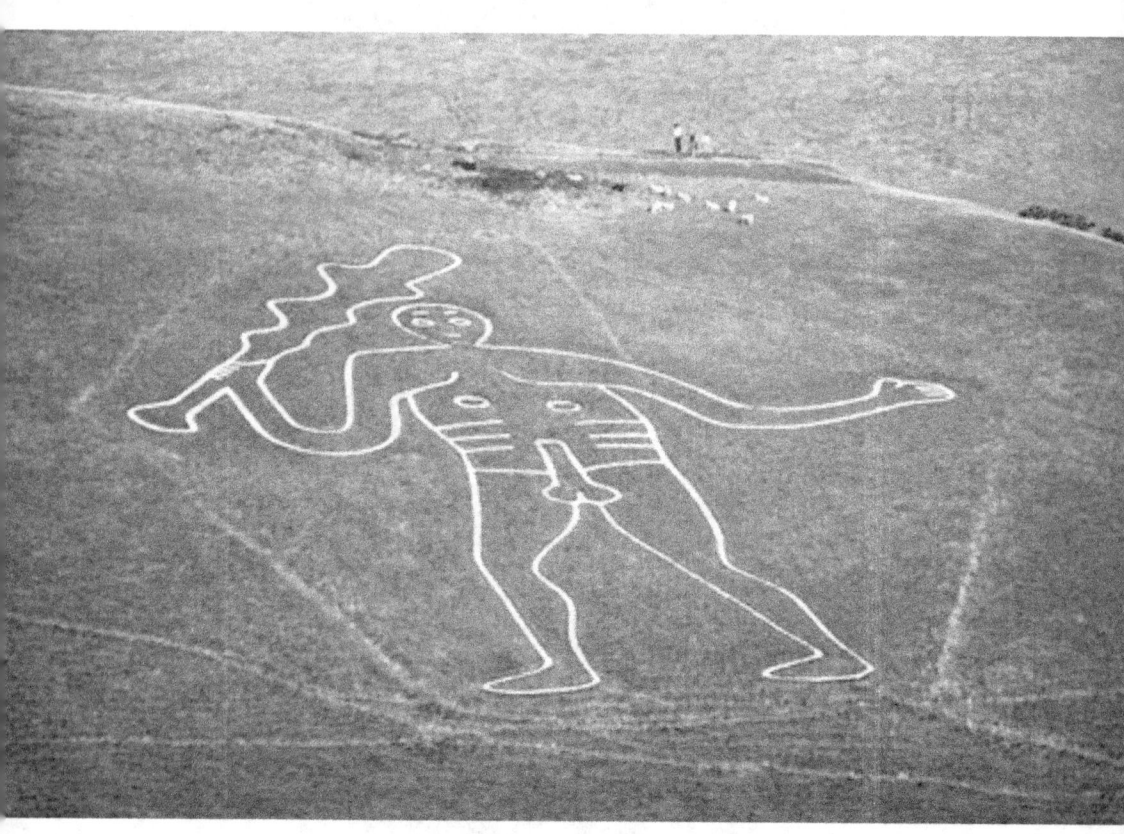

Cerne Giant, Dorset, England

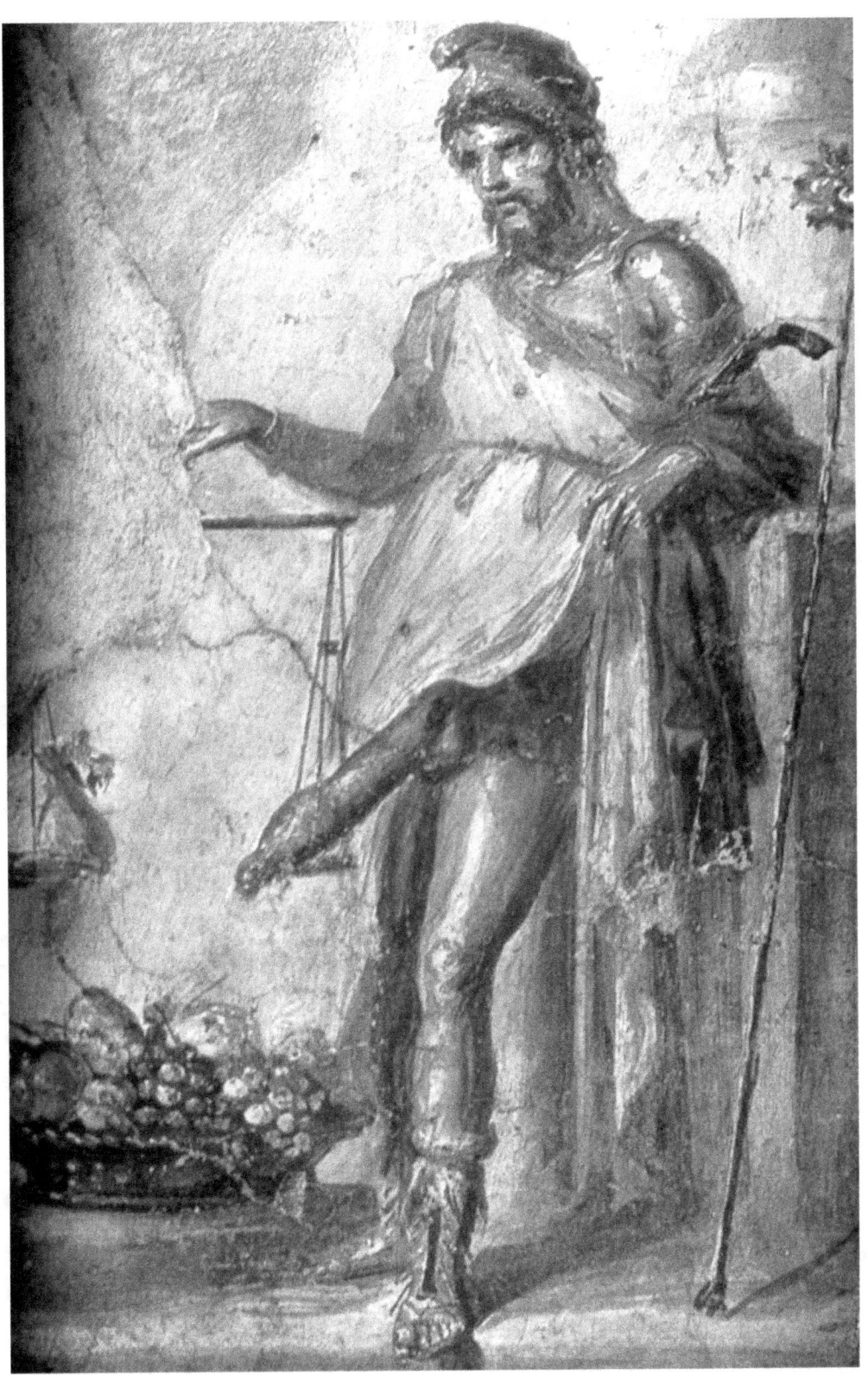

Fresco, Ancient Roman

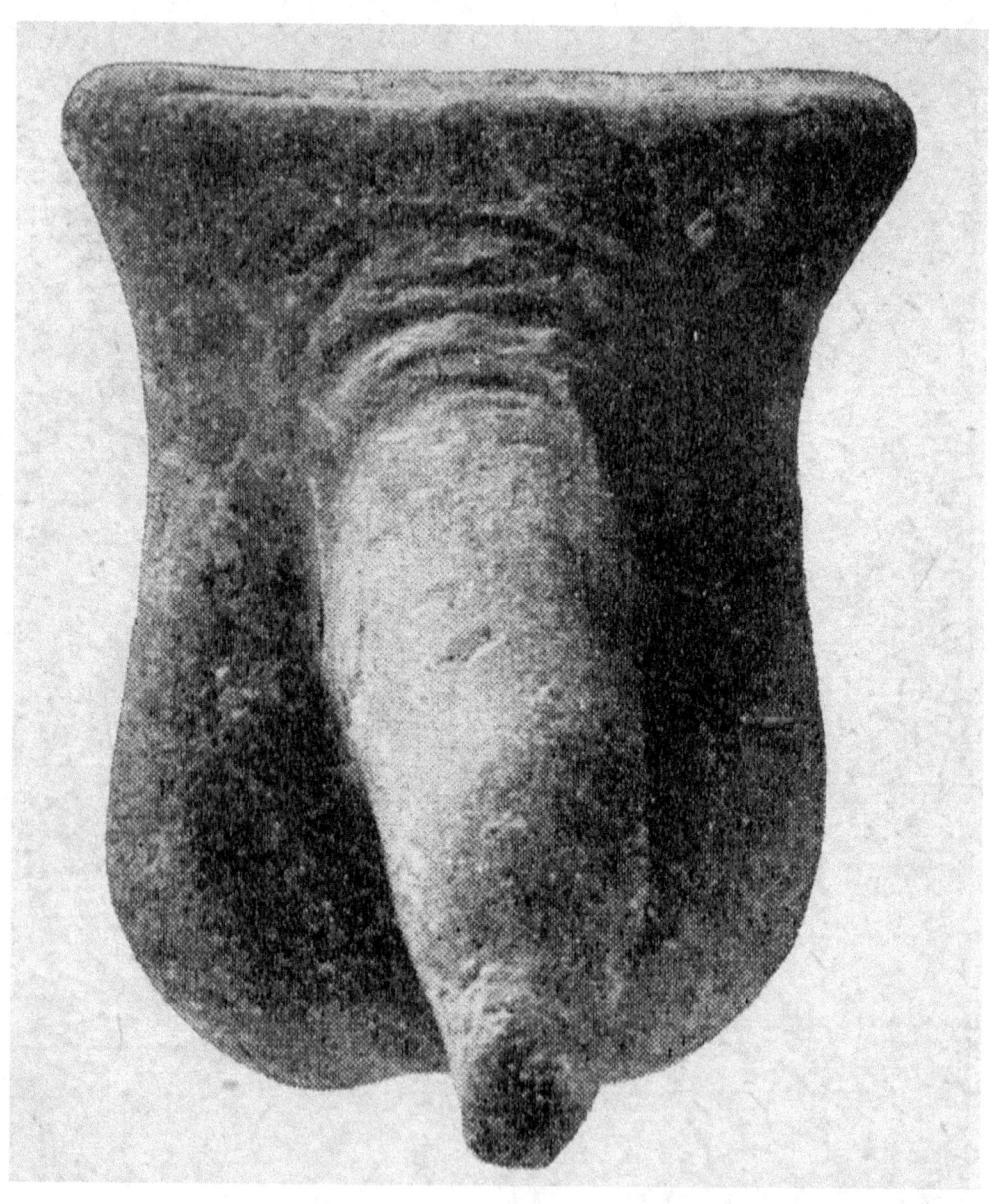

Ancient Votive Phallus, from Albert Moll, Handbuch der
Sexualwissenschaften, Verlag Von F.C. Vogel, Leipzig, 1921

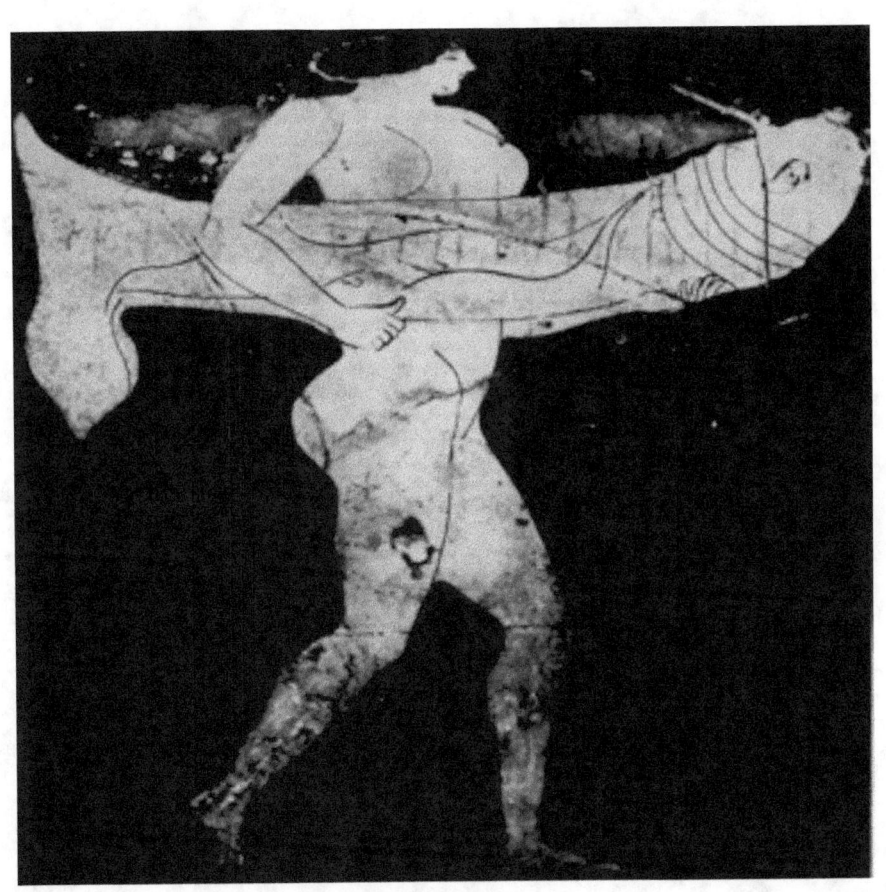

Vase, Ancient Greek

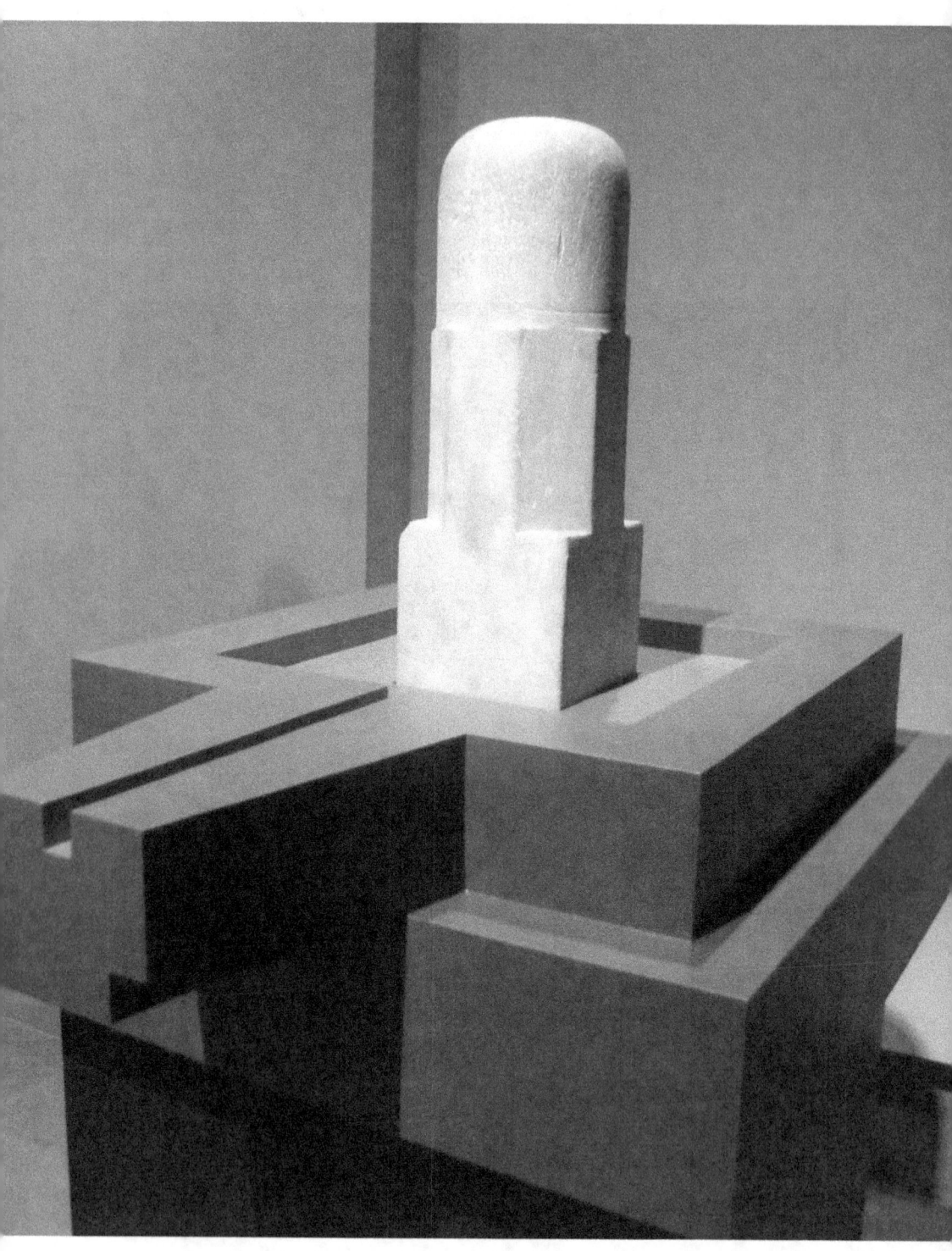

Lingam and Yoni, Cambodian, Norton Simon Museum, Pasadena, CA

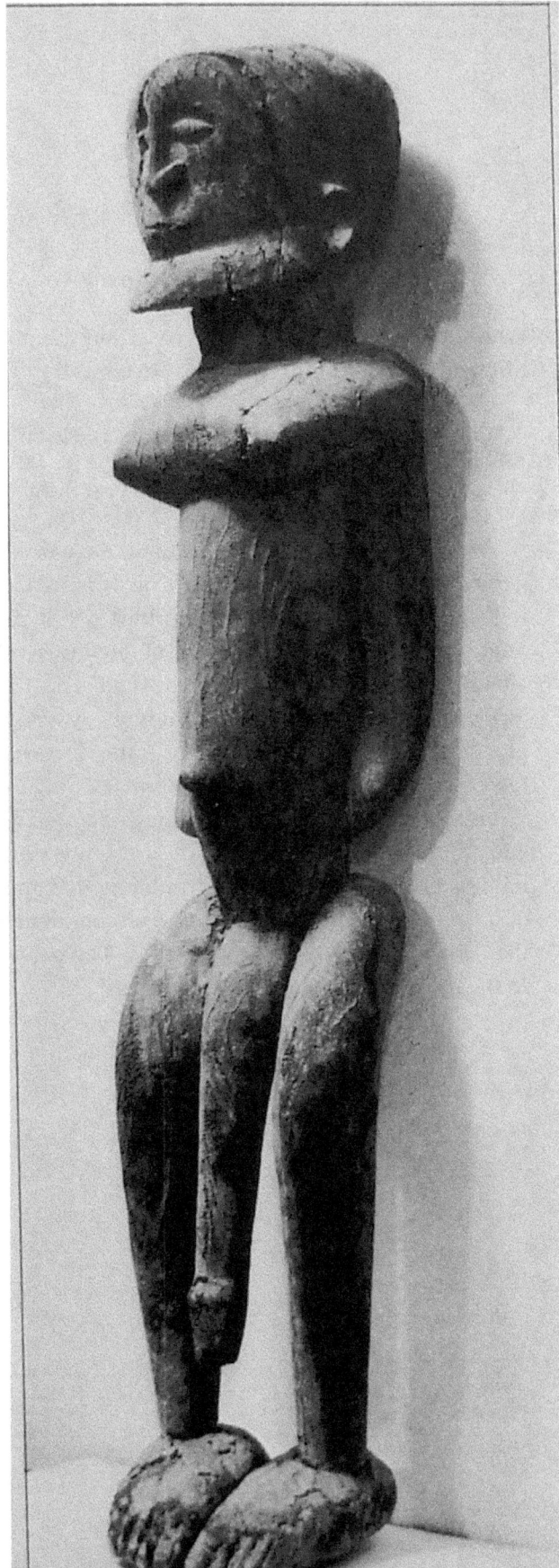

Wood figure, Ivory
Coast

THE PHALLUS

Whole philosophic systems are based on the phallus, yet, as Juliet Mitchell remarked in "Feminine Sexuality':

> It's extraordinary what happens when you get rid of the centrality of the concept of the phallus. I mean, you get rid of the unconscious, get rid of sexuality, get rid of the original psychoanalytic point.[1]

If men reduce people to their sexual identities, as some feminists claim, then at the heart of this is the penis. Women are reduced to 'cunt', as Kate Millet put it, while men are all phallus. There are certainly no shortage of phallic symbols and artifacts about. The real thing, the real penis, is censored, carefully guarded – it's not much to look at anyway – so men displace their phallic sexuality onto thrusting cars, lorries, missiles, bombs, towers, cameras, computers, guitars, cigarettes, telephones, swords, guns, eyes, etc. These things abound in (patriarchal) art, and throughout the history of art (and pornography adds a million further fetishes). The trouble is that the penis ain't much of a thing, after all. As Richard Dyer commented: 'the fact is that the penis isn't a patch on the phallus. The penis can never live up to the mystique implied by the phallus'.[2]

1 J. Mitchell: "Feminine Sexuality: Interview with Juliet Mitchell and Jacqueline Rose", *m/f*, 8 (1983), 15.
2 R. Dyer: 'Don't Look Now", *Screen*, vol. 23, 3/4, 1983, and in A. McRobbie, 206.

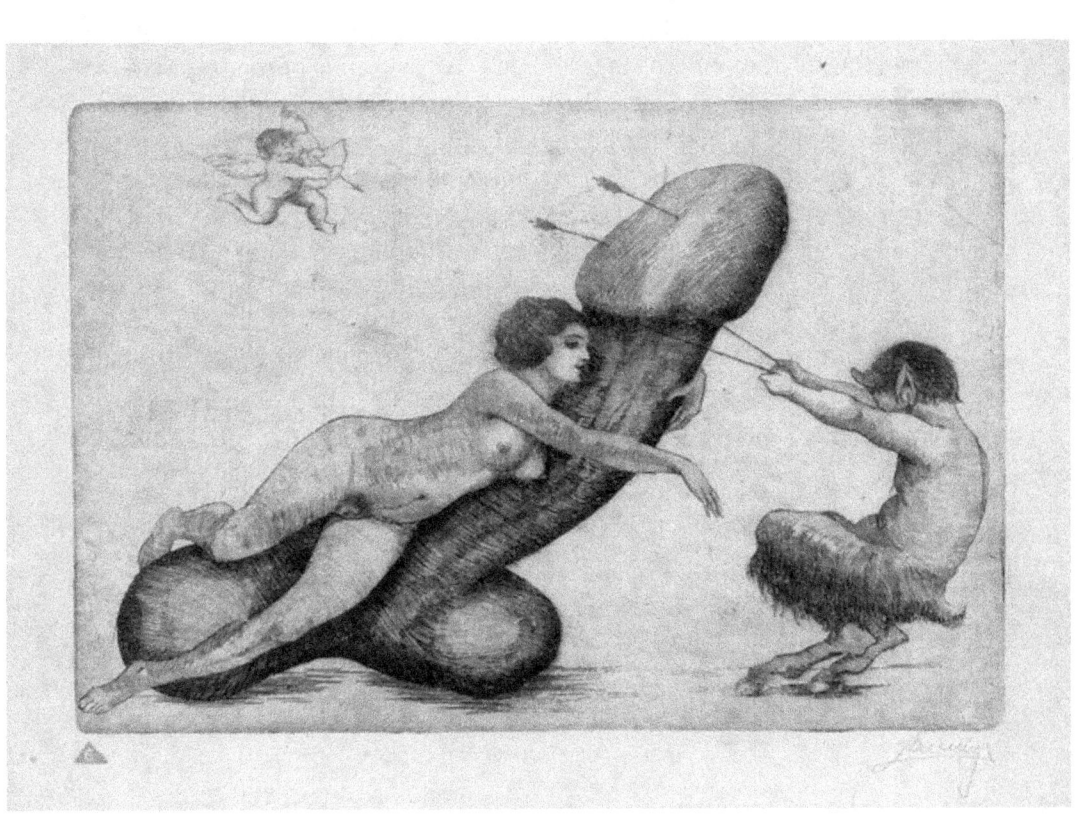

After Max Klinger (1857-1920)

In the (second wave) feminist view, the pornographer creates with his penis – the paintbrush, camera, computer or pen – these things are called 'tools', a common euphemism for the penis (there are thousands of other phallic control devices, such as game consoles, TVs, digital cameras, hi-fis, factory machinery, aeroplanes, etc). The quill, stylus or 'sharp projective' is a crucial element in the male's manufacture of art and pornography.[1] When Pierre Renoir was asked how he painted when he hands were crippled by arthritis he replied, '[w]ith my prick'.[2]

In pornography, the eye becomes the phallus, and looking is equated with caressing the obscure object of desire with the phallus (in the Lacanian system). Throughout Western art the phallus has been that visually absent but psychologically and ideologically present object. It is central in erotic art. Look at the Western art nudes – by Titian, Picasso, Ingres, Boucher: the phallus is there even though one doesn't see it. It's the same in any number of books, poems, sculptures, plays, operas, installations.

1 See J. Derrida: *Spurs: Nietzsche's Styles*, tr. B. Harlow, University of Chicago Press, Chicago 1979, 37-9; on the penis as a paintbrush, see Carol Duncan: "The Esthetics of Power in Modern Erotic Art", *Heresies*, 1, 1977, 46-50.
2 In J. Hobhouse, 135.

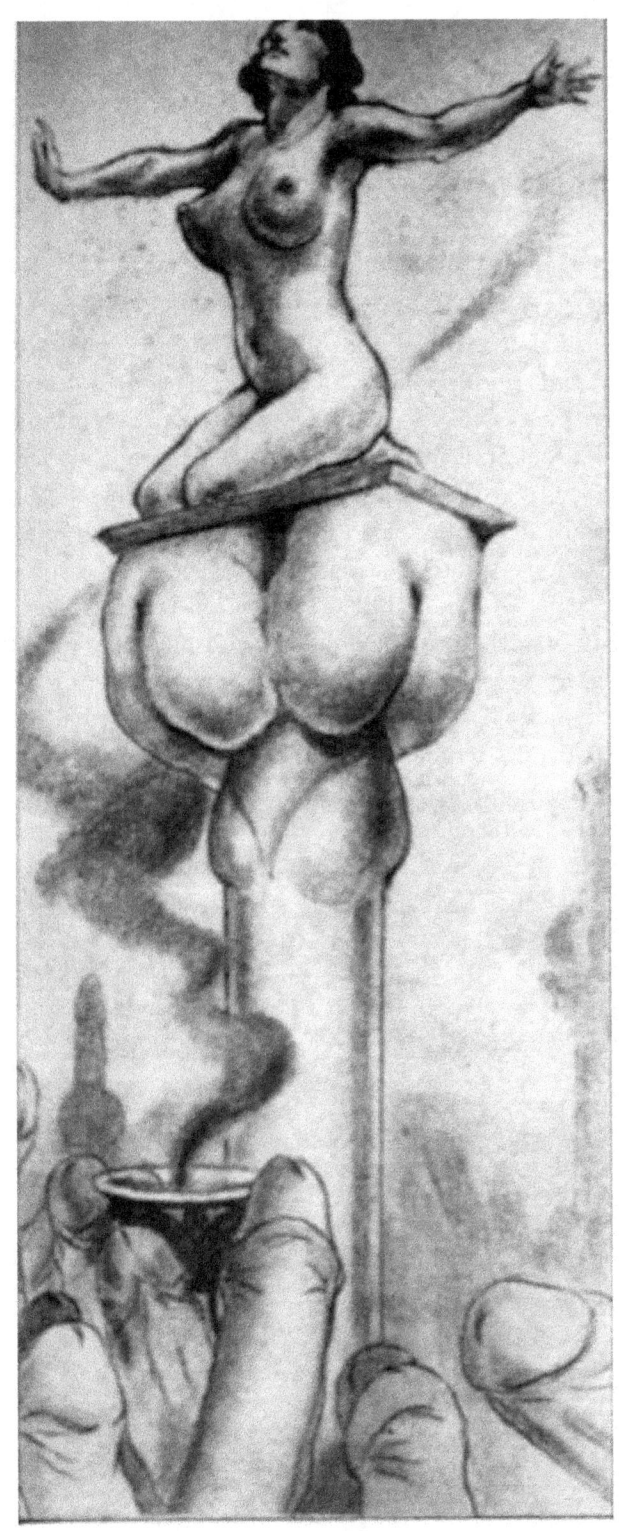

Anonymous, 19th century

LESBIAN EROTICA

In heterosexual pornography, lesbian eroticism is often introduced, but always controlled by a patriarchal force. Typically, in a soft porn scenario, two bisexual women cavort on a bed overseen by a male ('I've always wanted to see ya with another woman' drools the man to his wife/ girlfriend; or, frequently, 'I got back from work an' saw my wife and her best friend writhin' on the bed'). Towards the end of the scene, the man makes love to both women. Why? Because they needed the phallus, they needed a man to be fulfilled. Variations on this scenario occur endlessly in pornography. The male presence (the phallus) is seen as necessary for the true satisfaction for women (for valorization, for authenticity: i.e., it's not *true* sex without the phallus).

Lesbian or women's pornography, made by women for women, disappoints some feminists. Elizabeth Carola, who called herself as a 'radical feminist lesbian', described magazines such as *On Our Backs, Bad Attitude, OW! – Outrageous Women: A Journal of Woman-to-Woman SM, Yellow Silk, The Power Exchange*:

> Like all porn, this new 'woman's' porn is neither about nor for women. Like all porn it is, in a most basic sense, *against* women and *about* male fantasy – the basic male fantasy of Woman as Wholly Sexual Object whose Purpose is To Be Fucked – which feeds men's egos, fuels their violence...

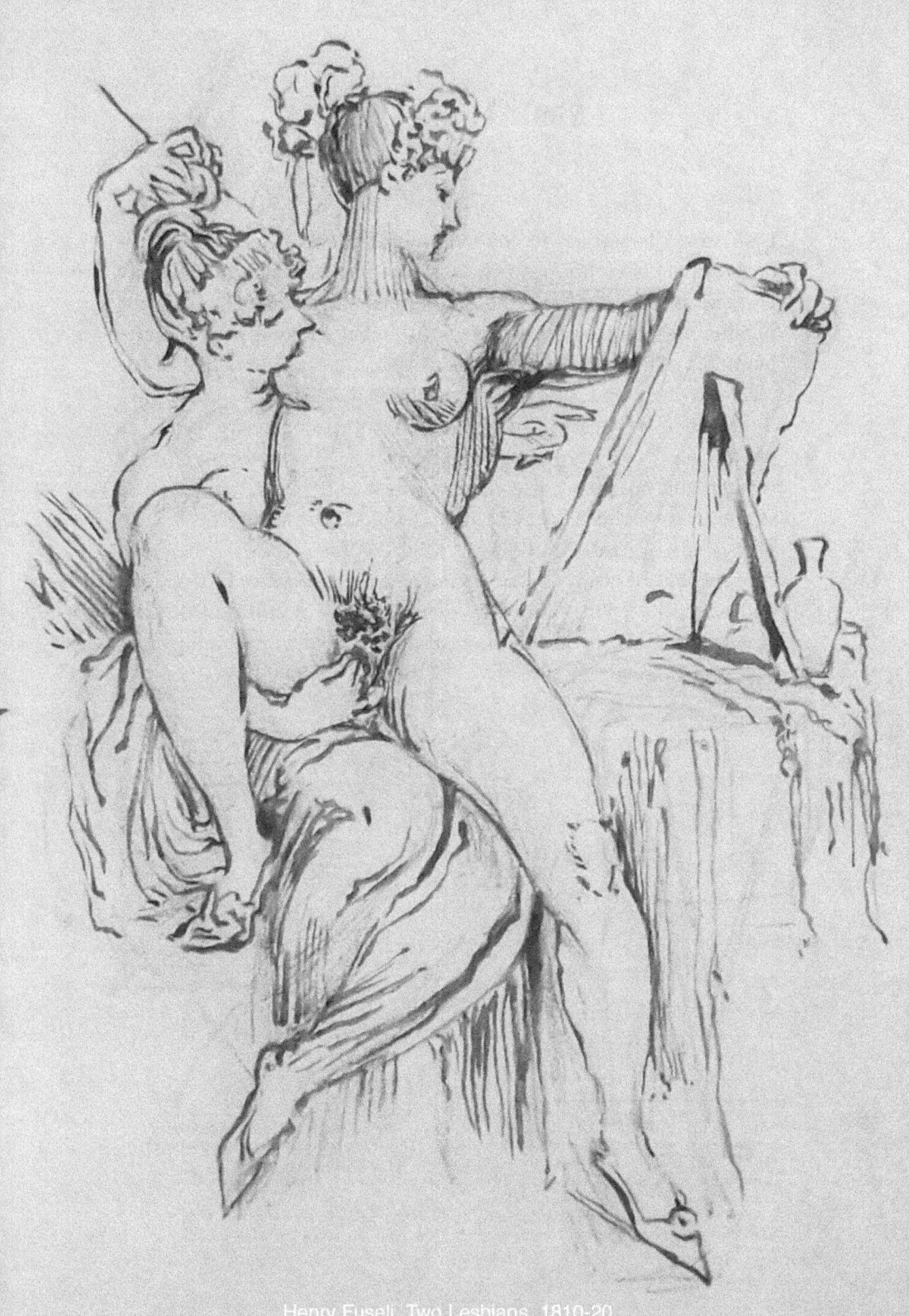

Henry Fuseli, Two Lesbians, 1810-20,
private collection

LESBIAN EROTICISM

Lesbian sex is marked in contemporary cultural theory by the *lack* of the phallus. Hence, lesbian eroticism must always be 'deviant', because it departs from the patriarchal norms which exalt the phallus. Lesbianism must always be 'other', sexually, and many feminists note that the otherness of lesbian sexuality is one of the reasons that men and their patriarchal institutions are very threatened by lesbianism.[1] Lesbian attacks patriarchy at its powerbase. Men cannot control lesbians: '[l]esbians, by loving women and not men, pose a direct threat to the very basis of male supremacy', write Alice, Gordon, Debbie and Mary.[2] The lesbian is crucial, argued Monique Wittig, because she 'is the only concept that I know of which is beyond the categories of sex (man and woman)'.[3] Wittig moved towards a view of culture that goes beyond gender, beyond 'biological dimorphism', and biology.

---

1 T. Atkinson: *Amazon Odyssey*, Links Books, New York 1974; Alice, Gordon, Debbie and Mary: "Separatism", in S.L. Hoagland & J. Penelope, eds: *For Lesbians Only: A separatist anthology*, Onlywomen Press 1988, 31-40; A. Rich: "Towards a woman-centred university", in *On Lies, Secrets and Silence*, Novotny, New York 1979; J. Johnston: *Lesbian Nation: The Feminist Solution*, Simon & Shuster, New York 1974; S. Rowbotham: *Beyond the Fragments: Feminism and the making of Socialism*, Merlin 1979.
2 Alice, Gordon, Debbie and Mary, op. cit., 31-40.
3 M. Wittig: "One is not born a woman", in S. Hoagland, op. cit., 446-7.

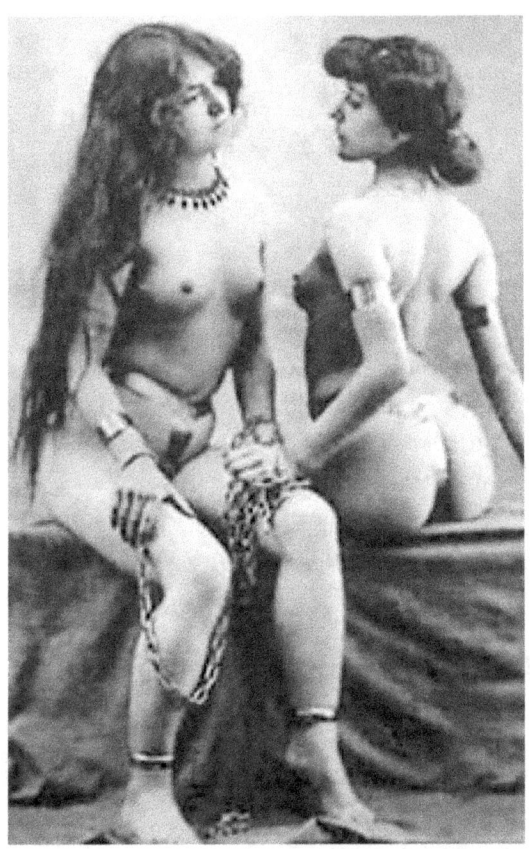

Anonymous, lesbian photograhs,
19th century

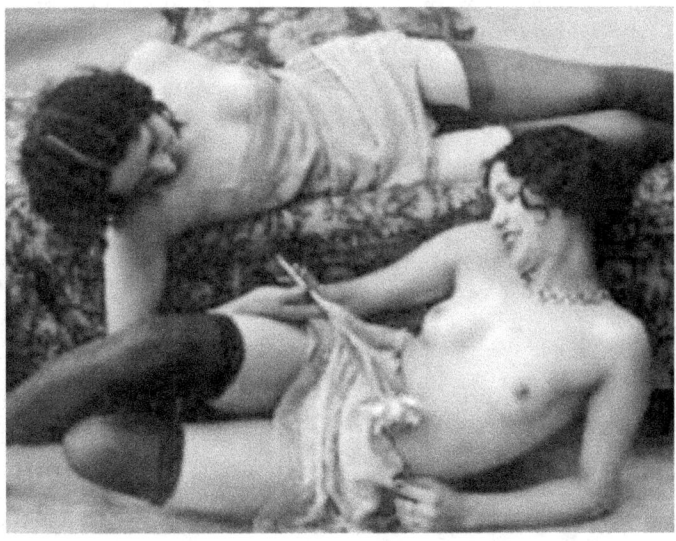

LESBIAN EROTICA

In heterosexual pornography, lesbian eroticism is often introduced, but always controlled by a patriarchal force. Typically, in a soft porn scenario, two bisexual women cavort on a bed overseen by a male ('I've always wanted to see ya with another woman', drools the man to his wife/ girlfriend; or, frequently, 'I got back from work an' saw my wife an' her best friend writhin' on the bed'). Towards the end of the scene, the man makes love to both women. Why? Because they needed the phallus, they needed a man to be fulfilled. Variations on this scenario occur endlessly in pornography. The male presence (the phallus) is seen as necessary for the true satisfaction for women (for valorization, for authenticity: i.e., it's not *true* sex without the phallus).

Lesbian or women's pornography, made by women for women, disappoints some feminists. Elizabeth Carola, who called herself as a 'radical feminist lesbian', described magazines such as *On Our Backs, Bad Attitude, OW! – Outrageous Women: A Journal of Woman-to-Woman SM, Yellow Silk* and *The Power Exchange* in "Women, Erotica, Pornography":

> Like all porn, this new 'woman's' porn is neither about nor for women. Like all porn it is, in a most basic sense, *against* women and *about* male fantasy – the basic male fantasy of Woman as Wholly Sexual Object whose Purpose is To Be Fucked – which feeds men's egos, fuels their violence...[1]

---

[1] Elizabeth Carola: "Women, Erotica, Pornography: – Learning to Play the Game", in G. Chester, 172.

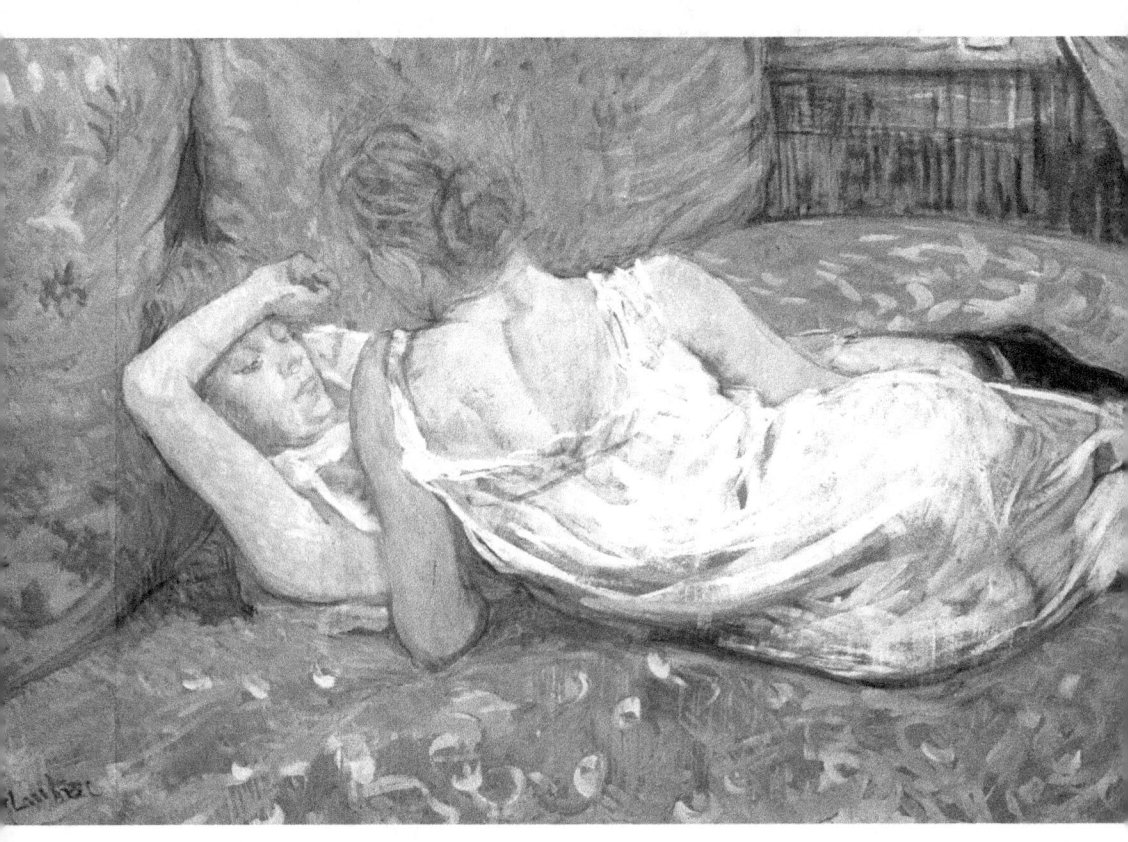

Henri de Toulouse-Lautrec (1864-1901), Two Friends

LESBIAN EROTICISM

Not all feminists agree about the revolutionary potential of lesbianism, if it is a lesbianism that keeps defining itself in terms of patriarchy. Elizabeth Mees reckoned that 'lesbianism, as an attack on hetero-relations, takes (its) place within the structure of the institution of heterosexuality. The lesbian is born of/ in it.'[1] There is no escape, it seems, from patriarchal and heterosexuality: the world is permeated with these ancient structures. As Sheila Jeffreys wrote: '[e]very woman grows up in a heteropatriarchal world',[2] while Ann Barr Snitow remarked in "Mass Market Romance':

> One of our culture's most intense myths, the ideal of an individual who is brave and complete in isolation, is for men only. Women are grounded, enmeshed in civilization, in social connection, in family and in love (a condition a feminist culture might well define as desirable) while all our culture's rich myths of individualism are essentially closed to them.[3]

1 E. Mees, in K. Jay & J. Glasgow: *Lesbian Text and Contexts: Radical Revisions*, New York University Press, New York, NY, 1990, 82.
2 S. Jeffreys: "The Censoring of Revolutionary Feminism", in G. Chester, 139.
3 A. Snitow: "Mass Market Romance: Pornography for Women Is Different", *Radical History Review*, no. 20, Spring/Summer, 1979.

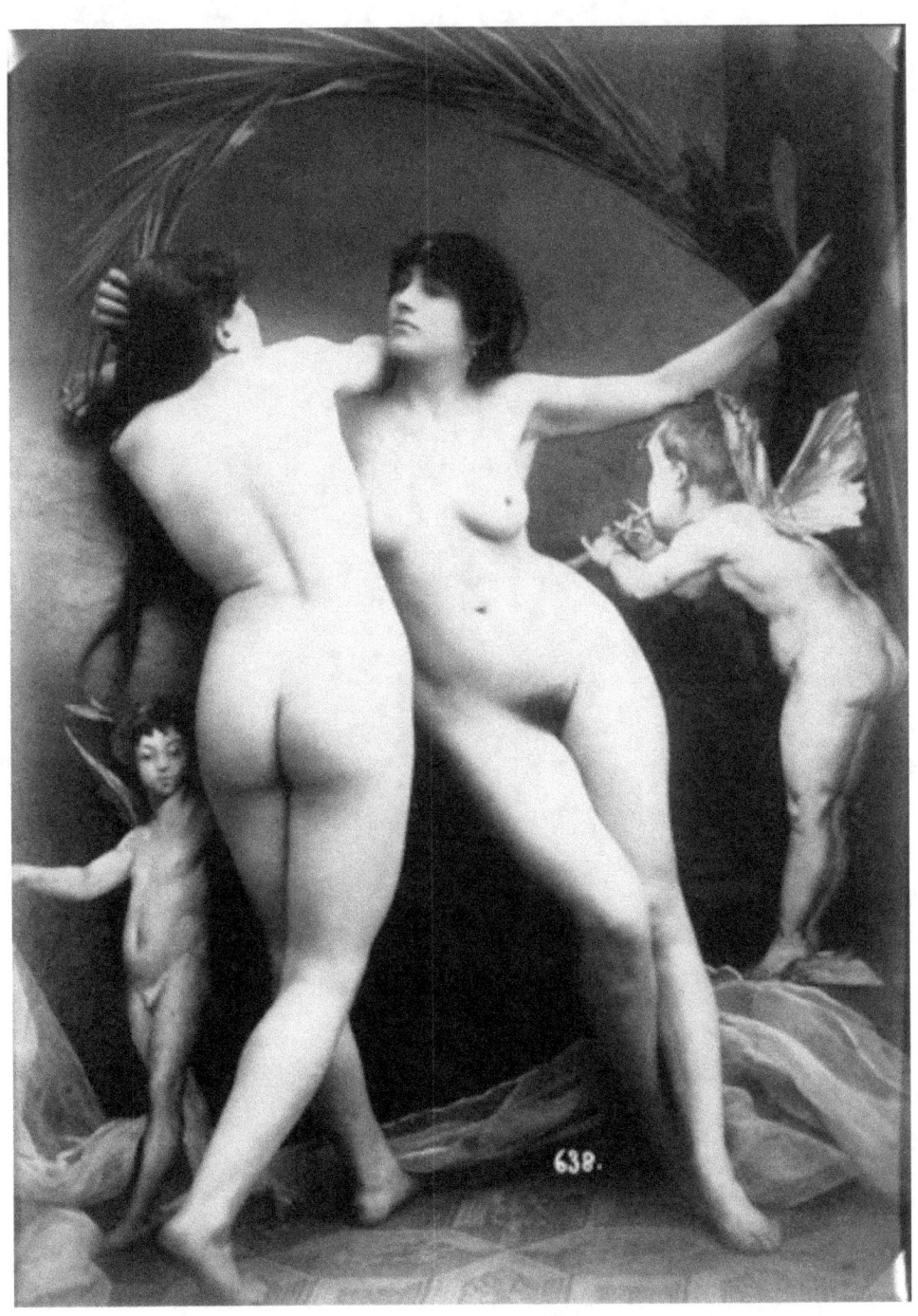

Gaudenzio Marconi (1841-85), Nudes and Angels, 1880s

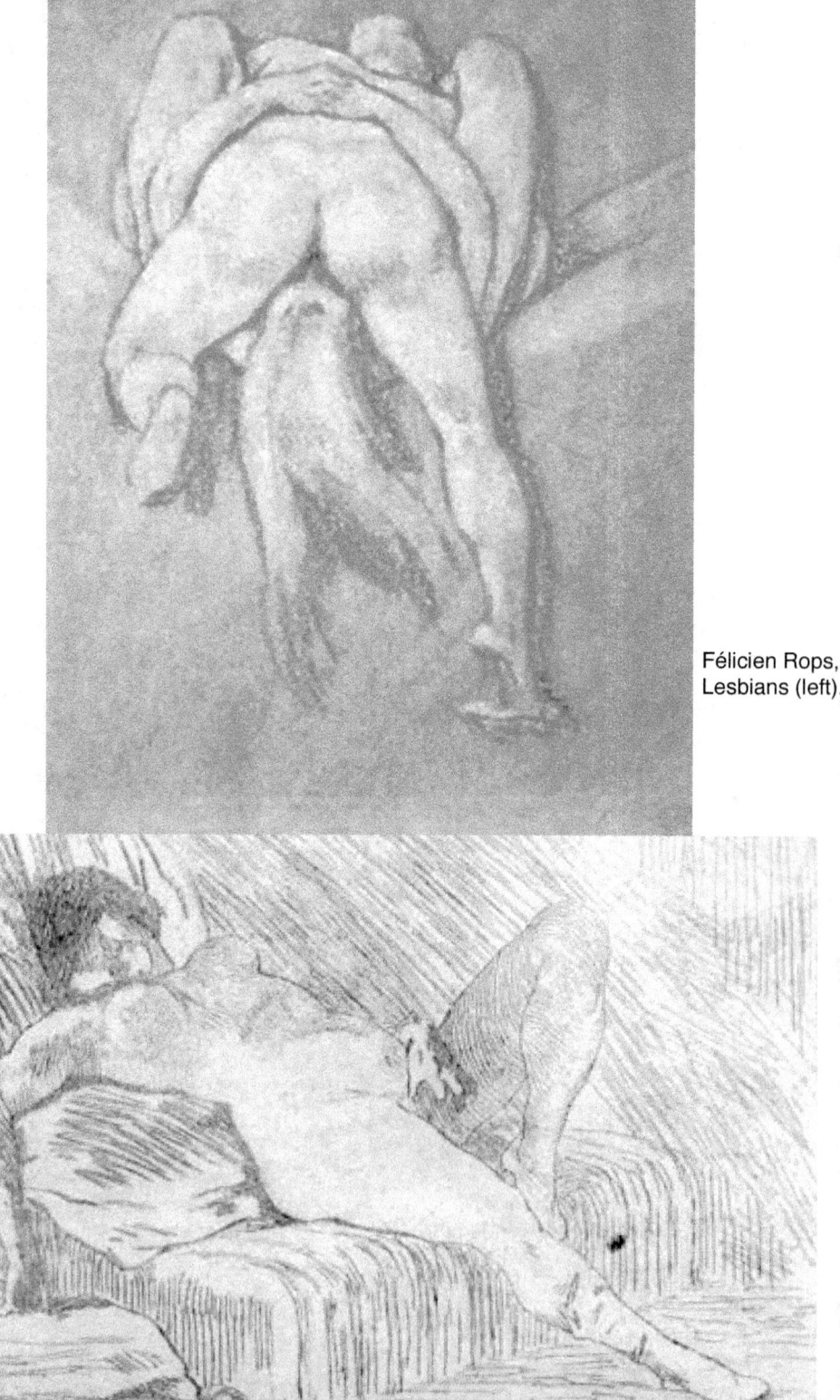

Félicien Rops,
Lesbians (left).

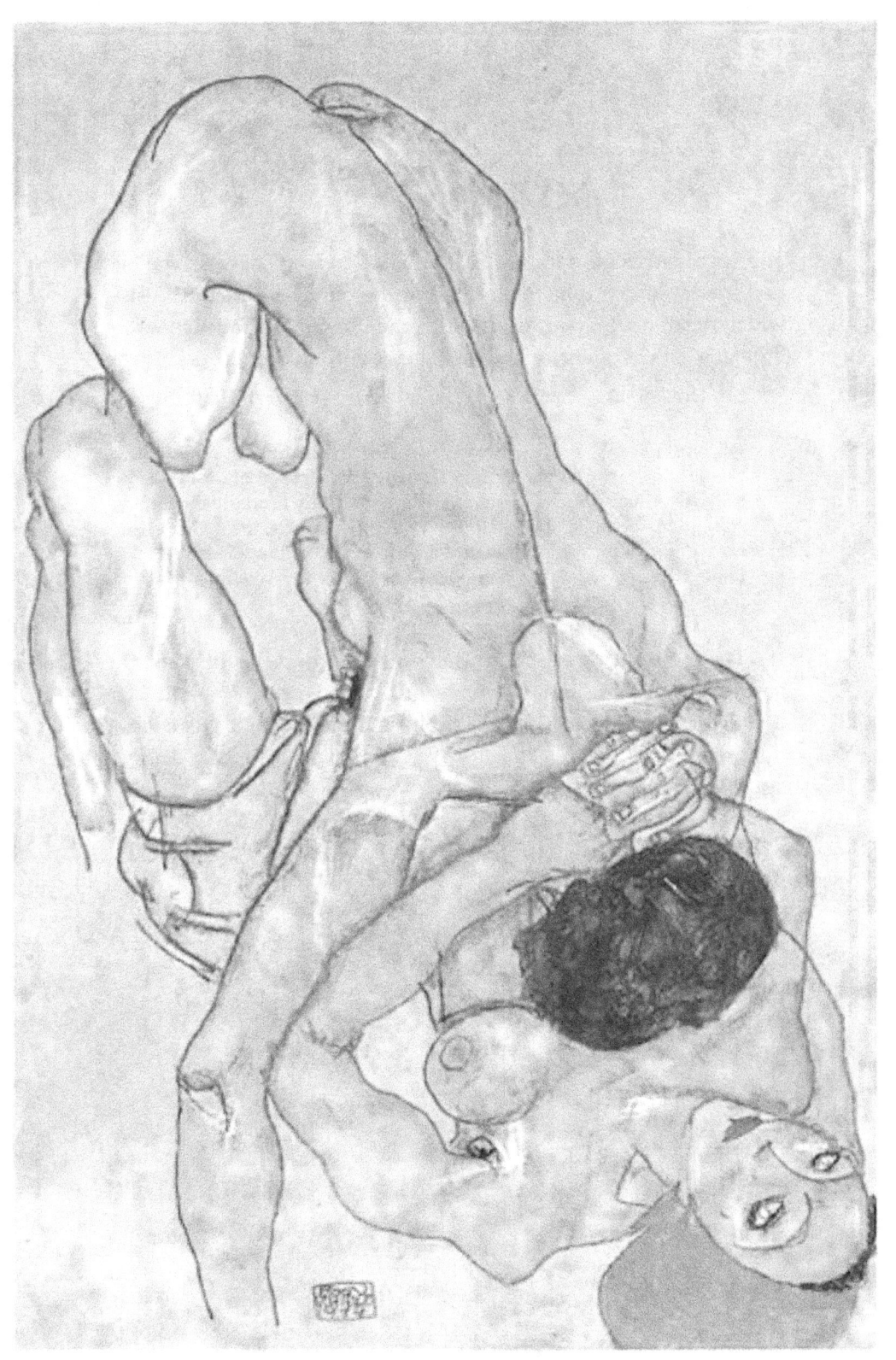

Egon Schiele, Two Women Lovers, 1914

VOYEURISM

The Lacanian Look emphasizes eroticism. Seeing is erotic, the eye becomes a kind of phallus, caressing the obscure object of desire, which it can never 'possess'. As the poet Rainer Maria Rilke wrote '[g]azing is a wonderful thing.'[1] The act of looking eroticizes the object. Jack Zipes describes it thus in *Don't Bet On the Prince*:

> For him [Lacan], seeing is desire, and the eye functions as a kind of phallus. However, the eye cannot clearly see its object of desire, and in the case of male desire, the female object of desire is an illusion created by the male unconscious. Or, in other words, the male desire for woman expressed in the gaze is auto-erotic and involves the male's desire to have his own identity reconfirmed in a mirror image.[2]

The look is an assertion of male power and sexuality. For the gaze is male, and feminists have grappled with the notion of a 'female' gaze, whether there can be such a thing as a 'female' or 'feminine' gaze.[3]

1 R. Rilke, letter to Clara Rilke, 8 March 1907, in *Gesammalte Briefe 1892-1926*, Insel Verlag, Leipzig 1940, II, 279f
2 Jack Zipes: *Don't Bet on the Prince: Contemporary Feminist Fairy Tales in North America and England*, Gower, Aldershot 1986, 258
3 Maggie Humm: "Is the gaze feminist? Pornography, film and feminism", *Perspectives on Pornography*, eds G.Day & C. Bloom, Macmillan 1988; Lorraine Gamran & Margaret Marshment, eds: *The Female Gaze*, Women's Press 1988; E.D. Pribram, ed: *Female Spectators: looking at film and television*, Verso, 1988

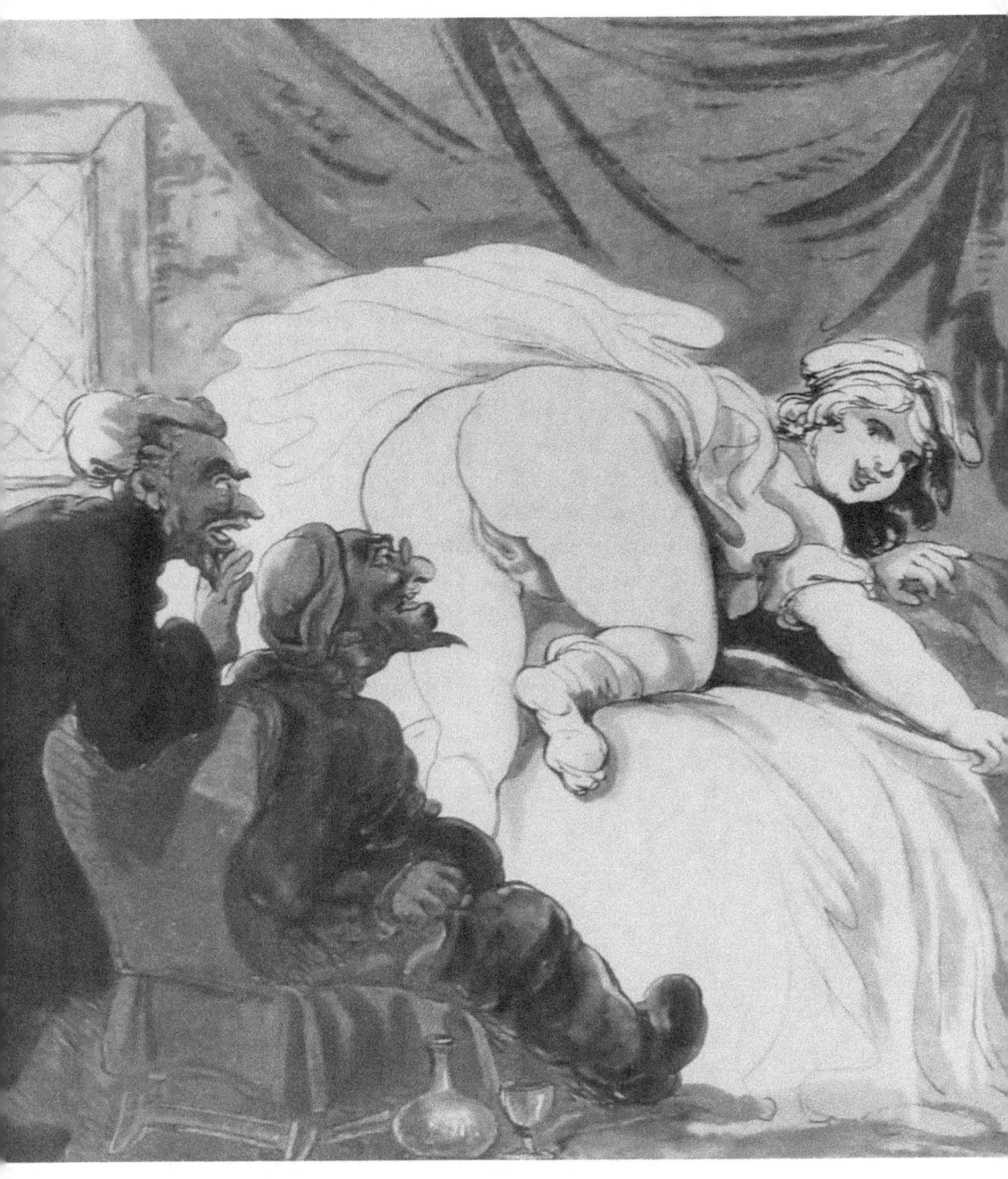

Thomas Rowlandson, Susannah and the Elders, 1820, London

SEX AND DEATH

Pain is good, because it means you are fully alive. This is the Existential view of patriarchal culture. 'Sensual pleasure is agony in the strictest meaning of the word', says C. Mauclair in a Freudian tone.[1] Suffering is holy, in the Christian tradition. The journey from martyrdom to sainthood and beatification is swift. The West exalts pain. Christ *suffered*, say theologians, so he must have been right, he must have lived hard, because he died hard. Death becomes heroic. Death transfigures people. Suicide is even better, if you can manage it. Hence Marilyn Monroe, Vincent van Gogh, Johann Wolfgang von Goethe's Werther, Virginia Woolf. Die young, and become famous (many artists have followed this equation: Egon Schiele, Frédéric Chopin, Wolfgang Amadeus Mozart, Georges Seurat, James Dean, Paula Modersohn-Becker, D.H. Lawrence, Jimmy Hendrix, Jim Morrison, Arthur Rimbaud, Raphael, John Keats, Percy Shelley, and Novalis.

---

1 C. Mauclair: *Magie de l'amour*, 145, quoted in Julius Evola, 84

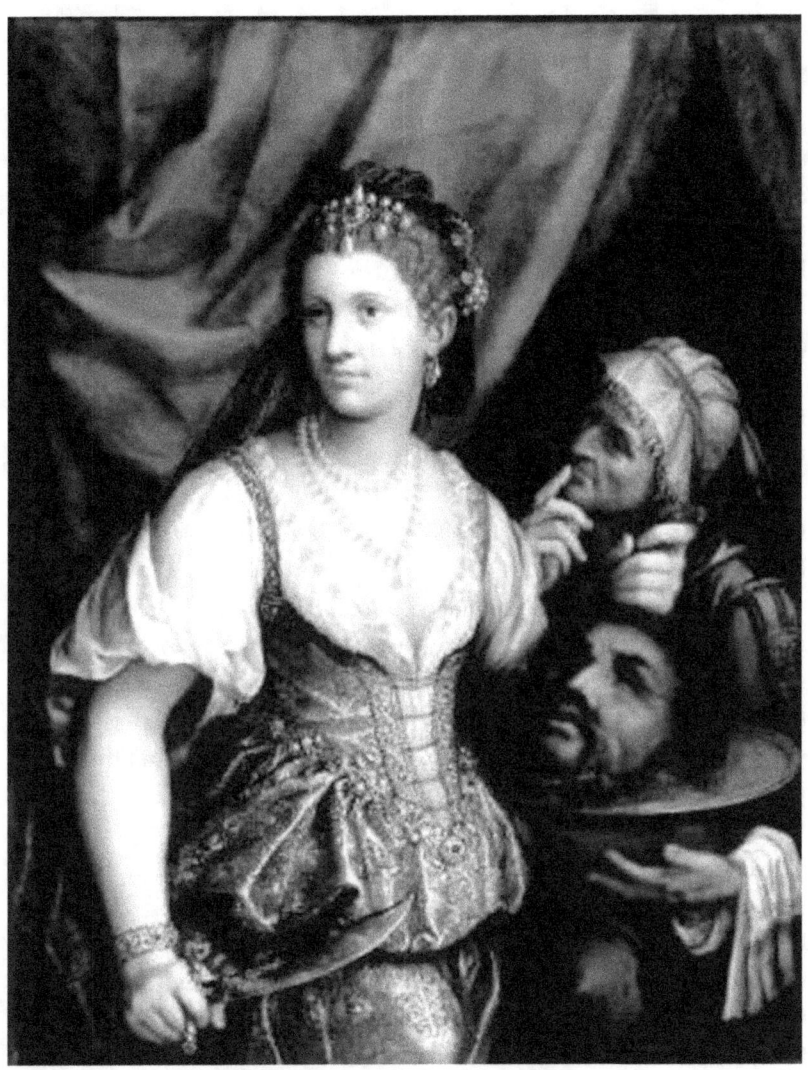

Fede Galizia, Judith with the Head of Holofernes,
Museum of Art, Sarasota, Florida

SEX AND DEATH

In the male system, sex and death are entwined. Further, death and the feminine, death and women are combined. Further, pain and sex are combined. Painful sex must be good sex, according to the male system. If it hurts, it works is a typical adage often bandied about. Pain is good, because it cuts through everything and makes acute the transitoriness and bliss of the human condition, according to the (male) existential view.

A lot of art of any kind comes out of pain, according to men. Love poetry flows from the emotional pain of being left by the lover. Thus, love poetry, from Sappho to the latest pop song, is a cry of pain from a bereft soul. Love songs come from loss, from losing the object of bliss, the beloved. Like babies, love poets sob forlornly.

Love is pain, death, sin, vice and fornication in the Christian view. Love poets transform the pain into art, as do creators of erotic art. There is a masochism at the heart of Western art, as there is at the core of Christianity. Christ on the Cross is the supreme example of masochistic pain in the West, and is the most painted image, apart from the Madonna and Child, in the Western world.

There is a link here: the Crucifixion is the end of life, the painful letting go, while the child in the Madonna's arms is the beginning of life, swathed in the softness and care of the mother figure. The two images, Virgin and Child and the Crucifixion, form the twin poles of Western art. Both images are dominated by the feminine, for the Cross in the Crucifixion is the Mother, the Goddess, the Cross being part of the Earth from which Christ is later reborn – the second, spiritual birth echoing his first, earthly birth, depicted in so many Nativity scenes and Madonna and Child images.

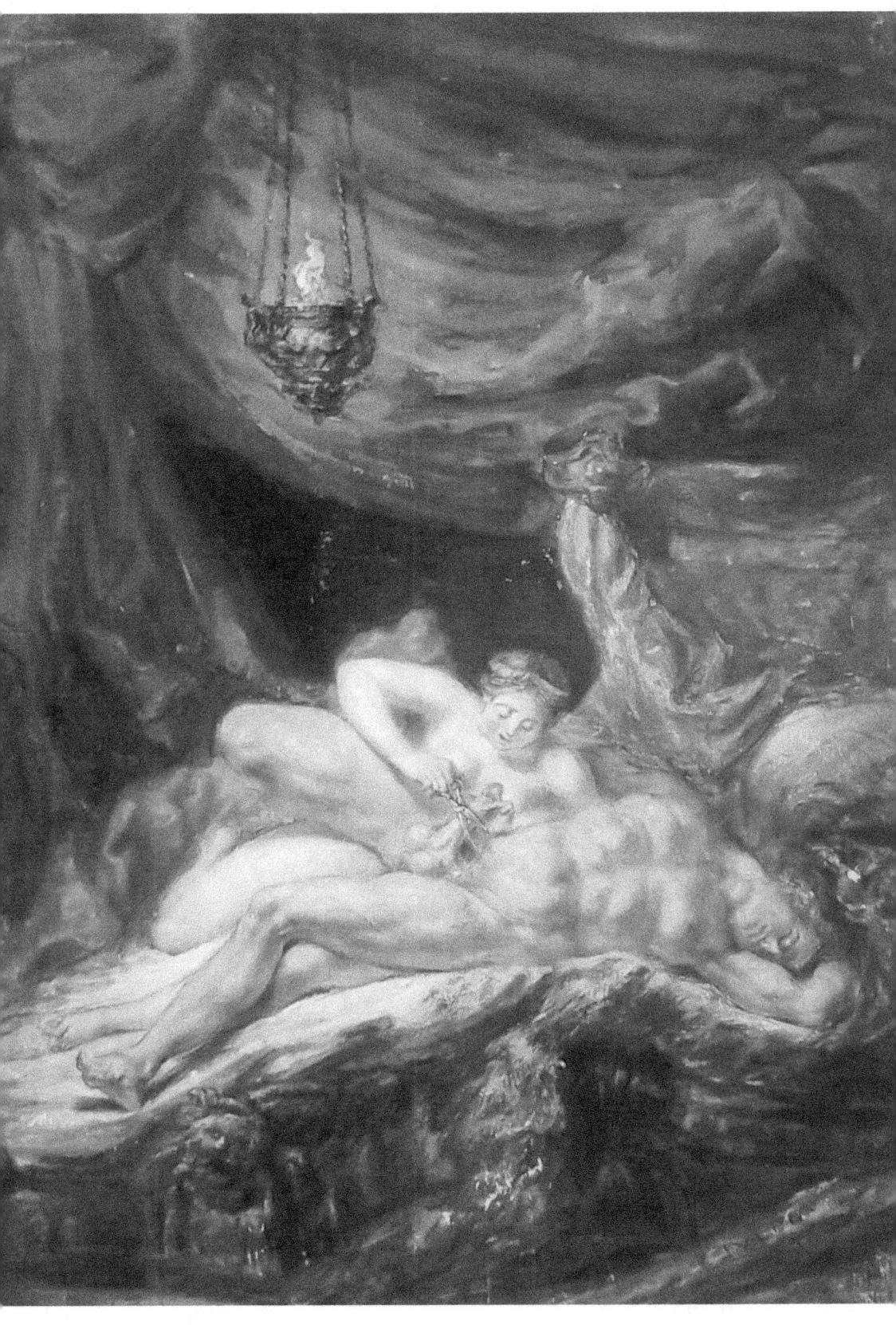

Anonymous, Samson and Delilah, 18th century, French, British Museum

Part Two

Erotic Art In the Renaissance

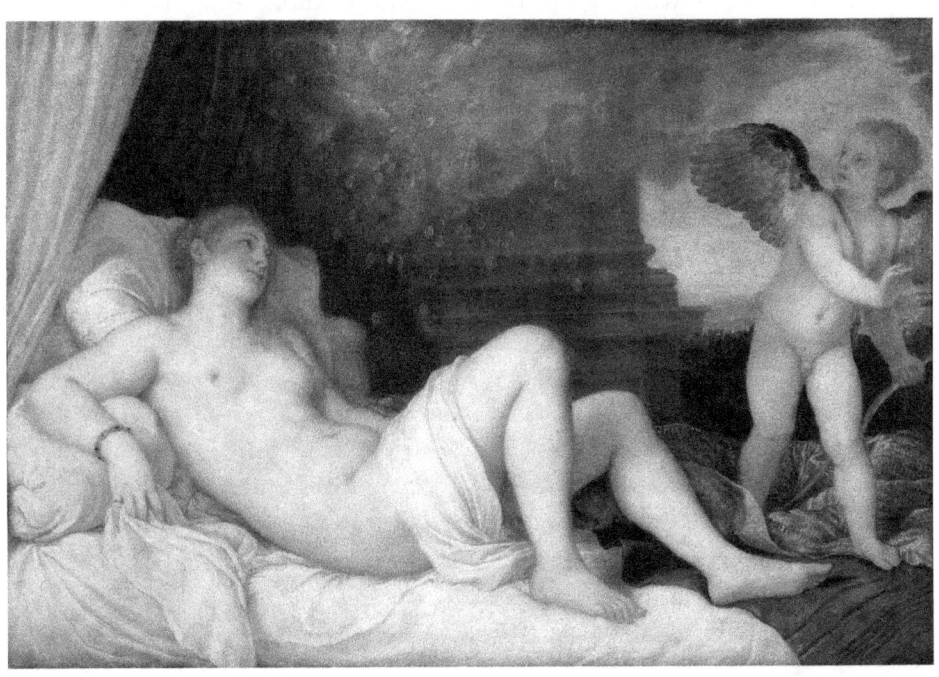

EROTIC ART IN THE RENAISSANCE

Imagine a nude painting of the Blessed Virgin Mary. The idea, to patrons, critics and consumers of Renaissance and mediæval art is shocking, as well as blasphemous. A naked Mother of God, it is unthinkable in terms of Renaissance and mediæval painting. There is a cult of the Virgin baring one breast, to suckle the baby Jesus. Here painters could depict breasts and nipples being sucked and it was all sanctified by the Catholic establishment. Anthony Van Dyck, Titian, Jan Gossaert (Mabuse), Hans Baldung, Joos van Cleeve, Rembrandt van Rijn and Peter Paul Rubens, among many others, painted the breasts of the Madonna.[1] The scene is usually a Holy Family, in Christ's childhood, with Jesus one or two years old, in some house, a room somewhere. Or the scene is a landscape in those paintings entitled *The Rest on the Flight Into Egypt*. Here, Joseph, always depicted as an old man, looks on longingly as Jesus is breast-fed. Joseph is an onlooker, a way into the picture, for the (male) viewer looks at the mother and child through Joseph's eyes. (The viewer is assumed to be masculine in most Renaissance paintings). In one painting of the Virgin breastfeeding Christ, by Orazio Gentileschi, Joseph has fallen asleep.[2] We do not see the mother and child through his vision. Instead, Jesus looks directly out at the viewer while he sucks his mother's nipple. The viewer is thus embroiled in this erotic mother-child relationship.

---

1 Titian: *The Virgin and Child,* c. 1570s, 75.6 x 63.2cm, National Gallery, London; Jan Gossaert: *The Virgin and Child,* c. 1530s, 47.7 x 38.2cm, Gemäldegalerie Staatliche Museen Preussicher Kulturbesitz, Berlin; Hans Baldung: *The Virgin and Child with an Angel,* 91 x 64cm, Gemäldegalerie Staatliche Museen Preussicher Kulturbesitz, Berlin; Anthony Van Dyck:*The Rest on the Flight into Egypt, c. 1627,* 134.5 x 114.5cm, Alte Pinakothek, Munich; Joos van Cleeve: *The Rest in the Flight into Egypt,* 54 x 67.5cm, Musées Royaux des Beaux-Arts, Brussels; Rembrandt van Rijn: *The Holy Family, c. 1640,* 41 x 34cm, Louvre, Paris; Peter Paul Rubens: *The Holy Family with the Apple Tree,* 1620-2, 353 x 233cm, Kunsthistorisches Museum, Vienna
2 Orazio Gentileschi: *the Rest on the Flight into Egypt,* 175.3 x 218.4cm, Birmingham Museum

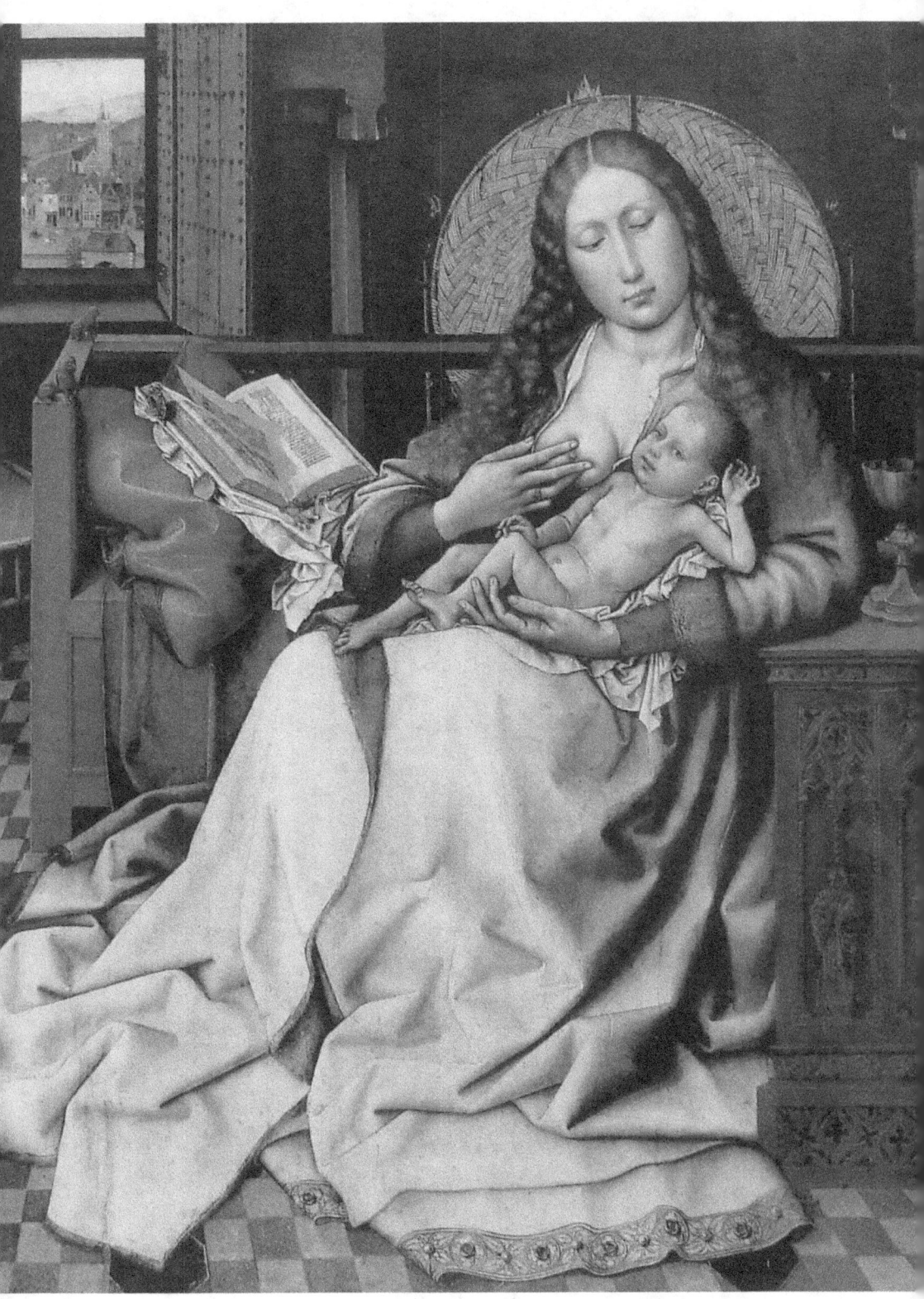

Robert Campin, Madonna With the Firescreen, National Gallery, London

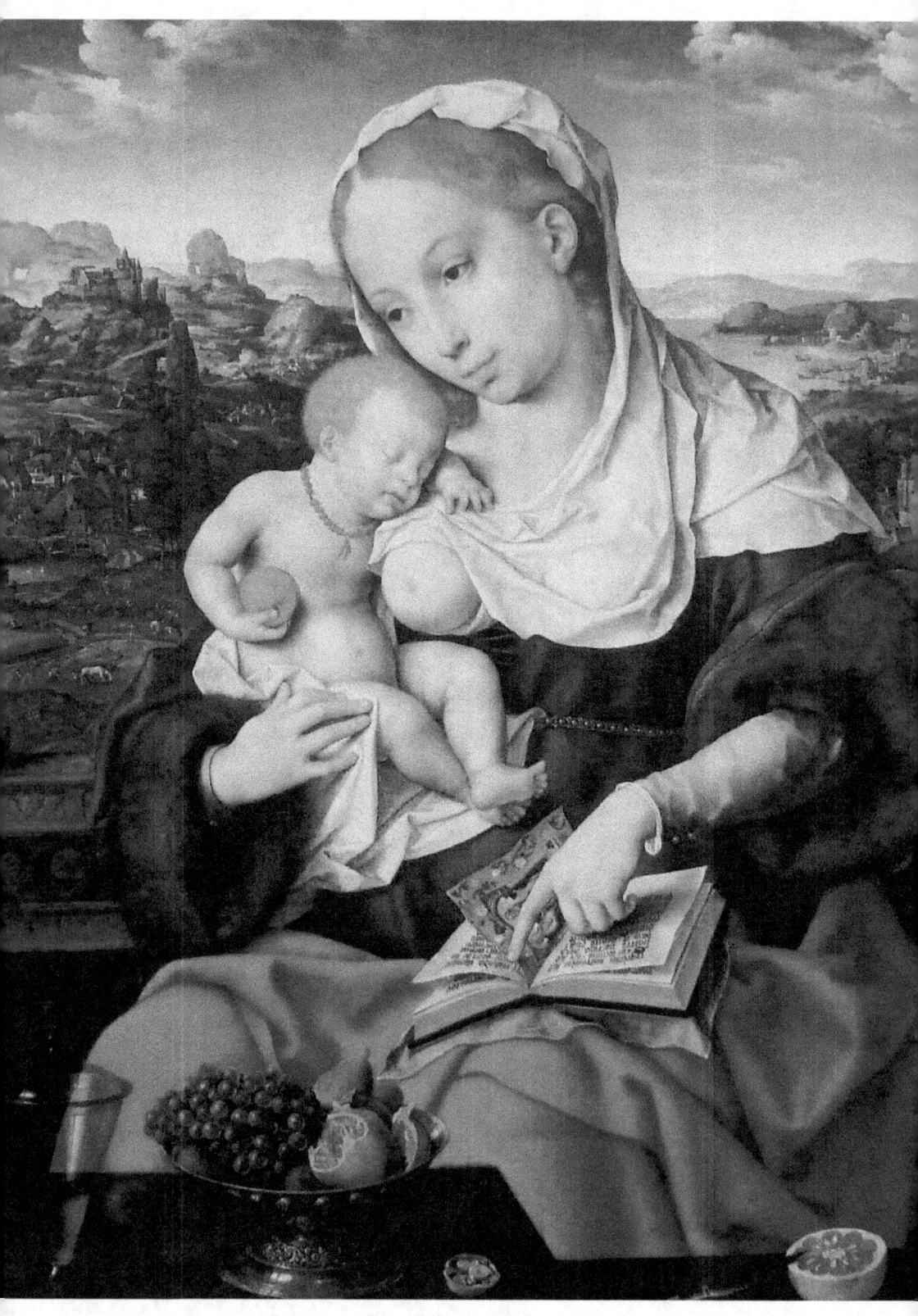

Joos van Cleve, Madonna and Child, Metropolitan Museum,
New York City

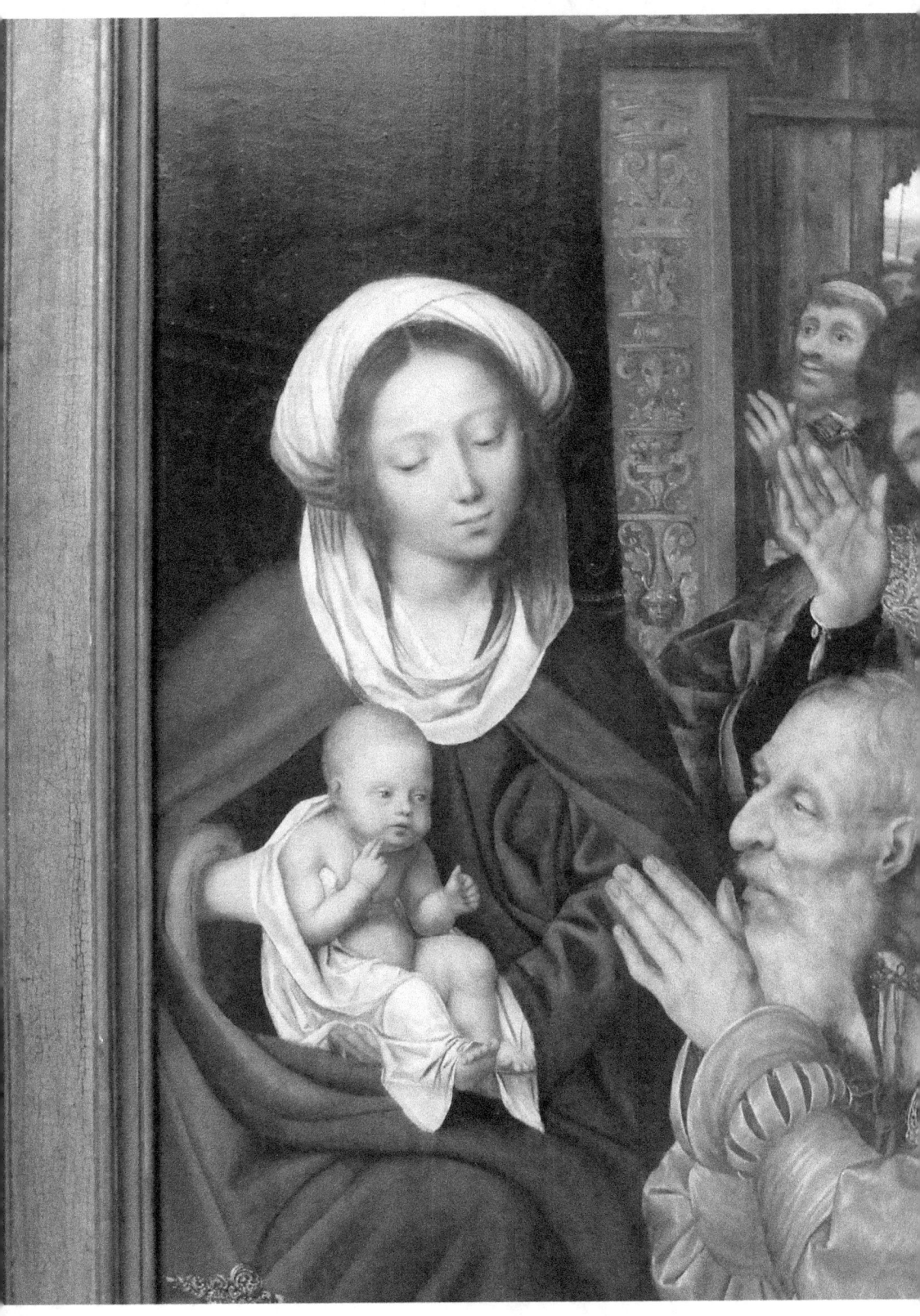

Gerard David, Adoration of the Magi, detail, Metropolitan Museum of Art

Greek mythology enabled Renaissance artists to use images and themes of a wilder, stranger and more erotic nature than the images, themes and codes of Christianity. While Catholicism suppressed sex at every opportunity, only allowing it to express itself in figures such as Mary Magdalene, who had to be portrayed as an eternal penitent, Greek mythology was fully human. The Greek gods and goddesses are playful, stupid, silly, deceitful, jealous, angry, wily, poetic, ignorant and erotic, quite unlike Jehovah or Jesus. Greek myths were subjects in which painters and sculptures could let themselves address erotic issues. The myths, drawn from Ovid, Plato, Apuleius and others, are contain many erotic moments, such as Zeus/ Jupiter making love to Leda in the form of a swan, or Apollo pursuing Daphne – to escape him, she changed into a laurel tree (this was a favourite myth of Francesco Petrarch's), or Actaeon seeing Diana naked, or Pygmalion falling in love with his statue of Venus which comes alive, or the god Zephyr chasing Chloris: when he embraces her, flowers spill from her mouth, as depicted in Sandro Botticelli's famous *Primavera*. Jean-Léon Gérôme painted an indubitably erotic depiction of Pygmalion: the statue comes alive and the sculptor embraces her passionately: the woman's legs are still white marble, but her upper body is already flesh. Typically, Gérôme makes sure that the groin and hips of the statue-becoming-woman are fleshly, for the woman is clearly destined to be the artist's whore, a statue made for sex.

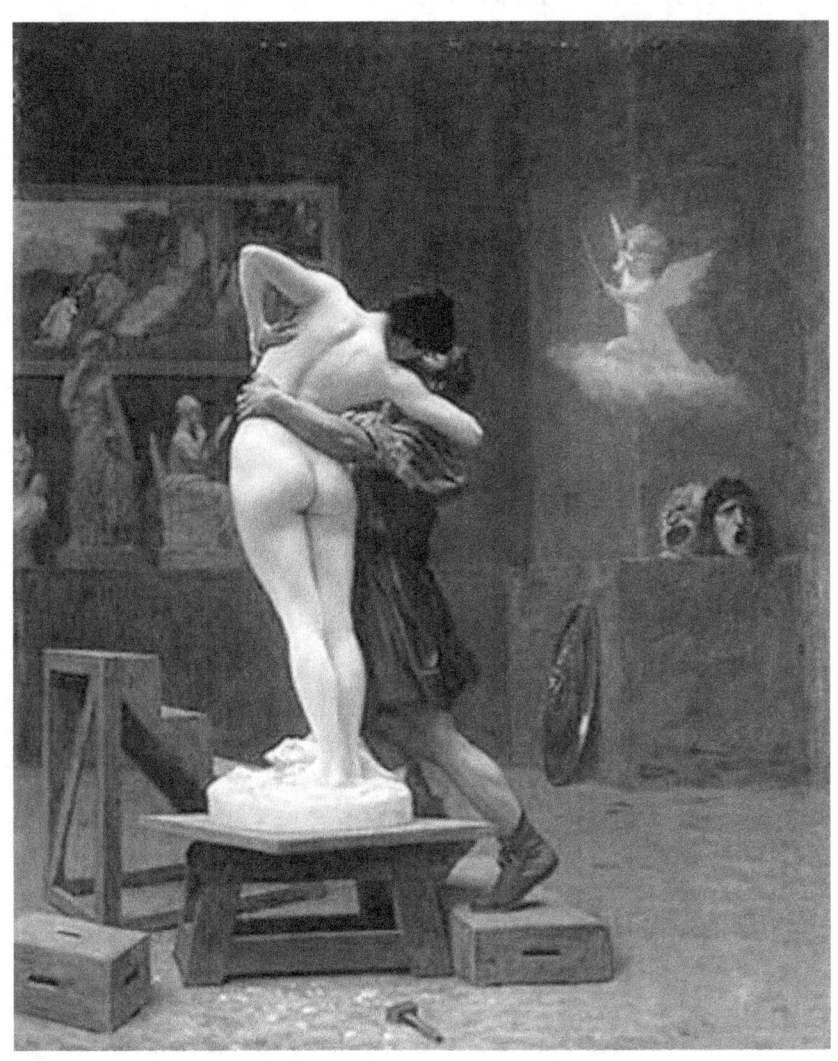

Jean-Léon Gérome, Pygmalion and Galatea,
Metropolitan Museum, New York

The common subject of the Renaissance nude was Venus. As the Goddess of Love in mediæval and courtly love poetry, Venus, with her phallic assistant, Cupid, as the cherub armed with bow and arrow, presided over erotic experiences. The poetry of the troubadours was distinctly erotic and physical, despite its insistence on manners, etiquette and morals. The aim of courtly love poetry was to get into the bed of the beloved woman, basically. Venus was called upon to aid the lover in this pursuit of the Holy Grail, the mystic cauldron of Woman, her womb. Venus is both Holy Whore and chaste Mistress of 'Love'. She is Love personified. The Louvre birth plate, *c.* 1400, shows the Goddess Venus hovering over a Tuscan Garden of Love attended by two angels. Below are six 'famous warriors'. All of them are staring intently at the genitals of the floating Goddess.[1] The lines of sight are marked on the painted salver. The Goddess is depicted in a mandorla, just like the Virgin Mary in *Assumption* images. The centre of the picture is Venus's vulva.[2]

Countless female nudes depict Venus in different poses of shyness and abandonment. Giorgione's *Sleeping Venus* makes the looking at the body easier, because she is asleep.[3] Yet this depiction is created very definitely for the pleasures of eroticism, made for the *jouissance* of looking. Other Renaissance Venuses, from Sandro Botticelli's *Birth of Venus* to Titian's *Venus of Urbino*, to the Master of Flora's *Birth of Cupid*, are offered as gorgeous depictions of women, of mythical women painted sublimely, of women who expose their 'looked-at-ness' for all to see.[4] Even 'unusual' visions of the female nude, such as the paintings of Lucas Cranach, come across, finally, as erotica.[5]

---

1 See Paul Watson: *The Garden of Love in Tuscan Art of the Early Renaissance*, Associated University Press 1979, 17, 23
2 *The Triumph of Venus*, anonymous, birth plate, School of Verona (?), c. 1400, Louvre, Paris
3 Giorgione: *Sleeping Venus*, c. 1508, oil on canvas, 108 x 175cm, Staatliche Kunstsammlungen, Gemäldegalerie, Dresden
4 Titian: *Venus of Urbino*, 1538, oil on canvas, 119.5 x 165cm, Uffizi, Florence; Sandro Botticelli: *The Birth of Venus*, c. 1482, tempera on canvas, 173 x 279cm, Uffizi, Florence; Master of Flora: *Birth of Cupid*, c. 1540/60, oil on wood, 108 x 130.5cm, Metropolitan Museum of Art, New York
5 Lucas Cranach: *the Nymph of Spring*, Palitz Collection, New York; *The Judgement of Paris*, panel, 40.2 x 27.8in, Metropolitan Museum of Art, New York

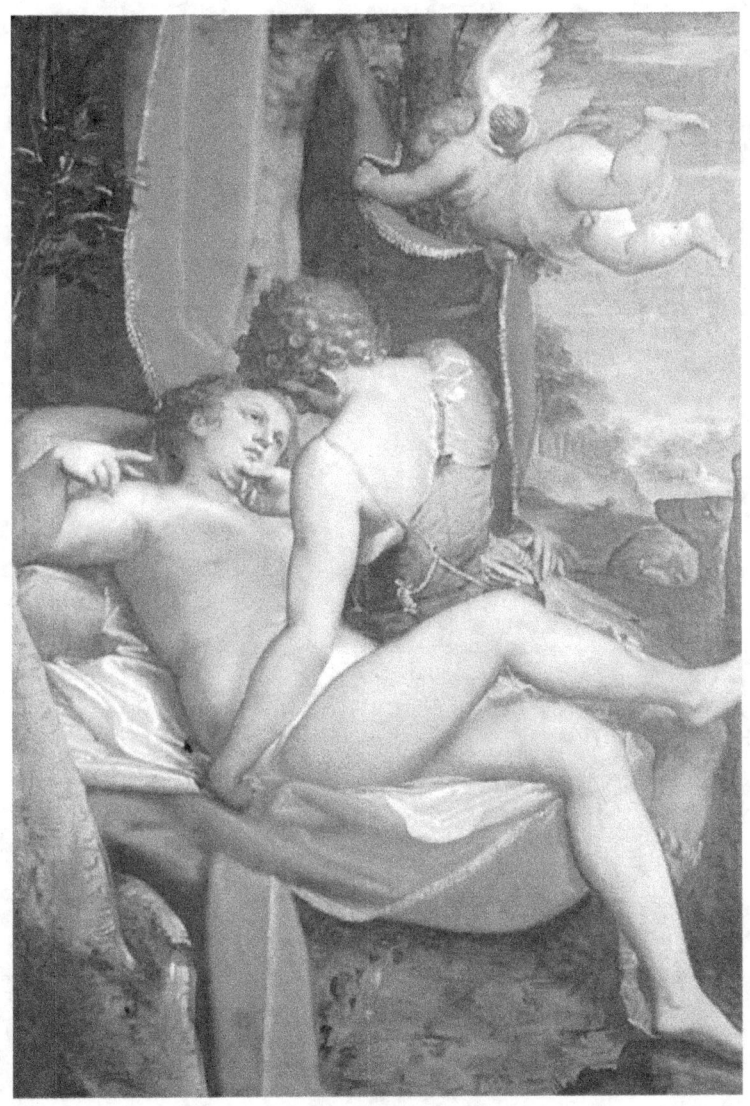

Luca Cambiaso, Venus and Adonis, 16th century

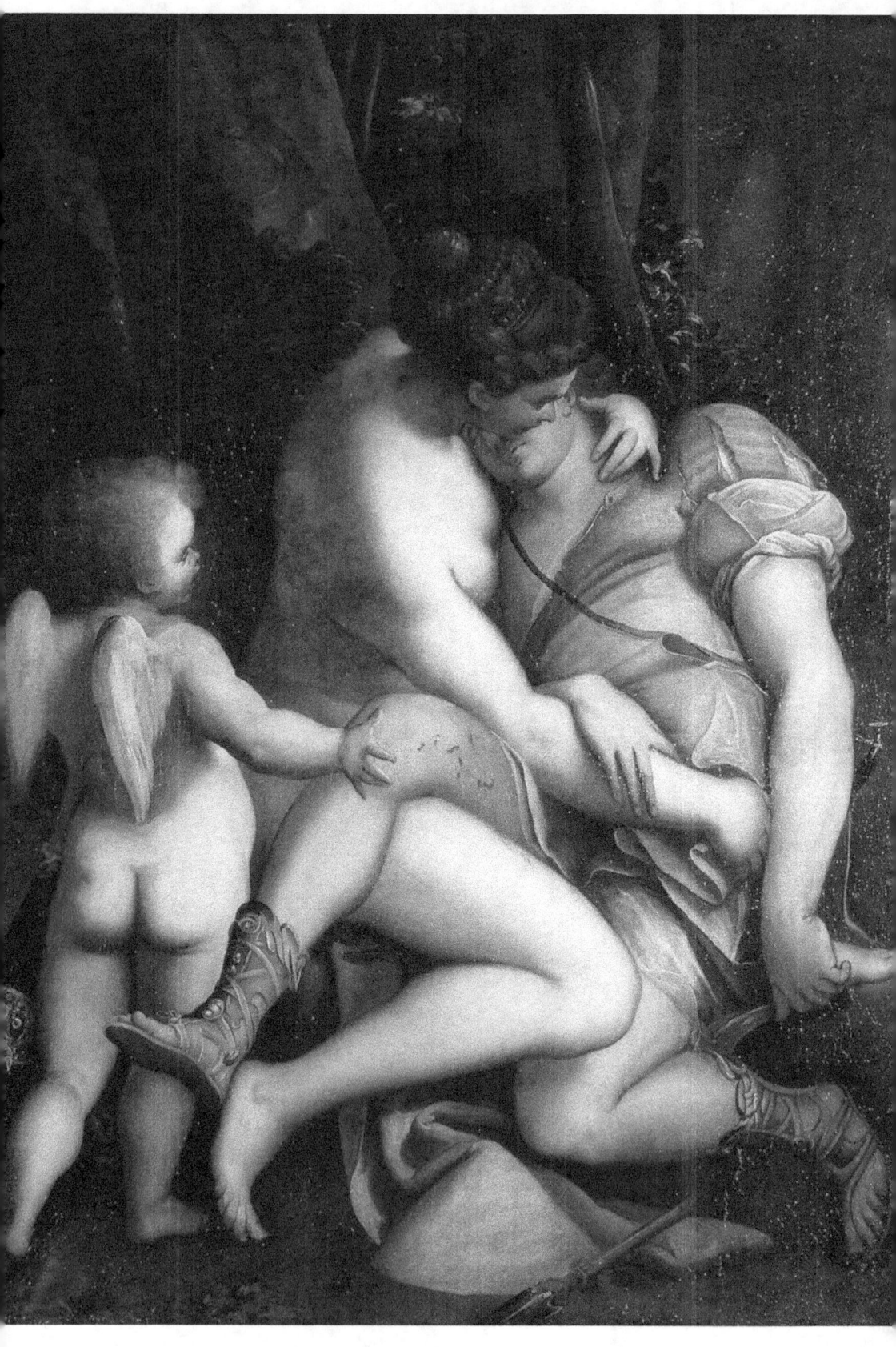

Luca Cambiaso, Venus and Adonis, c. 1565

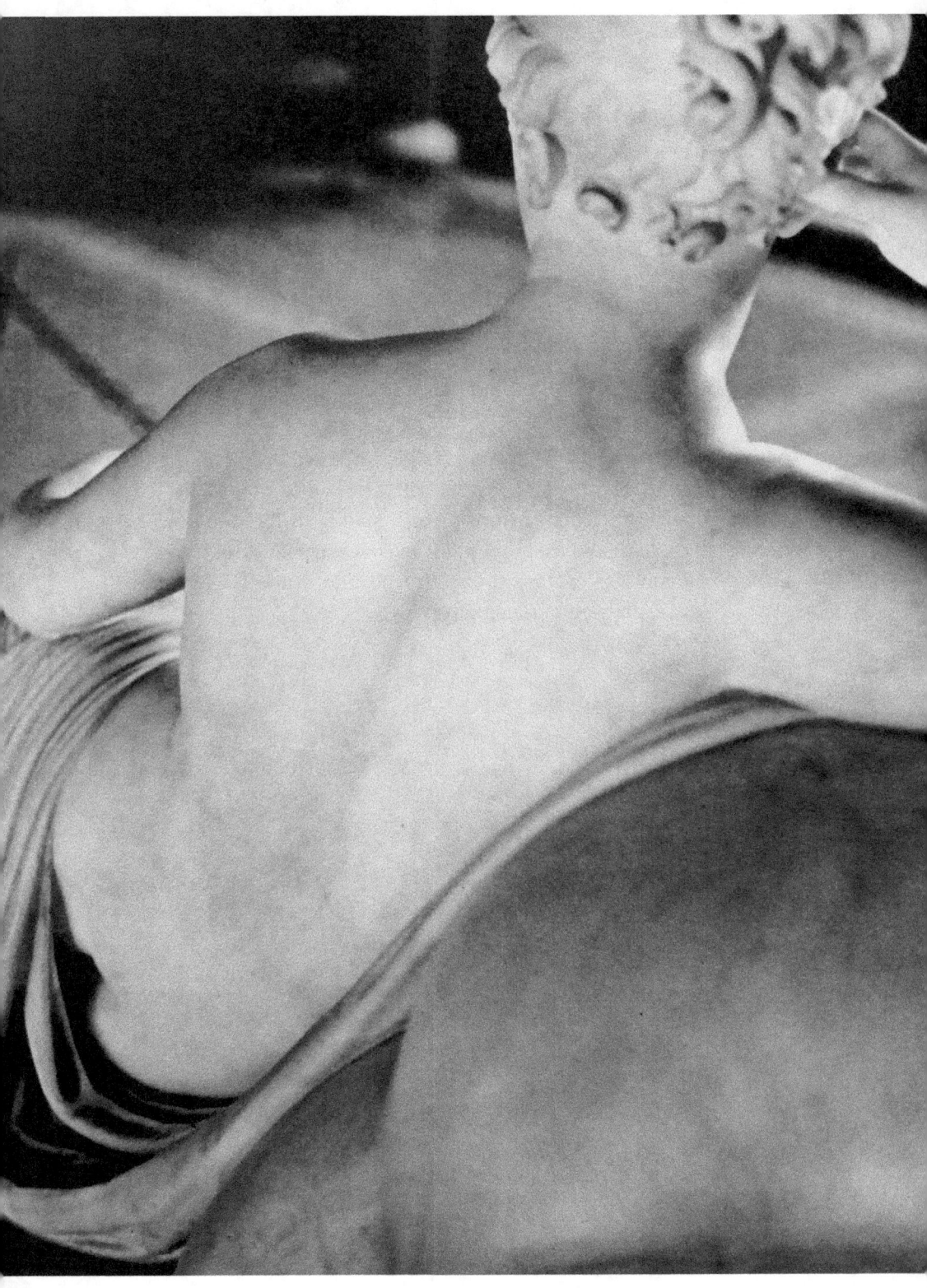

Antonio Canova, Venus Victorious, 1808

Even in unexpected places, such as in Early Italian Renaissance art, such as Pietro Lorenzetti, one finds erotic objectifications of women that look towards the 'high art' nude. And otherwise chaste and sober painters, such as Giovanni Bellini, produced female nudes made to be looked at erotically.[1] Piero di Cosimo's Neoplatonic, mythological paintings are called 'mysterious' by critics, but they also contain female nudes that are pornographic.[2] Antonio Pisanello's drawing of the personification of 'Luxury' undoubtedly depicts a prostitute: his drawing is a form of Renaissance pornography, given 'high art' status because Pisanello was a 'major' artist.[3] Some images of the Renaissance and later nudes contain men in the picture, who modulate the viewer's gaze.[4] The man in the picture stands in for the viewer, and the gaze is distinctly erotic (and male, except in certain cases, such as Simon Vouet's image of Psyche and Amor, where the female contemplates the male body).[5]

1 Ambrogio Lorenzetti: *Peace*, in *Good Government*, c. 1338-40, Palazzo Publico, Sienna; Giovanni Bellini: *A Young Woman at Her Toilet*, 1515, Kunsthistorisches Museum, Vienna
2 Piero di Cosimo: *Simonetta Vespucci*, c. 1477, tempera on panel, 22.4 x 16.5in, Condé Museum, Chantilly; *Venus, Mars and Cupid*, c. 1490, panel, 72 x 182cm, Staatliche Museen, Berlin
3 Pisanello: *Allegory of luxury*, drawing, Albertina, Vienna
4 Antonio Allegri de Correggio: *The Sleep of Antiope*, c. 1525, oil on canvas, 189.8 x 124.1cm, Louvre, Paris; Peter Paul Rubens: *Angelica and the Hermit*, c. 1625-8, oil on wood, 43 x 66cm, Kunsthistoriches Museum, Vienna
5 Simon Vouet: *Psyche Looking at the Sleeping Amor*, 1626, oil on canvas, 112 x 165cm, Musée des Beaux Arts, Lyons

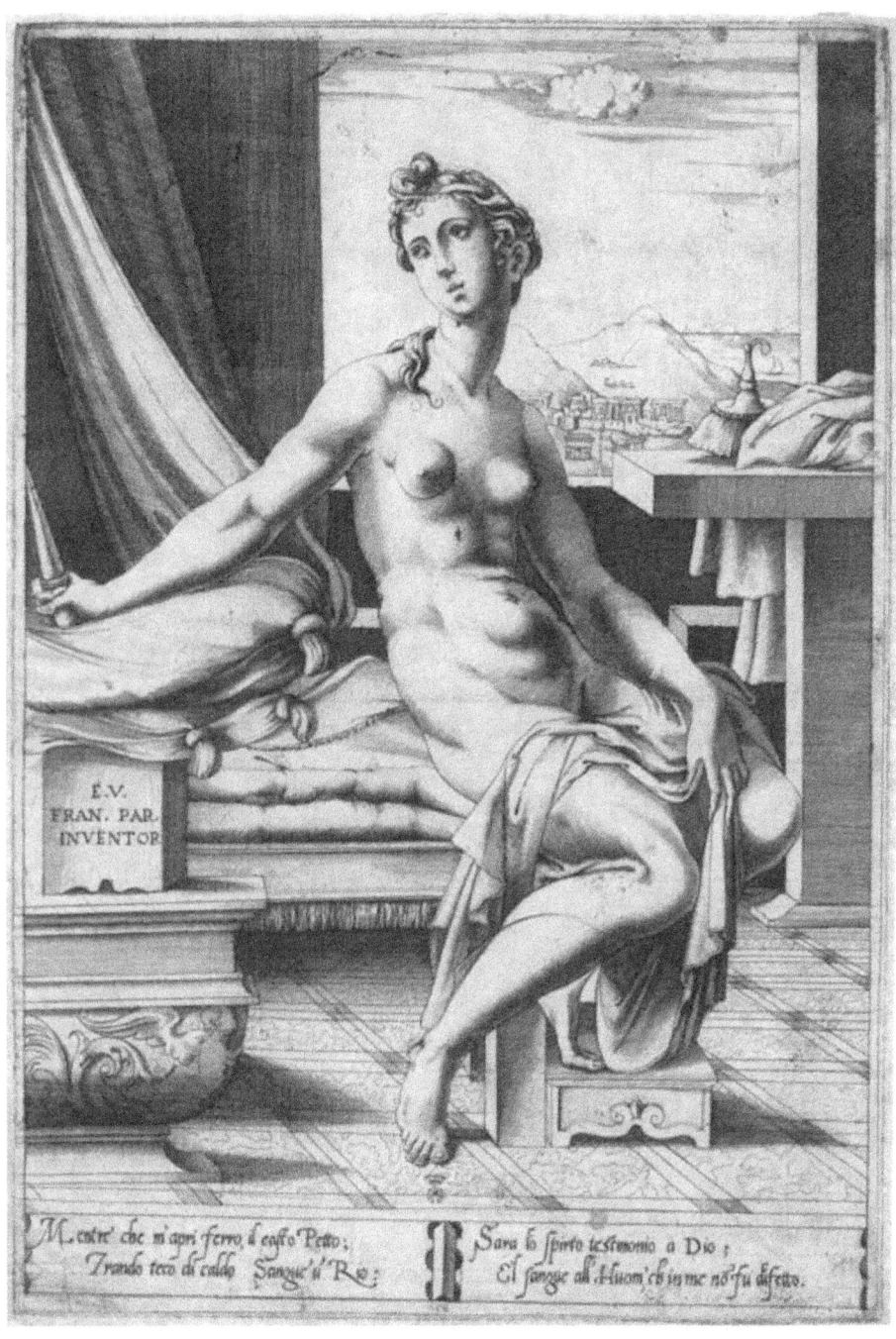

Enea Vico

VENUS AND VIRGIN

In the Neoplatonic, Aristotlean, Renaissance view of the fine art establishment, there is good art and bad art, there is art of 'taste', 'decency', 'refinement', 'purity' and 'civilization', and there is the vulgar, the uncouth, the disrespectful, the unornamental, the unlearned. Pornography falls into the latter category. In mediæval culture, there is Sacred and Profane love, drawn from Plato's *Symposium*, and the Venus Vulgaris (Earthly Venus) and Venus Coelestis. The Heavenly Venus is the one to aspire to, even though the Earthly Venus may be much more exciting.

These dichotomies are found throughout art. There is the chaste, passive, motherly Virgin Mary and the sexual, active, lascivious Mary Magdalene.[1] There is good and evil. There is Heaven and Hell. There is male and female. Throughout the history of Western culture we come across the same dualities, in one form or another. The female is clearly on the 'left' side, on the wrong side of the 'right' way. Women are the 'second sex', 'second class citizens': Sherry Ortner writes there is an opposition between culture and nature, and women are lower down in the male-made hierarchy:

> my thesis is that woman is being identified with – or, if you will, seems to be a symbol of – something that every culture devalues, something that every culture defines as being of a lower order of existence than itself.[2]

---

1 See Marina Warner: *Monuments and Maidens*; Kenneth Clark: *The Nude*; Lynda Nead, 19;
2 Sherry B. Ortner: "Is Female to Male as Nature is to Culture", in M. Evans, ed: *The Woman Question*, Fontana 1982

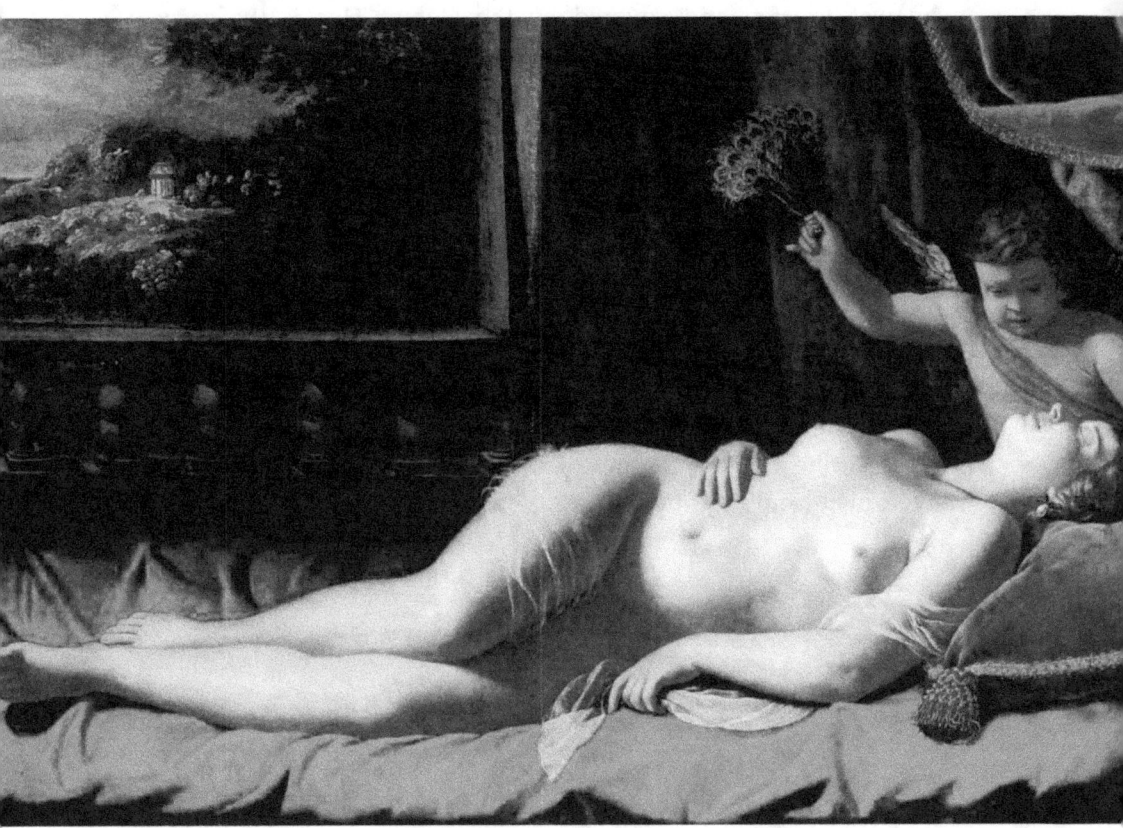

Artemisia Gentileschi, Sleeping Venus, 1625-30,
Barbara Piasecka Johnson Foundation, Princeton, New Jersey

The myth of Venus is based on that of the Greek Goddess Aphrodite. According to Homer, Aphrodite, the 'foam-born', was birthed from the severed, castrated genitals of the god Uranus, which were cast into the sea, creating white foam. The Goddess was blown ashore by the West wind, Zephyrus, to Cyprus, where she was greeted and covered by the Horae. This is the scene Sandro Botticelli depicts, and the sexual origin of Venus lies behind all those female nudes of the Renaissance.

Venus and the Virgin thus represent the twin poles of patriarchal culture: the sexual and asexual, the naked and the clothed, the lover and the mother, etc. The two merge, confusedly and ambiguously, in many Renaissance artworks. The Virgin is both Mother and Lover of Christ, just as, according to psychoanalysis, the mother is the child's first lover. The cults of the milk and breasts of the Madonna emphasize the erotic nature of the child-mother relation. The structure of the Madonna and Child image, with the child seated on the other's lap, echoes that of Osiris sitting on the 'throne' of his mother Isis, who is also his lover, in ancient Egyptian art.

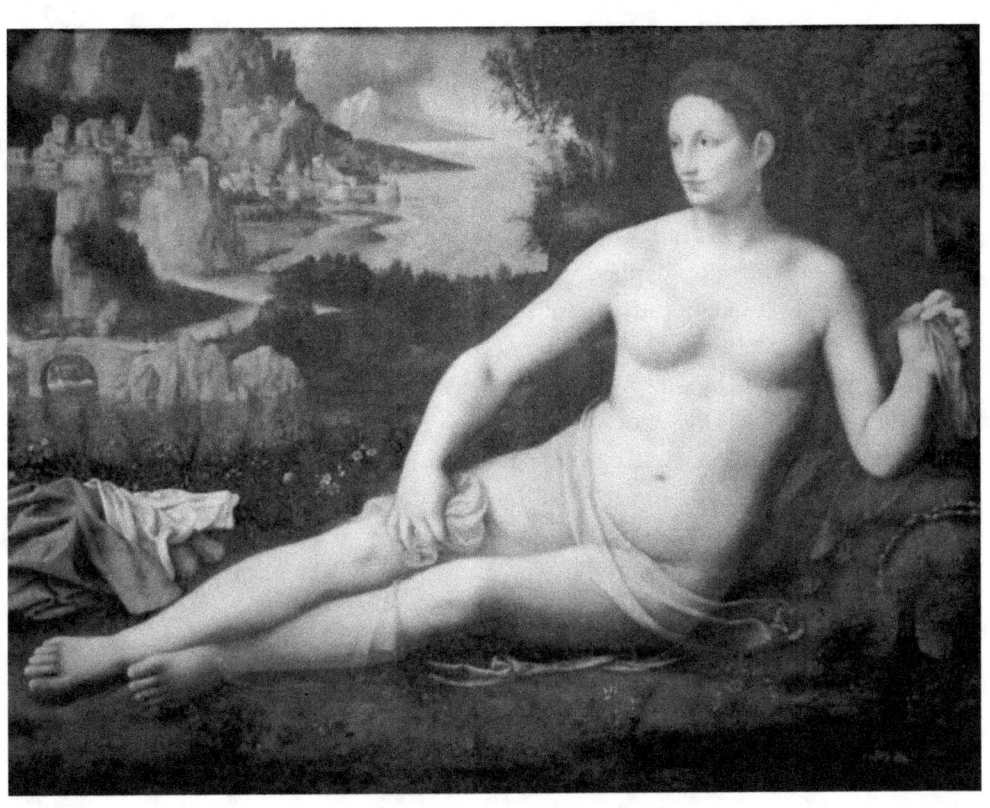

Bernardino Luini, Venus, 1530

FRAGONARD, DAVID, INGRES

After the astonishing output of Leonardo and Michelangelo, Renaissance art lost some of its passion, although it became increasingly openly erotic. Images such as Peter Lely's *Nymphs by a Fountain*, anything by Peter Paul Rubens, Jean Honoré Fragonard's *Bathers*, Jacques-Louis David's *Cupid and Psyche*, and Jean Auguste Dominique Ingres' study for *Ruggiero and Angelica* are openly erotic, displaying the body as a sensual object.[1] Myths such as that of the Judgement of Paris and the Three Graces allow ample opportunity for painting acres of quivering female flesh, as in paintings by Raphael, with his Neoplatonically idealized figures, or in the work of Rubens, Lucas Cranach and Hans Baldung Grien.[2] Artists such as Tintoretto, Veronese, Boucher, Tiepolo, Watteau, Reni, Rembrandt, Guercino, Correggio, Gros, Girodet, Géricault, and Delacroix do not hide their depictions of erotic bodies behind mythological narratives. Their images often put eroticism in the foreground: the pretence at mythological or historical painting is not longer upheld, and the nude form becomes primary.

---

1 Peter Lely: *Nymphs by a Fountain*, c. 1650-5, canvas, 129 x 144.8cm, Dulwich Picture Gallery, London; David: *Cupid and Psyche*, 1817, canvas, 184.1 x 241.6cm, Cleveland Museum of Art; Jean-Honoré Fragonard: *Bathers*, canvas, 64 x 80, Louvre, Paris; Jean-Auguste-Dominique Ingres: *Study for Ruggiero and Angelica*, c. 1819, canvas, 84.5 x 42.5cm, Musée Ingres, Montauban

2 Rubens: *The Judgement of Paris*, c. 1638-9, Prado, Madrid; Lucas Cranach: *The Judgement of Paris*, 1530, Staatliche Kunsthalle, Karlsruhe; Hans Baldung Grien: *The Three Graces*, c. 1540, Prado, Madrid; Raphael: *The Three Graces*, c. 150, panel, 6.6 x 6.6in, Condé Museum, Chantilly

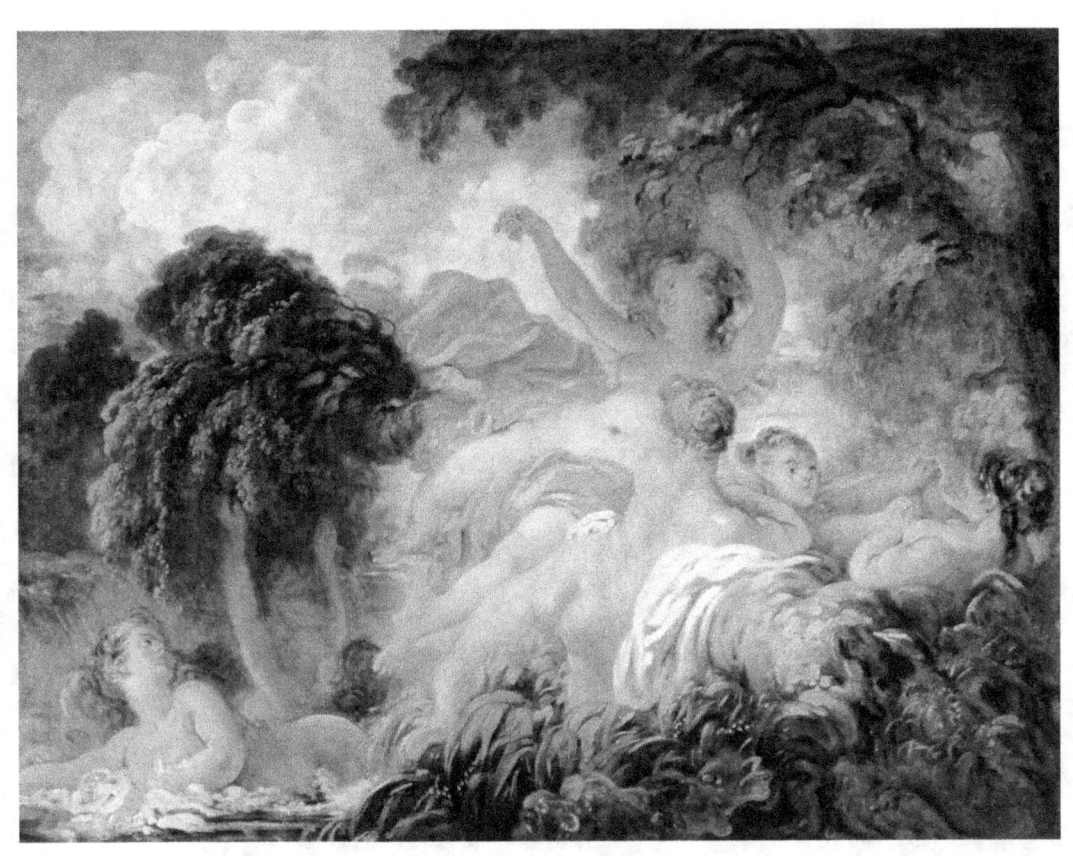

Jean-Honoré Fragonard, Bathers, 1756

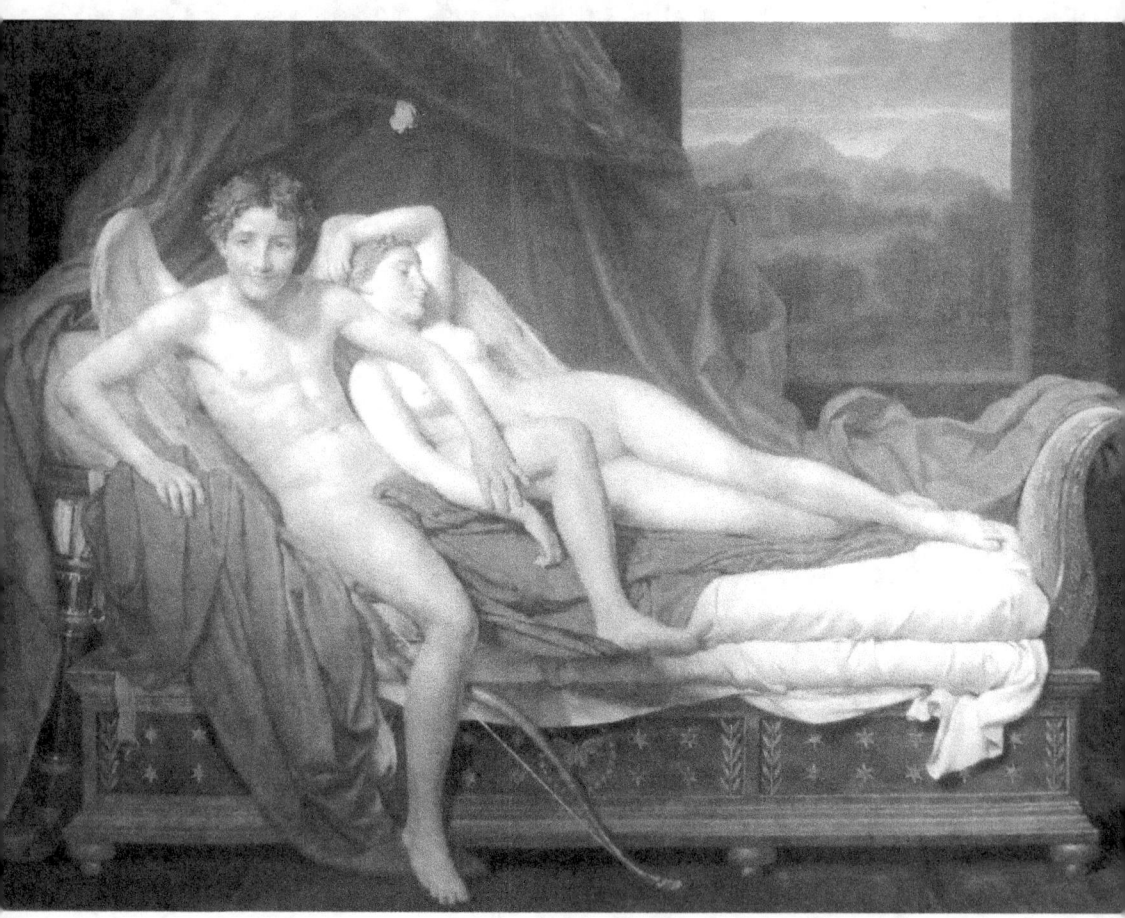

Jacques-Louis David, Cupid and Psyche, 1817,
Cleveland Museum of Art

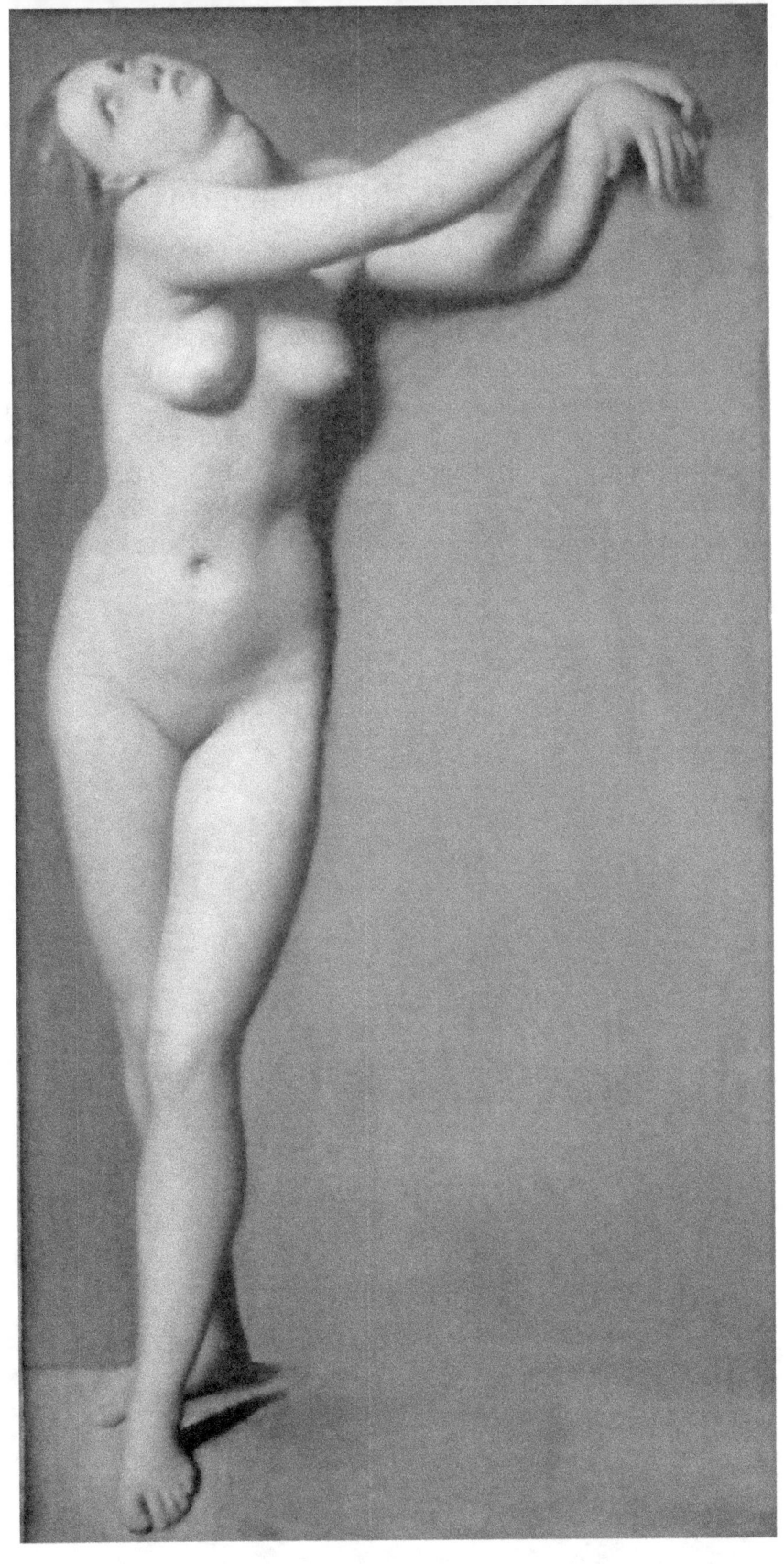

J.A.D. Ingres, study for Ruggiero

TINTORETTO, CORREGGIO, BALDUNG

See, for instance, the voluptuous nude in Correggio's *Jupiter and Antiope*, the acres of female flesh in *The Three Graces* by Tintoretto, or in his *Susannah and the Elders*, where the image of a woman admiring herself in a mirror occurs, to shift the focus from masculine vanity, or the ample back view of a woman, nude of course, stared at by two men, clothed of course, or the luminous skin of the women, nude of course, in Hans Baldung's *Adam and Eve*.[1]

1 Tintoretto: *Susannah and the Elders*, c. 1560, oil on canvas, 76 x 95.6in, Kunsthistorisches Museum, Vienna, *The Three Graces*, 1578, oil on canvas, 57.5 x 61in, Ducal Palace, Venice; Correggio: *Jupiter and Antiope*, c. 1525, oil on canvas, 74.8 x 48.8in, Louvre, Paris

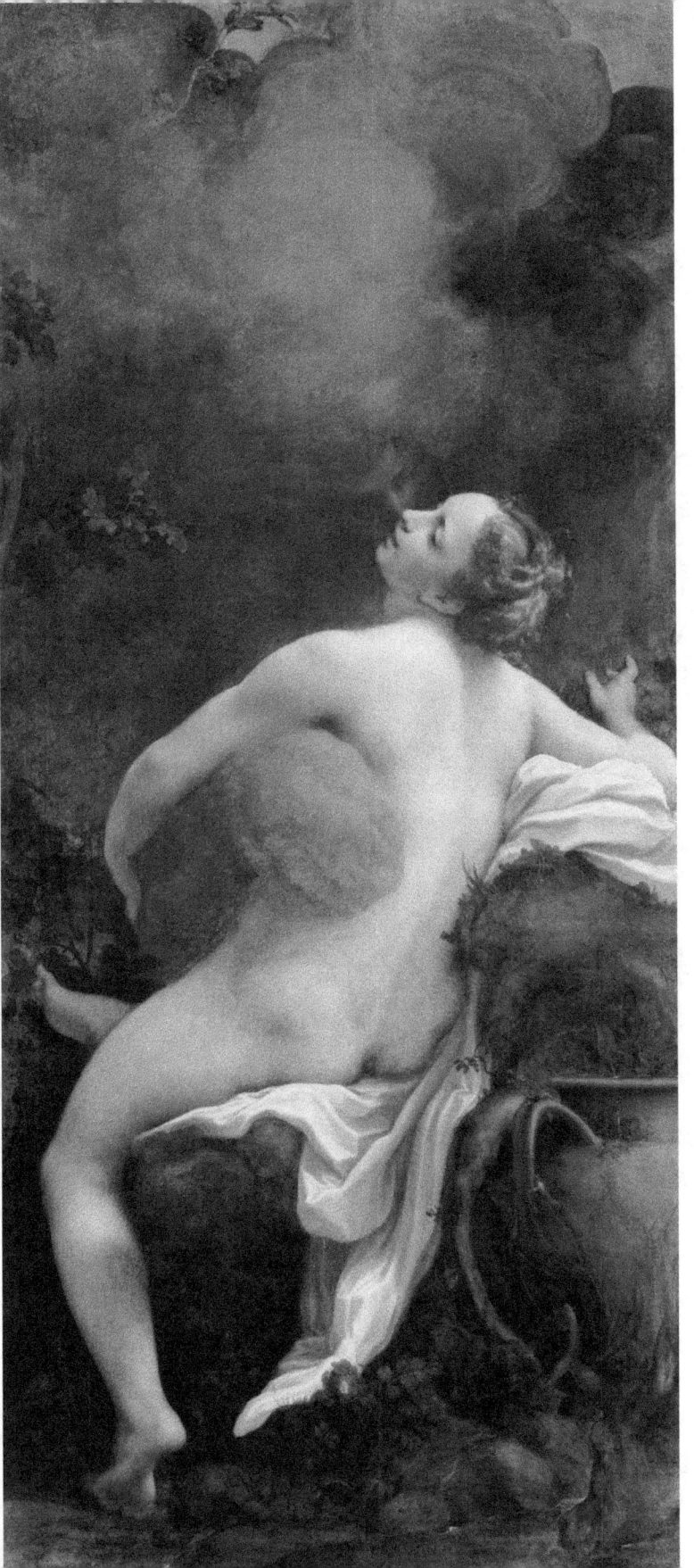

Correggio,
Jupiter and Antiope

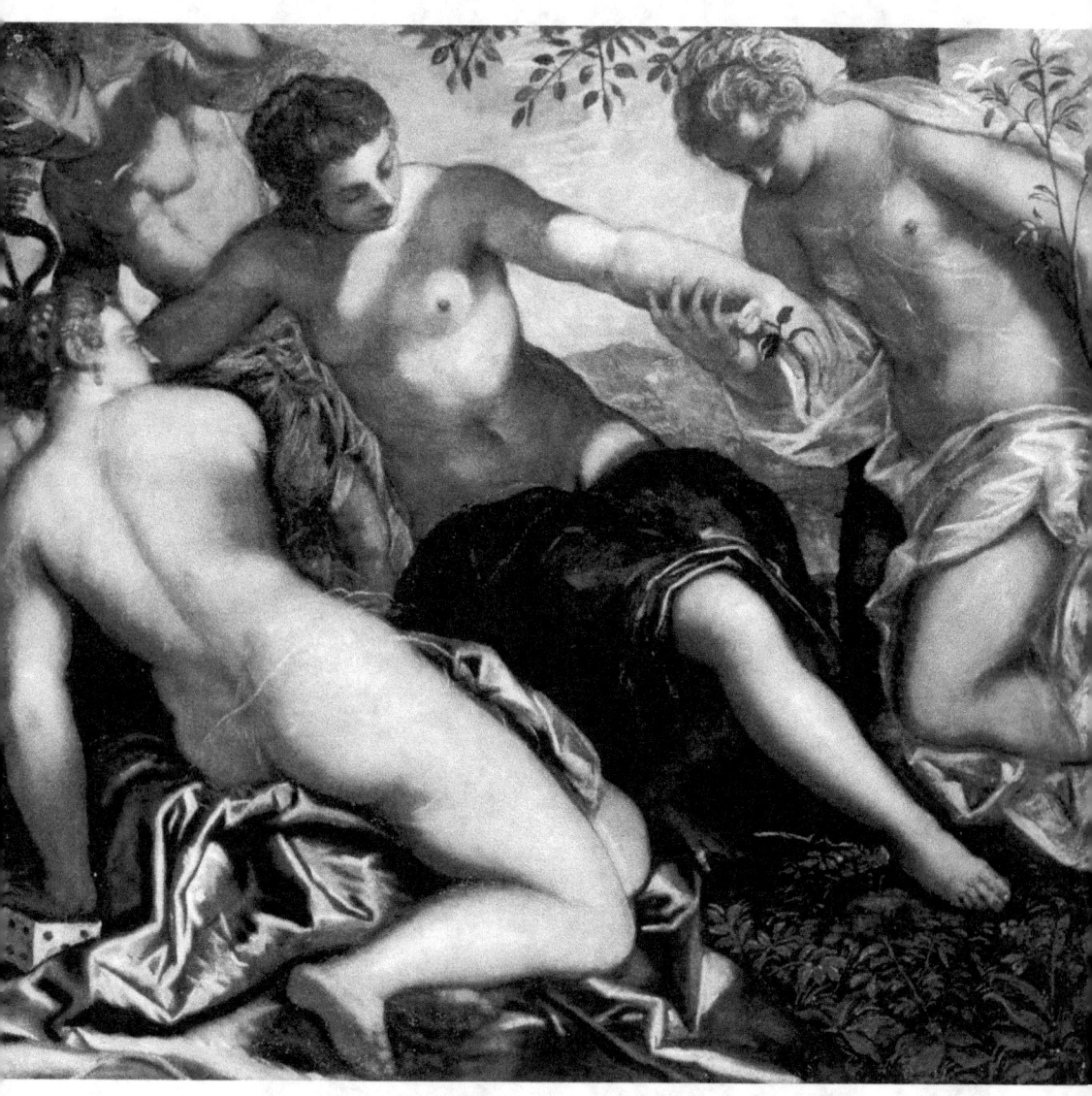

Jacopo Tintoretto, Mercury and the Graces, 1577

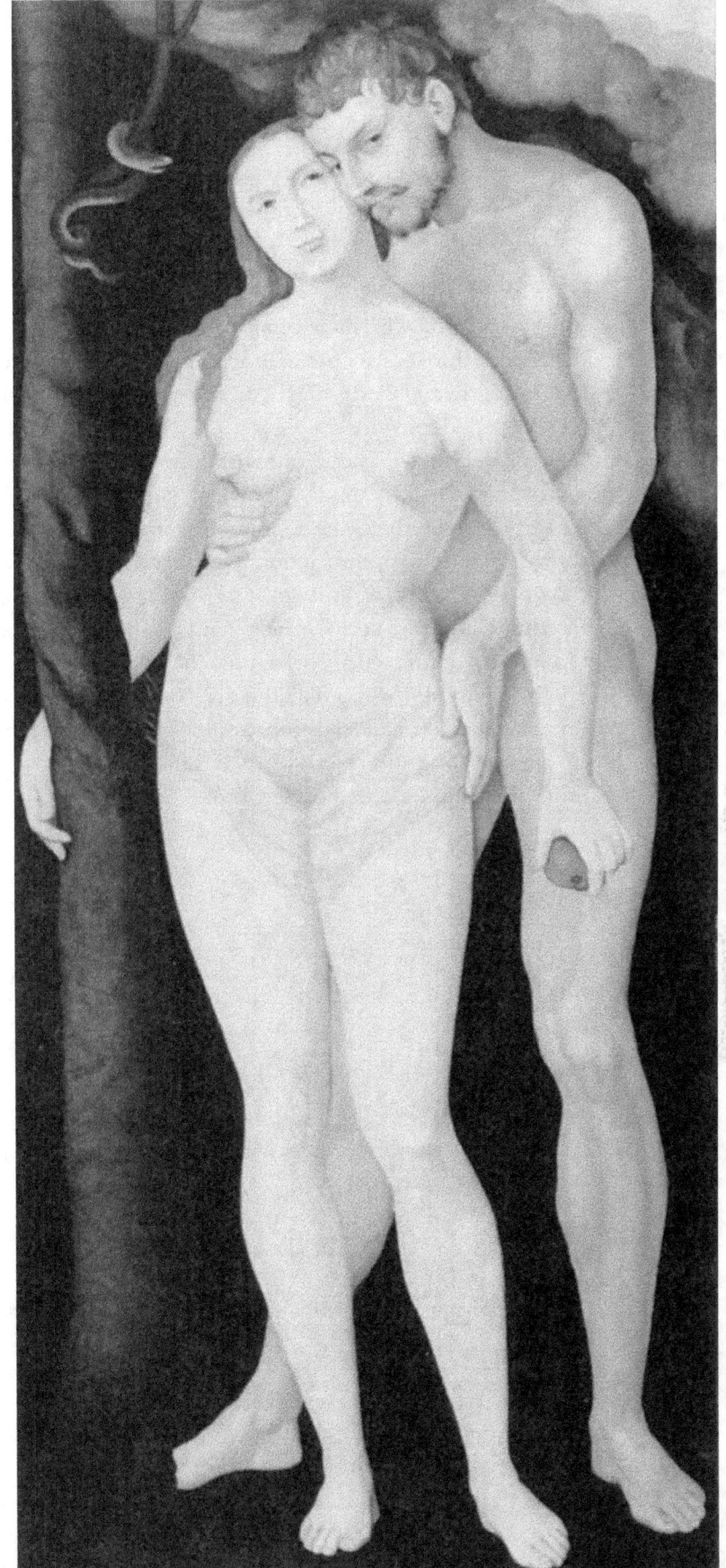

Hans Baldung,
Adam and Eve,
1531-35

CHRIST

One aspect of Christian imagery and Renaissance art that most Christian thinkers would not acknowledge is the eroticism of the Saviour's naked body. It is certainly a significant element in the celebrated depictions of Christ on the Cross: by Peter Rubens, Diego Velásquez and Andrea Mantegna, among many others.[1] Christ's nakedness sends conflicting signals. Clearly, nudity has a religious or mythic aspect, connoting nature/ naturalness, purity, birth, creation, renunciation, unveiled reality, truth.[2] In art, however, nudity is ambiguous: in religious contexts it is both spiritual and sexual.[3] Christ's body is often sexless, or androgynous, or feminized.[4] Christianity is an ambivalent cult; it has a clothed, virginal woman as the object of worship on the one hand, and a naked, equally virginal and chaste man on the other. In the most holy of churches, nudity is sanctified by the statues, icons and paintings of Christ on the Cross.

1 Andeas Mantegna: *Calvary*, 1459, 67 x 93cm, Paris, Louvre; Rubens: *Christ Between the Two Thieves (Coup de Lance)*, 1620, 429 x 311cm, Musée des Beaux Arts, Antwerp; Velásquez: *Christ Crucified*, 1630, 248 x 169cm, Prado, Madrid
2 See J.C. Cooper: *An Illustrated Encyclopaedia of Symbols*, 112-3
3 See Marina Warner: *Monuments and Maidens*, 304
4 See William Thompson: *The Time Falling Bodies Take to Light*, 109

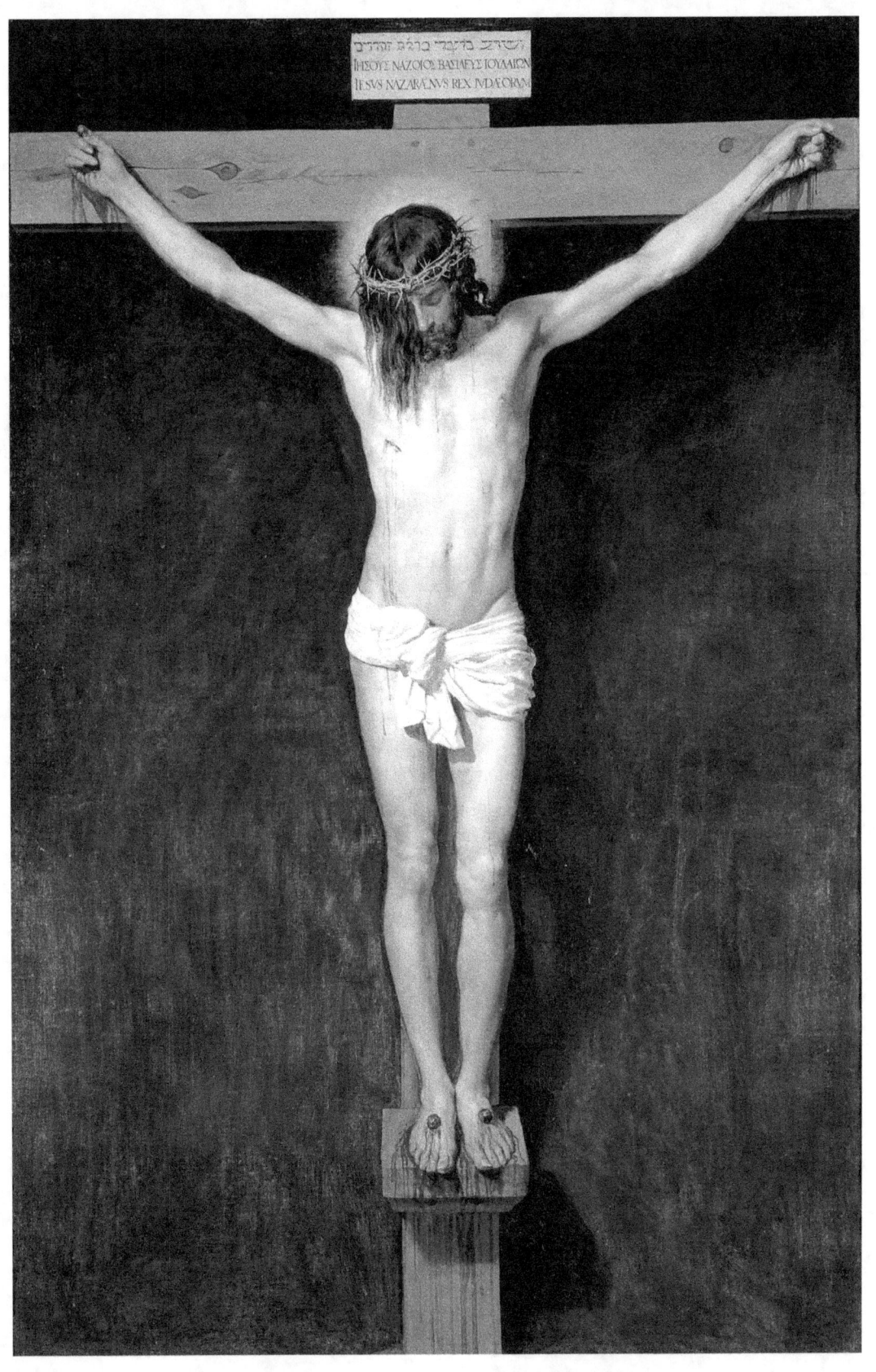

Diego Velásquez, Christ Crucified, 1632, Prado, Madrid

CHRIST

Christianity cannot deal with expressions of sexuality; or it prefers not to. It has a long history of suppressing sexuality, of body-hating, of repressing eroticism and erotic art. What Christianity does is to ignore erotic feelings, or to marginalize them in the outpourings of mystics. Other religions, such as Hinduism, acknowledge eroticism. There is room for the expression of sexual feelings in Hinduism; there are many gods, for a start. Such polytheism allows, as in the Greek pantheon of deities, for all manner of feelings. Renaissance painters understandably looked to the *Old Testament*, to historical figures and the Greek and Roman mythologies.

The dying or dead Christ, naked but for a slip of cloth and sometimes depicted entirely naked but with his legs bent to one side, hiding the 'transcendent signifier', the phallus, is an image of homoeroticism. Theologians and art historians down the ages did not or would not admit that Christ was or could have been an object of lust. Yet this is clearly the case in some depictions of the naked Saviour, such as paintings by Giovanni Battista Rosso, Michelangelo Merisi da Caravaggio, or Antonello da Messina.[1] These nude figures send a mass of signals, from the pathetic to the narcissistic, from the erotic to the spiritual.

---

1 Antonello da Messina: *Crucifixion*, 1475, 52.5 x 42.5cm, Musée des Beaux Arts, Antwerp; Caravaggio: *Entombment*, 1604, 300 x 203cm, Vatican, Rome; Rosso: *Dead Christ Supported by Angels*, c. 1524-7, oil on wood, 133.6 x 104.4cm, Museum of Fine Arts, Boston

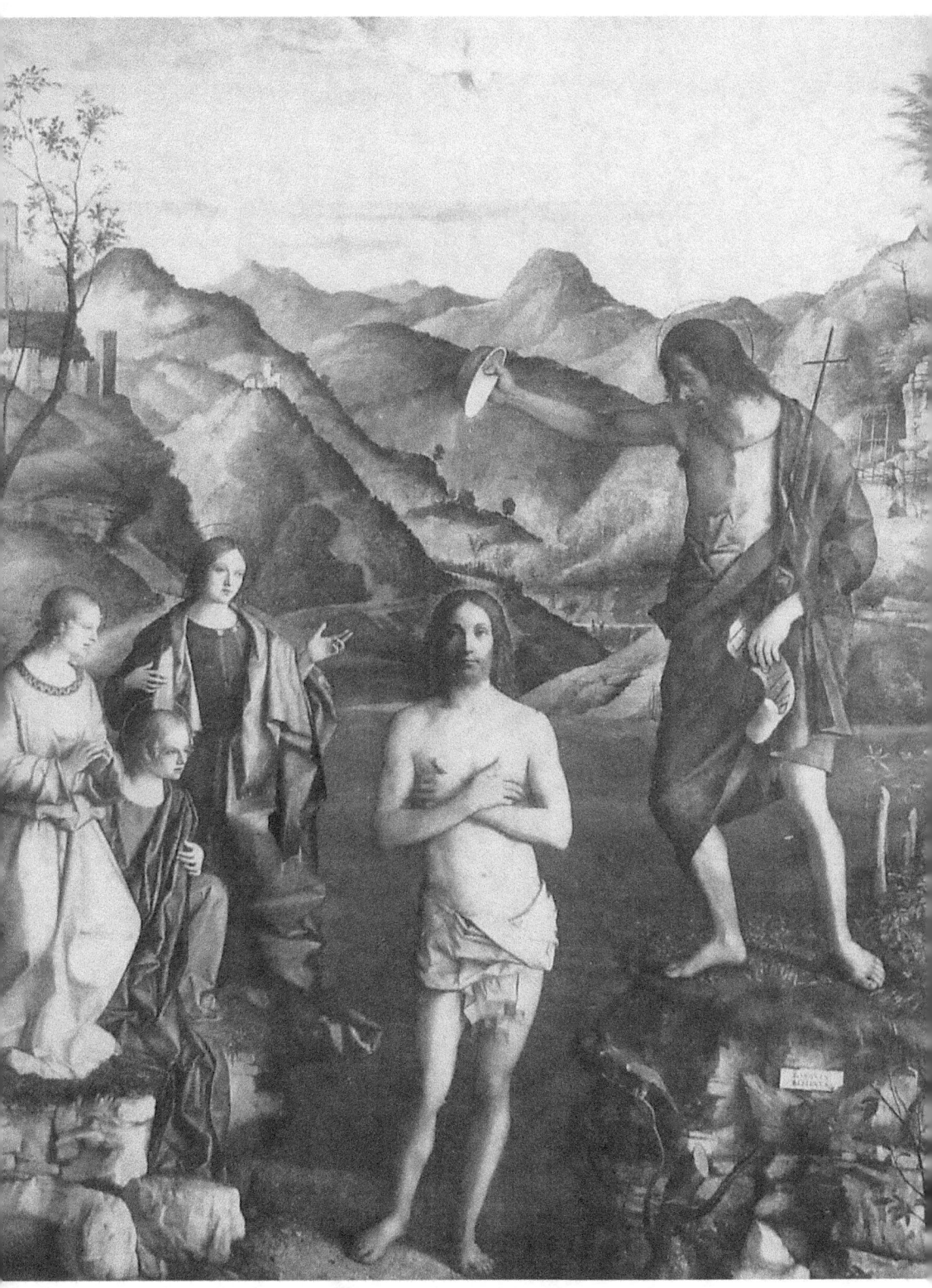

Giovanni Bellini, Baptism, early 16th century

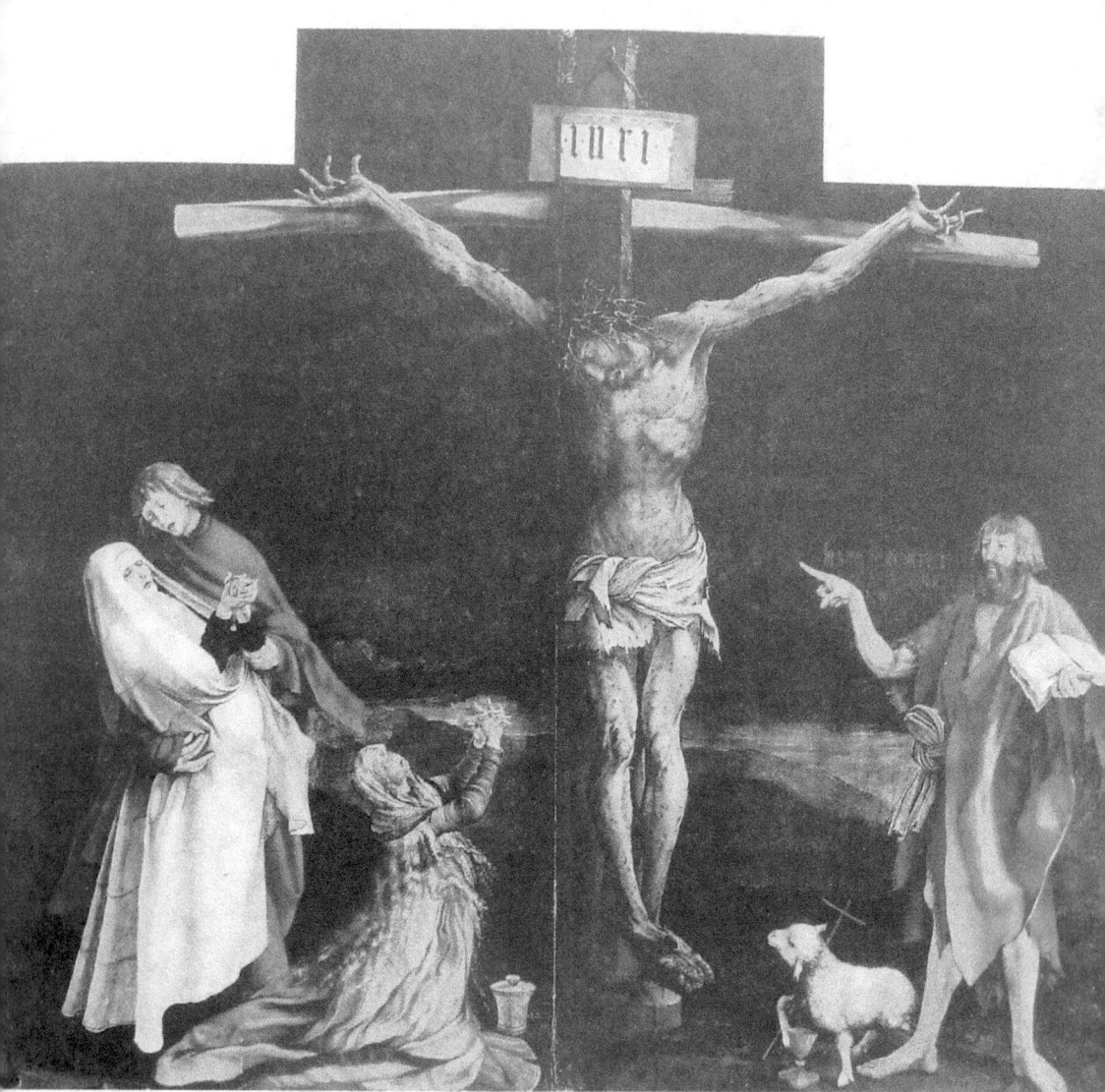

Matthias Grünewald, Crucifixion, Isenheim Altarpiece

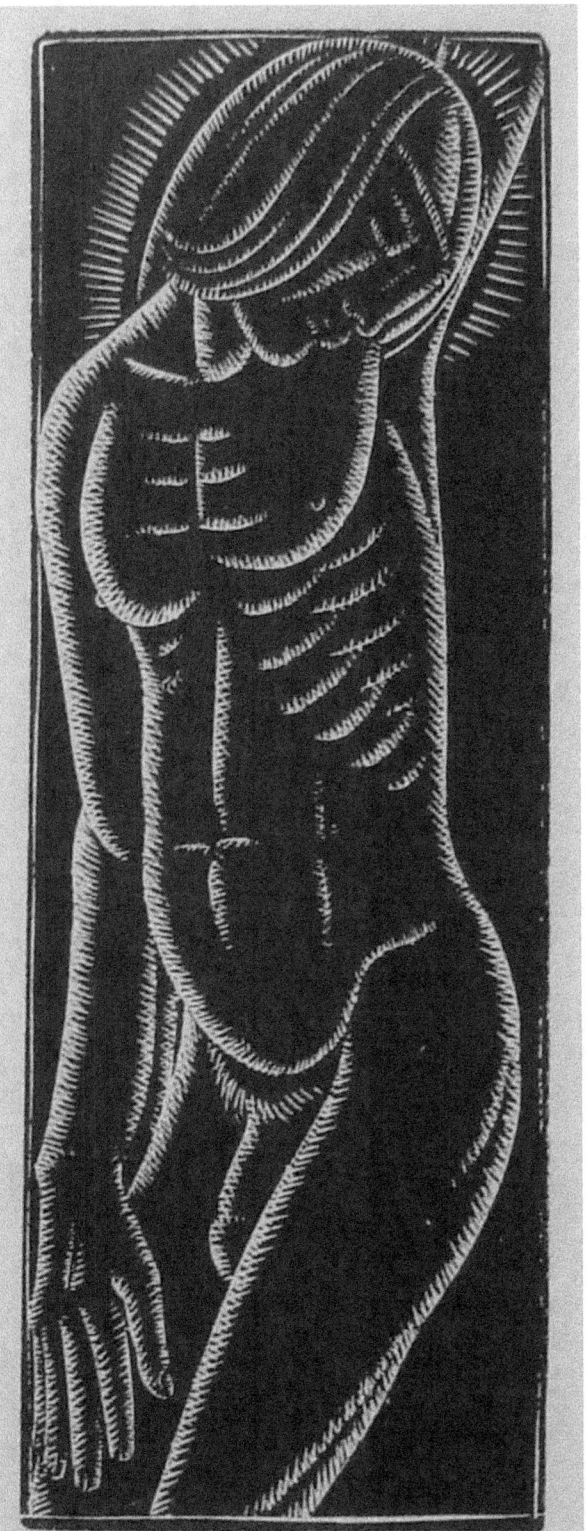

Eric Gill, Deposition, 1924

CHRISTIANITY

In the patriarchal view, religion is sexy, and sex is religious. Artists in the Renaissance often combined sexual and religious imagery. Western art, like pornography, draws on of the Judæo-Christian insistence on sin, death, vice, fornication, dirt and suppression. The father of Christianity is not Jesus but St Paul. Jesus wrote nothing; St Paul wrote everything, setting down the views of Christianity in that fanatical prose in the *Corinthians* and *Galatians* and *Romans*, which gets so many things wrong about flesh and spirit and marriage. Michael Foucault writes of some of the strictures of Christianity:

> Christianity associated it ['the sexual act'] with evil, sin, the Fall, and death, whereas antiquity invested it with positive symbolic values.[1]

In Christianity, women are the 'gateway to Hell' as the early theologian Tertullian poetically put it; women are evil, sinful, lustful ('the Devil is a woman' is a common theme in mediæval philosophy as well as pop songs). From Eve in the *Old Testament* to the Virgin and Magdalene in the *New Testament*, women are definitely second class citizens in the eyes of Western religion. Women-hating is startling in its violent manifestations – not just in wife-beating, which occurs everywhere and, one supposes, at every moment of human history, but also in the mass movements, such as the fight against witchcraft in the Middle Ages and later, when, armed with the *Malleus Maleficarum*, the Witchfinder Generals hunted down and tortured and killed hundreds or thousands, some say millions, of women.

---

1 M. Foucault: *The Use of Pleasure*, 14

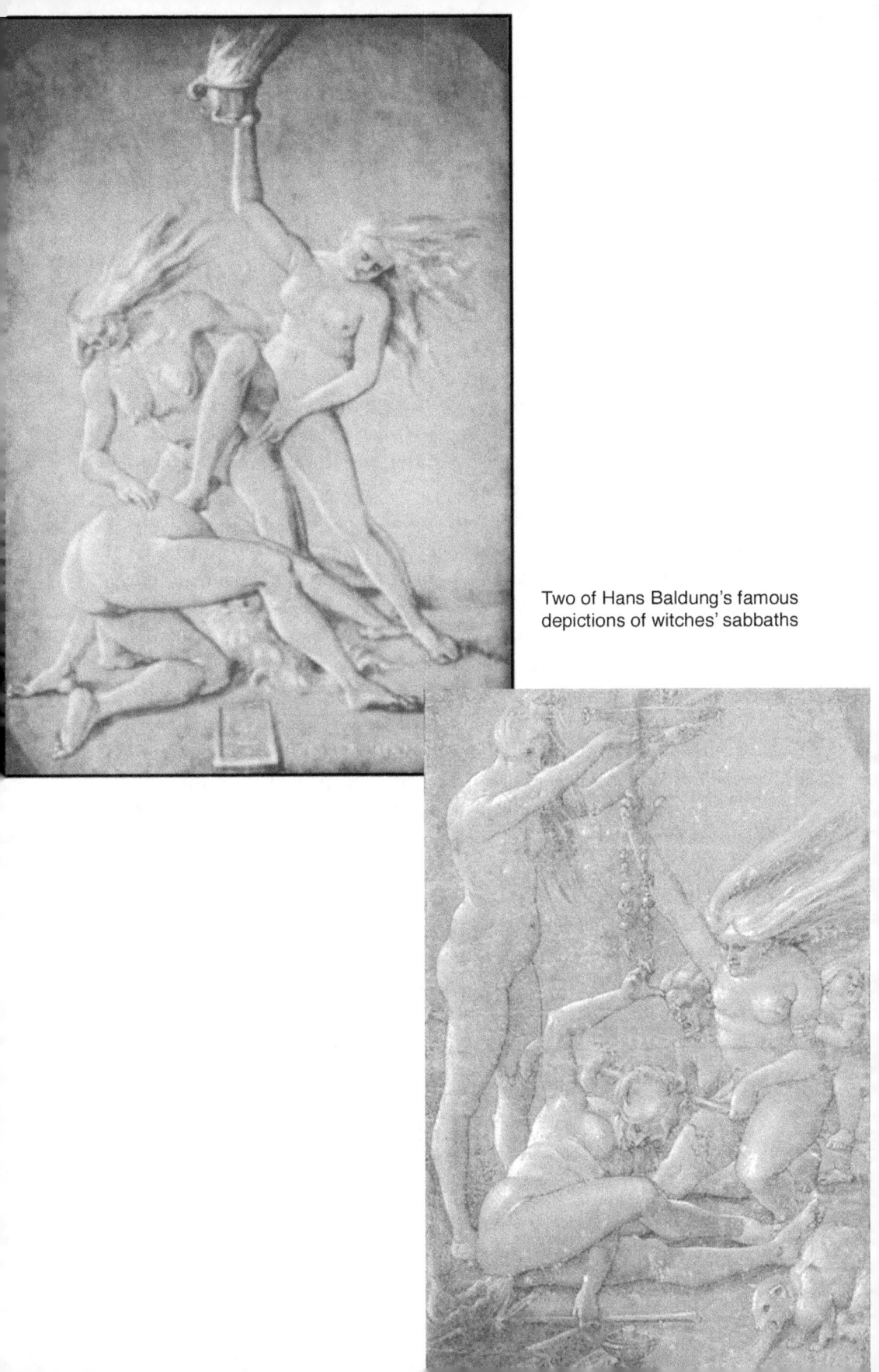

Two of Hans Baldung's famous
depictions of witches' sabbaths

CHRISTIANITY AND PORNOGRAPHY

A good bout of flagellation goes down well with Christians too, and many Renaissance painters painted Christ being whipped or tortured by the guards, and being crowned with thorns. Examples include Titian's two *Christ Crowned with Thorns* paintings, which make suffering a sublime, heroic experience,[1] or the ritualized whipping in Piero della Francesca's *The Flagellation of Christ*, a much-discussed Renaissance painting, or Luca Signorelli's more staid approach to the torture.[2]

Not to be out-done, Vittore Carpaccio painted a bizarre picture: the crucified Jesus sitting on a throne, dead, with his eyes closed, with two semi-naked old men sitting on either side of him. The title is *Meditation On the Passion of Christ*.[3] There's the Saviour, looking very dead, on a throne, in a ruined landscape, while two old men sit right next to him and muse upon his death. Bizarre.

Sebastiano del Piombo goes even further: his *The Martyrdom of St Agatha* depicts the saint, nude of course, being tortured by a bunch of men, fully clothed of course.[4] They are applying gigantic metal pliers to her nipples. This is a depiction of sadism (in Christianity the euphemism is 'martyrdom'). Naturally, it seems, this is *sexual* torture, painted in such a straightforward fashion, the woman centre frame, the men surrounding her intent on brutalizing her. The rape, which must follow this torture, is not shown, and it is never shown in Renaissance art, and rarely in Western art. When rape occurs, as it must have done millions of times through the Christian era, men dragging away women are depicted, or Jupiter as a swan screwing Leda, but not the rape itself.

---

1 Titian: *Christ Crowned with Thorns*, mid-1450s, panel, 303 x 180cm, Louvre, Paris; *Christ Crowned with Thorns*, c. 1570-6, canvas, 280 x 181cm, Alte Pinakothek, Munich
2 Piero della Francesca: *The Flagellation of Christ*, c. 1450, panel, 59 x 81.5cm, Ducal, Urbino; Signoreli: *Flagellation*, c. 1480, canvas, 80 x 60cm, Brera, Milan
3 Carpaccio: *Meditation on the Passion of Christ*, c. 1505, panel, 70 x 86cm, Metropolitan Museum of Art, New York
4 Sebastiano del Piombo: *The Martyrdom of St Agatha*, 1520, 31 x 175cm, Pitti Palace, Florence

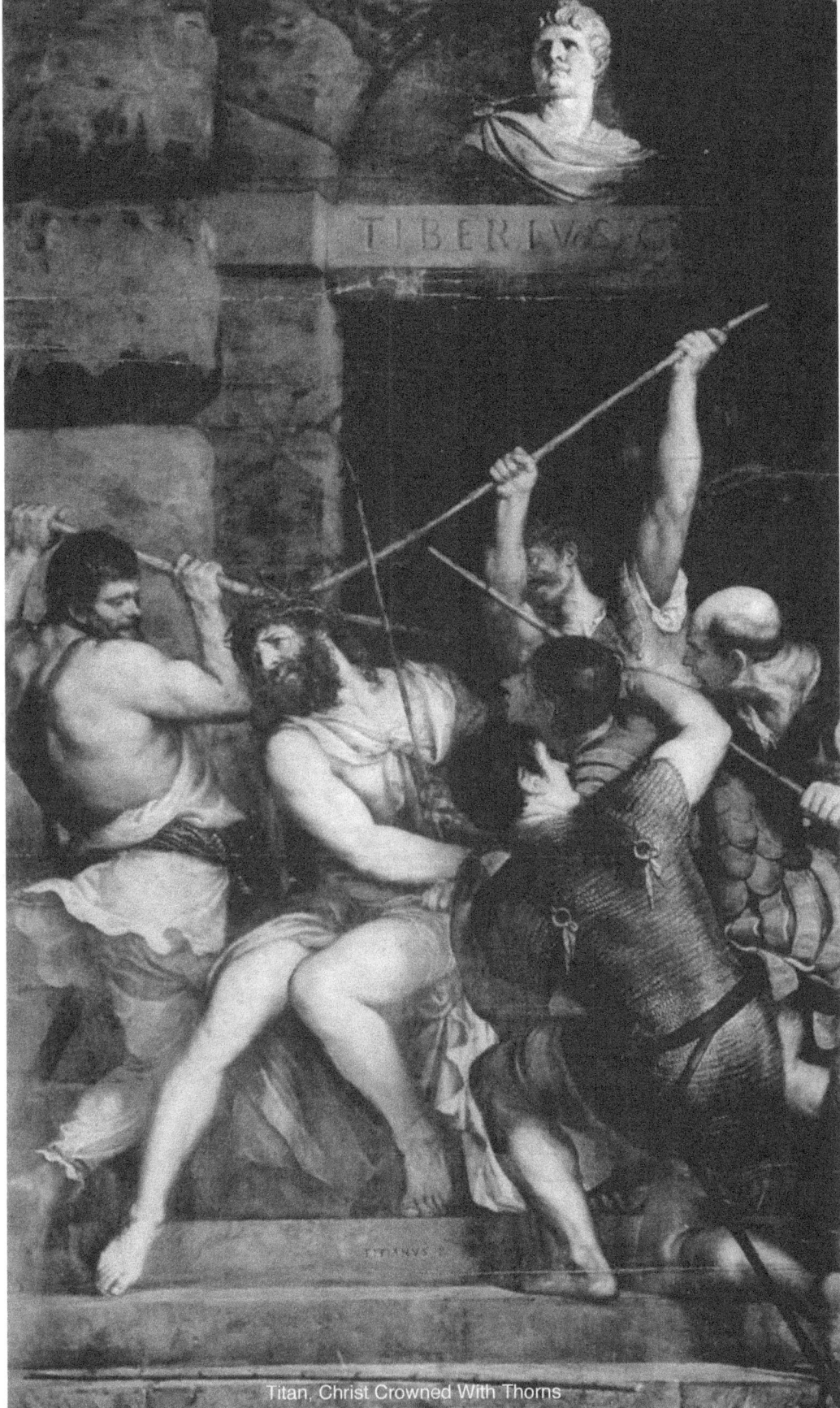

Titan, Christ Crowned With Thorns

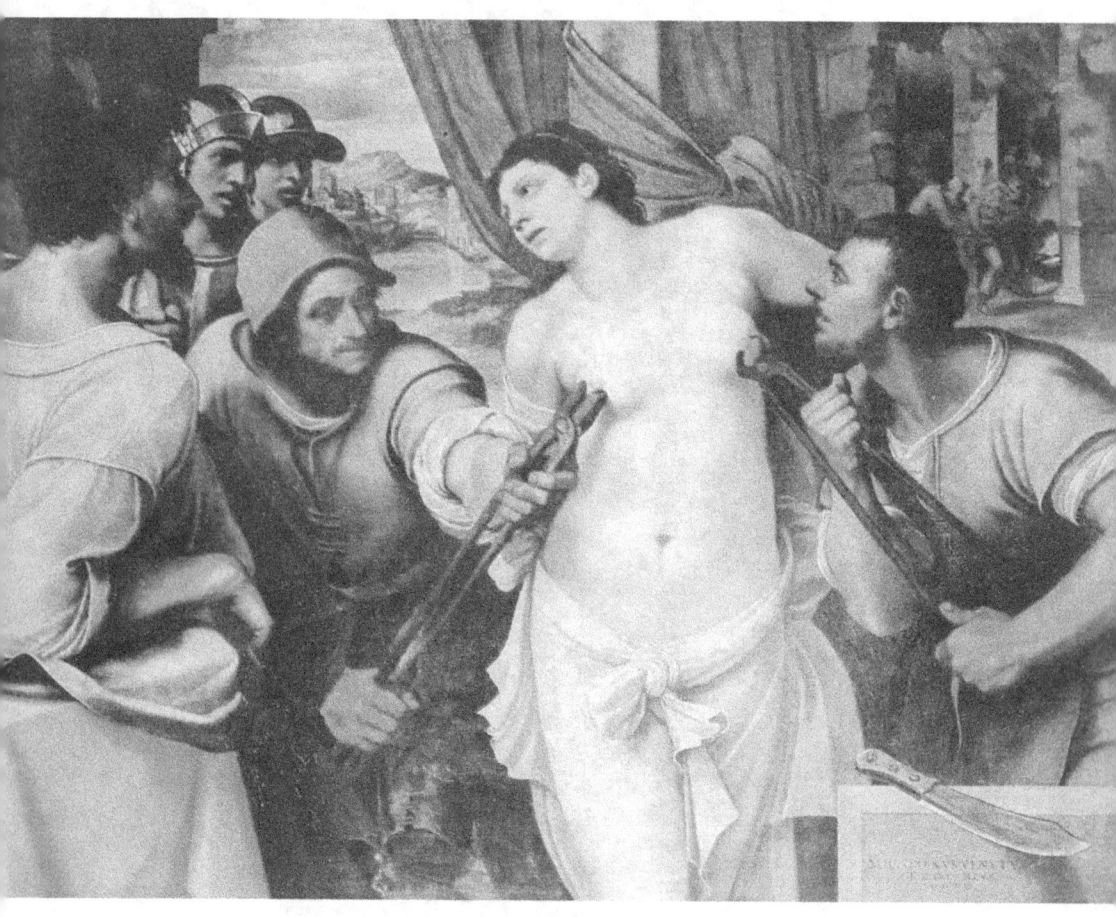

Sebastian del Piombo, The Martyrdom of St Agatha, 1520, Pitti
Palace, Florence

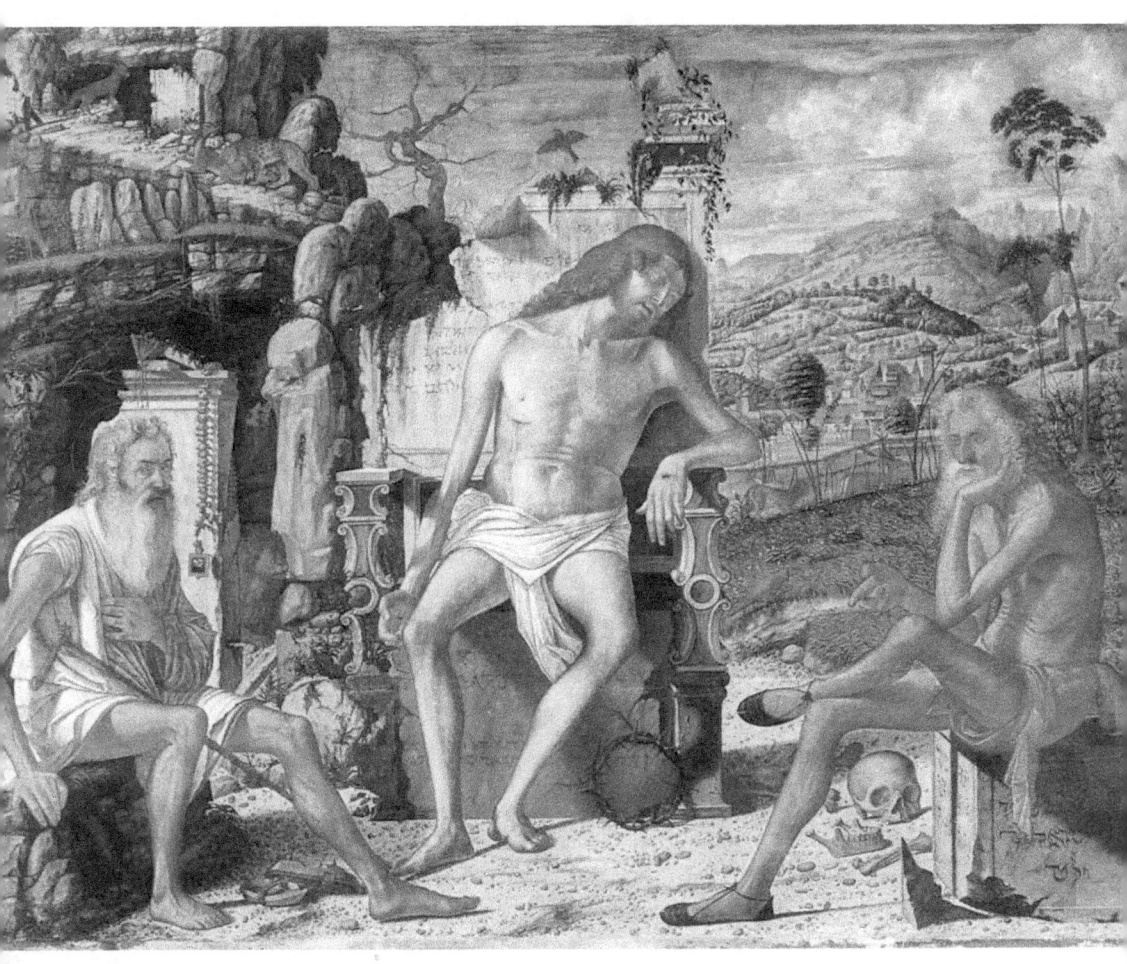

Vittorio Carpaccio, Meditation On the Passion

CRUCIFIED WOMEN

Artistic transgressions of Christian religion upset some people. Witness, for instance, the complaints of the clergy and the church about women priests. In 1984 an artwork of a crucified woman, *Christa*, was taken out of a church in New York because it was 'theologically and historically indefensible'.[1] A crucified *woman*, now there's a blasphemous image to conjure with. It's the not the first time a woman's been seen in a satire on the crucifixion. Félicien Rops often used the motif.

---

1 K.A. Briggs: "Cathedral Removing Statue of Crucified Woman", *New York Times*, 28 Apl, 1984.

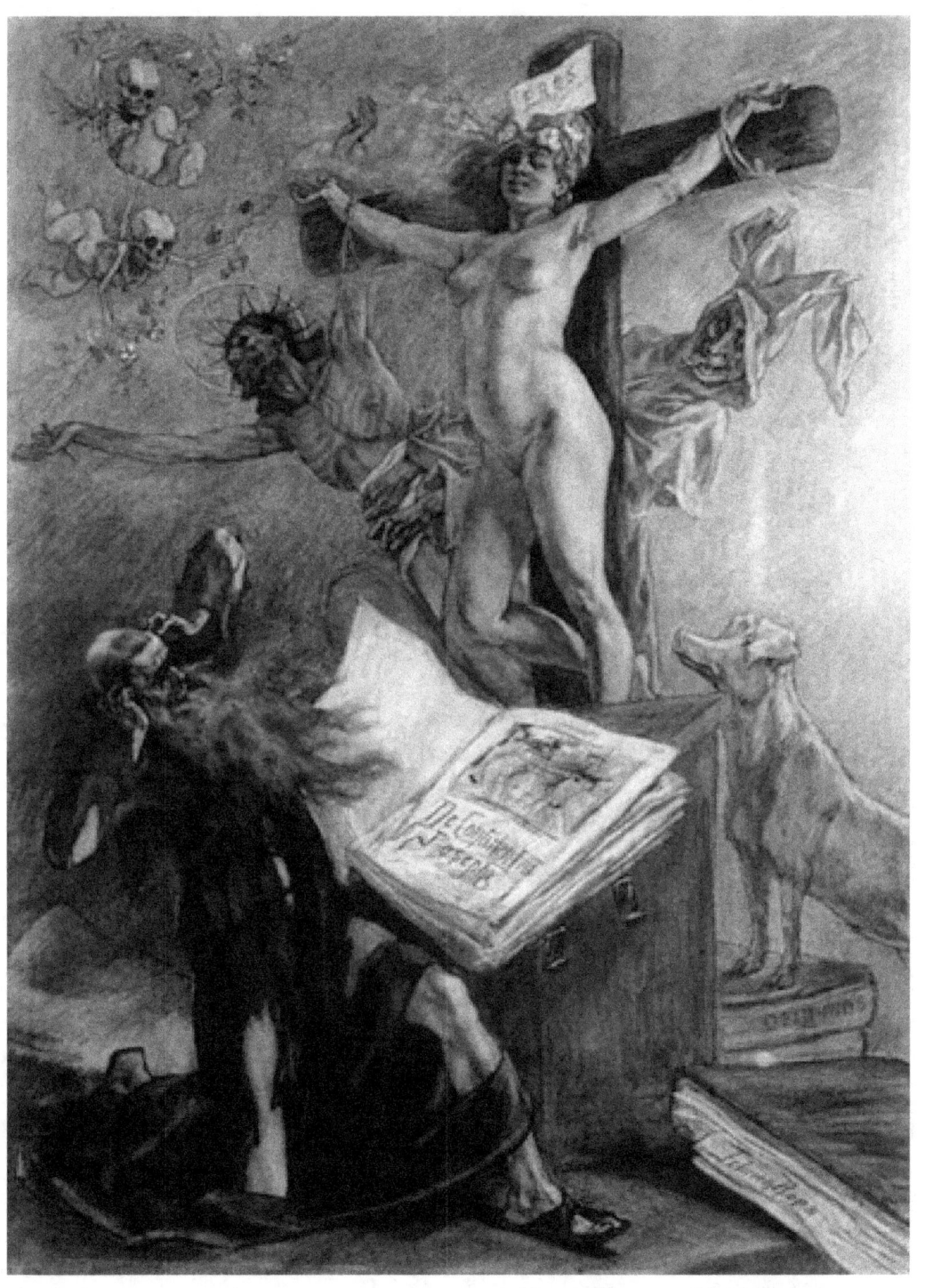

The Temptation of St Anthony, a popular subject of the era, by Félicien Rops

ANIMA

In the Jungian system, Beatrice, Laura, Cleopatra, Isolde, Eurydice, Ariadne and all those women of myth, poetry and legend, are incarnations of the *anima*, which is, as Carl Jung explains, something all males possess: '[e]very man carries with him the eternal image of woman, not the image of this or that particular woman, but a definitive feminine image.'[1] The *anima* is 'a personification of the unconscious in a man, which appears as a woman or a goddess in dreams, visions and creative fantasies', write Emma Jung and Marie-Louise von Franz, glossing Jung's *anima* concept.[2]

Male painters throughout history have depicted their version of the *anima*, it seems. Each (male) painter has a version of the 'inner feminine figure', as Carl Jung calls it.[3] For painters, this idealized *anima* figure seems to be another manifestation of that obscure object of desire, the eroticized woman, a mirror for male lust. The equation is: the more sublime and voluptuous the woman is painted, the more sublime and voluptuous is the artist's desire. The artist's model, then, can be seen as a Jungian *anima*, heavily eroticized, a Lacanian phallic mirror.

1 C. Jung: *The Development of Personality*, vol. 17, Routledge, 1954, 198; Marie-Louise von Franz: *The Psychological Meaning of Redemption Motifs in Fairy Tales*, Inner City Books, Toronto 1980, 39f
2 Emma Jung & Marie-Louise von Franz: *The Grail Legend*, tr. Andrea Dykes, Sigo Press, Boston, Mass., 1980, 64
3 C. Jung: *Memories, Dreams, Reflections*, Collins 1967, 210-1

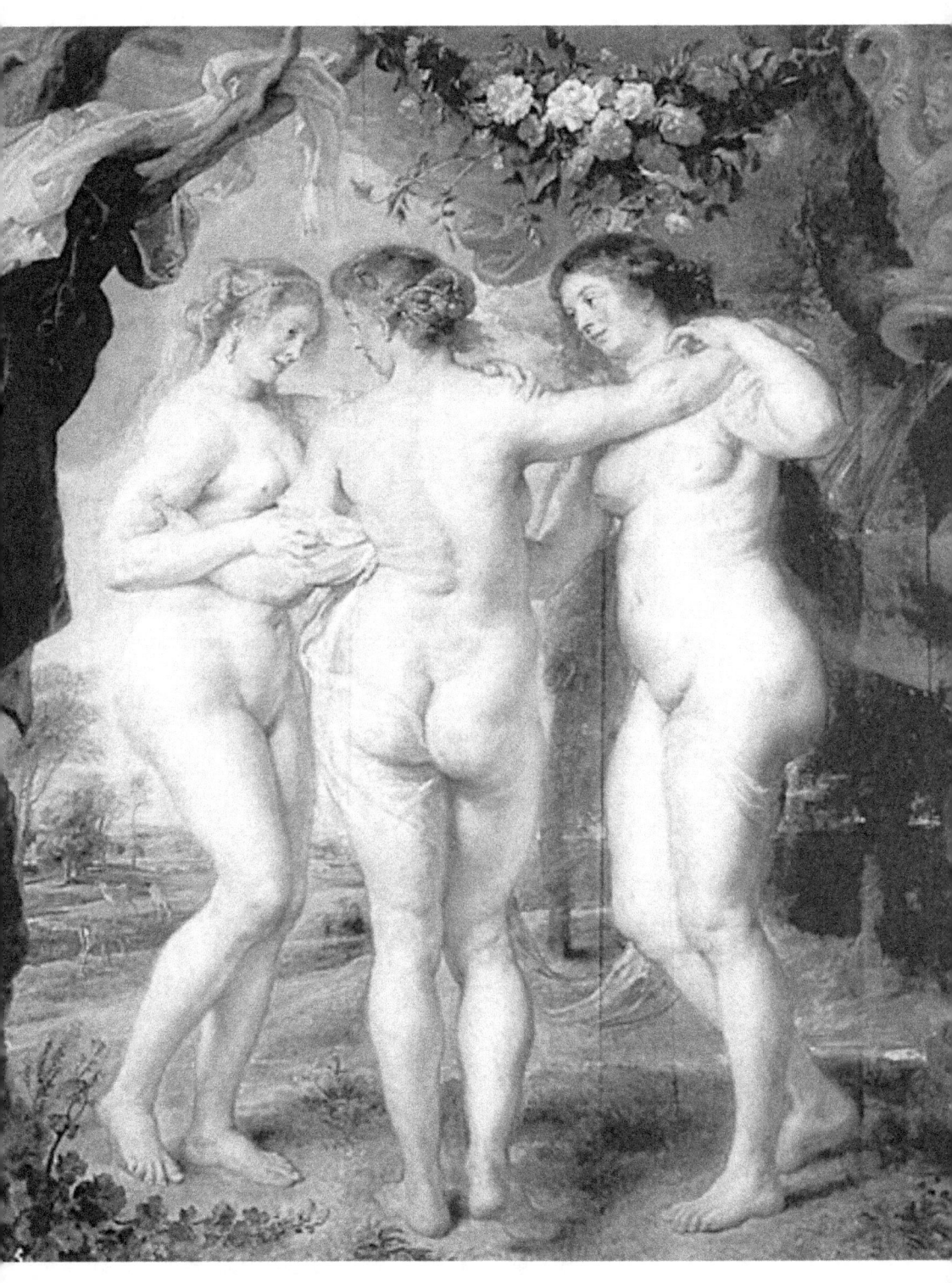

Peter Paul Rubens, The Three Graces, 1638-40, Prado, Madrid

ARTISTS AND MODELS

Seen in Lacanian theory, the female model becomes the 'obscure object of desire' feared and desired, ever unreachable, the manifestation of eternal loss.[1] We can see elements of the Lacanian lack, desire, repression, mirror stage, Symbolic Order and œdipal anxiety in the modern artists who create specifically erotic images. In the output of Renaissance artists such as Titian, Tintoretto and Peter Paul Rubens one finds loss, desire, repression and anxiety quite clearly. The art they produce is heterosexual, glorifying women, even as, in some case the paintings seem to denigrate women. The soft flesh is available but also distinctly not available; there is acres of skin, but it is not touchable either.[2] These nude paintings remain chimeras, never to be possessed, always to be yearned for. As Nicolas Poussin wrote of painting: '[p]ainting is nothing but an imitation of human actions, which alone are, properly speaking, inimitable'.[3] Poussin recognizes that painting is always an imitation, a mirror; the real thing can never be possessed in art. It is the same in erotic art – indeed, it is most dramatically expressed in erotic art – this paradoxical fear and desire, this simultaneous desire and loss, this ambiguous conflict between possession and dispossession.

1 Toril Moi: *Sexual Textual Politics*, 99f; Anika Lemaire: *Jacques Lacan*, Routledge & Kegan Paul 1977; Elizabeth Wright: *Psychoanalytic Criticism*, Methuen 1984
2 Pierre Renoir: *Bather Arranging Her Hair*, 1885, canvas, 92 x 73cm, Sterling and Francis Clark Institute, Williamstown, Mass.; Lawrence Alma-Tadema: *In the Tepidarium*, 1881, wood, 24 x 33cm, Lady Lever Art Gallery, Port Sunlight; Jules Pascin: *The Prodigal Son*, 1928, oil on board, 15 x 18in, private collection, Switzerland
3 In R. Goldwater, 154.

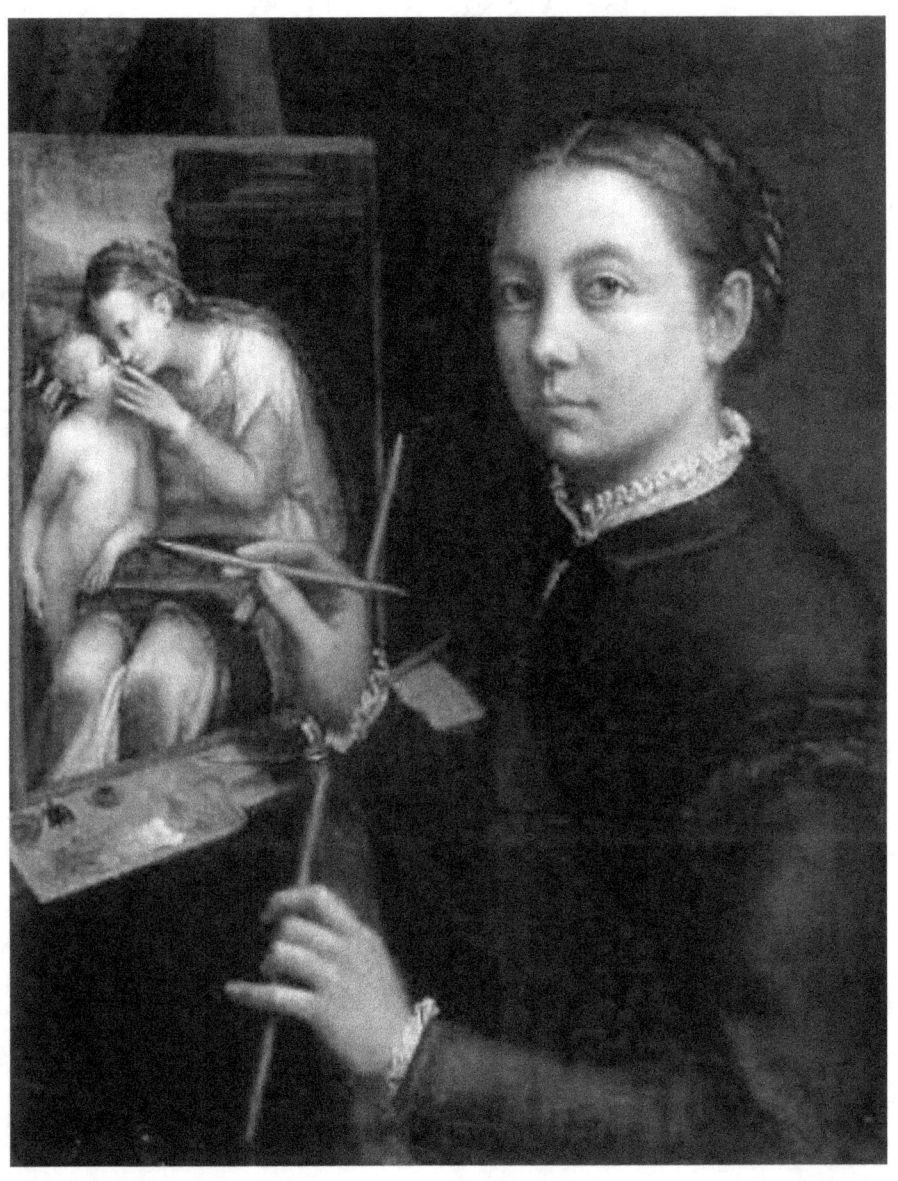

Sofonisba Anguissola, Self-Portrait, 1556, Lancut Museum, Poland

THE ANNUNCIATION

Even such seemingly gentle occasions such as the Annunciation are not free of sexist, patriarchal and erotic/ porn connotations. For a start, Mary is simply living her life when the Archangel Gabriel rushes in and tells her she is to bear the Son of God. Mary replies: 'how can this be, seeing I know not a man' (*Gospel of Luke*). As soon as she accepts, in the very moment she assents, she conceives Christ in her womb. It is literally the Word become Flesh.

Renaissance painters, such as Fra Angelico, depict the Annunciation as a delicate, silent moment, the two figures, Gabriel and Mary, kneeling together in spiritual communion. Angelico's Virgins are shy, passive, sad creatures.[1] For Mary in the *Gospels* is a 'good wife'; she accepts the Word of God.

Yet the Annunciation is clearly also a spiritual coercion. The woman is passive and humble. Her opinion or sanctity or dignity is not taken into account: she is forced to accept God's seed inside her. She cannot refuse the Word of the Lord. So it is sex by force for some feminists, because it is sex without consent (but is it sex? Or is it conception? These are theological paradoxes which much concerned theologians in the mediæval era).

---

1 Angelico: *The Annunciation*, c. 1440, fresco, San Marco Museum, Florence; *The Annunciation*, late 1440s, 194 x 194cm, Prado, Madrid; *The Annunciation*, c. 1443, fresco, 187 x 157cm, cell three, San Marco Museum, Florence

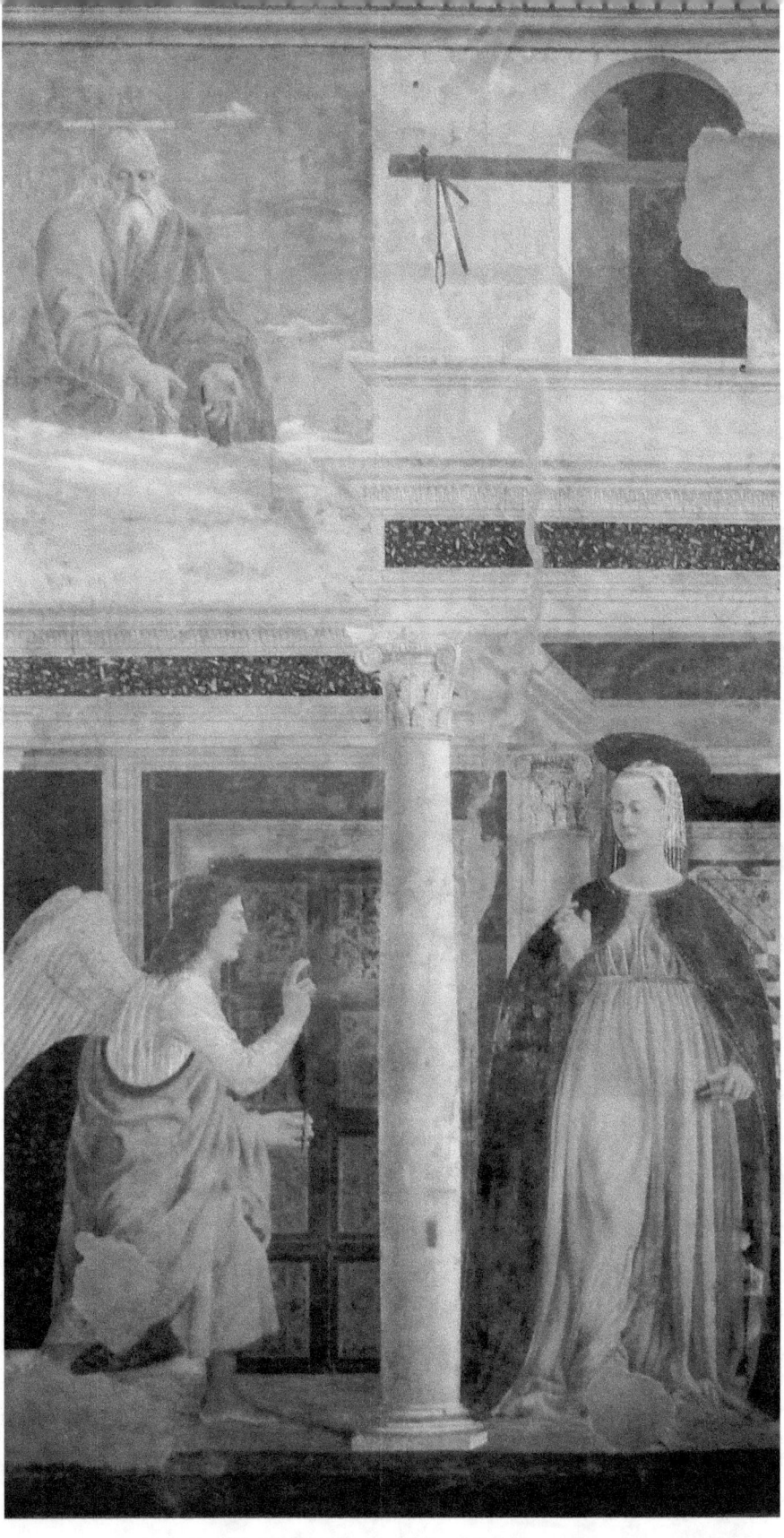

Piero, The Annunciation, Arezzo

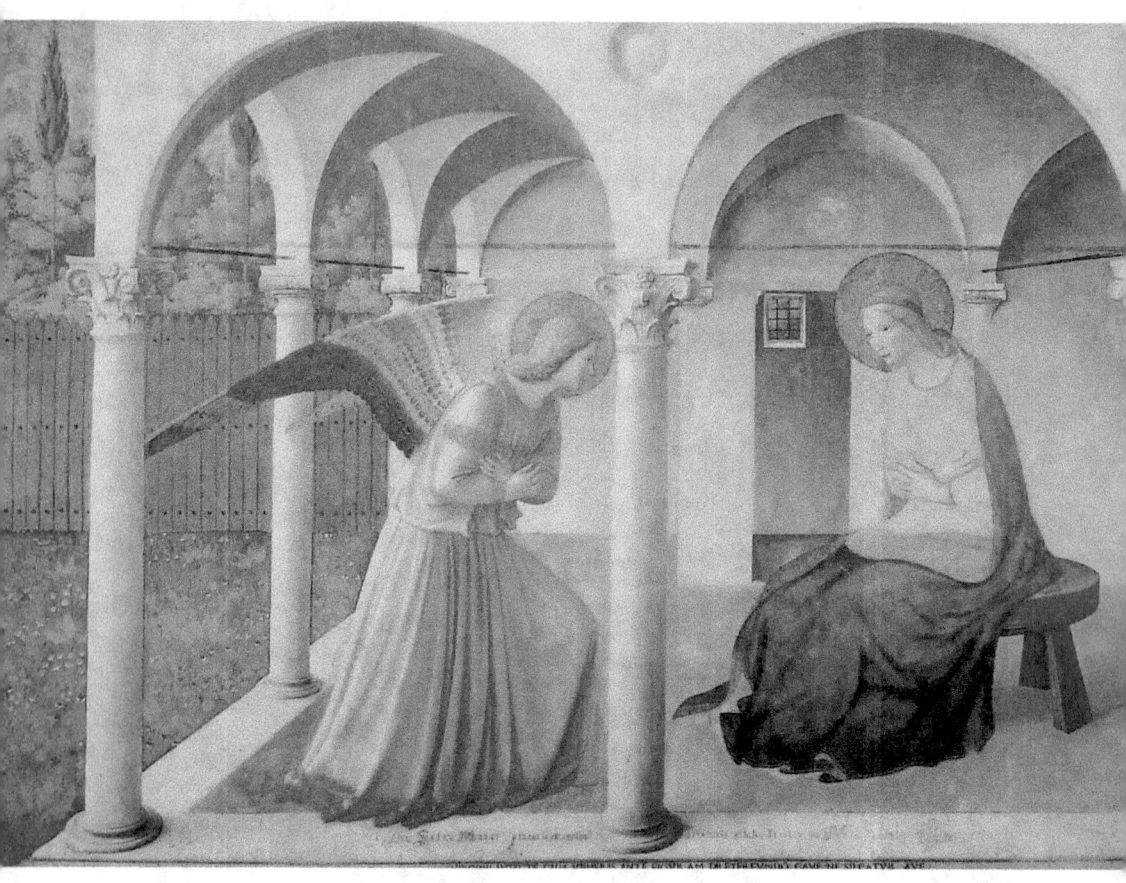

Fra Angelico, The Annunciation, San Marco, Florence

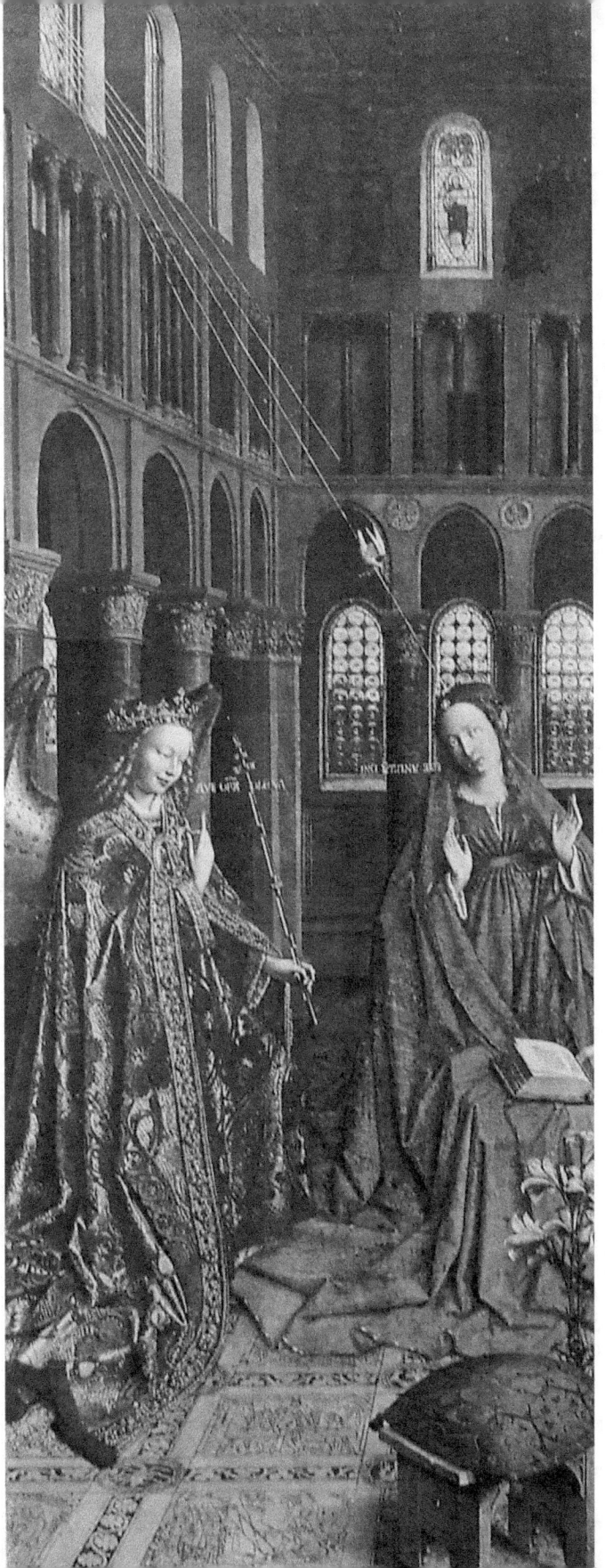

Jan van Eyck, The Annunciation, National Gallery of Art, Washington, DC

DEMONS AND NUNS:
RELIGION AND EROTICA

A good deal of erotica in the West of the early modern period revolves around religion (and Catholicism in particular). Demons, nuns, monks, crosses and churches are the familiar background. All of the reasons for employing religious imagery and settings are obvious. One is that creatures such as devils or monsters are obviously unreal or supernatural, and thus can be used to depict far more extreme sexual acts than 'realistic' portrayals of humans.

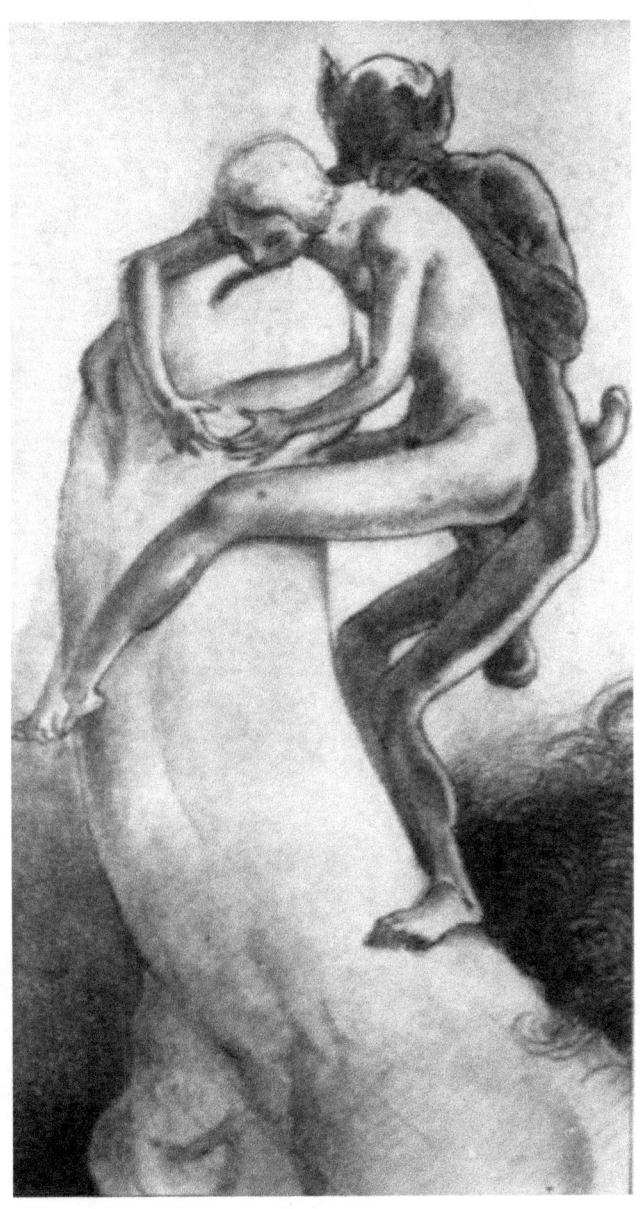

Anonymous, 19th century

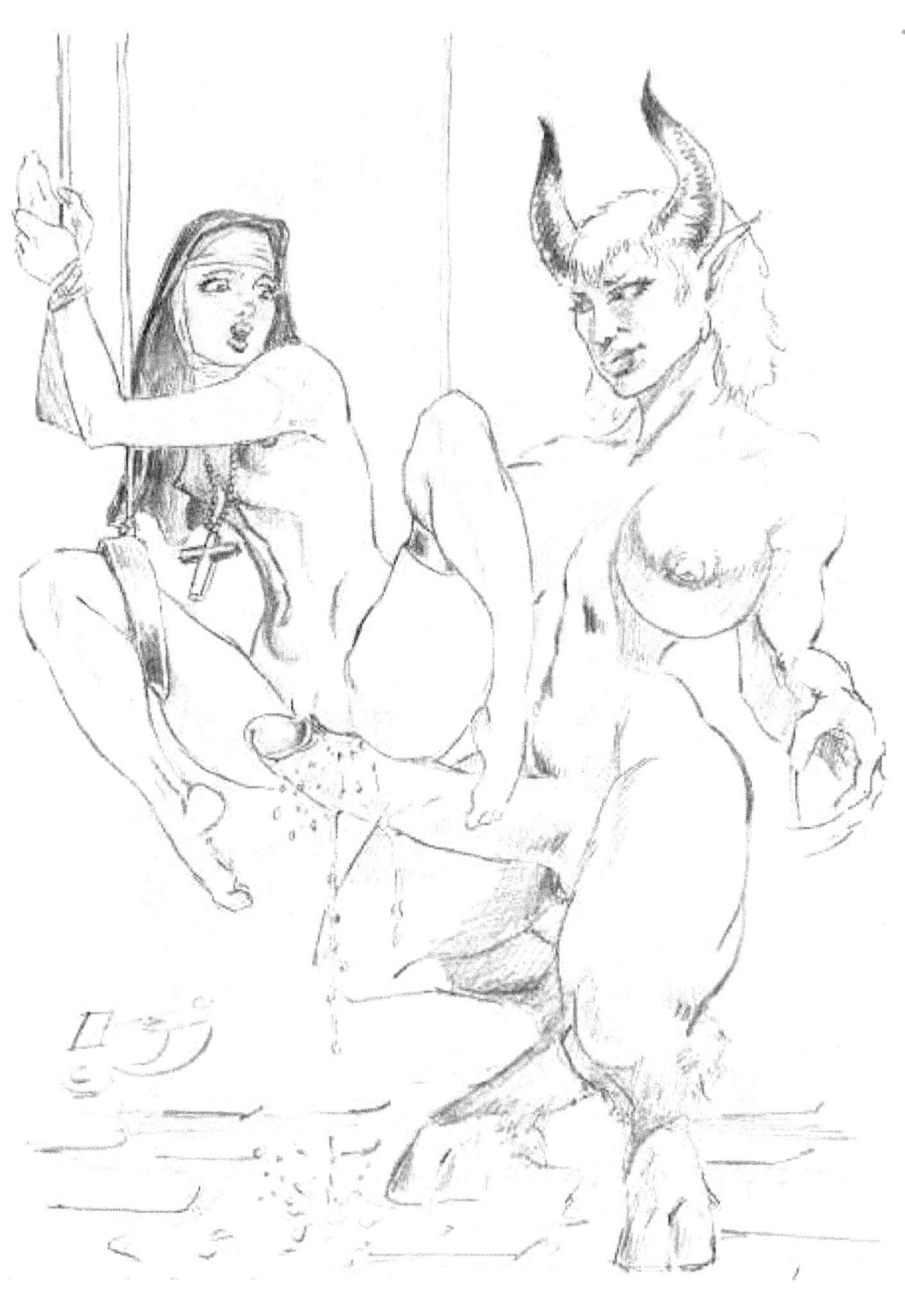

Anonymous, early 20th century

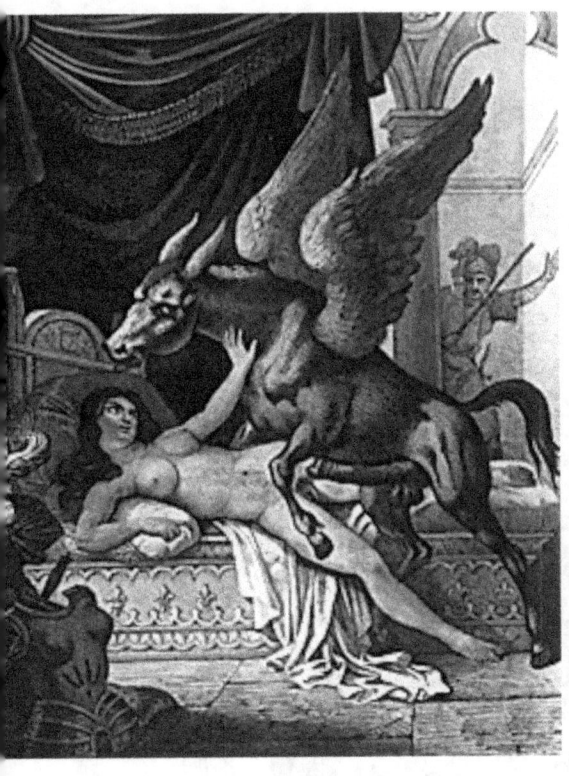

Puccelle d'Orleans

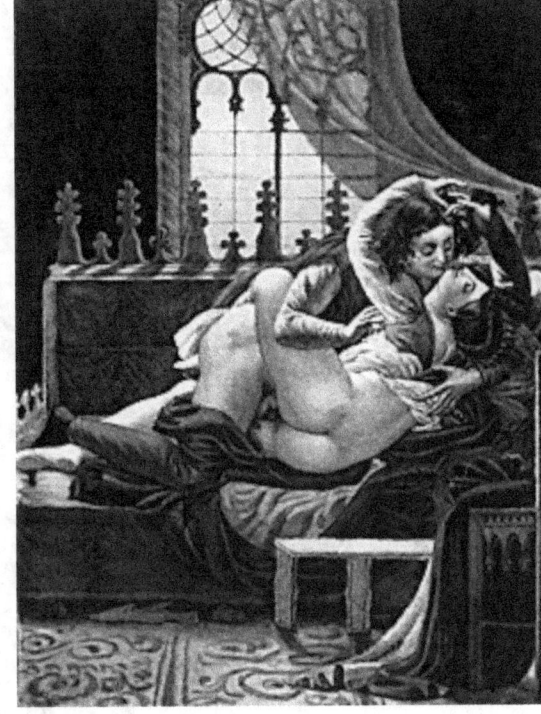

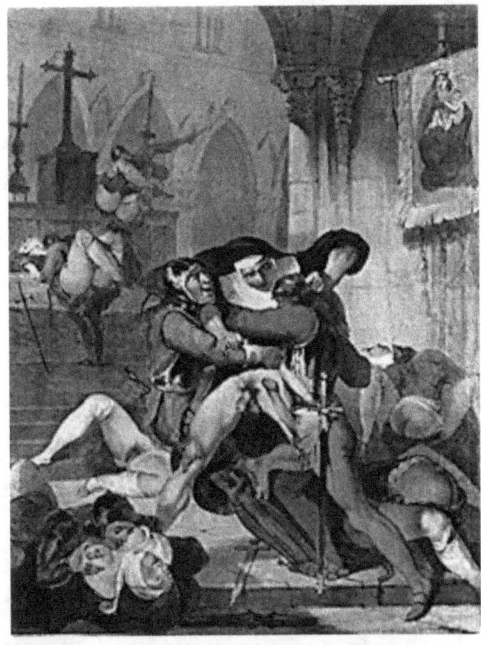

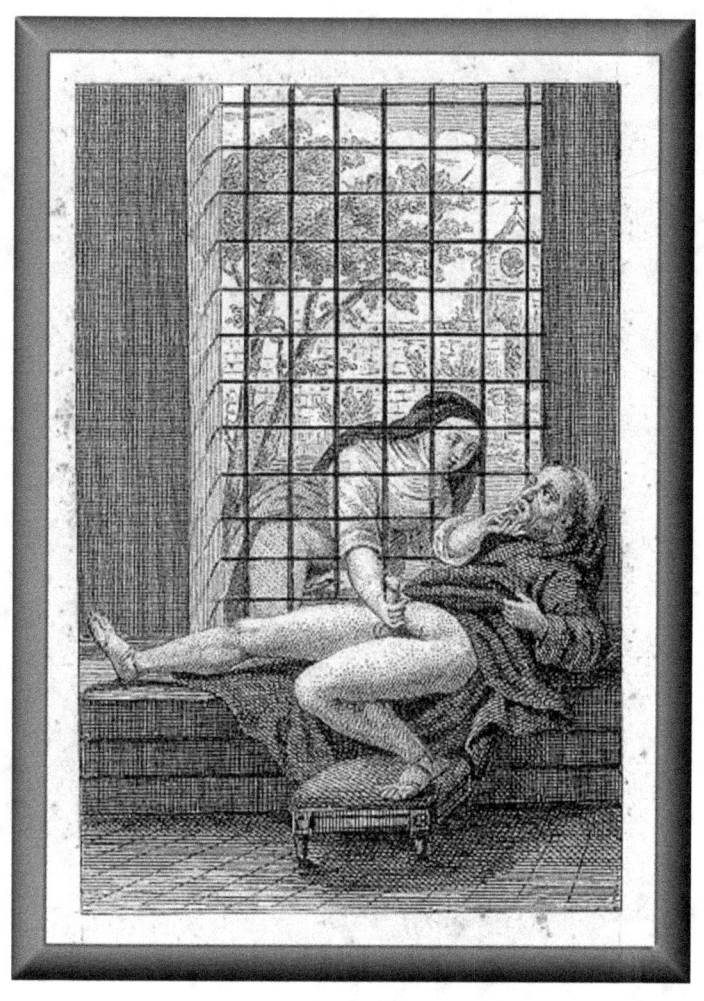

Anonymous, early 19th century

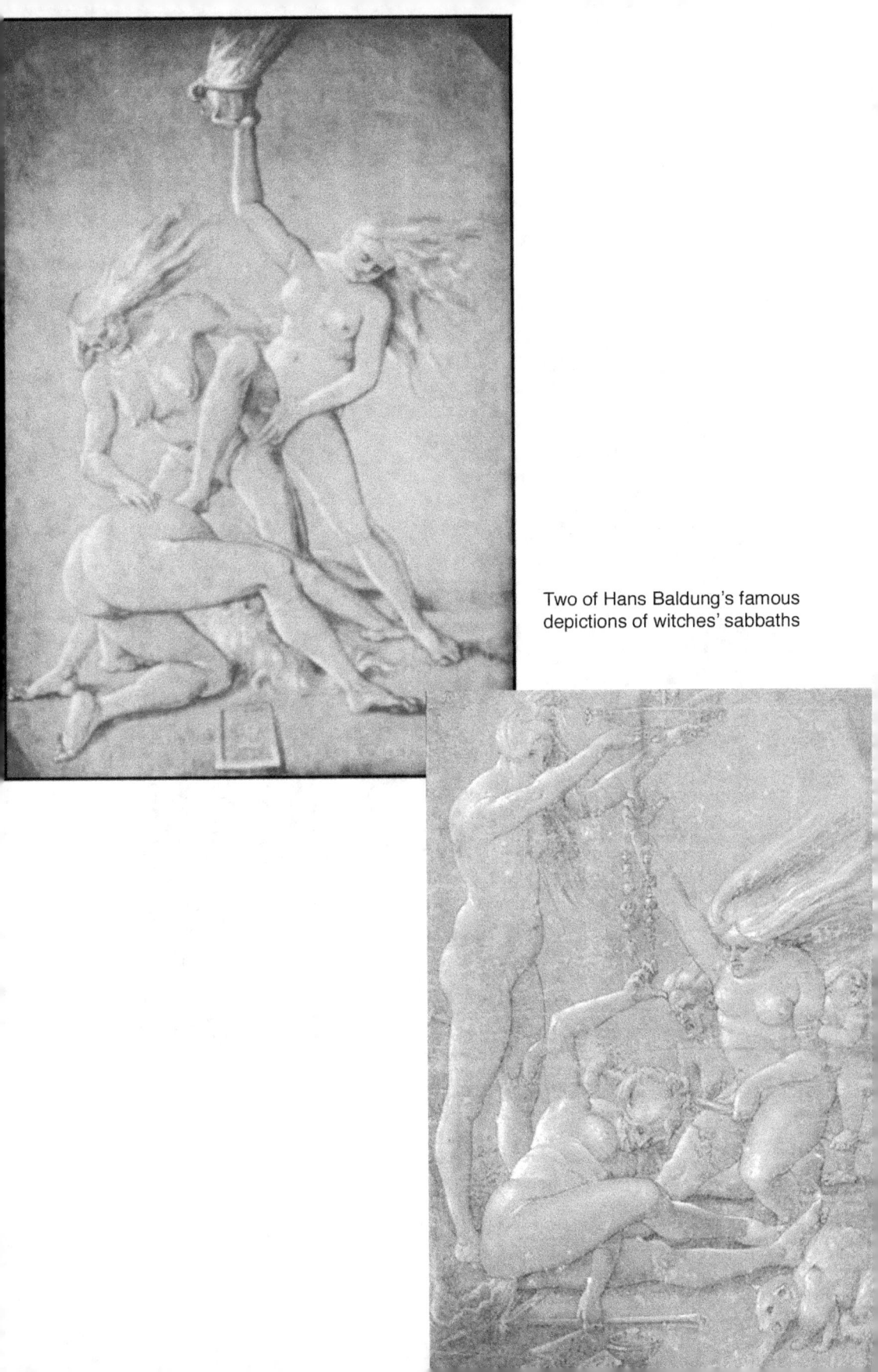

Two of Hans Baldung's famous
depictions of witches' sabbaths

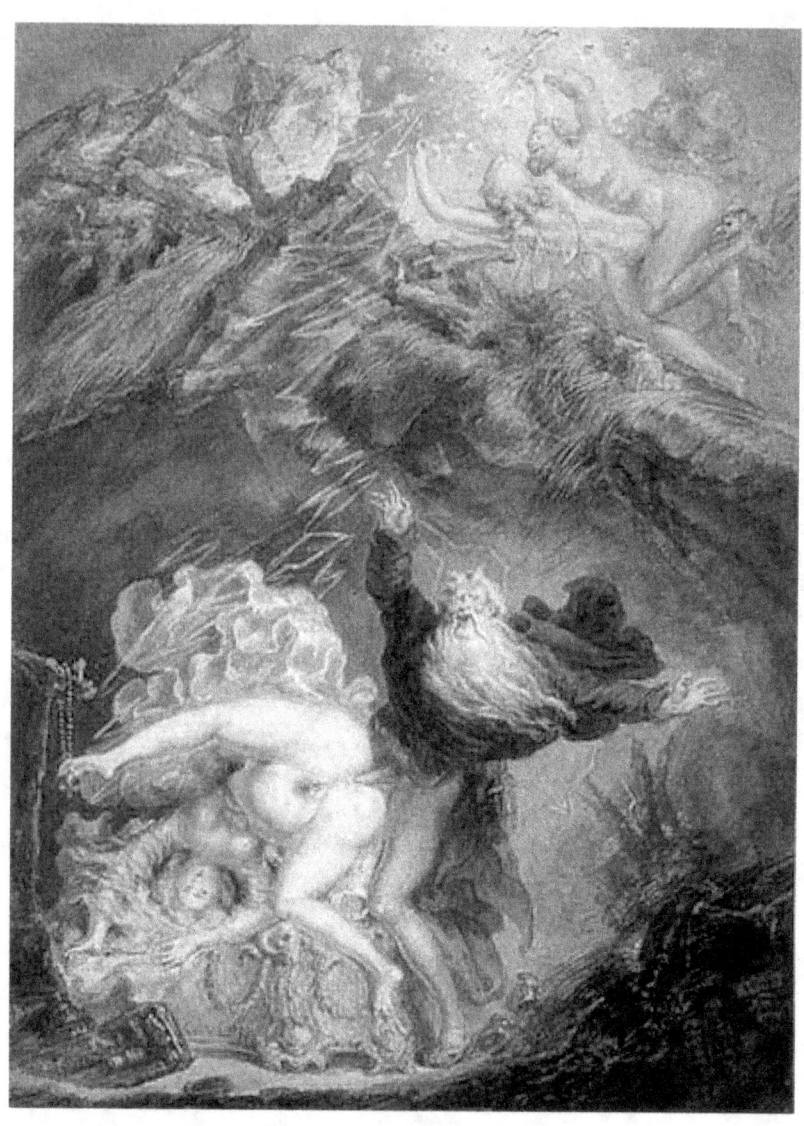

Giove Pluvio, Histoire Sainte

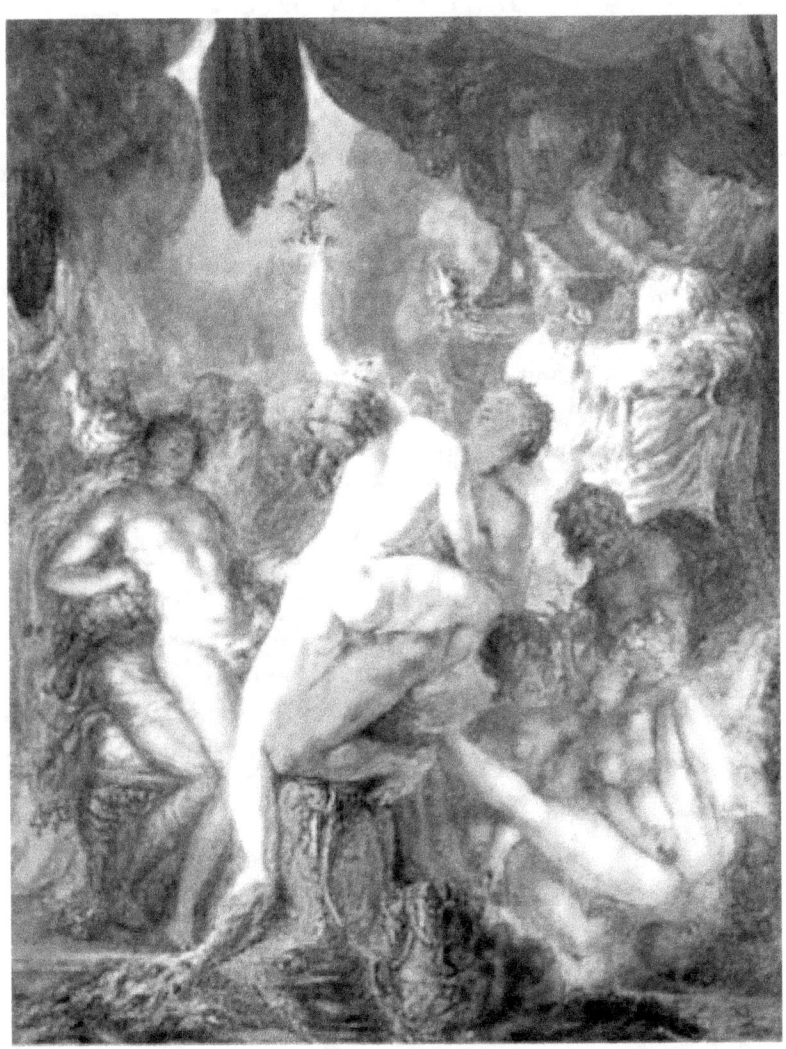

From Histoire Sainte, Adorazione del vitello d'oro

SANDRO BOTTICELLI:
THE ANNUNCIATION

Sandro Botticelli's *Annunciation* is violent. It depicts an aggressive sexual approach of a woman, though the pressure here is psychological and spiritual: the Archangel, as in all other depictions of the Annunciation, does not touch the Virgin. That would be too lascivious, if the Archangel's hand were placed on the breast or belly of the Virgin Mary. That would be too direct. So Gabriel does not touch the Madonna, but makes love to her from a distance, as God makes love to the Virgin from a distance, from the privileged position of Heaven. God sits on his heavenly throne, spiritually penetrating and impregnating the Virgin, who remains a Virgin, despite the physicality and pain of pregnancy and labour. The Virgin is too passive, fatally passive, for feminists. *Ecce Ancilla Domina* she says: 'behold the handmaid of the lord' (J. Metford, 28). The Virgin Mary moves from being a virgin, from 'knowing not a man', to becoming pregnant, in one anguished moment. Like Tess Durbeyfield in Thomas Hardy's 1892 novel *Tess of the d'Urbervilles*, she knows little of men. Then, the first time she knows 'love' (i.e. sex) she gets pregnant. This, then, is for some feminists a vicious kind of possession, which has the blessing of the top guy in the West, God.

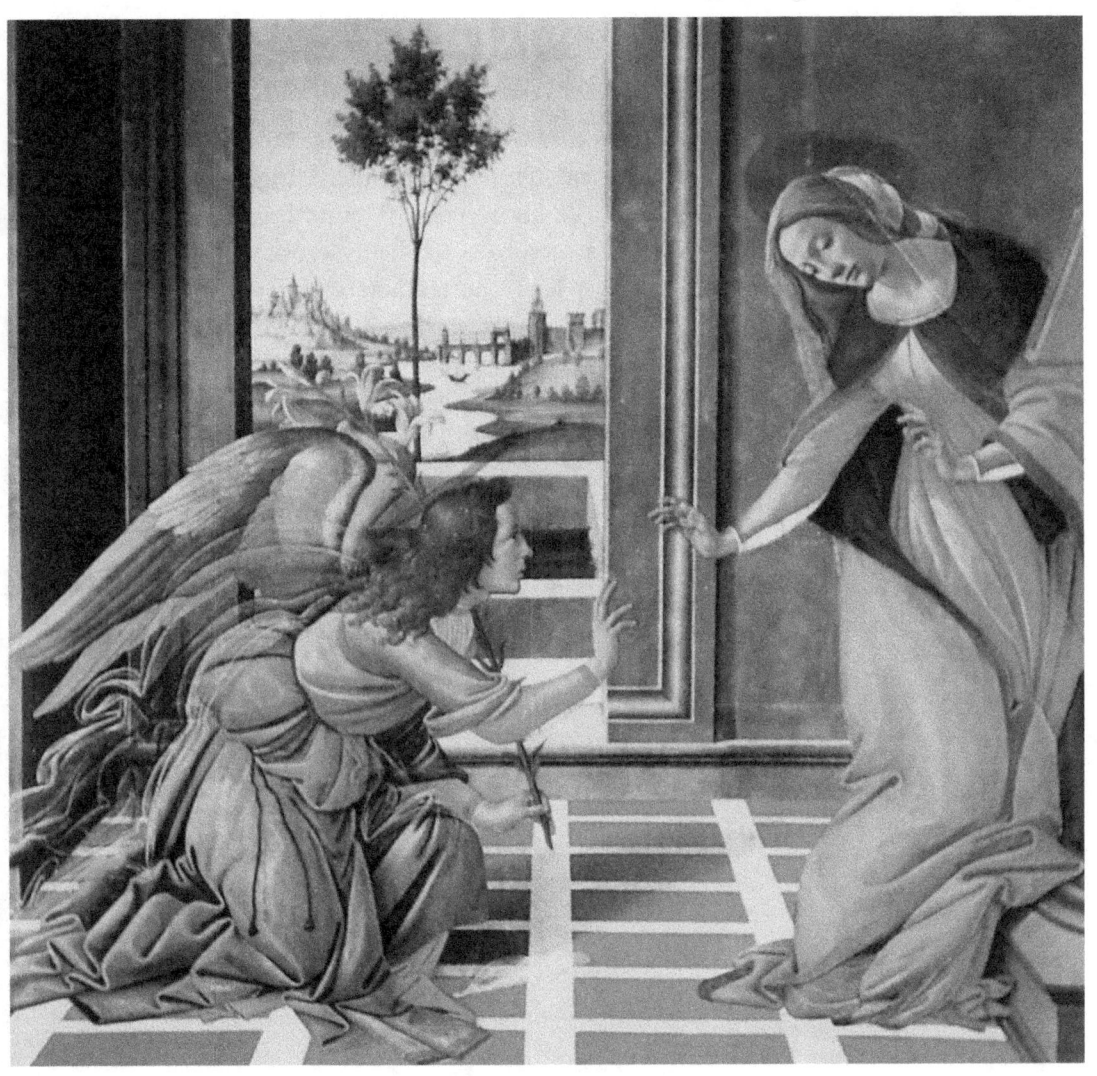

Sandro Botticelli, The Annunciation, Uffizi Gallery, Florence

LEDA AND THE SWAN

Like Michelangelo Buonarroti, Leonardo da Vinci produced an erotic version of *Leda and the Swan*. Both Michelangelo's and Leonardo's images are lost. We know both, though, because they were copied.[1] Michelangelo's picture is explicitly erotic: the huge swan lies between the deity's legs, the feathers of his wing over her vulva, a touch that expresses male 'possession' of the woman's sexuality.

Leonardo da Vinci made his *Leda and the Swan* as erotica is made; at the request of a (male) client: 'I executed the painting... for a lover. He wished to see the features of his goddess mirrored so that he might kiss them without arousing suspicion', Leonardo wrote.[2] In Antoine Coypel's (?) picture of *Leda and the Swan*, Jupiter's genitals are again the focus of the image, as the woman sits astride his legs.[3]

1 After Michelangelo: *Leda and the Swan*, 16th century, Royal Academy, London
2 quoted in Peter Webb, 112
3 Antoine Coypel (?): *Jupiter with Leda and the Swan*, from *Histoire Universelle*, c. 1750, British Museum

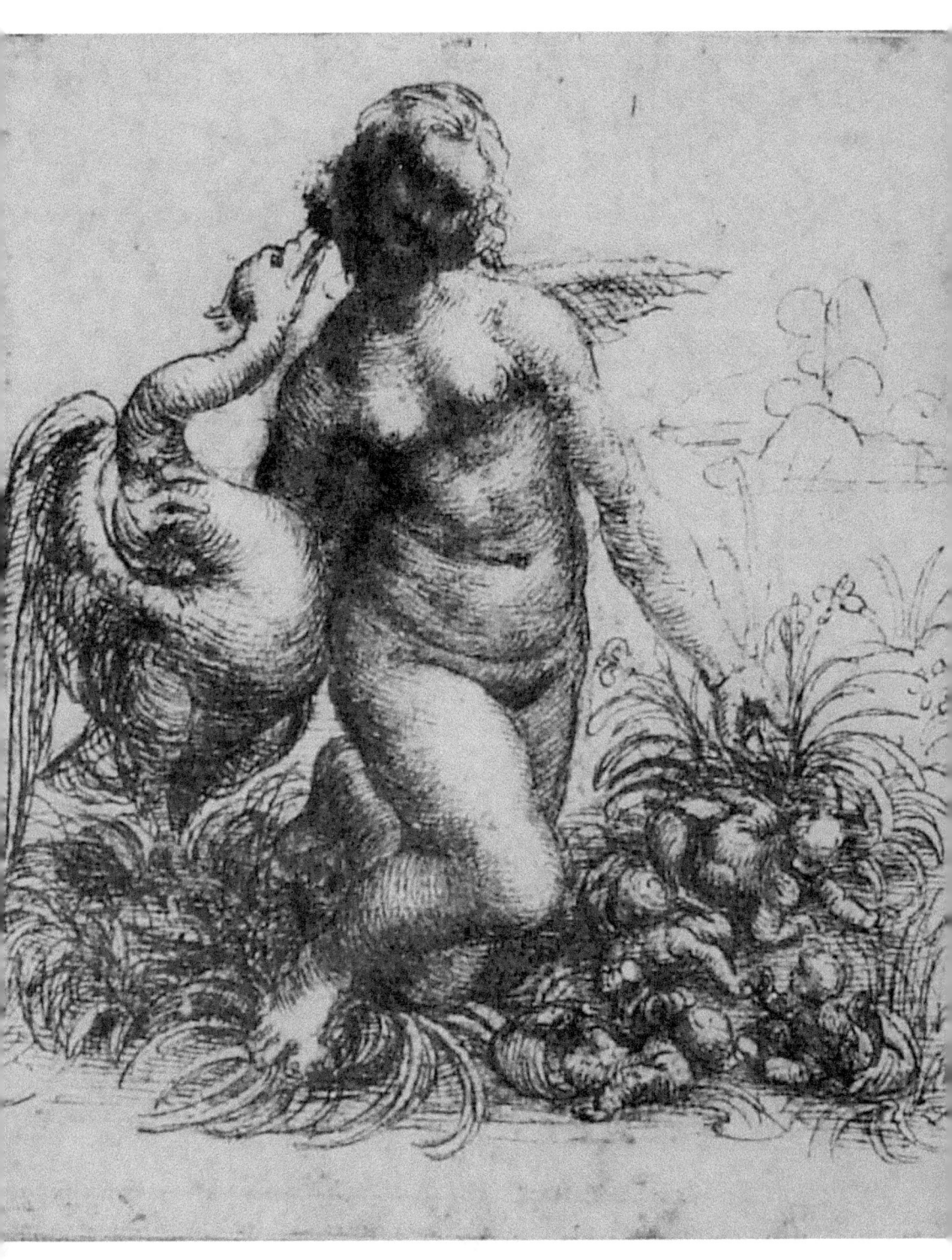

Leonardo da Vinci, Study for Leda and the Swan

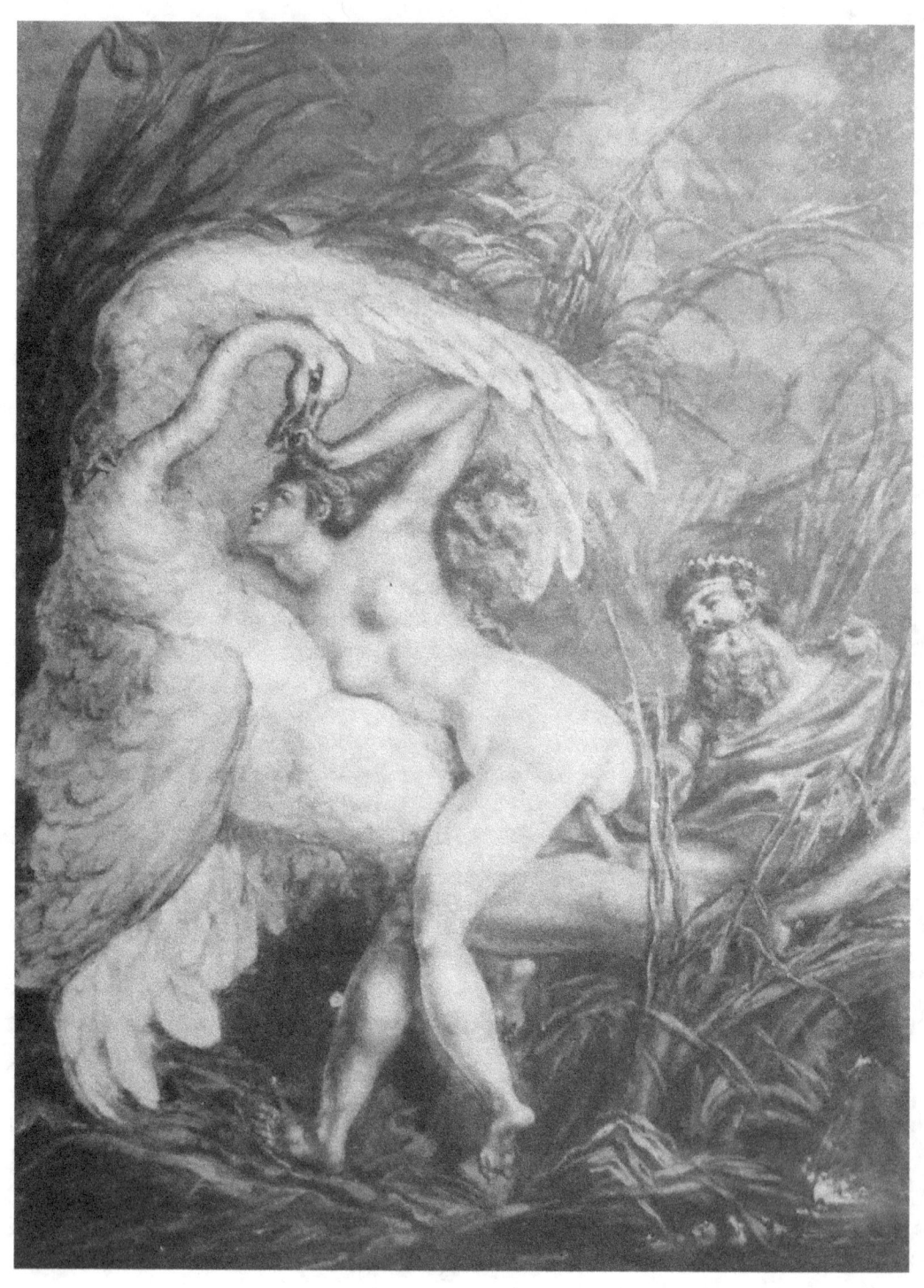

Antyoine Coypel, Jupiter With Leda and the Swan, c. 1750

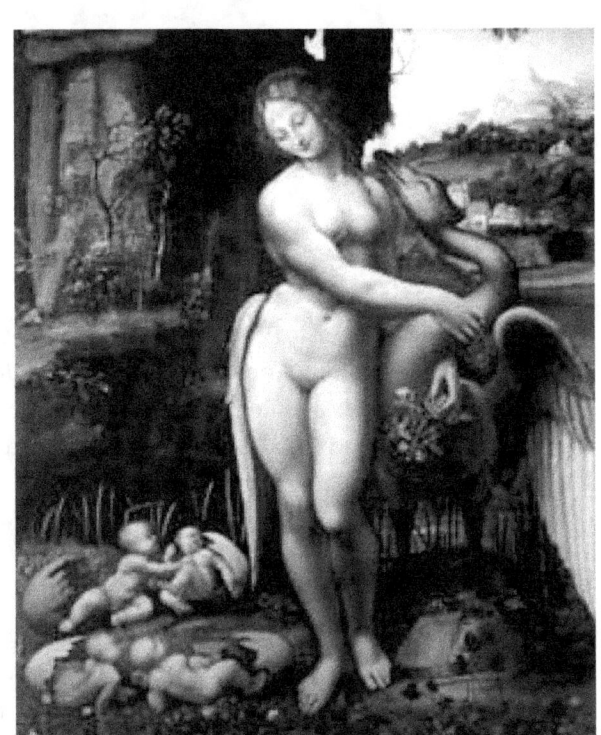

Leda and the Swan.
After Leonardo da Vinci (right).
After Paolo Veronese (below).

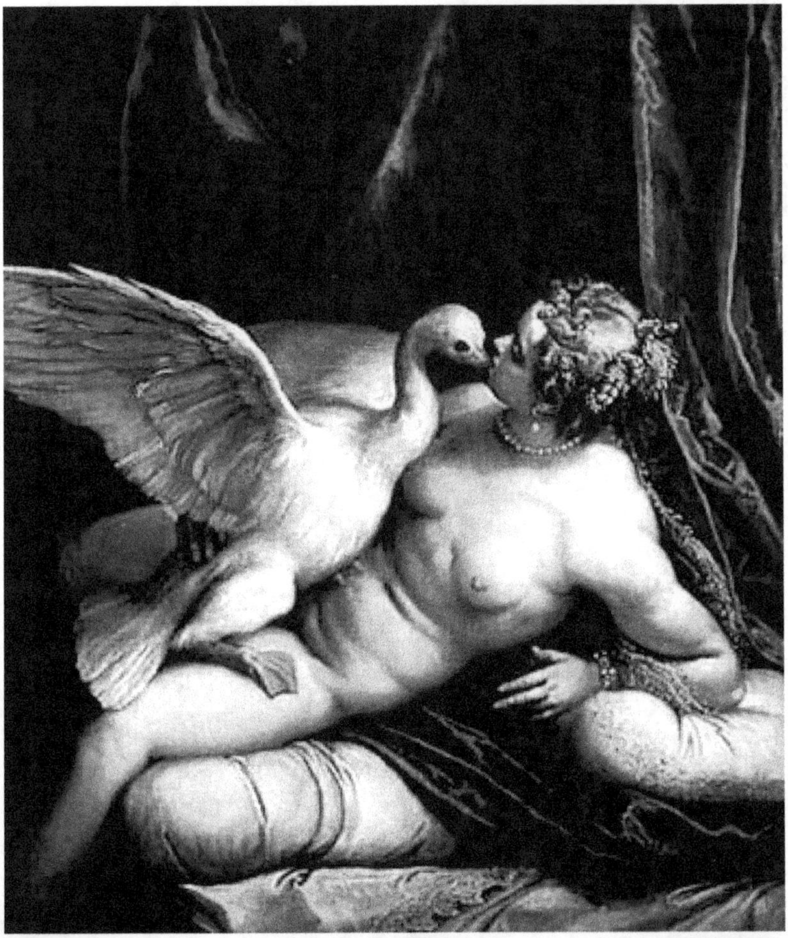

TITIAN: *NUDES*

Throughout history, female nudes of the high art type have been made for clients and connoisseurs – Titian made many nudes for such private, privileged consumption. Pornography too has been manufactured for the same clients and connoisseurs. When does a refined, rarefied enjoyment of erotic art become the vulgar, debased gratification of pornography? When does the connoisseur become the pornographic consumer?

In the art of Titian, as in Leonardo da Vinci, the sensuality of the paint surface is primary in the 'genius' of the art, in the critical acclaim the art generates. Whatever the subject, Titian manages to produce marvellous paintings.[1] Titian's soft colouring, his blurring of forms, his use of luminous lighting and his open use of paint look towards Impressionism and modern painting. Paintings such as *Venus Anadyomene* can stand happily beside Pierre Renoir as a modern depiction of a woman, a typical representation of 'woman' as erotic object, of 'woman' as Goddess and earthbound, flesh-and-blood being.[2]

Titian's nudes are the highpoint of the 'high art' nude; his nudes are as voluptuous as possible, for instance the woman reclining in bliss in the foreground right-hand corner of Titian's *Bacchanal of the Andrians*.[3]

1 Titian: *The Pesaro Altarpiece*, 1519-20, canvas, 478 x 268cm, Santa Maria Gloriosa dei Frari, Venice; *Christ Crowned with Thorns*, mid-1540s, 303 x 180cm, Louvre, Paris; *Pietà*, up to 1576, 353 x 348cm, Galeria dell' Academia, Venice
2 Titian: *Venus Anadyomene*, c. 1520, canvas, 76 x 57.3cm, Duke of Sutherland Collection, on loan to the National Gallery of Scotland, Edinburgh
3 Titian: *Bacchanal of the Andrians*, 1523-4, canvas, 175 x 193cm, Prado, Madrid

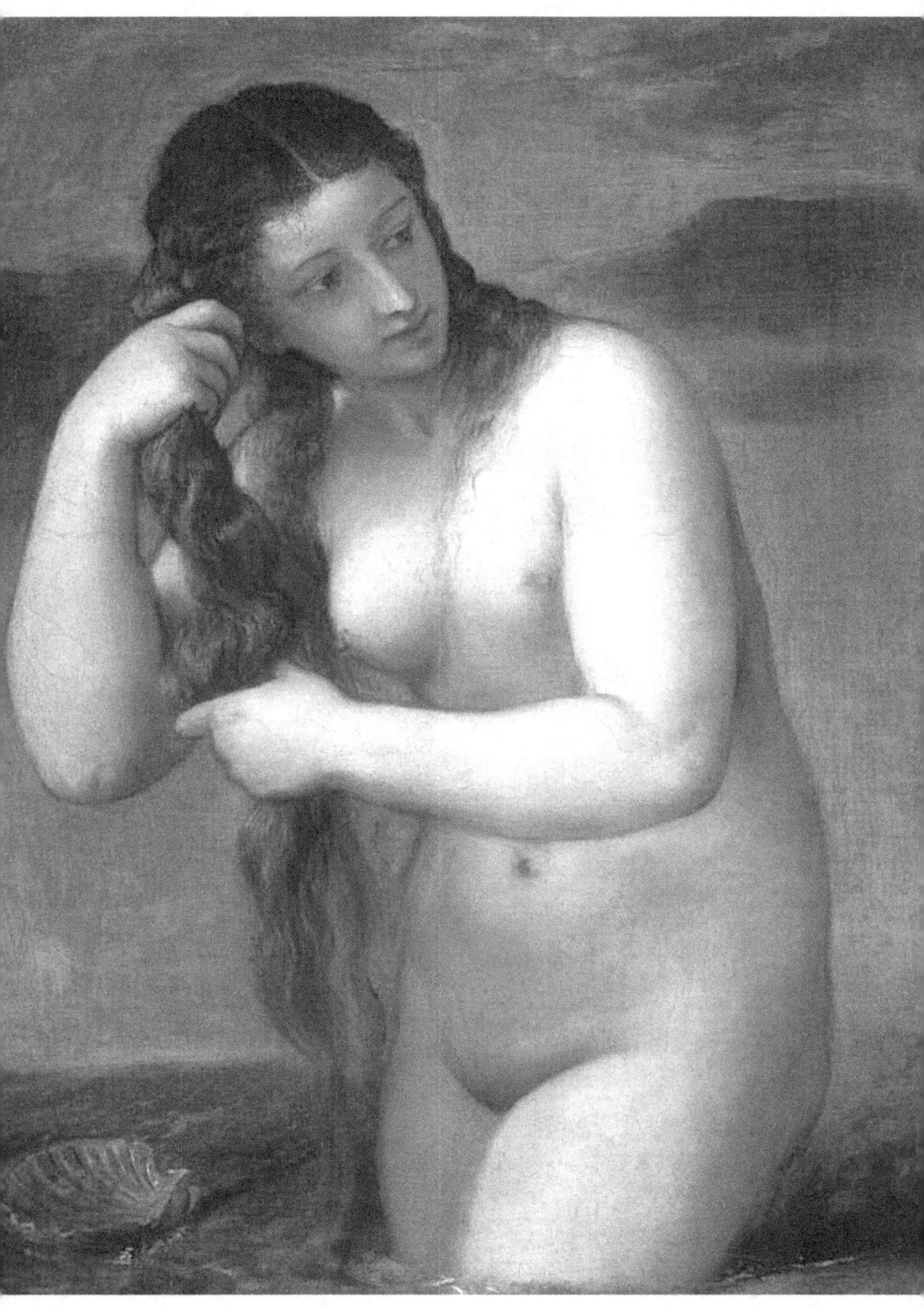

Titian, Venus Rising From the Sea, 1520, Scotland

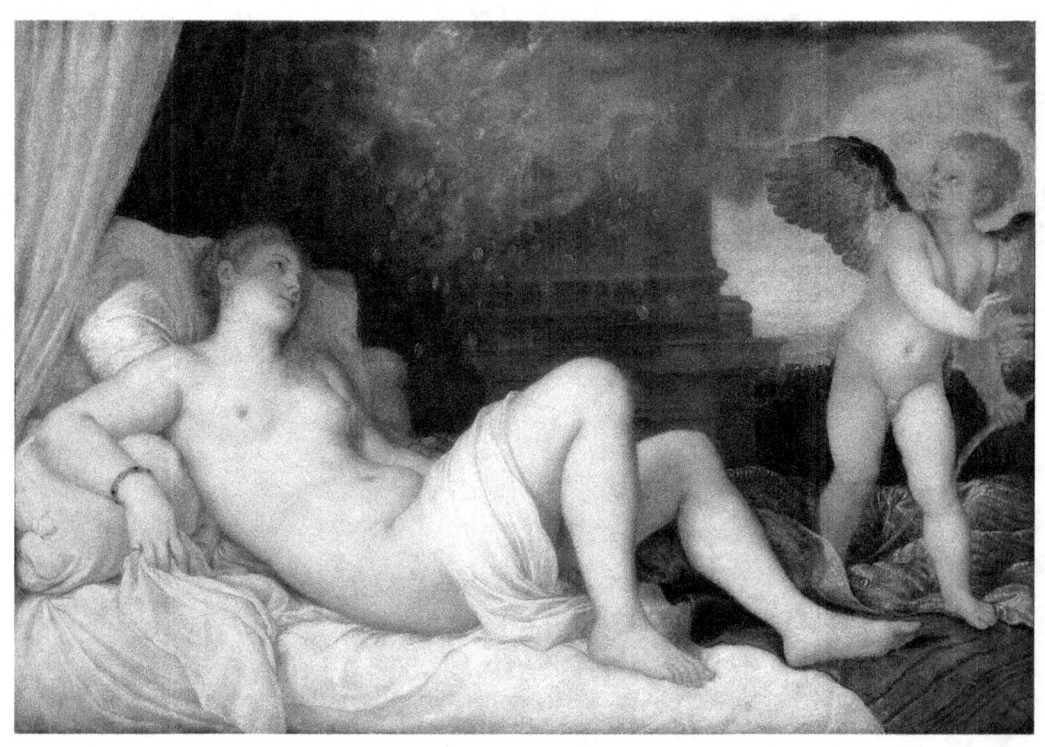

Titian, Danaë, 1544, Naples

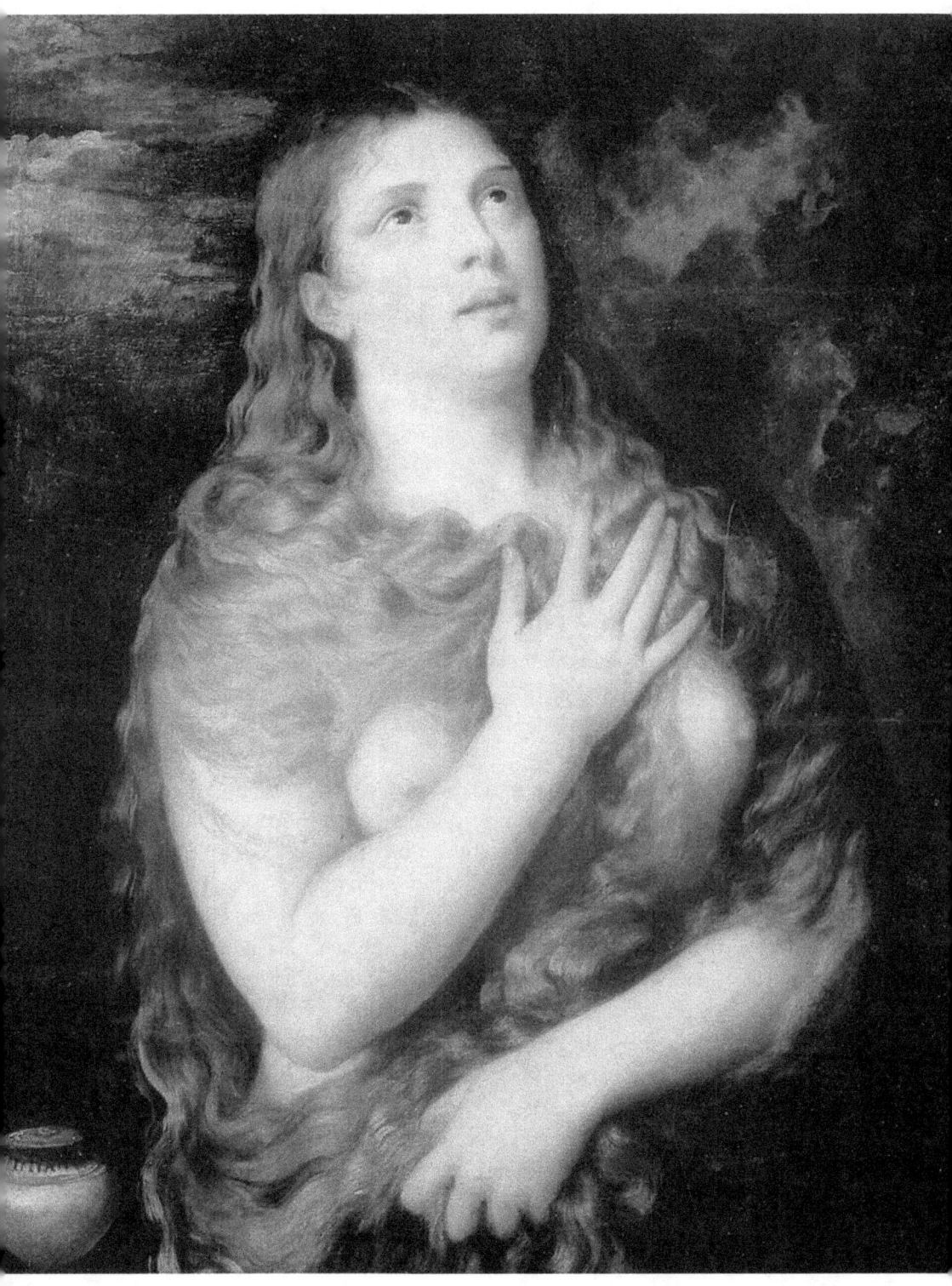

Titian, Mary Magdalene, 1533, Pittit Palace, Florence

MICHELANGELO MERISI DE CARAVAGGIO

When you enter one of the biggest galleries in the Louvre Museum in Paris, you can halt on your way following the crowds to the *Mona Lisa* to have a look at numerous masterpieces on either side. You should definitely spend some time in front of Michelangelo Merisi de Caravaggio's *The Death of the Virgin,* of course, but be sure you don't miss the remarkable picture *The Fortune-teller* (1594, a.k.a. *The Good Fortune*). Luckily, *The Fortune-teller* is hung (at the moment) not too high up, so you can get a good view (why do so many museums and galleries hang major, major works of art way too high? Are we giants all of a sudden?).

Without a doubt, *The Fortune-teller* is a fabulous image of romance and sexuality and erotic love. It might not appear so at first, but have a closer look. On the top level, the painting portrays a woman and man, both young. The woman is a fortune teller and the man is a client, a punter, someone who's going to have their fortune told.

So the youth offers his hand, and the young woman takes it. In the act of telling his fortune from his palm, she is stealing his ring. So already this is fabulously erotic stuff, because all of the time it is written in neon signs by the exchange of *looks* between the two protagonists. In other words, the guy *knows* that the young woman is stealing his ring, and the young woman *knows* that the man *knows* she's trying to take his jewellery. And that's one of the reasons this painting is so erotic – it's the tease, the unspoken gestures, the eye contact, it's the guy saying, 'I know what you trying to do and you shouldn't be doing it, but I'm going to let you do it', and it's the woman saying, 'I'm going to take your ring, though you might not want me to, but really, *really* you do.'

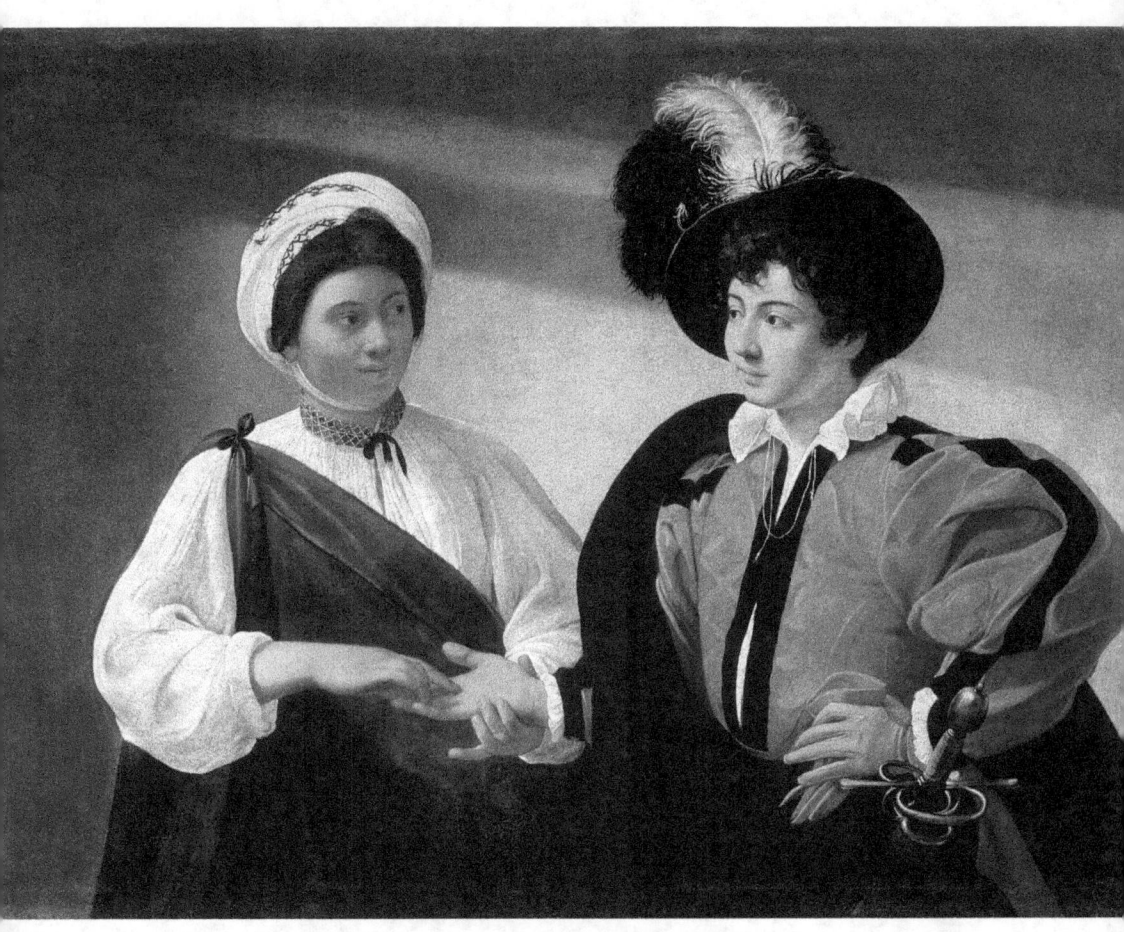

Michelangelo Merisi da Caravaggio,
The Fortune-Teller, Louvre, Paris

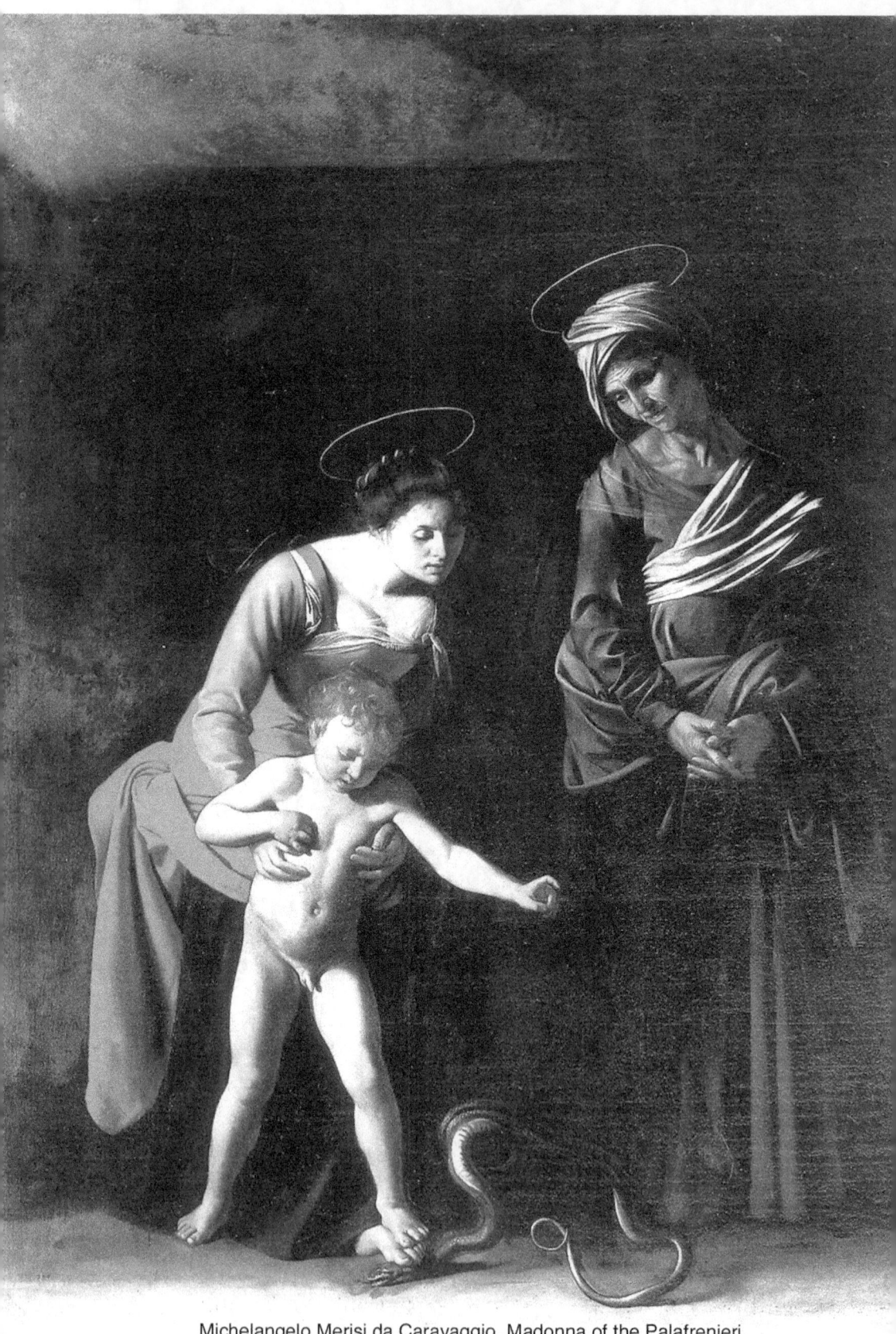

Michelangelo Merisi da Caravaggio, Madonna of the Palafrenieri,
1605-06, Galleria Borghese, Rome

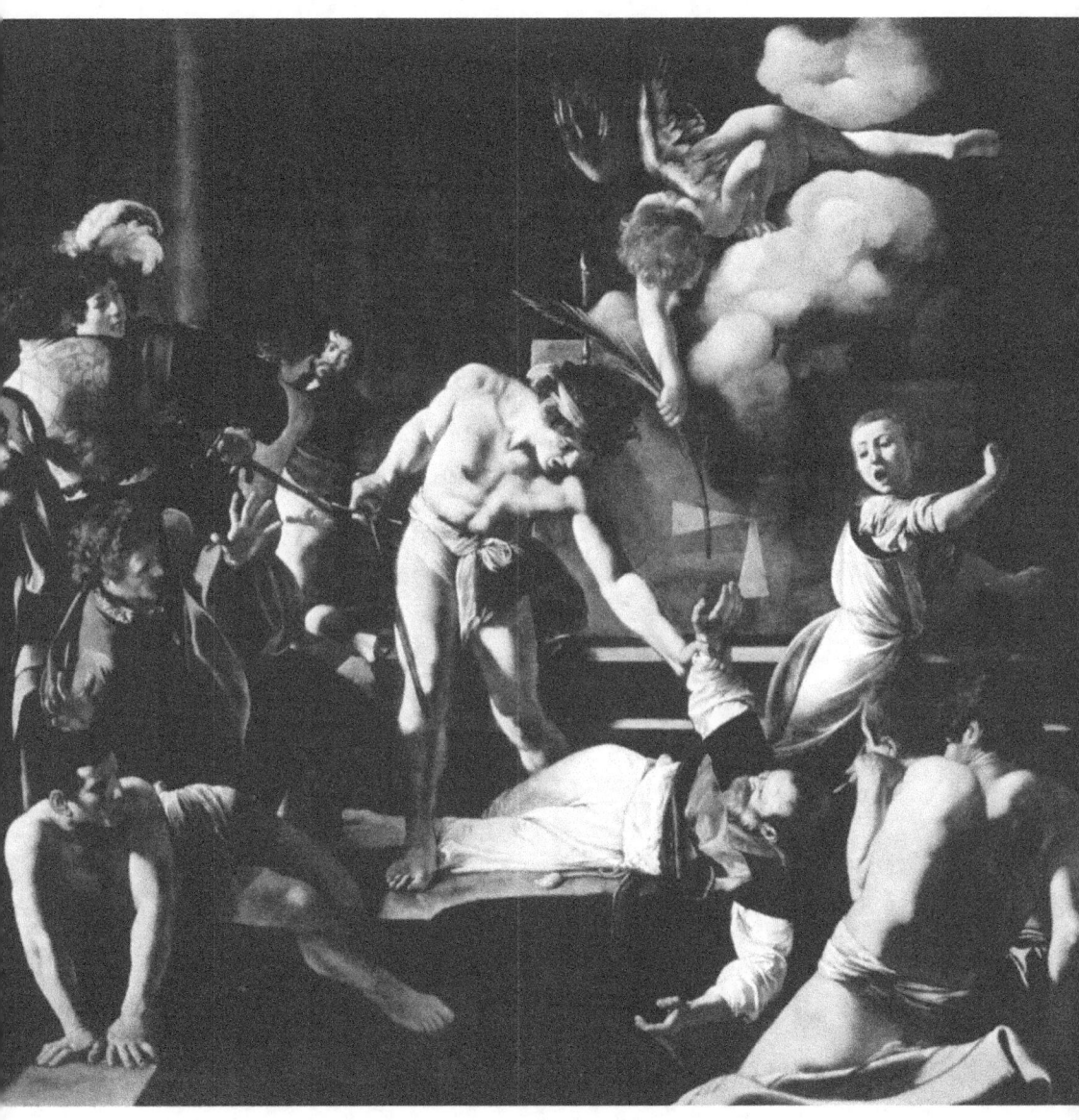

Caravaggio, The Martyrdom of St Matthew, 1600-01,
San Luigi dei Francesci, Rome

LUCAS CRANACH

The *Adam and Eves* and Venuses of Lucas Cranach (1472-1553, born in Vienna) are utterly distinctive: nobody in the history of painting has portrayed the human form quite like this. The nudes of Cranach (and other Northern Renaissance painters) are nudes that are not aware of their bodies being portrayed as spectacle. Yet Cranach's nudes must be conscious of their nudity too. Indeed, surely any Renaissance nude must be aware of its nakedness, otherwise it could not be a 'Renaissance' artwork. A mediaeval nude might be able to display itself without erotic self-awareness, but not a Renaissance nude, for Renaissance art is always aware of itself *as art*. It knows what it is doing.

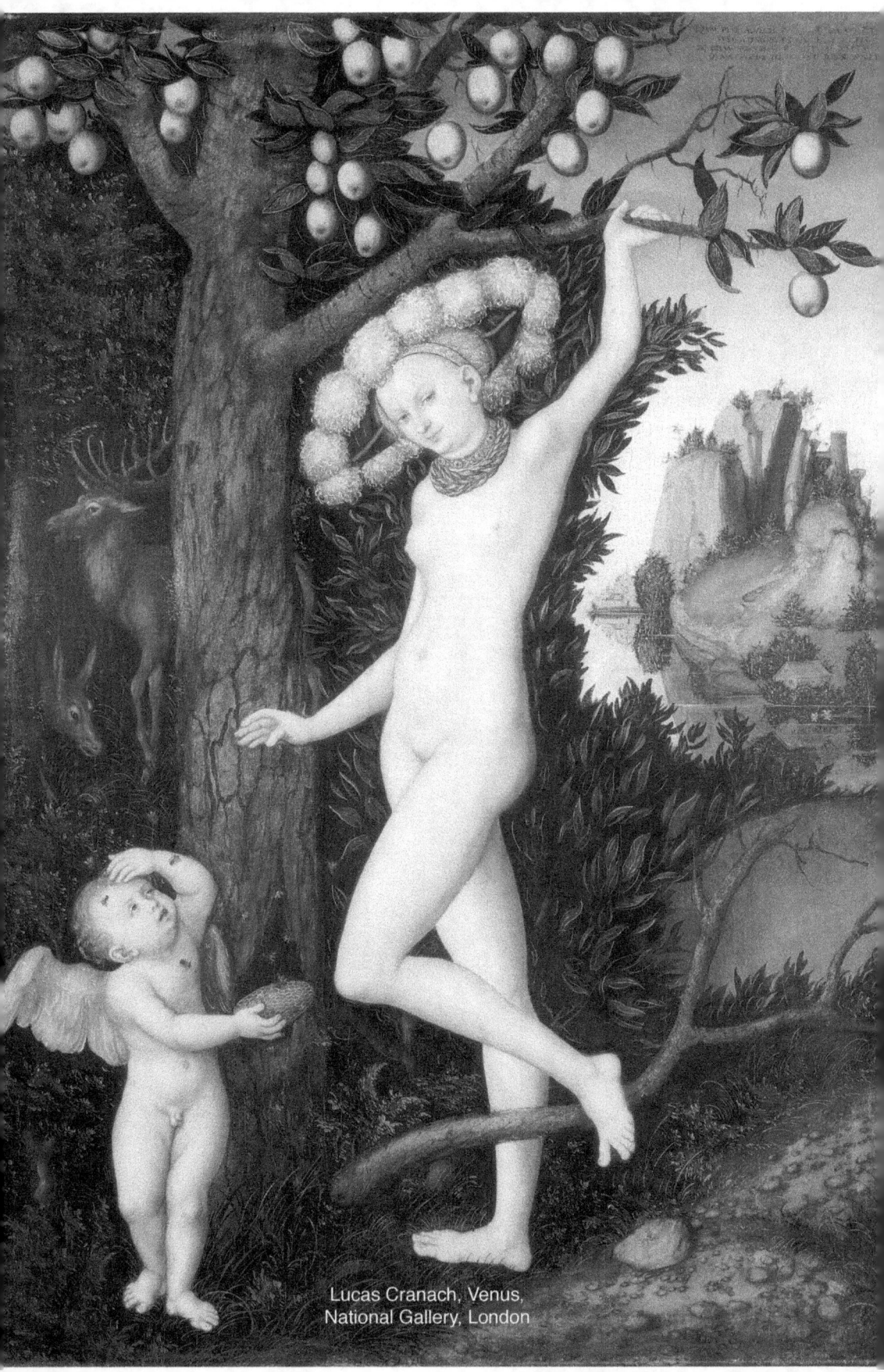

Lucas Cranach, Venus,
National Gallery, London

ARTEMISIA GENTILESCHI

Artemisia Gentileschi (1593-1653) is one of the celebrated women artists of the late Renaissance period, well-known for her marvellous *Judiths*, and her luminous *Self-Portrait*. Daughter of the painter Orazio Gentileschi, Artemisia was involved in a famous rape trial: Agostino Tassi was accused by her father of raping Gentileschi when she was 19 (Tassi was subsequently imprisoned). Inevitably, critics have linked the rape trial to the depictions of the *Old Testament* heroines that Gentileschi painted, including of course Judith cutting off the head of Holofernes.

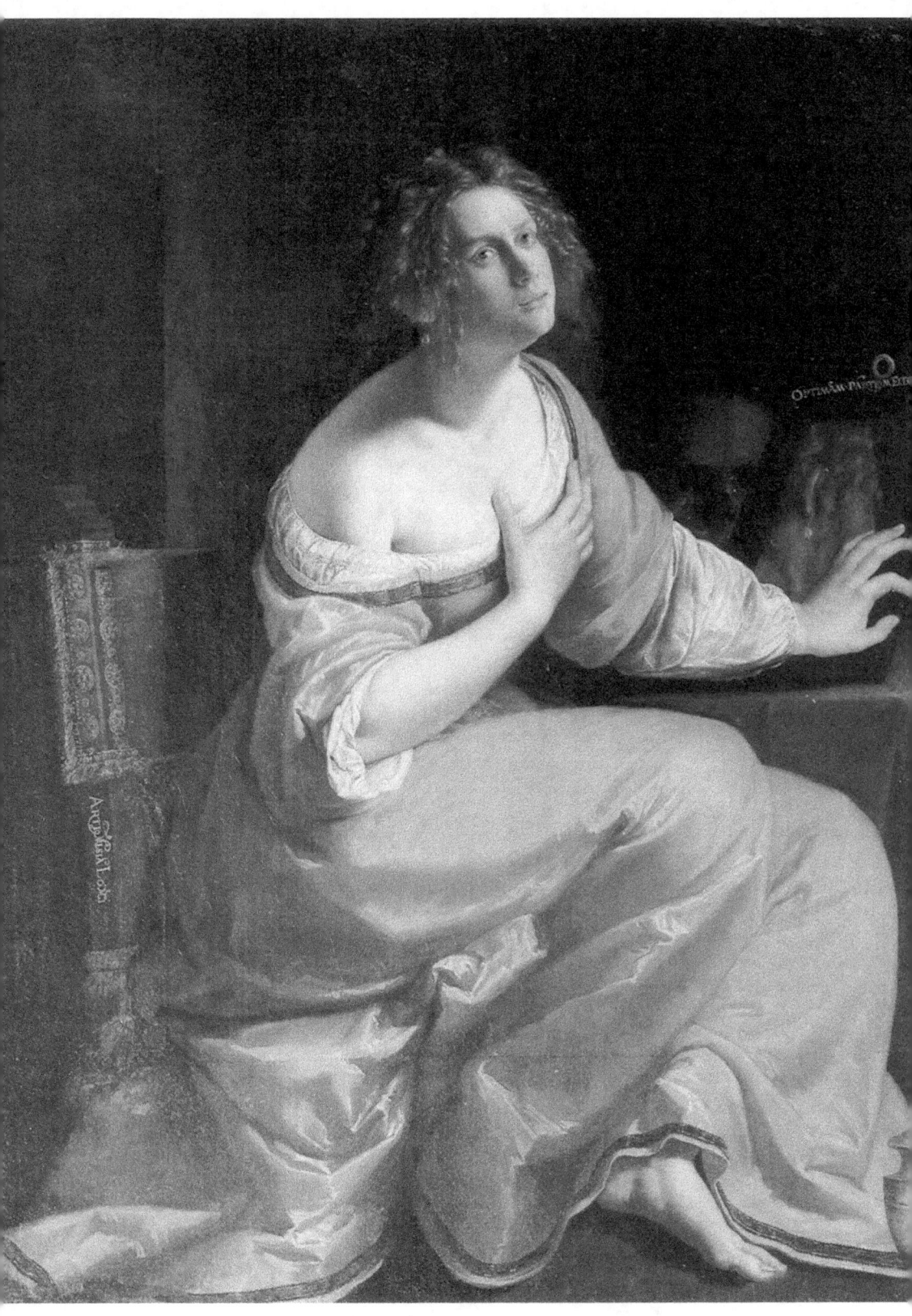

Artemsia Gentileschi, Mary Magdalene

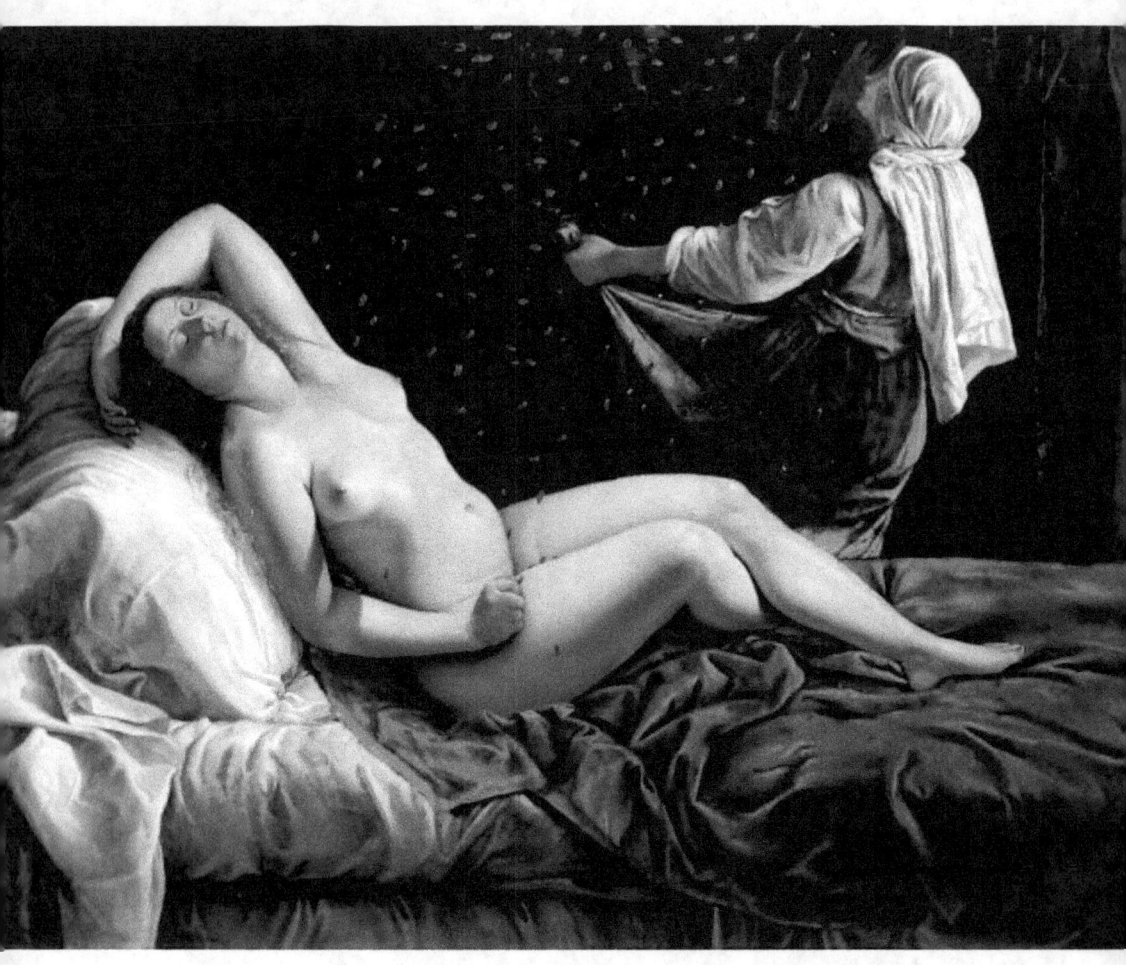

Artemisia Gentileschi, Danaë, c.1612, St Louis Art Museum.

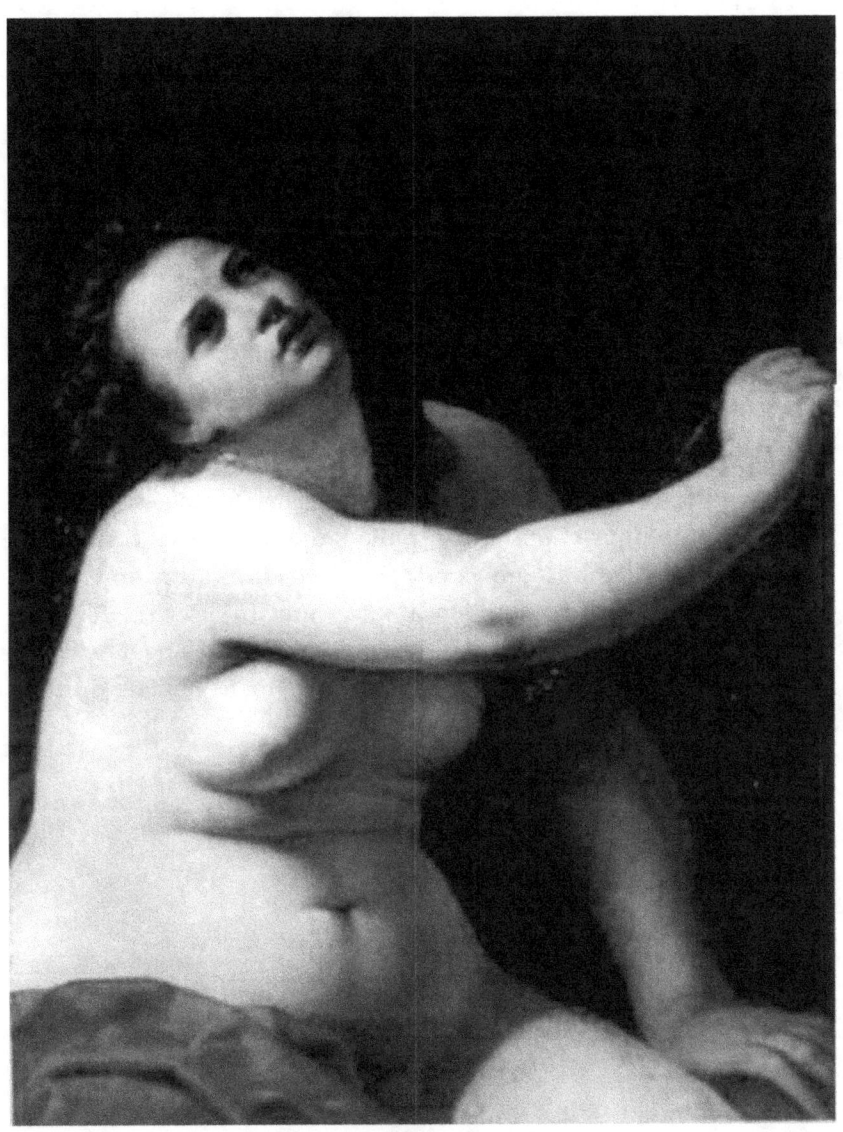

Artemisia Gentileschi, Cleopatra,
Cavallini-Sgarbi Foundation, Ferrara

MICHELANGELO BUONARROTI

Beside Michelangelo Buonarroti (1475-1564), the precocious, religious, obsessive hero of the era, other Renaissance sculptors often seem lightweight, insubstantial or hackneyed. Michelangelo's sculptures are full of the spirit of life which is expressed with an assurance of touch and modelling that is in itself erotic. His sculptures assert their eroticism, whatever the subject, from the superb *Dawn* and *Dusk* of the Medici tomb, to the late *Pietà*.[1]

There is undeniably a vivacious enjoyment of the male form in Michelangelo Buonarroti's *Ignudi* in the Sistine Chapel,[2] while his *Dying Slaves* are among the most sensual images of eroticism combined with death in Western art.[3] Michelangelo's slave dies utterly voluptuously, his arms pulled up to expose his body. Michelangelo's figures are confident in their nudity and their sexuality. They exude confidence – too much, it seems, for the owners of the Sistine Chapel: figures in Michelangelo's *Last Judgement* had to have drapes painted over their genitals during the Counter-Reformation.[4] And in 1970 the use of Michelangelo's *David* on a poster was banned.[5]

---

1 Michelangelo: *Tomb of Lorenzo de' Medici*, h. 173, Medici Chapel, Florence; *Pietà*, late 1550s, marble, 226cm high, Florence cathedral
2 Michelangelo: *Ignudi*, 1508-10, fresco, Sistine Chapel, Vatican, Rome
3 Michelangelo: *Dying Slave*, 1513, marble, 229cm high, Louvre, Paris
4 Michelangelo: *The Last Judgement*, 136-41, fresco, 1375 x 120cm, Sistine Chapel, Vatican, Rome
5 'In 1970, a bookseller in Sydney, Australia, was arrested for displaying a poster of the nude *David*, and the same happened in South Africa in 1973.' Peter Webb, *The Erotic Arts*, 4-5

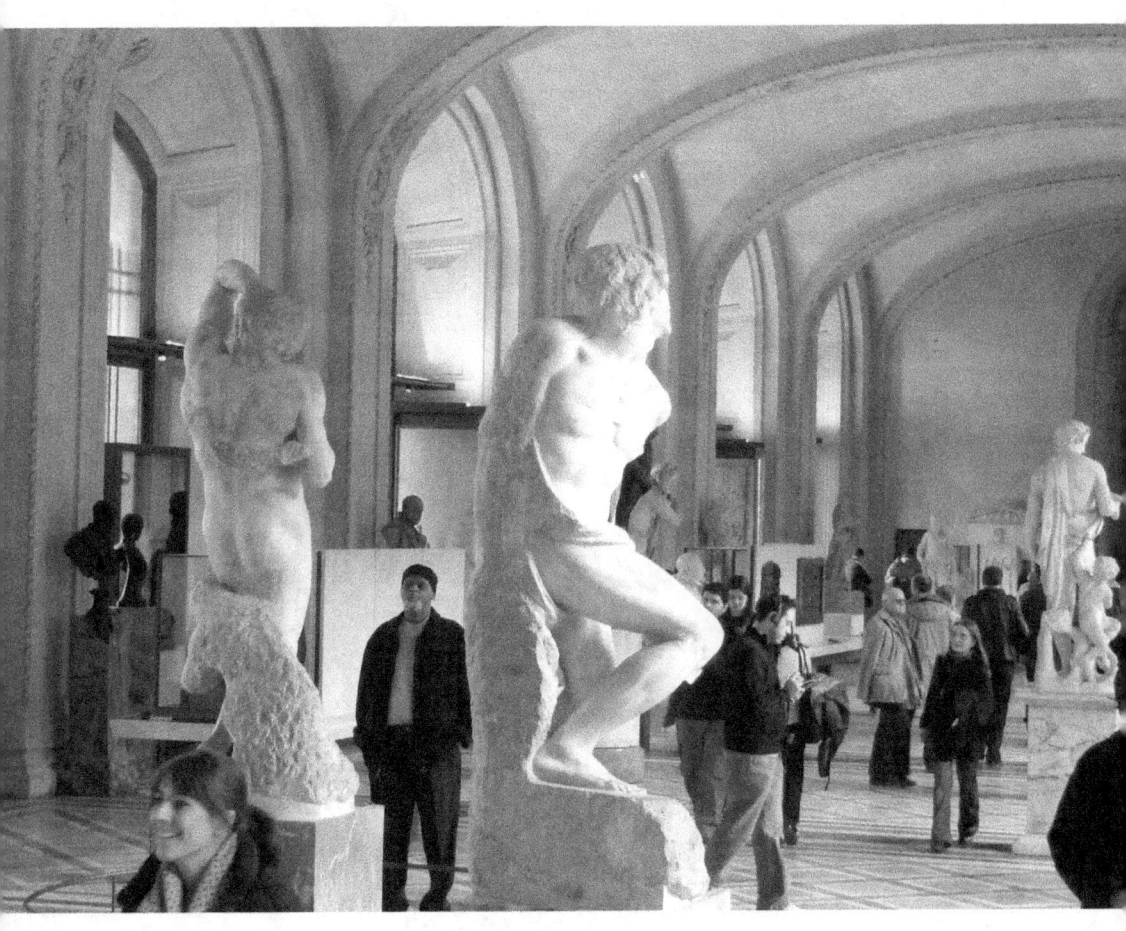

Michelangelo Buonaroti, Dying Slaves, Louvre, Paris
(This page and over)

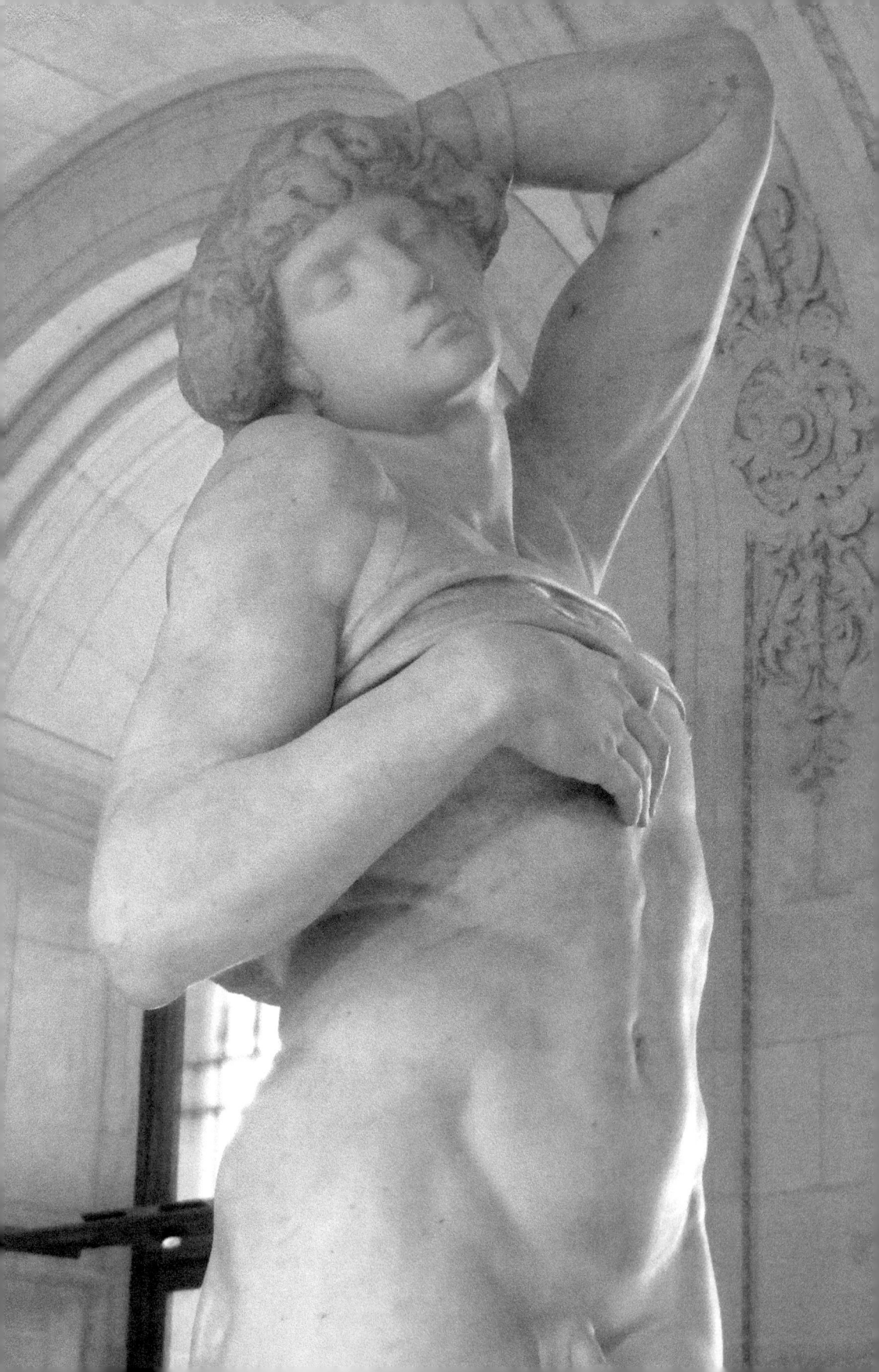

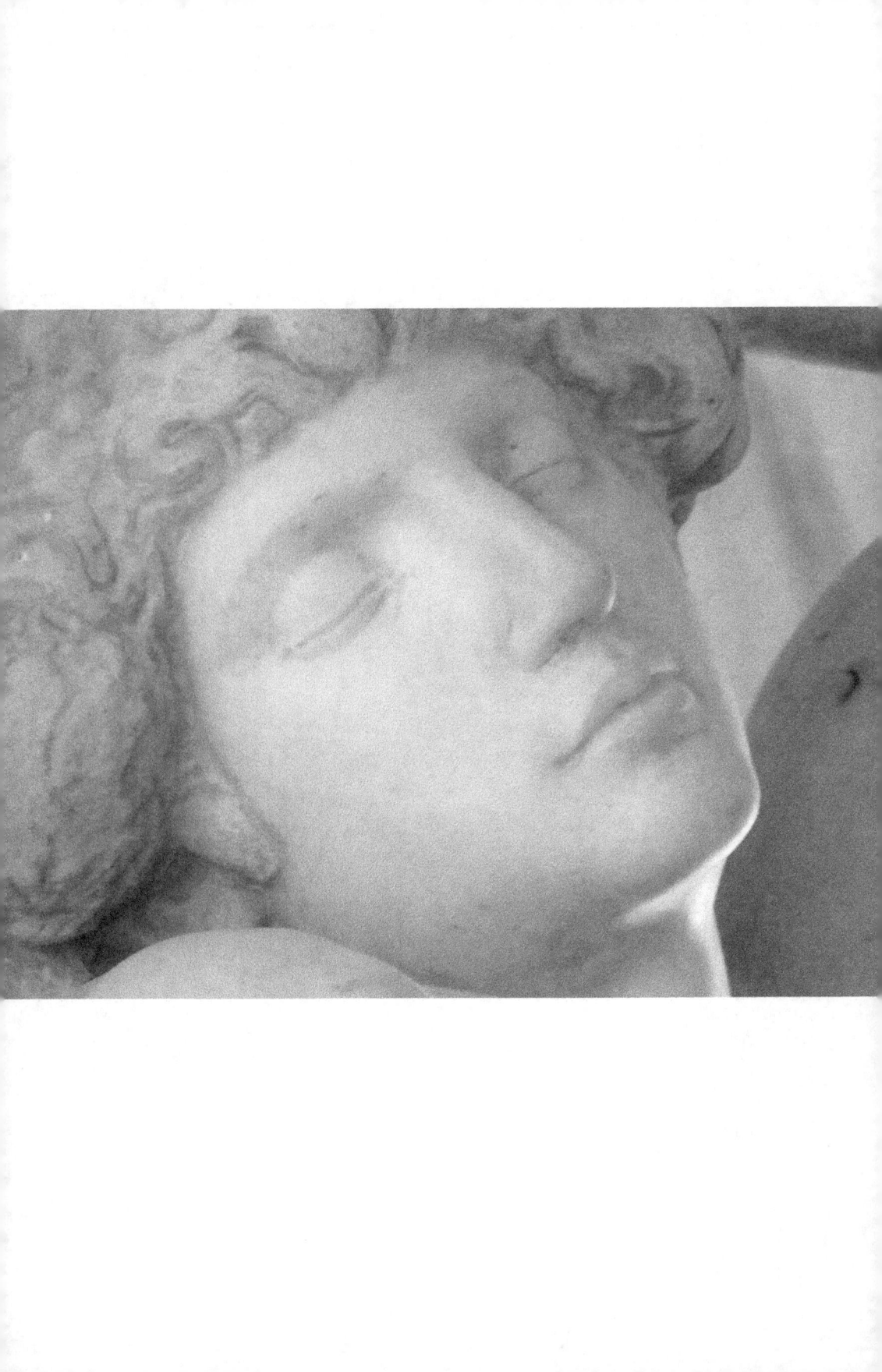

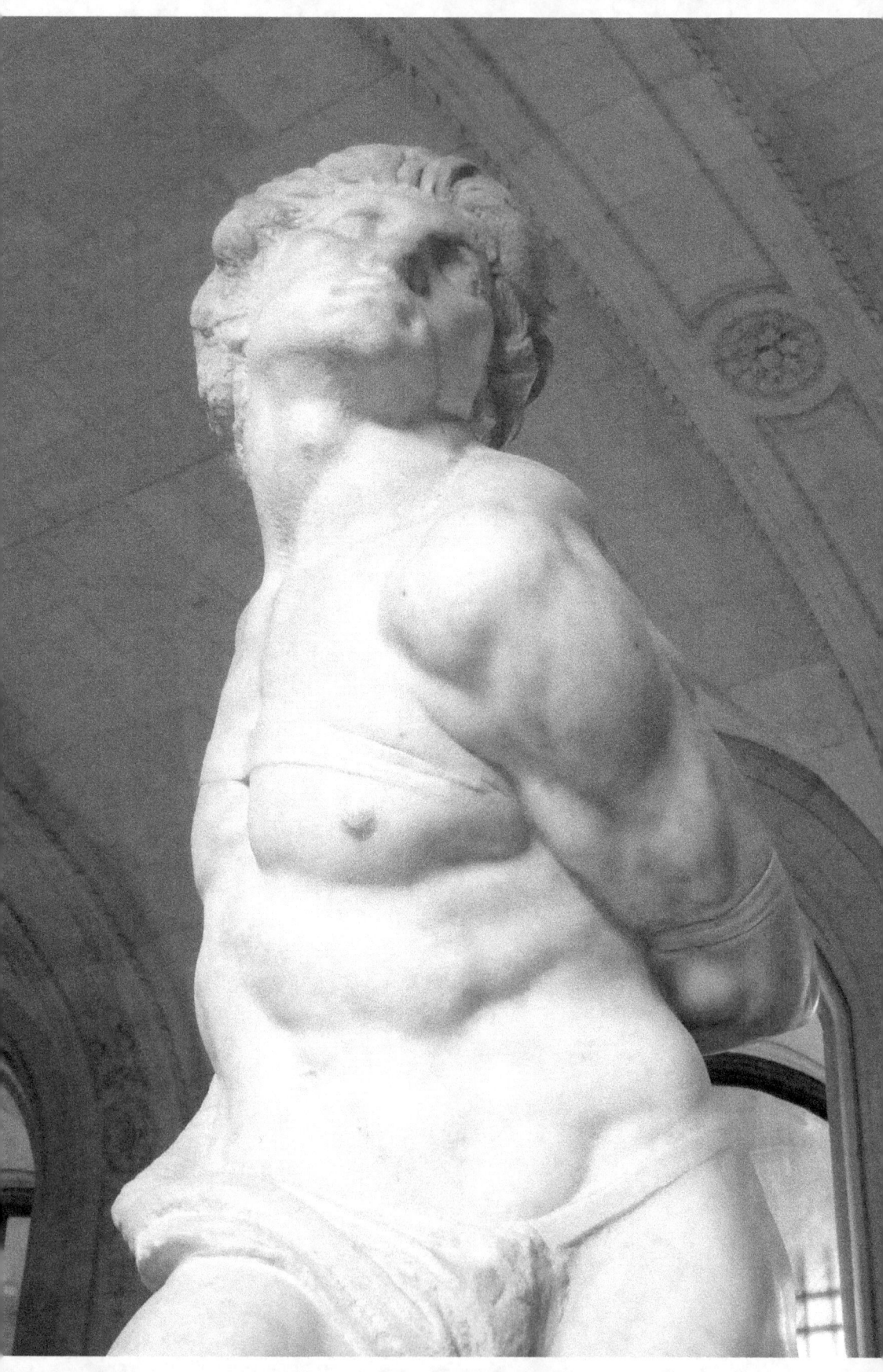

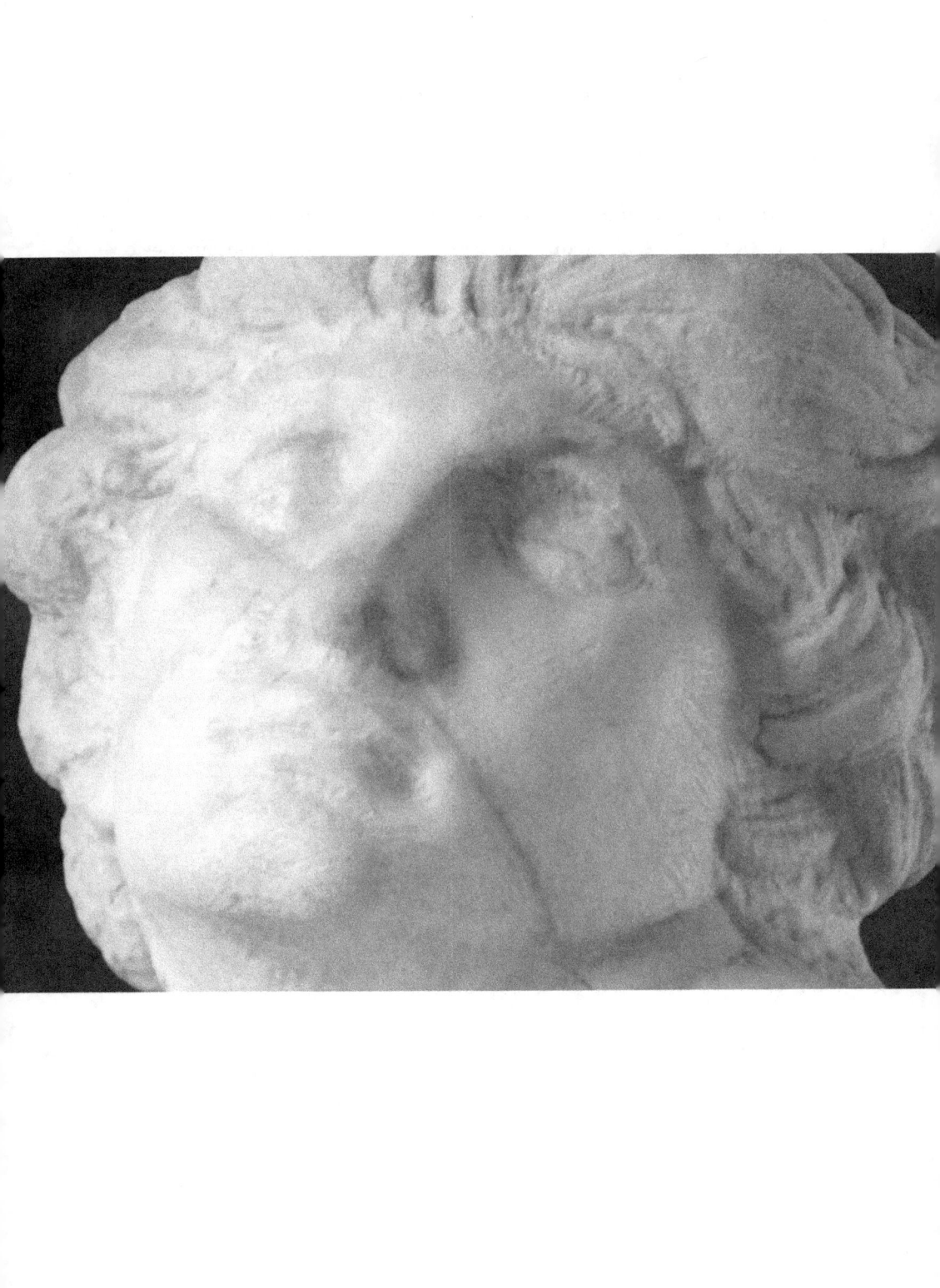

MICHELANGELO BUONARROTI

Michelangelo Buonarroti's figures add angst-ridden and 'modern' tensions – of self, identity, passion and Existential awareness – to the basically life-affirming gestures of ancient Greek sculpture. Michelangelo takes the anonymous, often indifferent eroticism of Greek statues and turns it into something modern or Renaissance, something decidedly individual and subjective. The anguish of (some of) Michelangelo's figures is that of a 'great' artist striving to achieve the Holy Grail or Philosopher's Stone of sculpture, the perfect form, that Neoplatonic impossibility. Beautiful as they are ('beauty' is precisely the right term for Renaissance's notions of perfection), Michelangelo's statues are not final, finished forms. They are fluid, aching for the touch of completion which nobody can give them. In Michelangelo's art, eroticism is passionately – sometimes desperately – asserted.

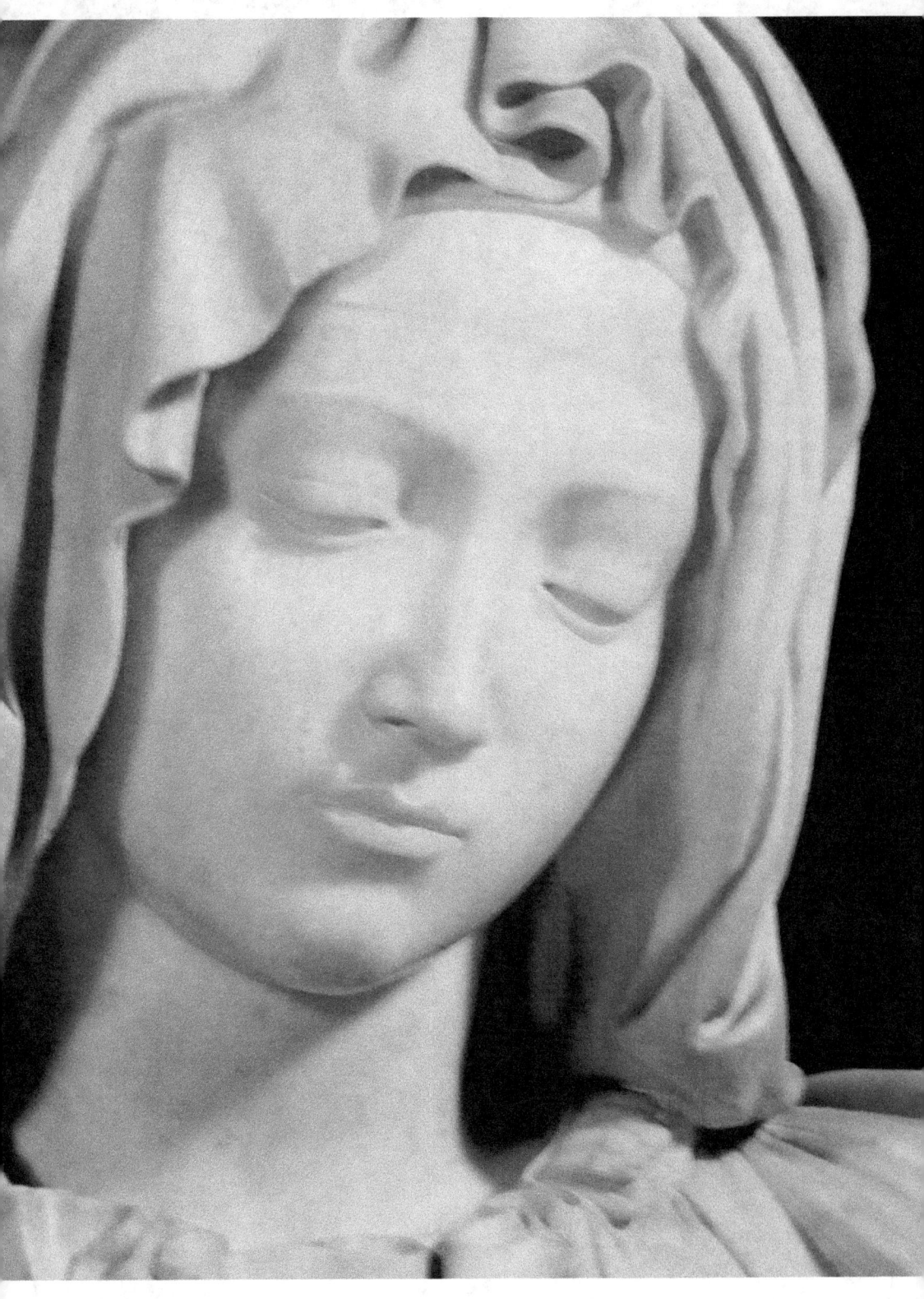

Michelangelo, Pietà, detail, Vatican, Rome

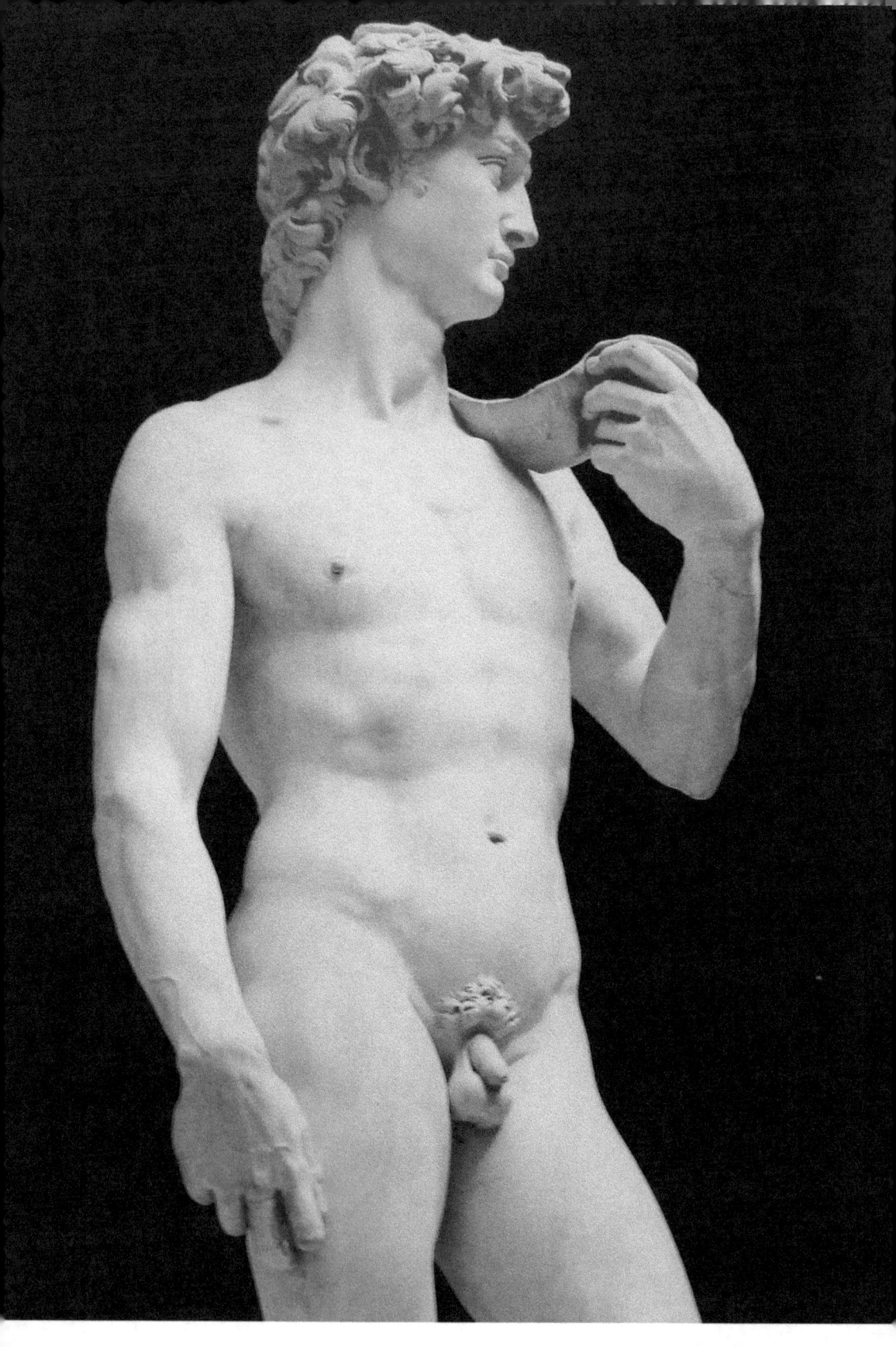

Michelangelo, David, 1501-04, Florence

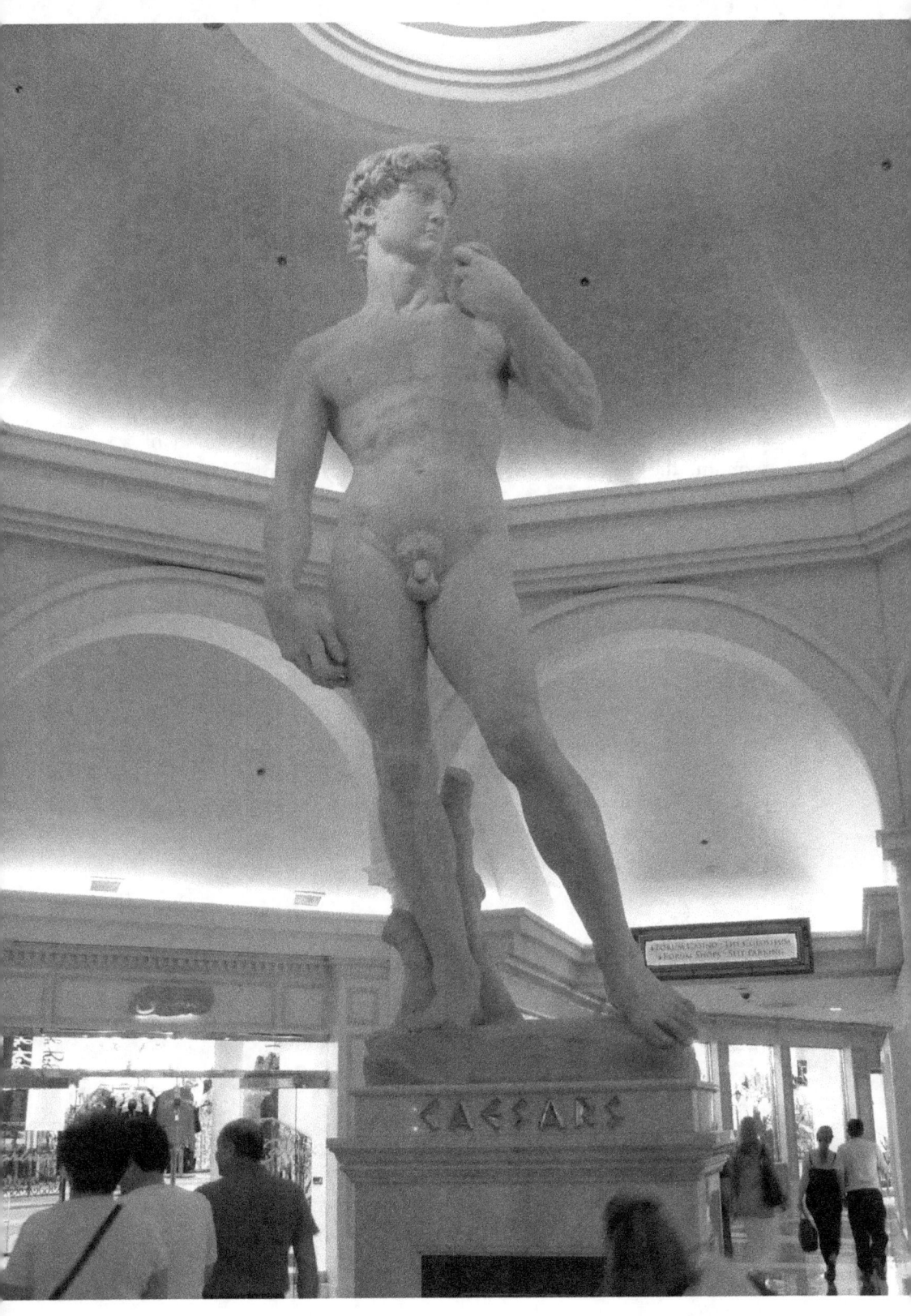

Michelangelo's David in Caesar's Palace, Las Vegas (photo: author)

MICHELANGELO BUONARROTI:
ADAM AND EVE

There is deep sexism in the Judæo-Christian Fall, for it is the woman who picks the apple and offers it to Adam. From the beginning, in the Judæo-Christian tradition, it is the woman who makes men 'fall'. In some depictions, the sexism is doubled, by having the serpent shown as a snake-woman – the torso of a woman, the legs, like those of a mermaid, as in Michelangelo Buonarroti's *Temptation and Expulsion* (1508-12).[1]

The symbol of the half-woman half-fish, still in use today,[2] is another manifestation of patriarchal people's projection of their sexual fears onto women, so that what lies 'below the waist' is feared and objectified as something slimy and fishlike, something dark, from the depths of the unconscious, which is the sea. The mermaid appears sculpted on mediæval churches, some of the mermaids expose their genitals, like the *sheila-na-gig* figure, which again fuses sacred and profane, spiritual and sexual, desire and fear.[3] The mermaid appears in much of Victorian art, as an image of men's ambivalent views of female sexuality – in E.M. Hale's *Mermaid's Rock* (1894), for instance, or John William Waterhouse's Pre-Raphaelite *A Mermaid* (1901).[4]

---

1 Michelangelo: *Temptation and Expulsion*, 1508-12, fresco, Sistine Chapel, Vatican, Rome
2 See the depiction of the Mary Magdalene in the wilderness sequence of Universal's film *The Last Temptation of Christ* (1988, USA)
3 See Anthony Weir & James Jerman: *Images of Lust: Sexual Carvings on Mediæval Churches*, B. T. Batsford, 1986, 48ff
4 John William Waterhouse: *A Mermaid*, 1901, 38.5 x 36.3in, Royal Academy of Arts, London; Edward Matthew Hale: *Mermaid's Rock*, 1894, 48 x 78in, City Art Gallery, Leeds

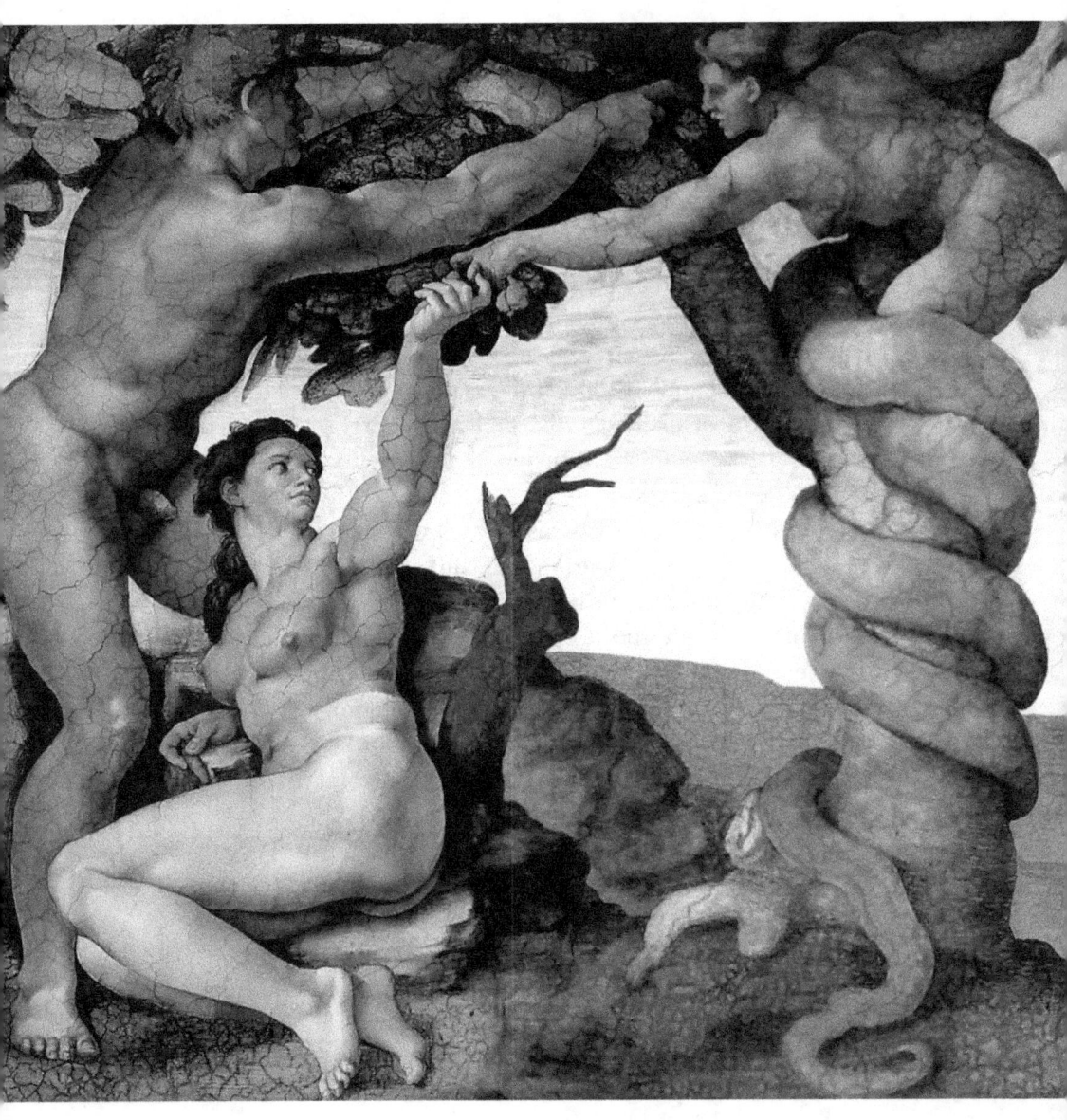

Michelangelo Buonarroti, from The Last Judgement, Rome

LEONARDO DA VINCI

The most erotic artist of the Renaissance, the one who created the darkest and the strangest images, who created the most hypnotic smile in art, who took Western painting to the highest point it has reached, was not Michelangelo Buonarroti, Andrea del Sarto, Fra Angelico, Sandro Botticelli, Piero della Francesca, Andreas Mantegna, Giovanni Bellini, Raphael Sanzio, Titian, Caravaggio, Simone Martini, Fra Bartolommeo, Lucas Cranach or Masaccio, but Leonardo da Vinci.

Leonardo da Vinci is one of the most celebrated of artists, he's perhaps the most exalted artist in the West. He is the artist-as-hero, the artist-as-genius, undisputed genius (like William Shakespeare or Sophocles). Leonardo is enshrined for his amazing mind, his scientific curiosity, his ideas on botany, anatomy, architecture, weaponry, engineering, etc. But it is Leonardo's *sfumato* painterly technique, his brilliant manipulation of oil colours, that makes him so profoundly erotic. Stendhal wrote of Leonardo's 'soft, melancholy tones, full of shadows'.[1] The most common adjective applied to Leonardo's art is 'mysterious'. Walter Pater wrote famously of the *Mona Lisa*, in a way which says more about Pater and late Victorian and Decadent art than it does about Leonardo:

> She is older than the rocks among which she sits... [she embodies] the animalism of Greece, the lust of Rome, the mysticism of the Middle Ages with its spiritual ambition and imaginative loves, the return of the pagan world, the sins of the Borgias.[2]

1 Stendhal: *Histoire de la peinture en Italie*, 1877
2 Walter Pater: *The Renaissance*, Fontana 1964, 123

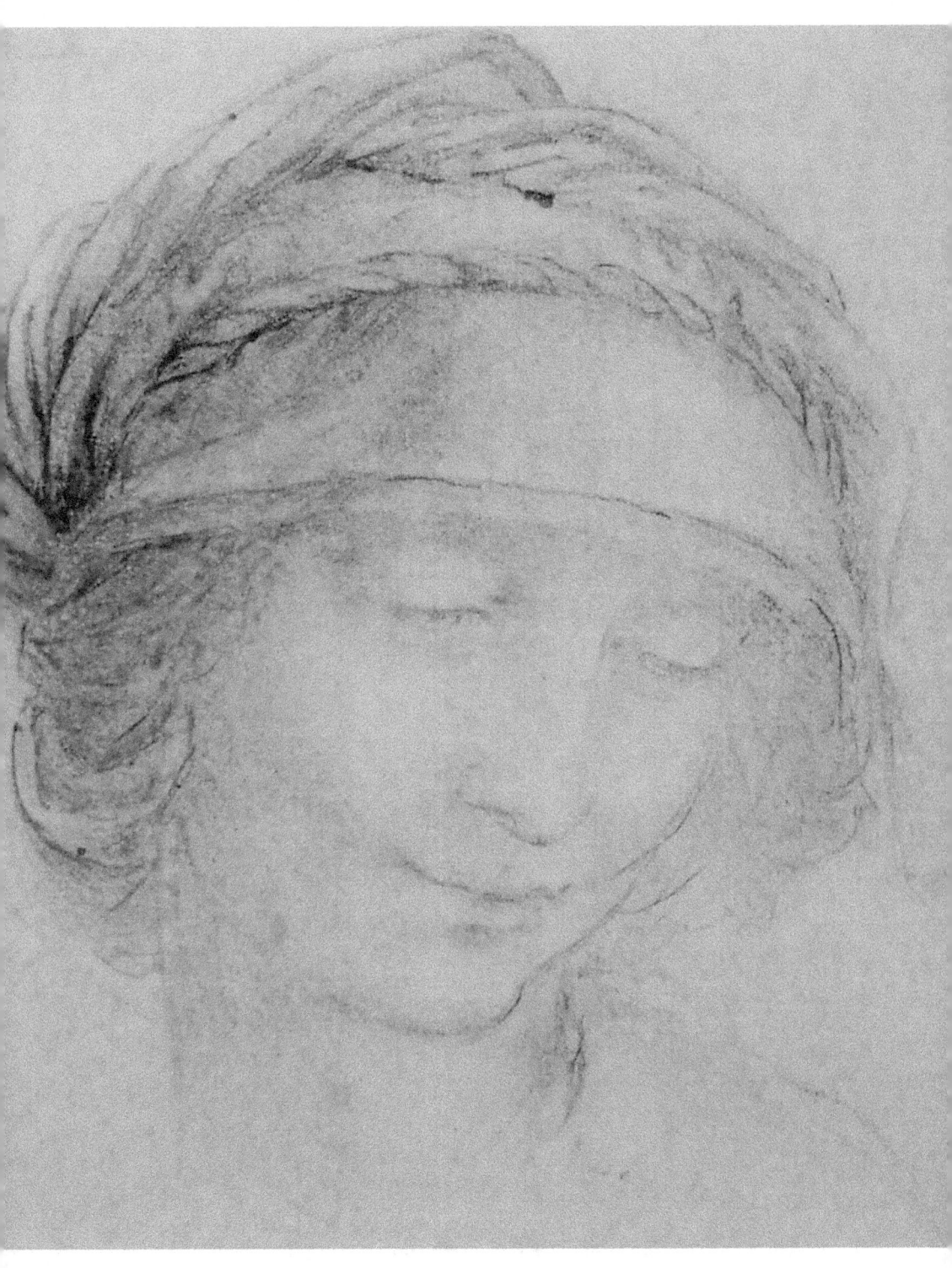

Leonardo, Study for The Virgin and Child With St Anne

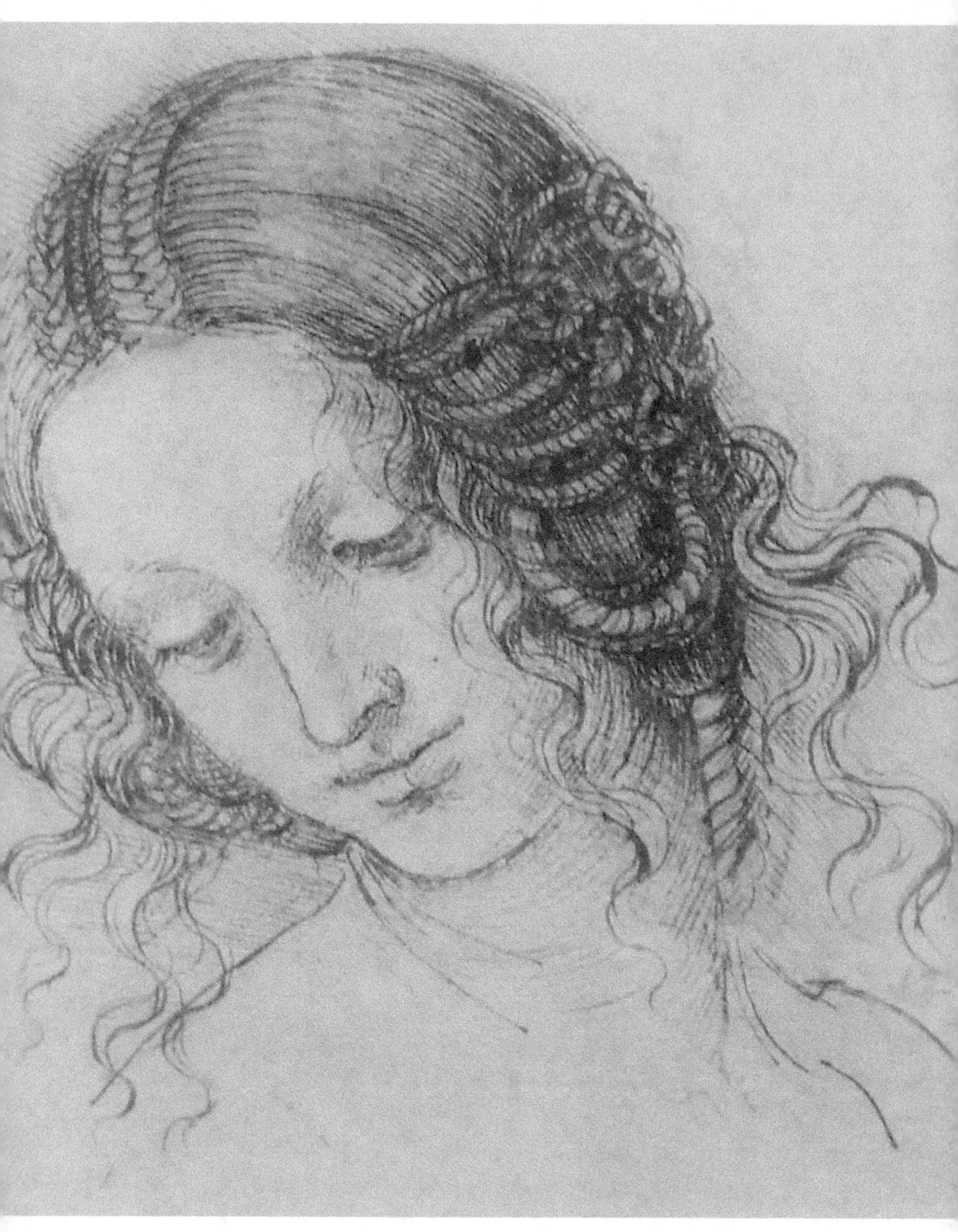

Leonardo, Study For the Leda and the Swan

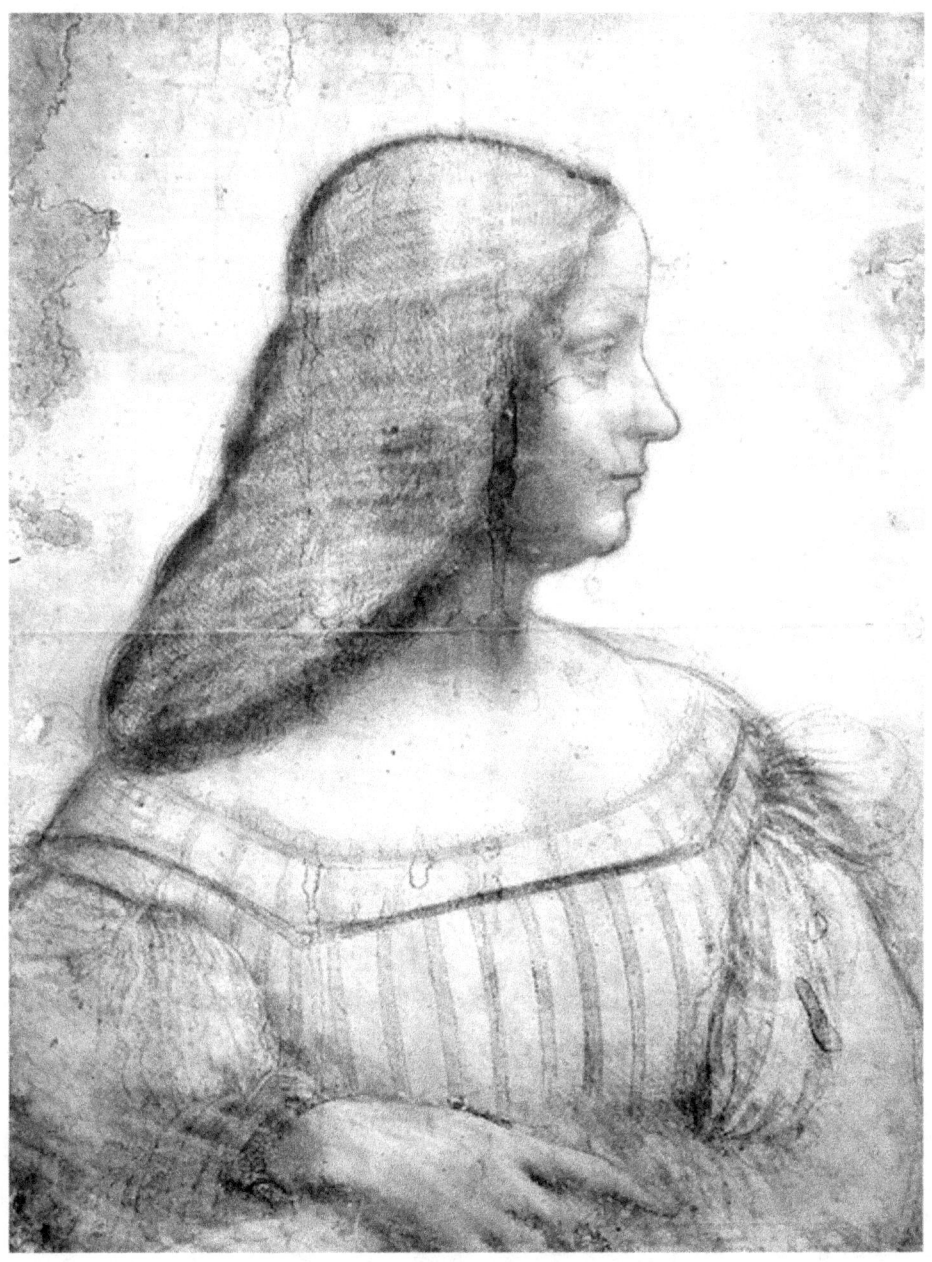

Leonardo da Vinci, Isabella d'Este, 1500, Louvre, Paris

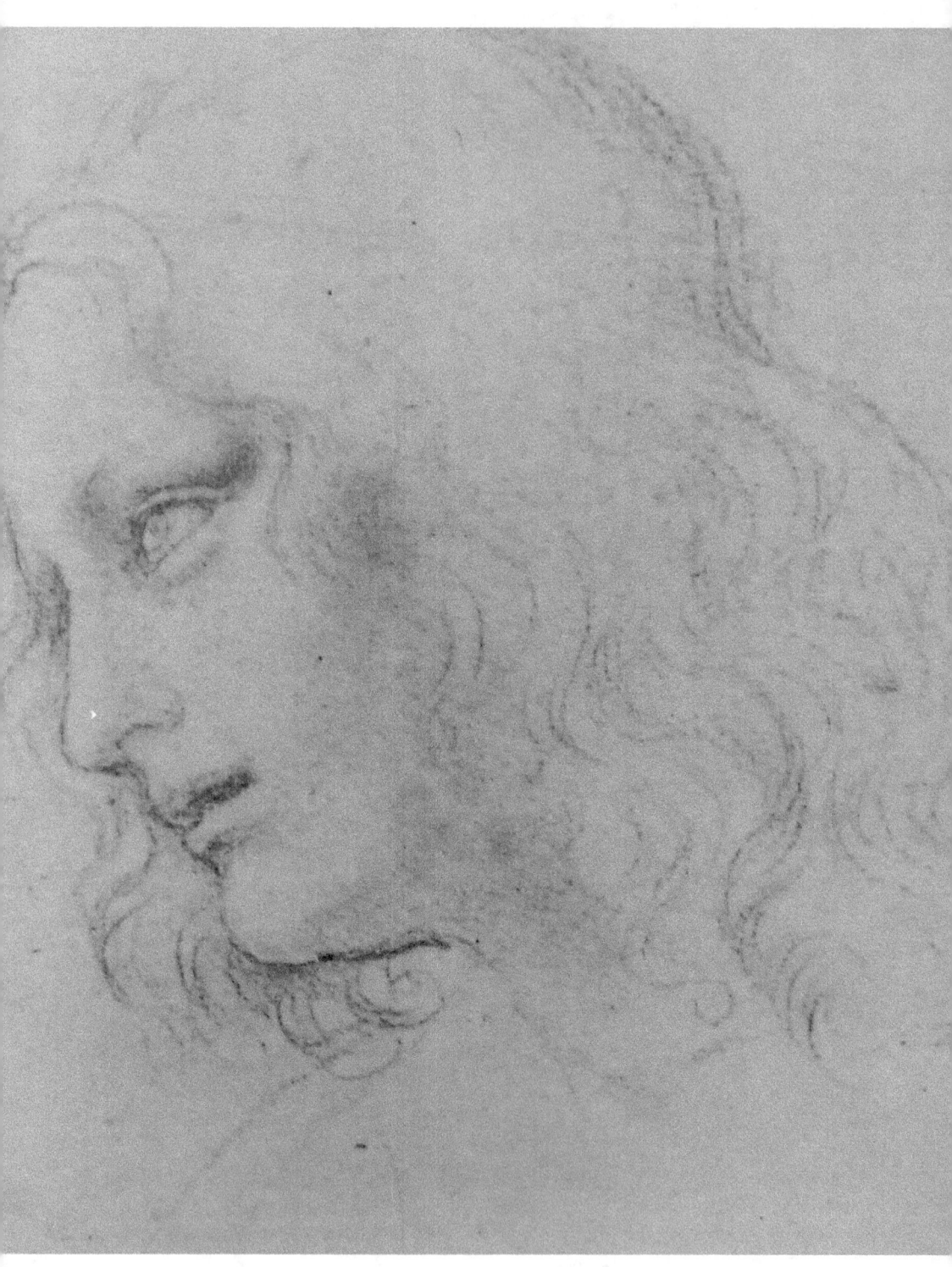

Leonardo, study for The Last Supper

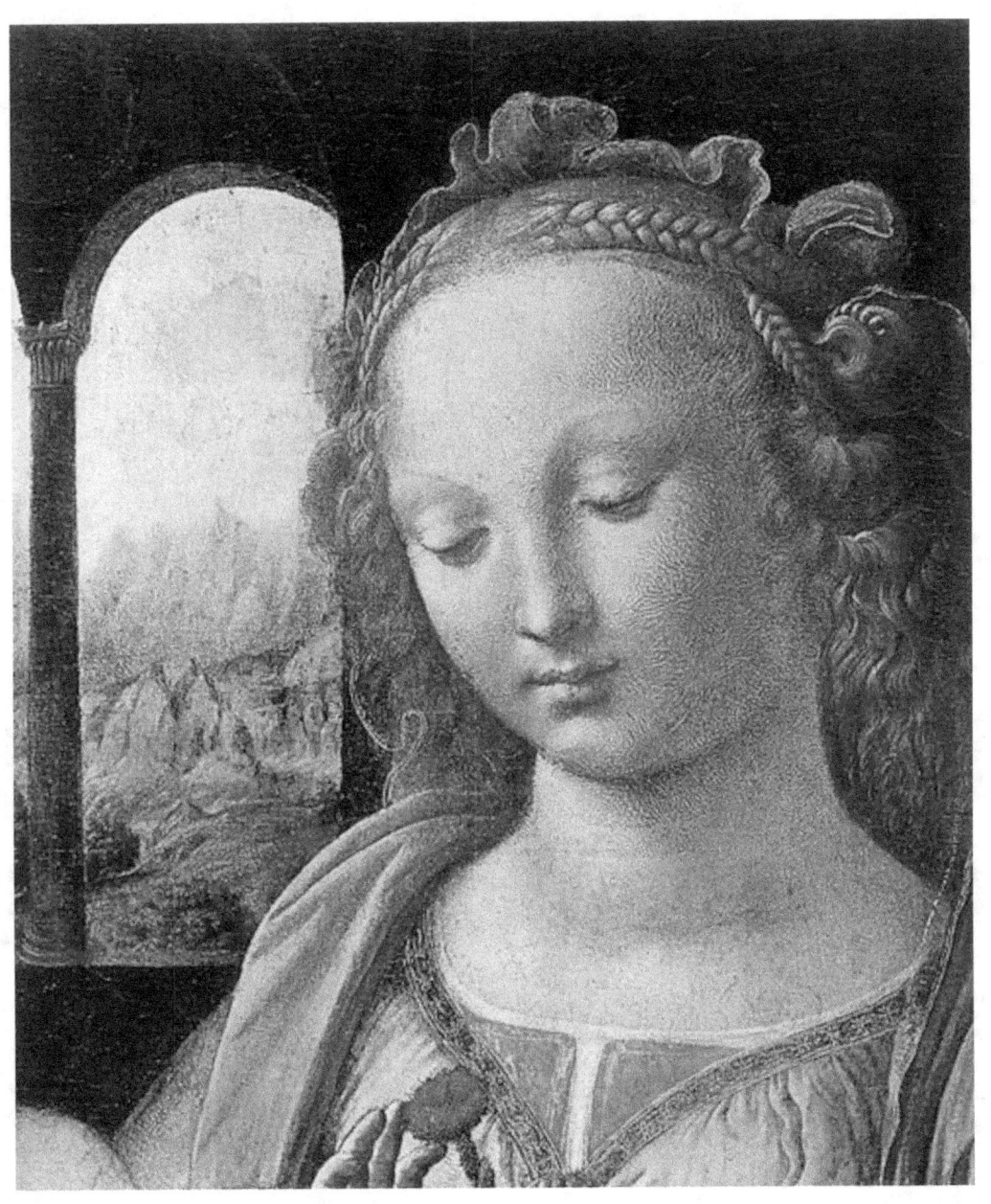

Leonardo da Vinci, Madonna of the Carnation, detail

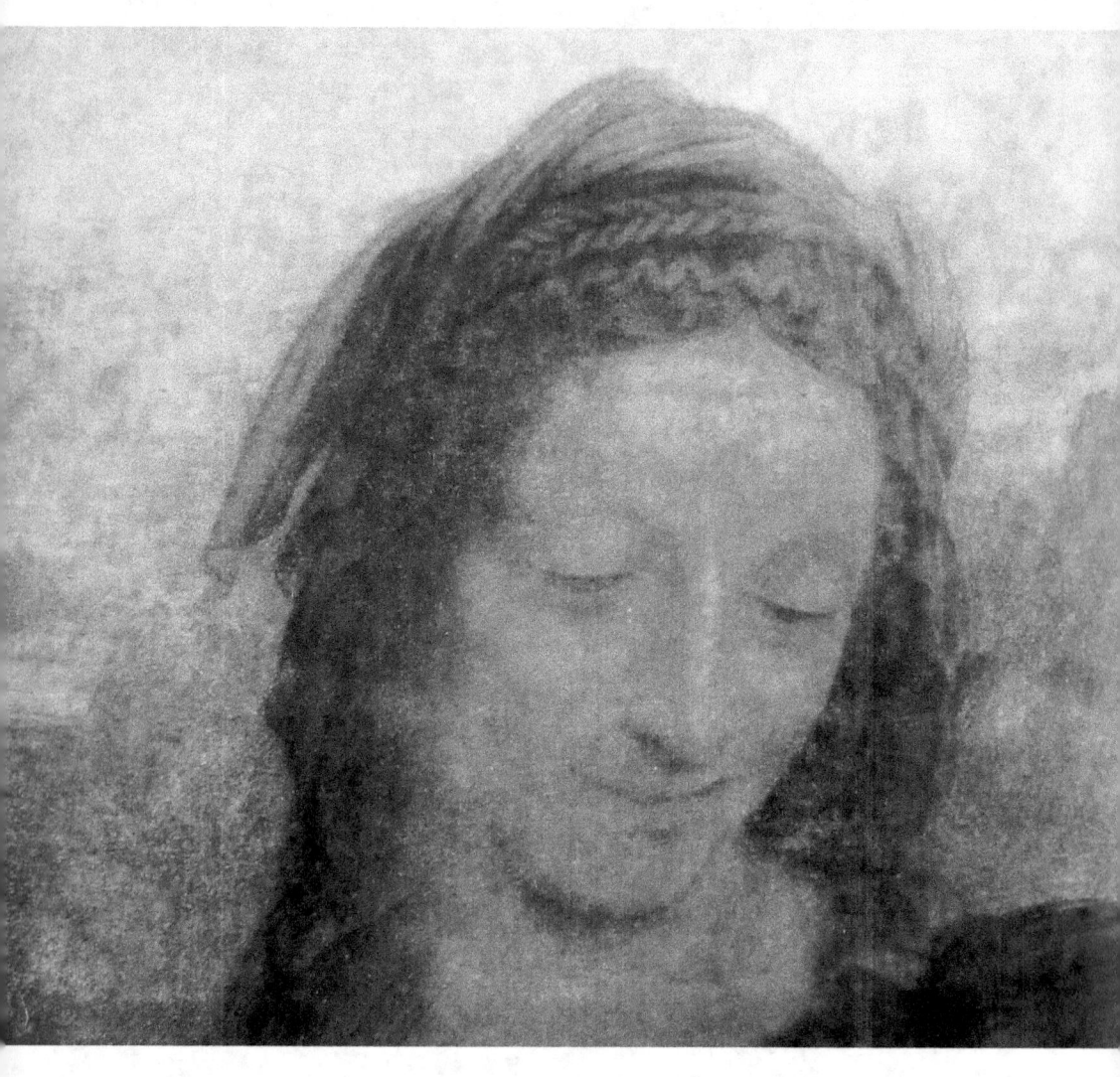

Leonardo da Vinci, Head of St Anne, from The Virgin and Child With St Anne,
Louvre Museum

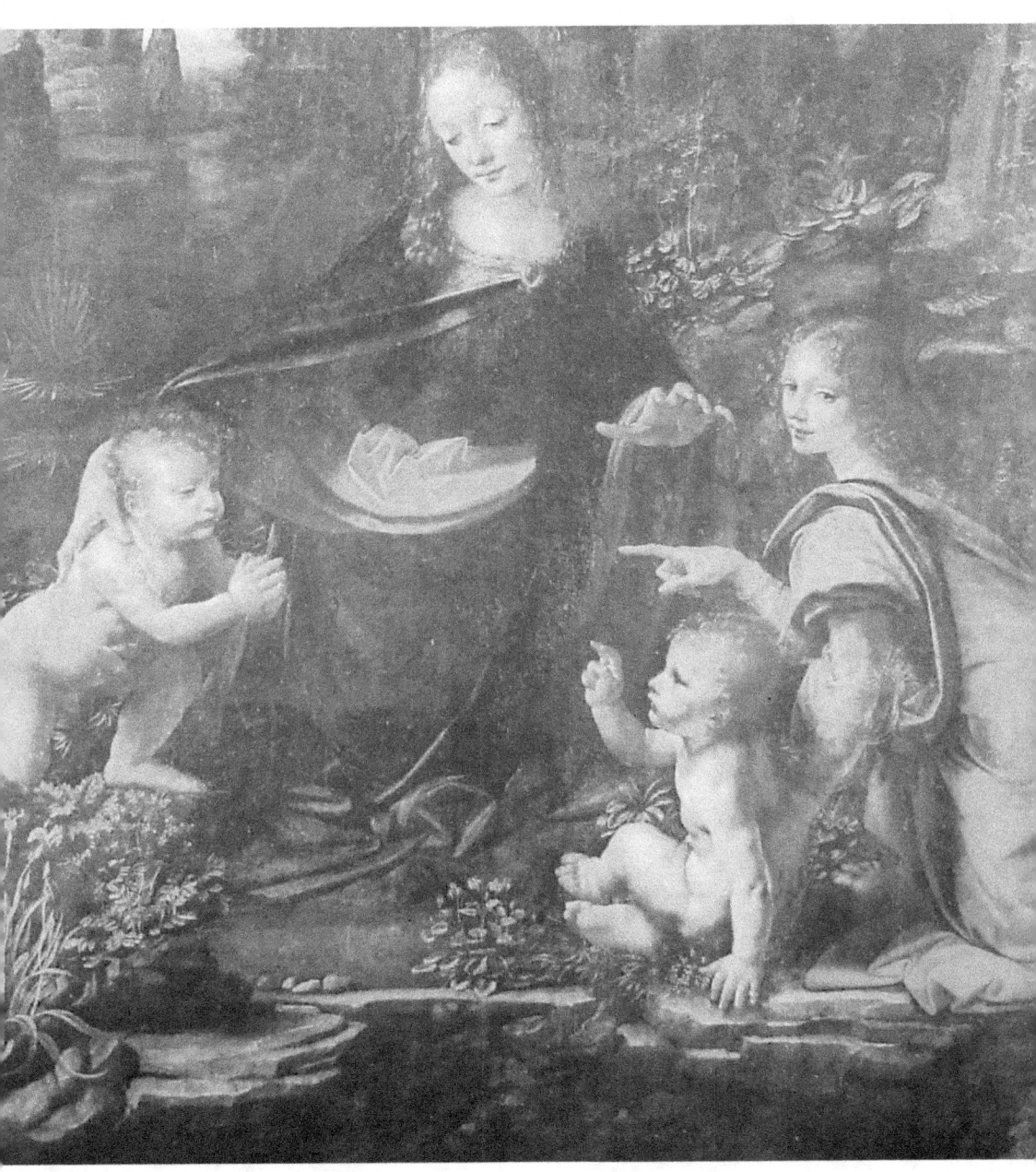

Leonardo, The Virgin of the Rocks, detail, Louvre, Paris

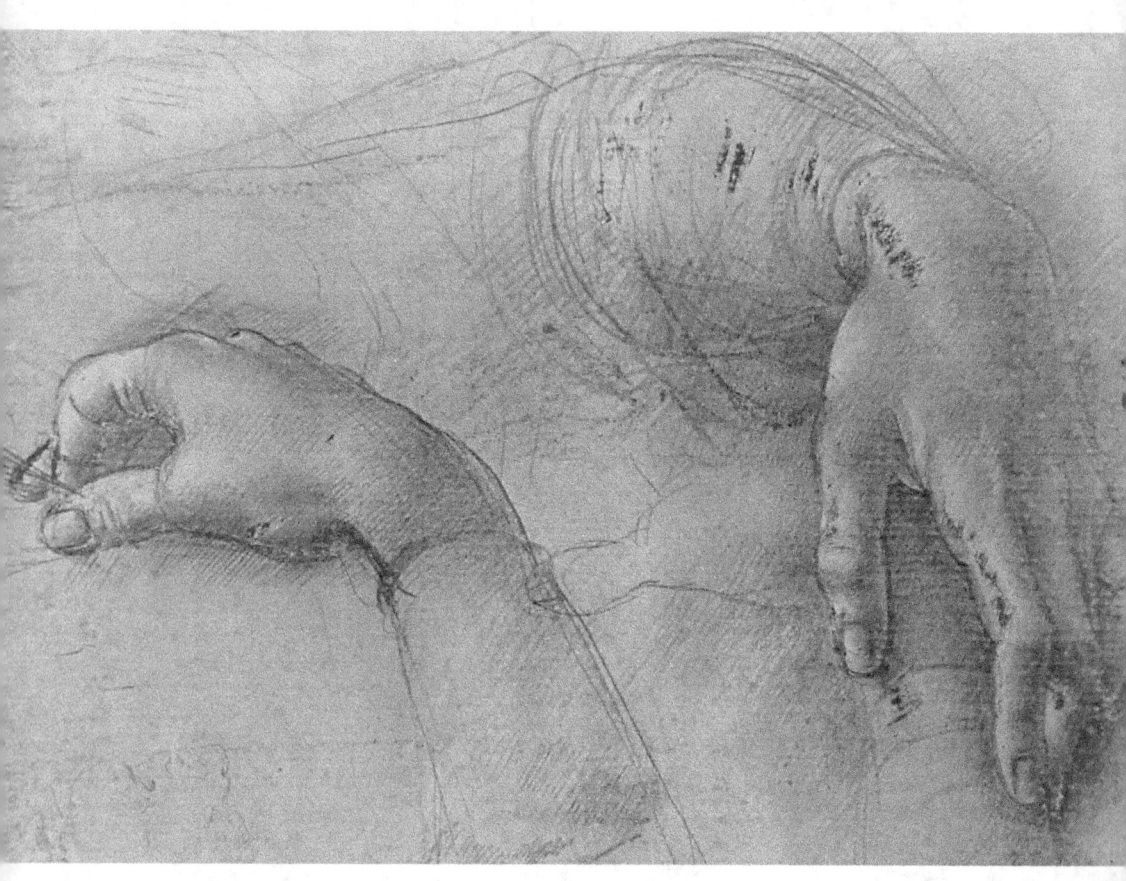

Leonardo, study of hands, Royal Collection, Windsor

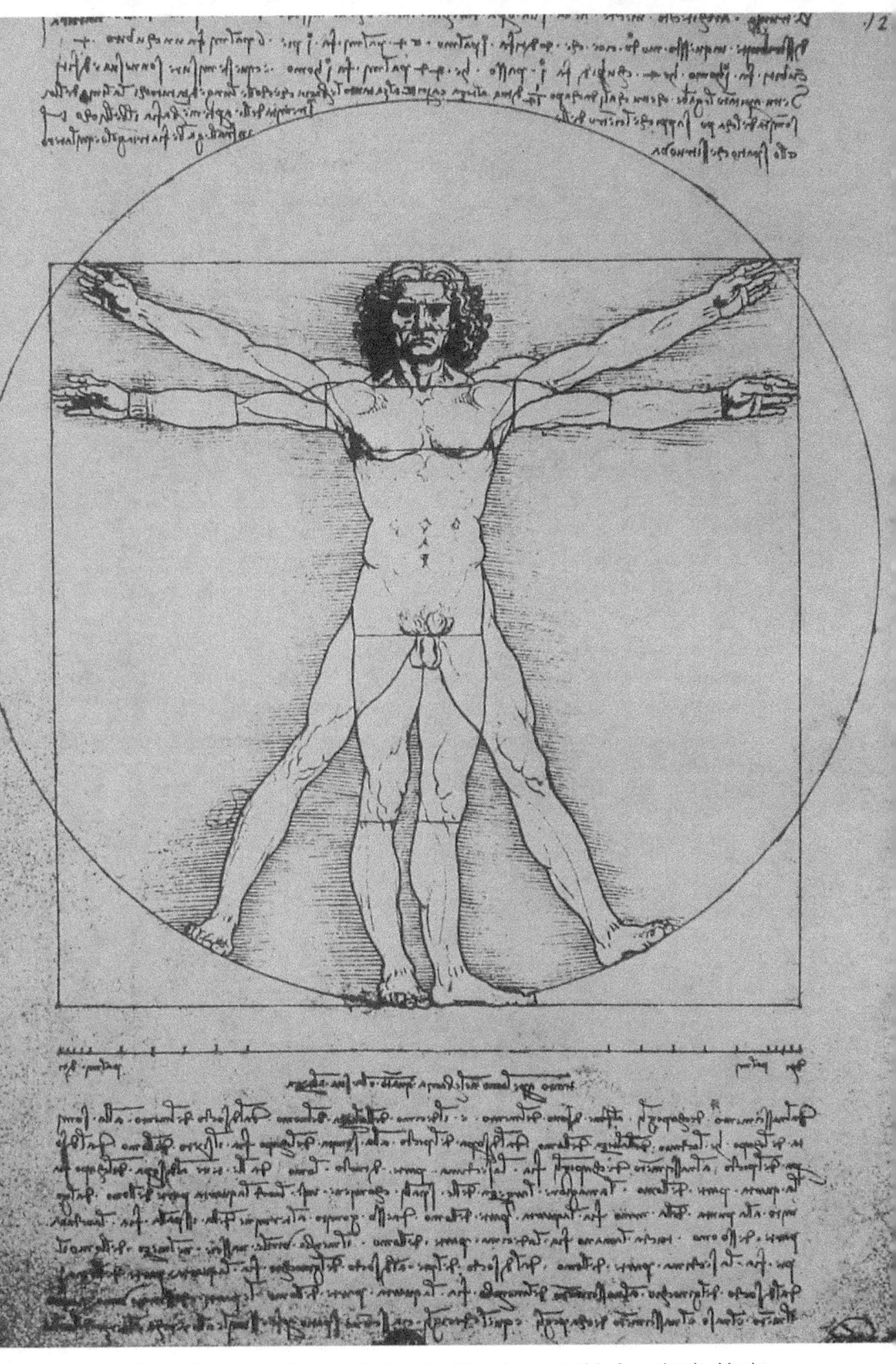

Leonardo, Proportions of the Human Body, after Vitruvius, c. 1492, Accademia, Venice.

FRANCISCO DE ZURBARÁN

Francisco de Zurbarán (1598-1664) was one of the central group of Spanish painters who formed the 'Golden Age' of Spanish painting (the others were El Greco, Diego Velásquez and Giuseppe de Ribera). Zurbarán's motifs included (aside from the usual Christian iconography of *Pietàs* and the like), monks in shadowy hoods and habits, and saints in meditation. Zurbarán's art is full of depictions of a devout Catholicism.

Francisco de Zurbarán's art is marked by the high contrast kind of lighting one finds in the art of Michelangelo Merisi de Caravaggio. Zurbarán, who lived in Seville, had never seen a Caravaggio painting in the flesh, but knew of Caravaggio's paintings from copies. As with Caravaggio's painting, Zurbarán's art aimed for a heightened realism, in which every detail of a person's clothing, for example, would be rendered sharply. The drive towards increased realism derived from the Church's demands: in the Counter-Reformation, 'extreme "spirituality" lay in extreme realism' (R. Hughes, 1990, 66).

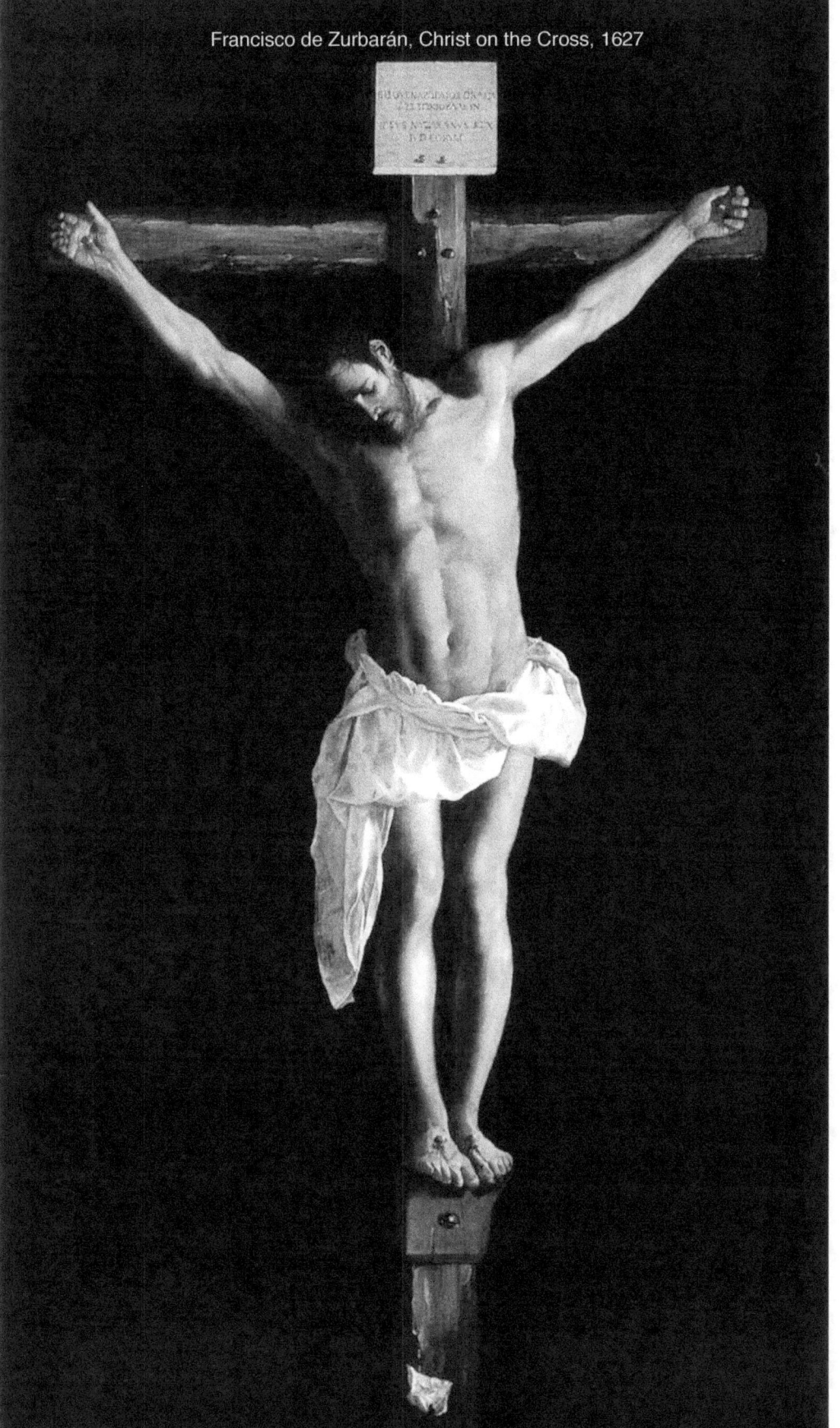

Francisco de Zurbarán, Christ on the Cross, 1627

GUILIO ROMANO

The sexploits of phallic deities such as Zeus/ Jupiter, whether he's chasing Leda as a swan or impregnating Danae as a golden shower, provide many opportunities for artists to make erotic art which is justifiably 'noble' because it comes from Classic mythology. It also means that sex with beasts can be depicted legitimately. Thus, one finds Guilio Romano depicting Jupiter with an erect penis about to tup Olympia.[1]

1 Guilio Romano: *Jupiter and Olympia*, 1525-35, Mansell Collection, London

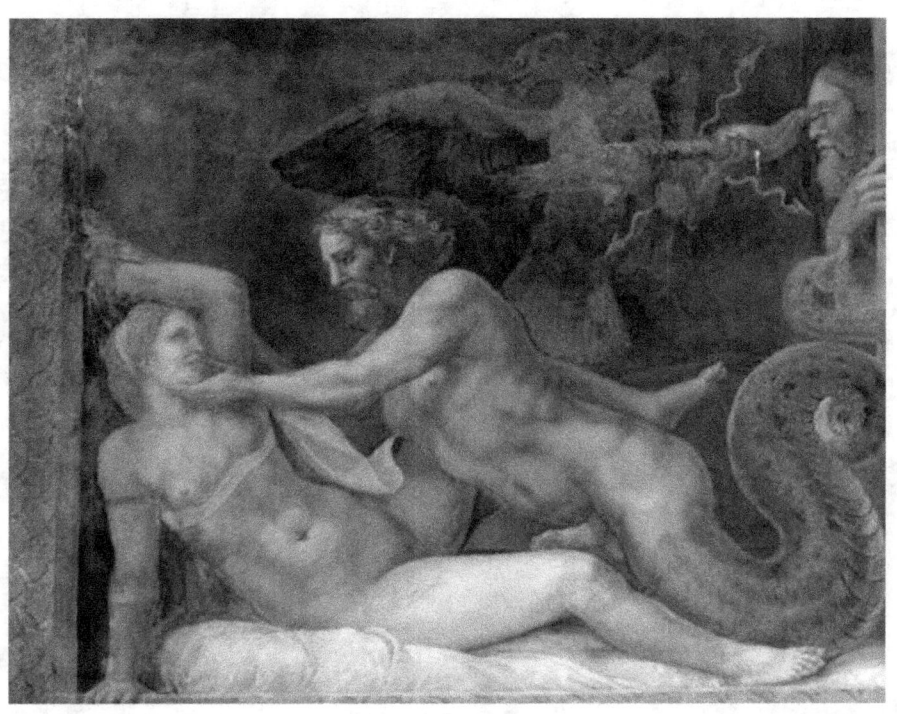

Giulio Pippi, a.k.a Giulio Romano

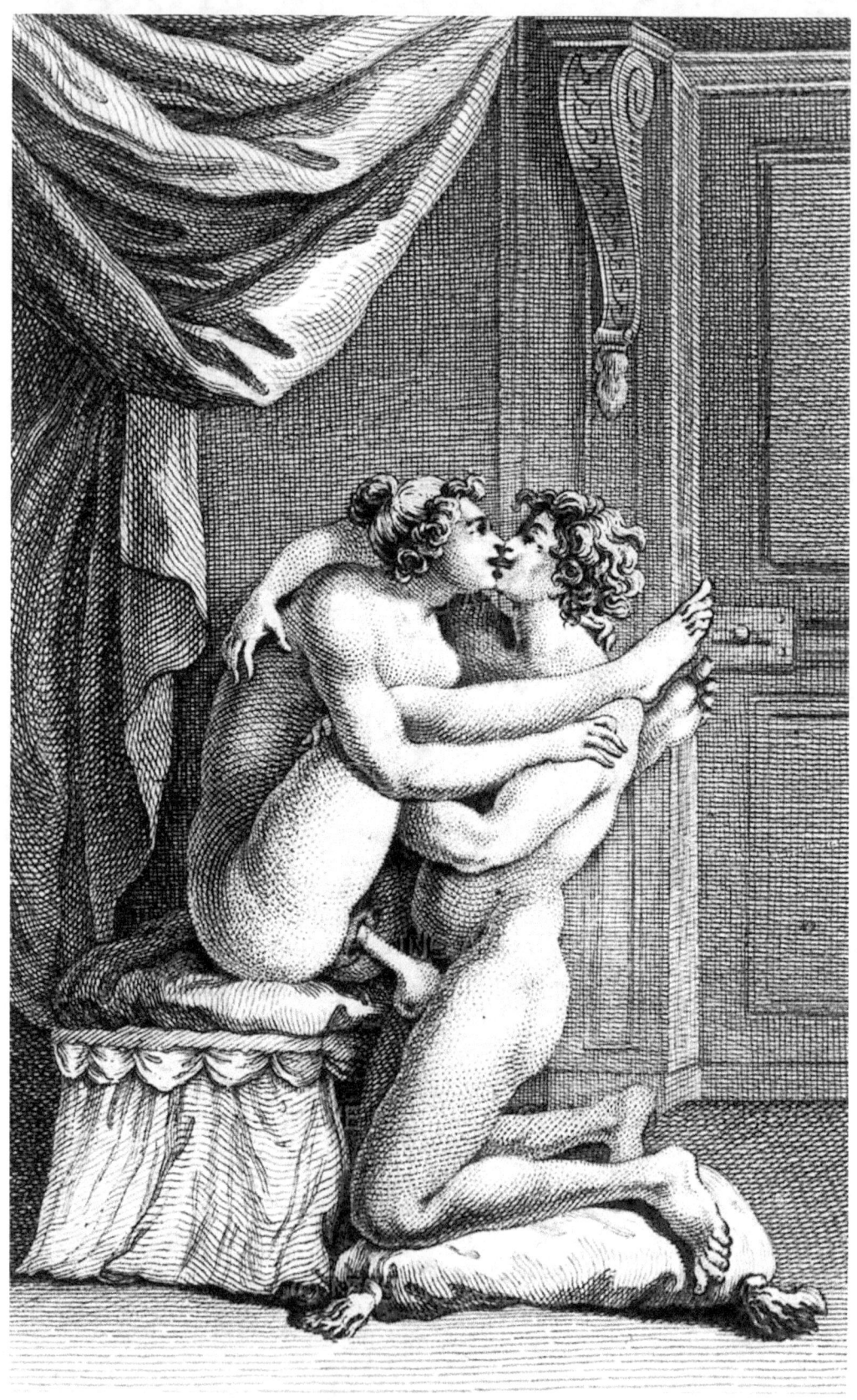

After Guilio Roman, 18th century

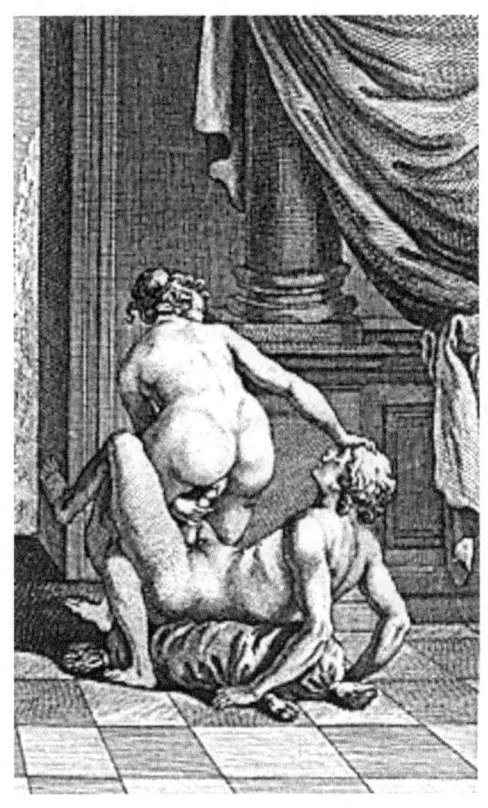

After Giulio Romano and Marcantonio Raimondi,
I Modi, 1524/ 27

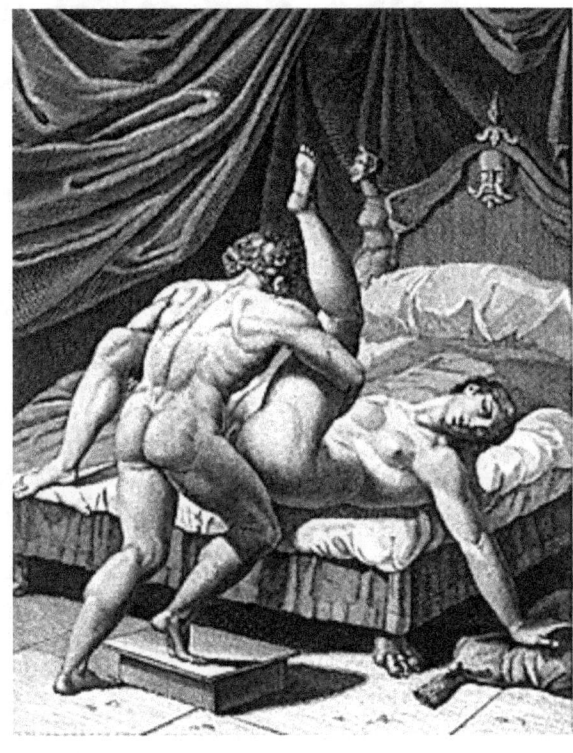

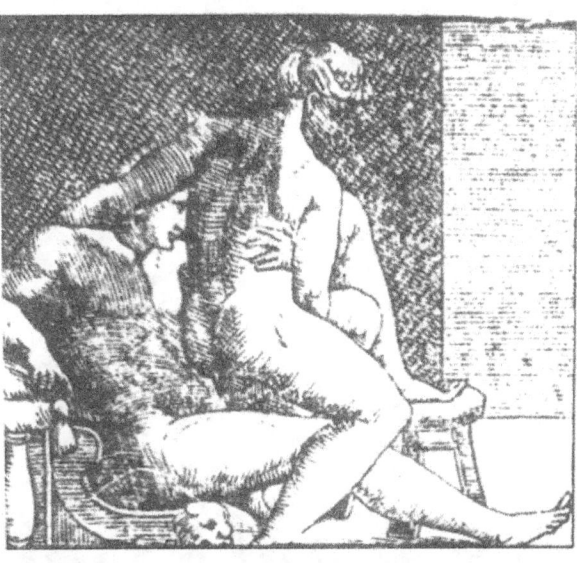

AGOSTINO CARRACCI: *THE WAYS*

The *I Modi* (*The Ways*) by Agostino Carracci is a celebrated 16th century collection of Italian Renaissance erotica. It has been much copied and pirated. It's a kind of Western, Renaissance version of the *Kama Sutra*. There's no denying the imagination and skill of the drawing on display here.

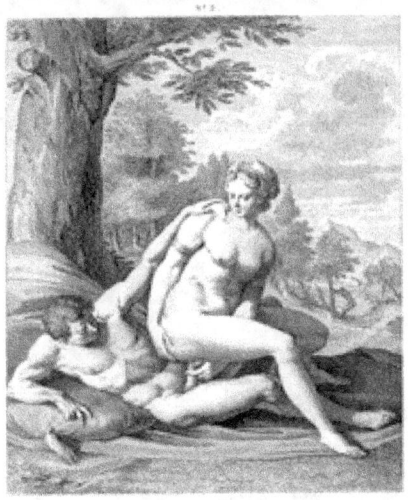

ANGÉLIQUE ET MEDOR.

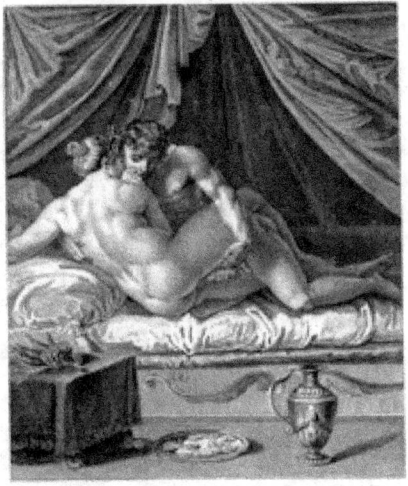

ANTOINE ET CLÉOPATRE.

Jacques Joseph Coiny, after Agostino Caracci,
I Modi, 1524, and Pietro Aretino

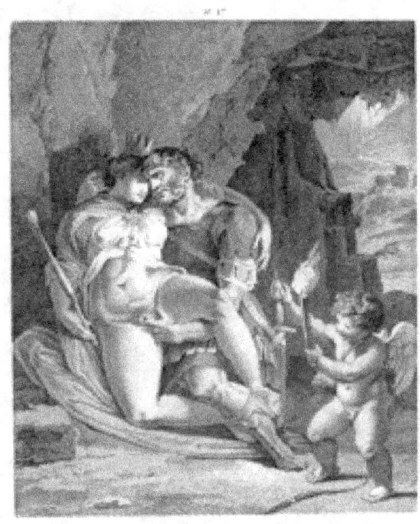

ENÉE ET DIDON.

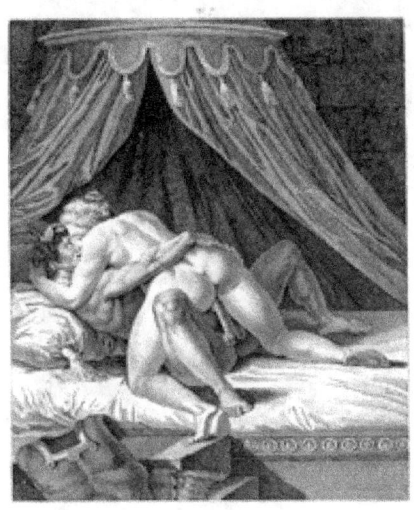

MARS ET VENUS.

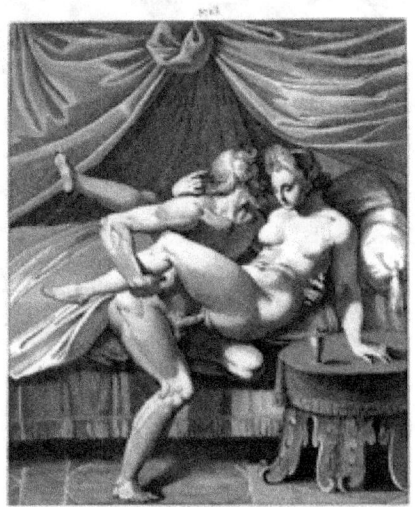

JUPITER ET JUNON.

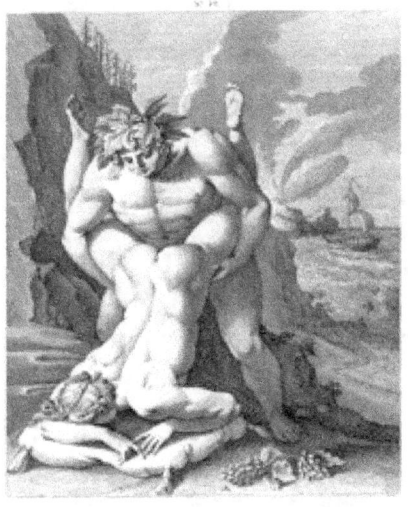

BACHUS ET ARIANE.

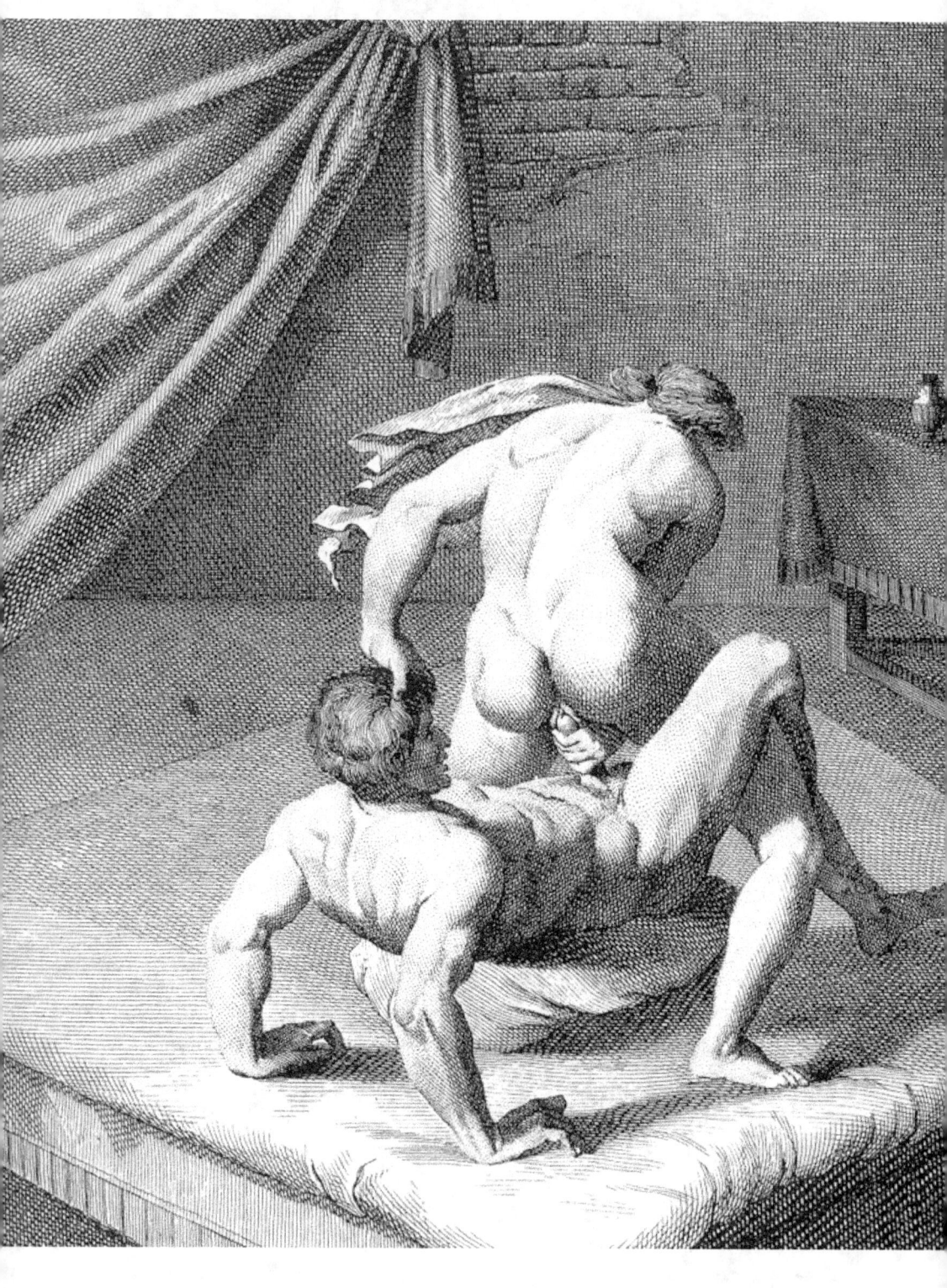

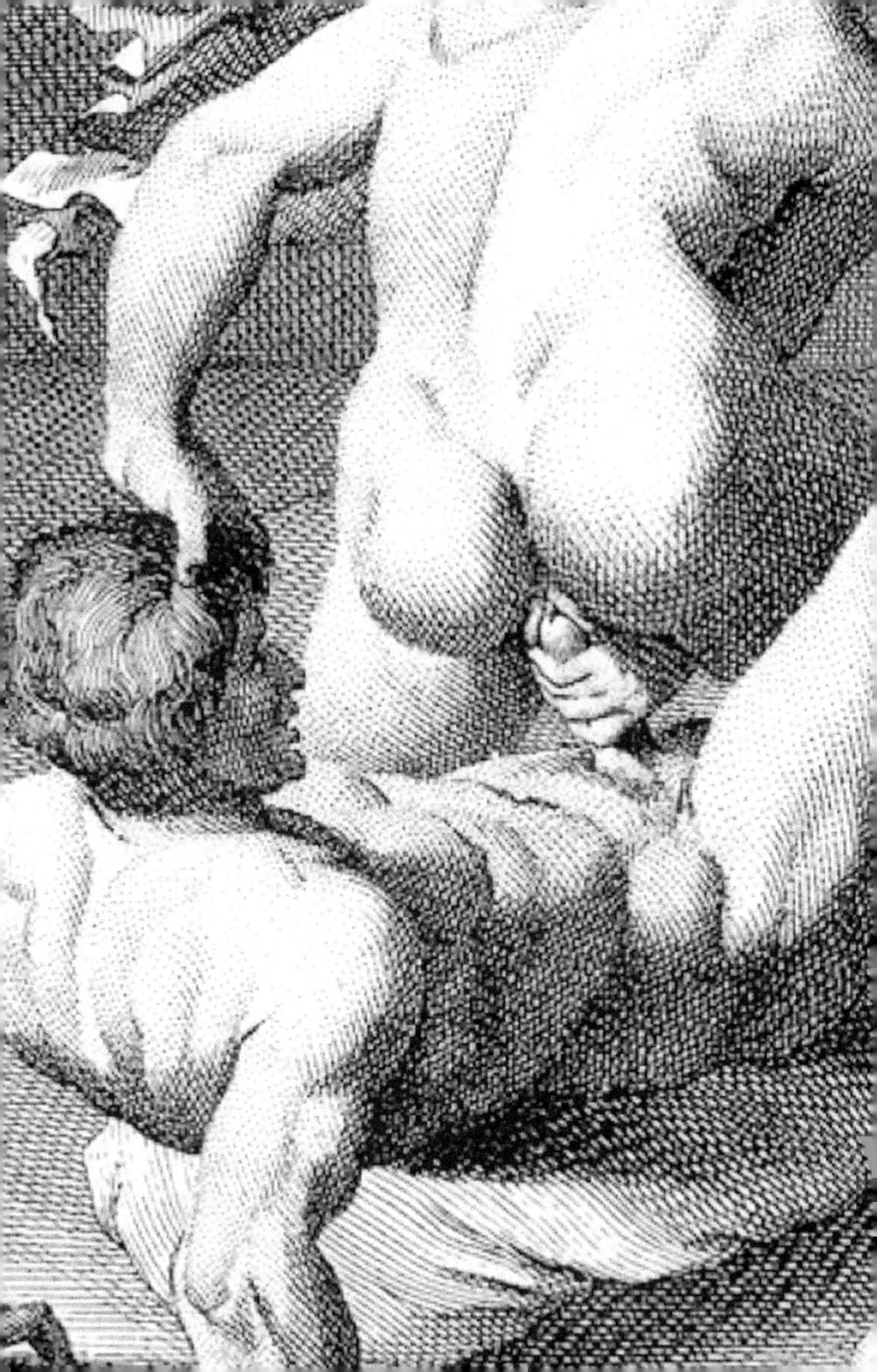

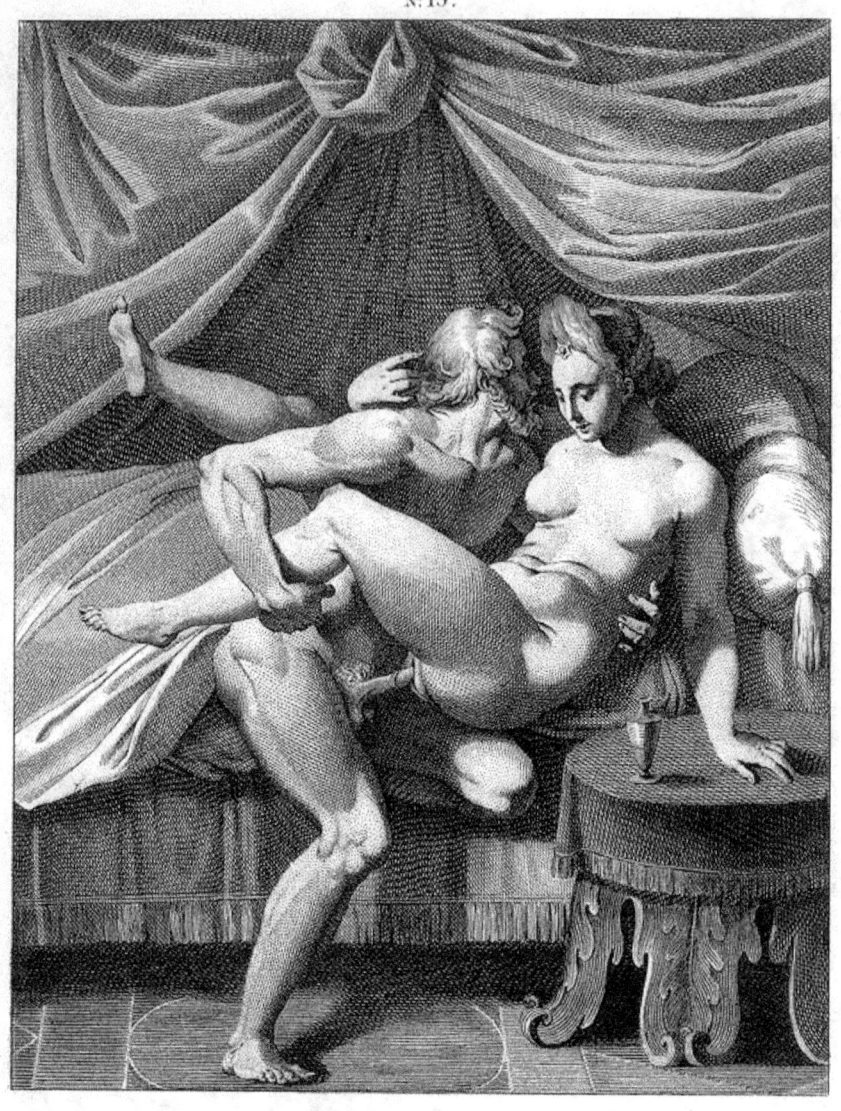

JUPITER ET JUNON

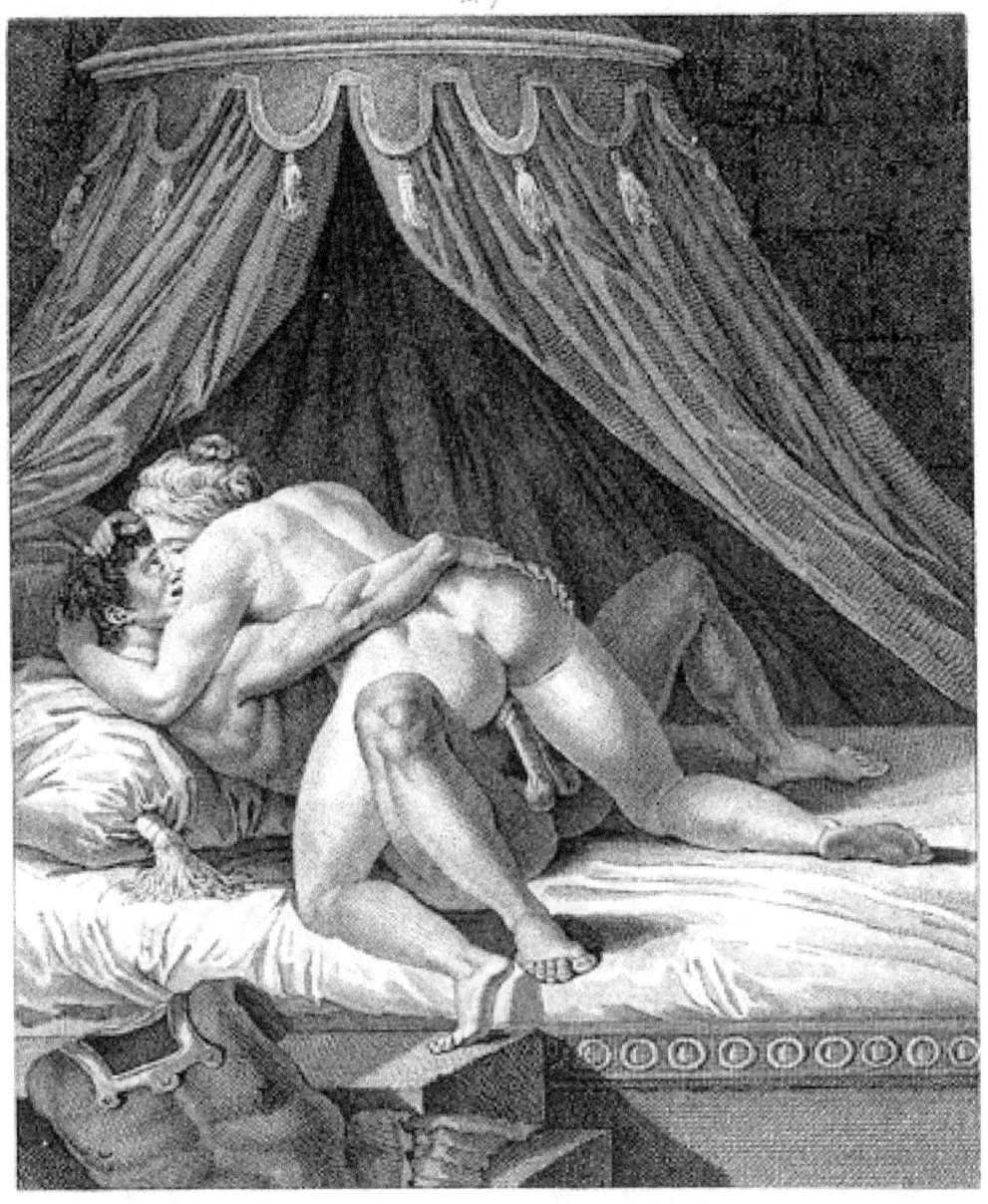

MARS ET VENUS

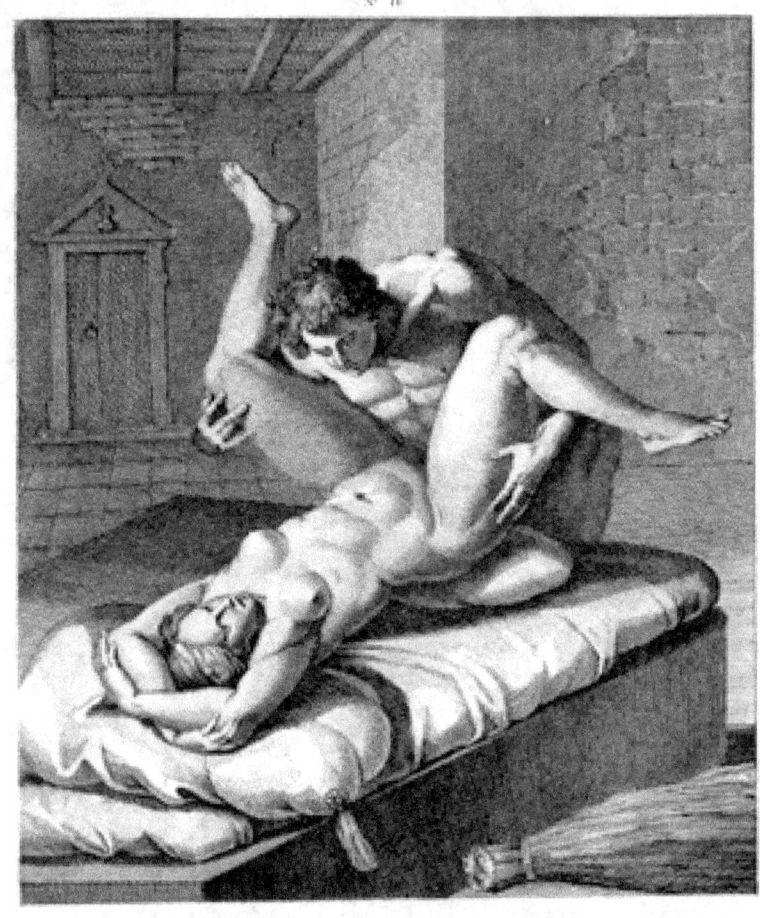

POLYENOS ET CHRISIS

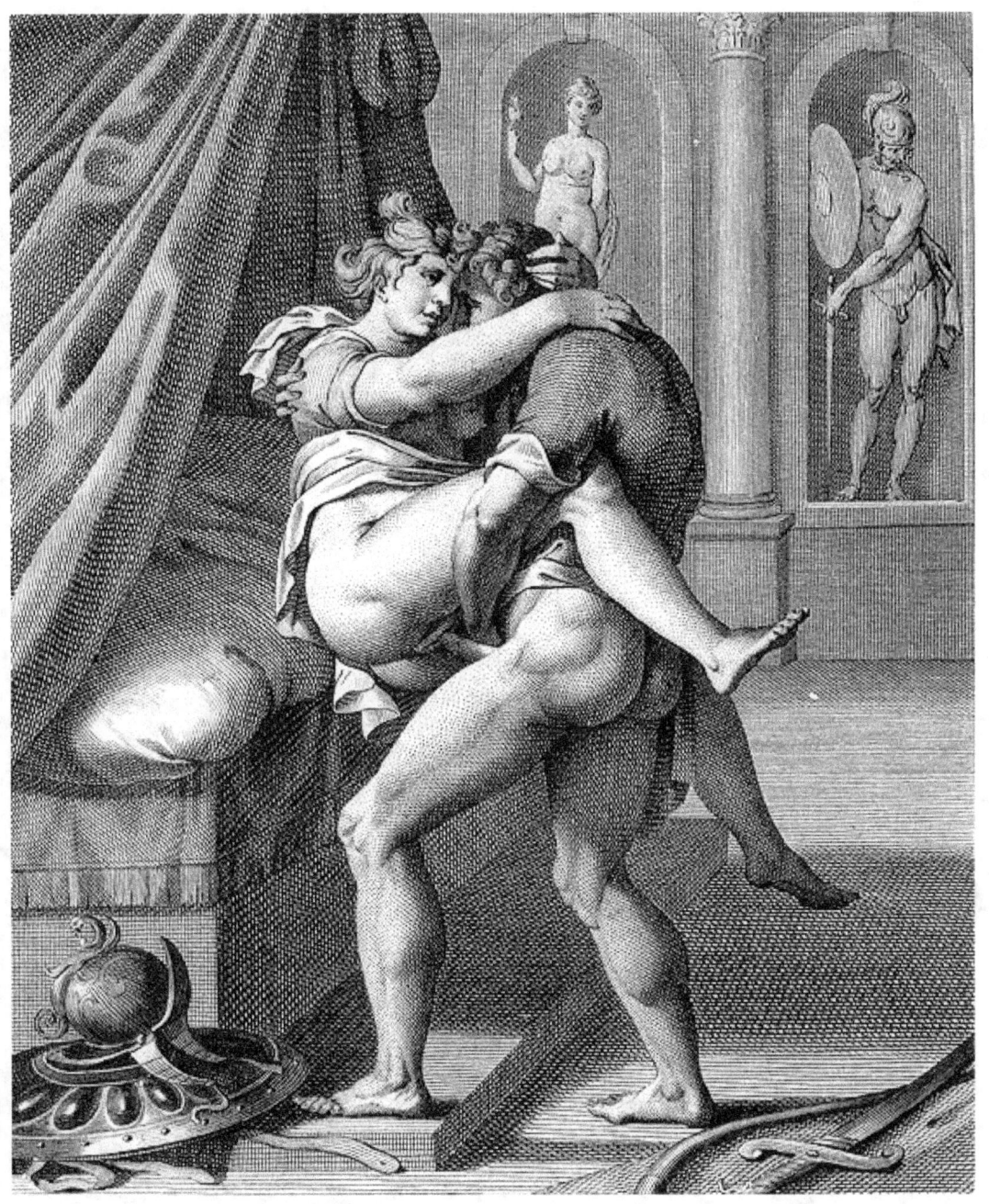

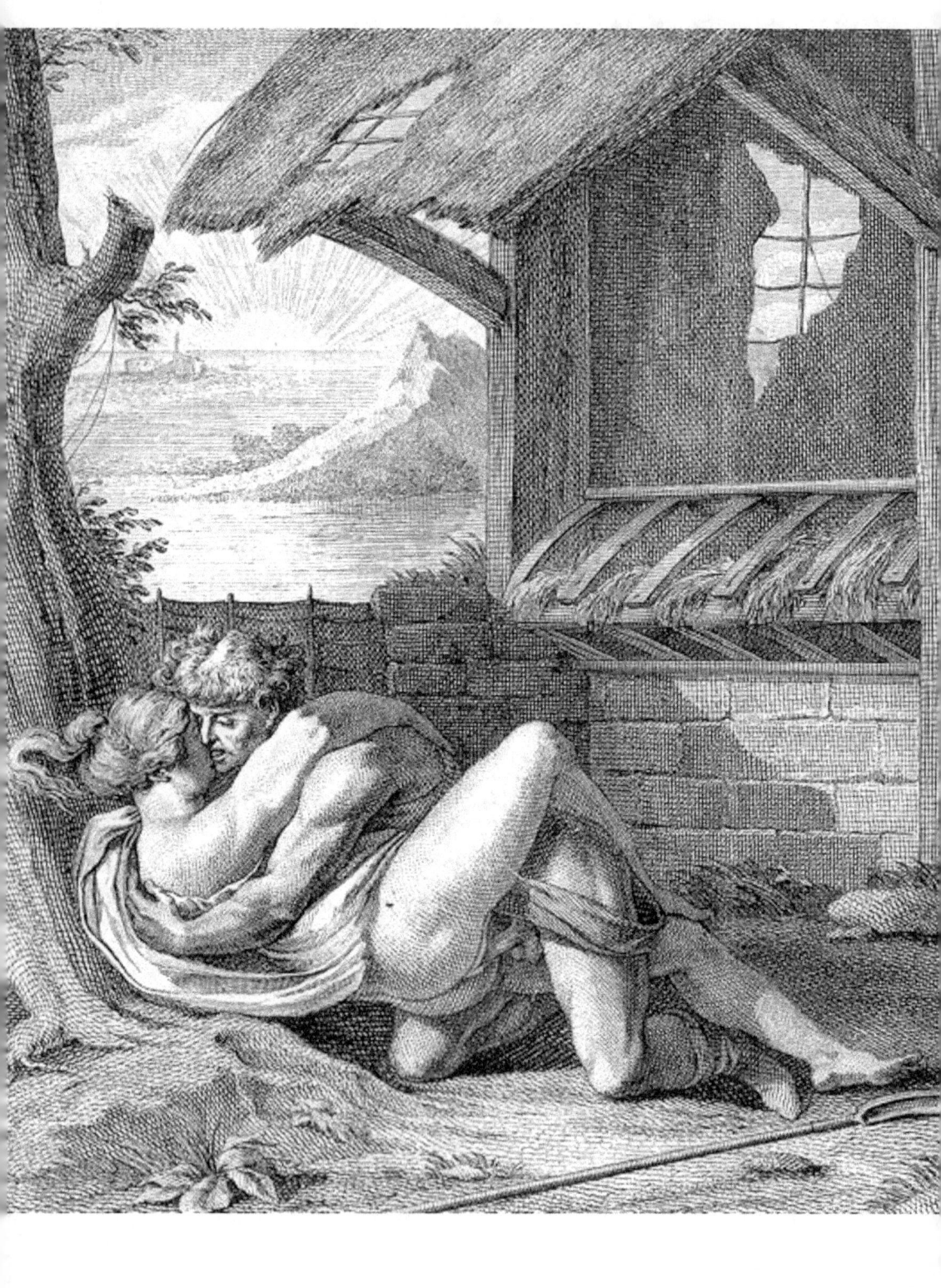

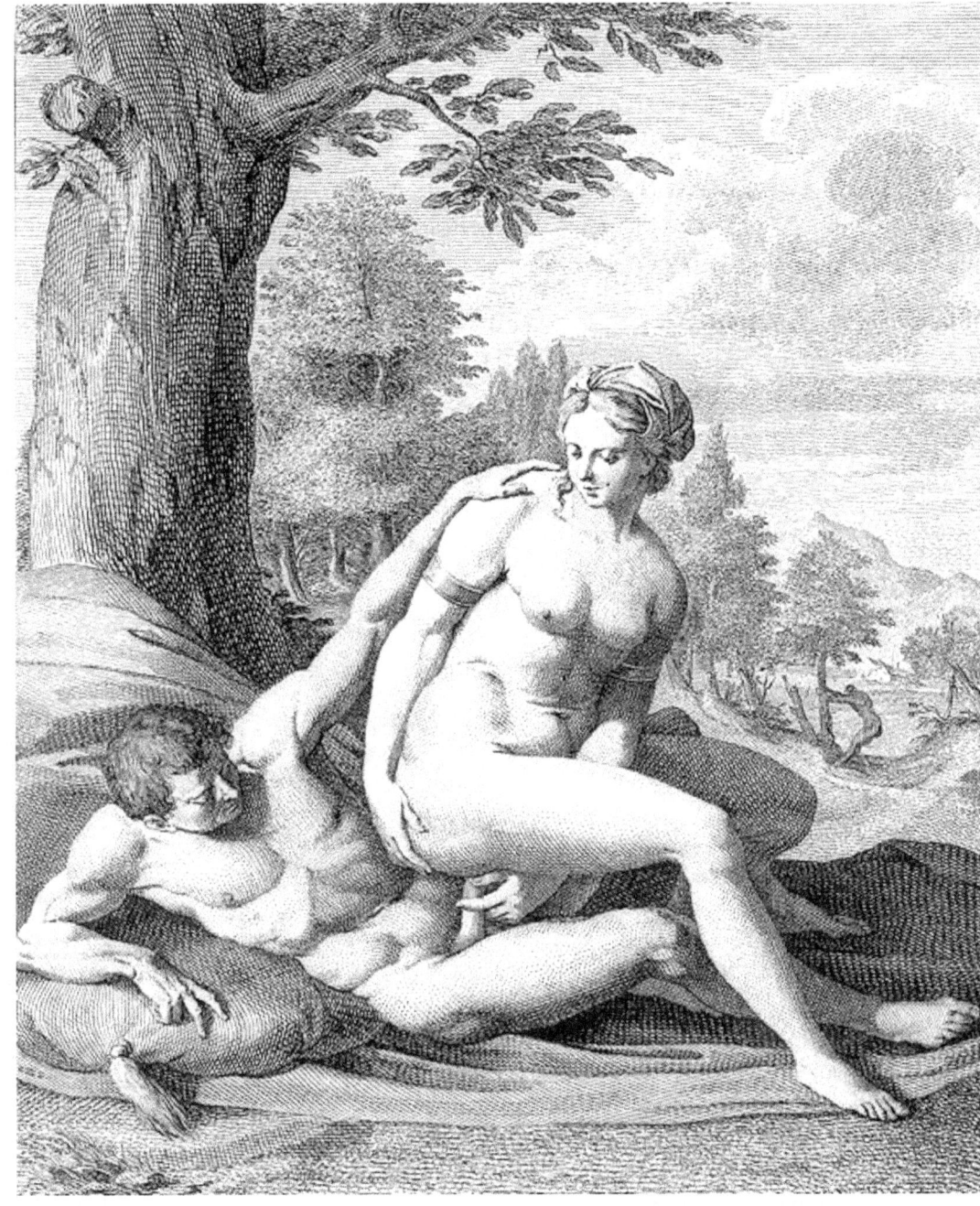

GIOVANNI LORENZO BERNINI

One of many ecstasies in Christian mysticism, of St Theresa, was the subject of Giovanni Lorenzo Bernini's famous 1640s statue.[1] More than a few commentators have noted that Bernini's saint is in orgasm. Jacques Lacan writes that 'you only have to go and look at the Bernini statue in Rome to understand immediately she (St Teresa) is coming'.[2]

1 Giovanni Lorenzo Bernini: *The Ecstasy of St Theresa*, 1645-52, S. Maria della Vittoria, Rome
2 Jacques Lacan in *Feminine Sexuality*; also Mervyn Levy, 32; also Président des Brosses, quoted in Howard Hibbard: *Bernini*, 1965, 241-2: 'If this is divine love, I know what it is'

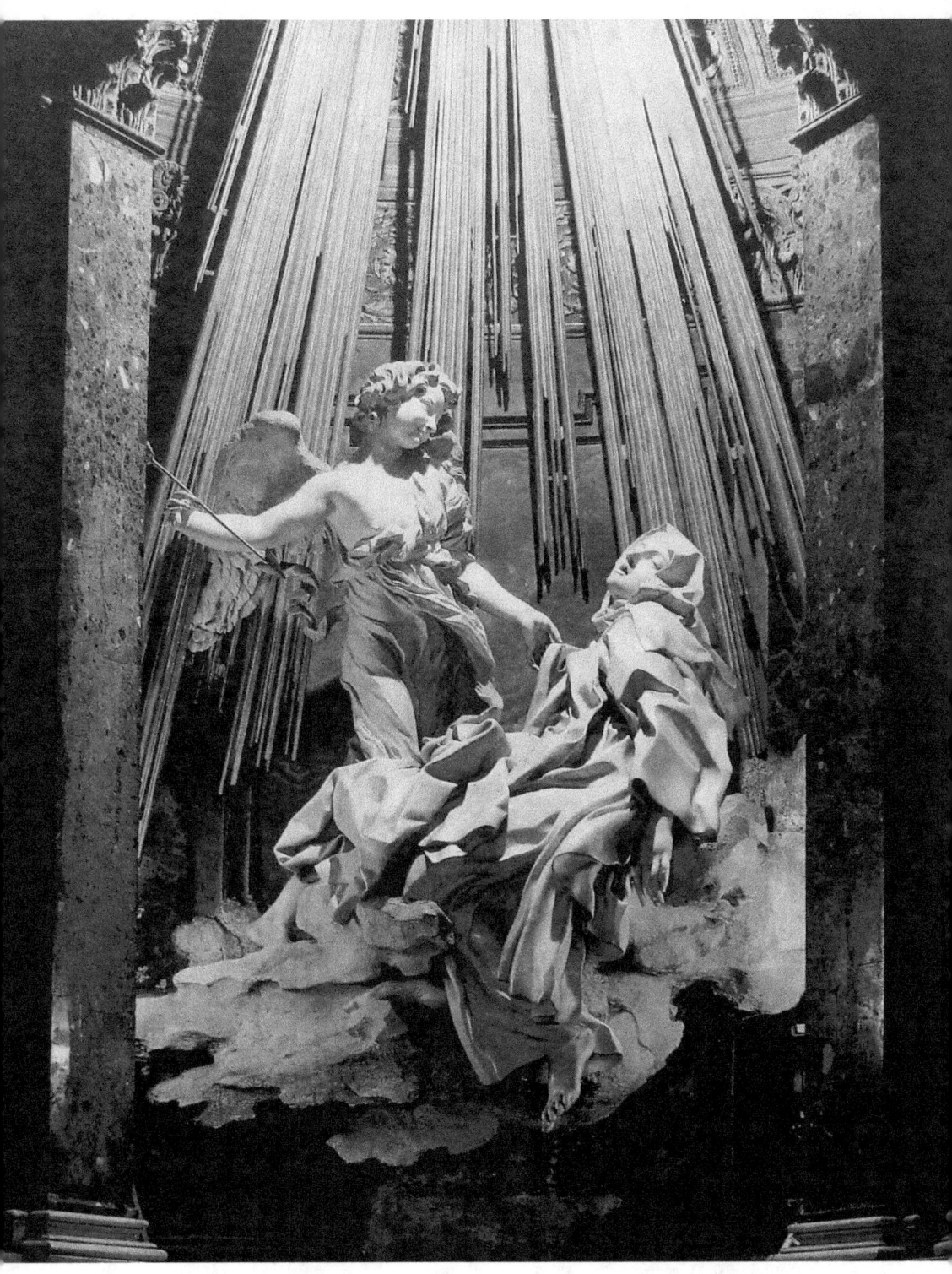

Gianlorenzo Bernini, The Ecstasy of St Theresa, 1652, Rome

FRANCESCO PARMIGIANINO:
WITCHES' SABBATH

As I've noted above, many of the 'great' artists of Renaissance and post-Renaissance art have produced 'erotic art', 'erotic art' meant for selected clients, not for mass consumption, in addition to the eroticism in their 'great' works. Thus, the 'great' Rembrandt van Rijn drew a couple copulating on a bed, Henri Fuseli drew a woman sucking the nipples of a woman, her hand on her clitoris, Francois Boucher drew half-naked people groping each other, Francesco Parmigianino drew a hilarious *Witches' Sabbath*, featuring a witch astride a gigantic phallus, Francisco de Goya drew two people sucking each other's genitals, Nicholas Géricault painted two people writhing under Caravaggesque drapes, and William Turner sketched people lovemaking.[1]

---

1 Henry Fuseli: *Lesbian Couple*, c. 1815-20, Edward Croft-Murray, London; François Boucher: *Pastoral Scene*, c. 1750s, Cary von Karwath, Vienna;Francisco de Goya (?): *Sixty-Nine*, c. 1790s, G. Lo Duca, Paris; Rembrandt: *Ledakant*, c. 1646, British Museum; J. M. W. Turner: *Sheet of Sexual Drawings*, c. 1820s, British Museum; Théodore Géricault: *Lovers*, 1815-6, oil on canvas, 24 x 32.5cm, private collection, Geneva; Francesco Parmigianino: *Witches' Sabbath*, 1530s, British Museum

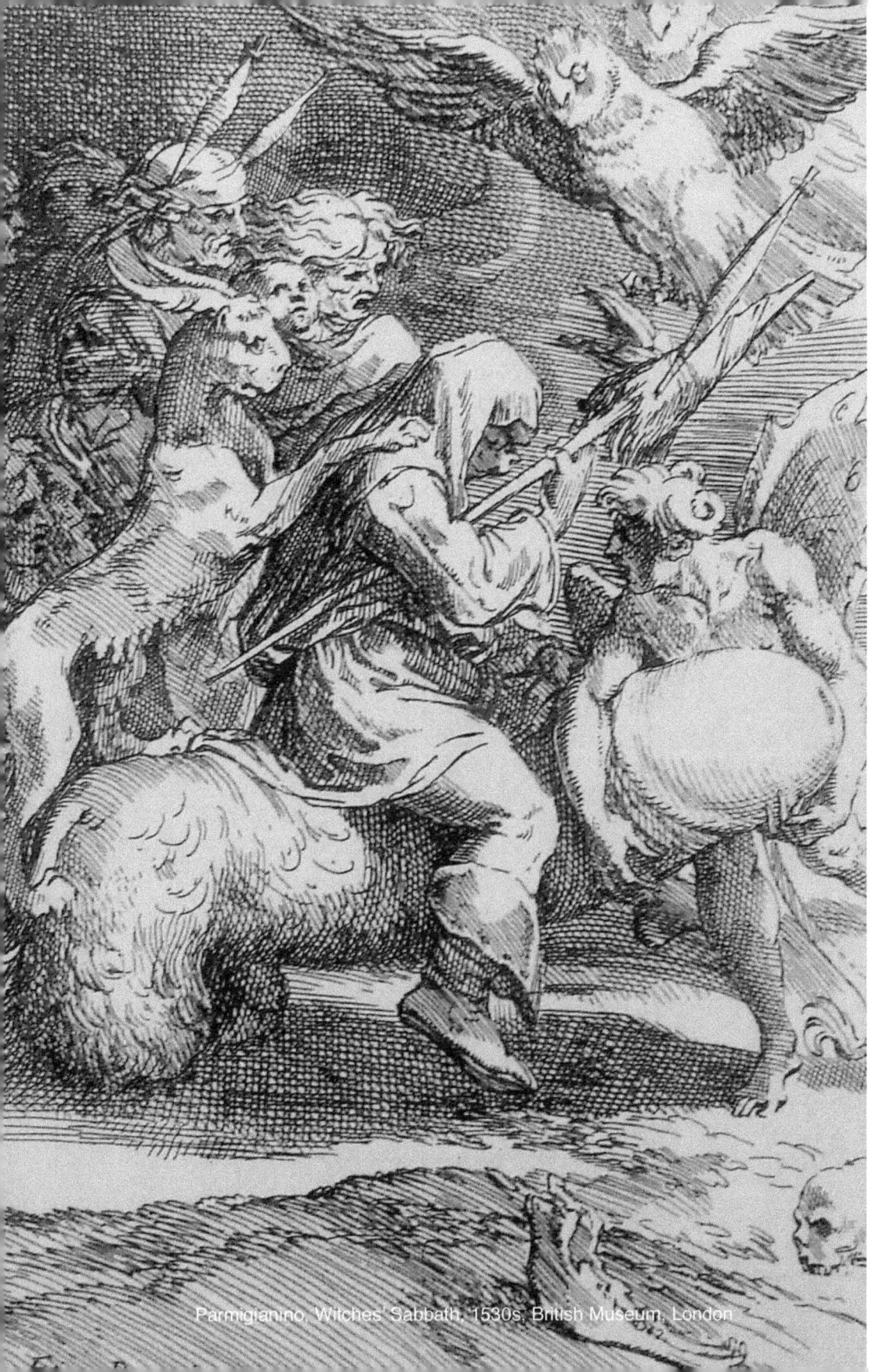

Parmigianino, Witches' Sabbath, 1530s, British Museum, London

PETER PAUL RUBENS

Painters such as Peter Paul Rubens do not hide their interest in the eroticism of art. Rubens' paintings are wild romps through fields of nakedness, through acres and acres of flesh.[1] When you see a large number of Rubens' paintings together, the effect is overwhelming: no other painter created such a shivering, trembling vision of shivering, trembling flesh. Among other post-Renaissance painters, there is a wealth of eroticism in Caravaggio, Ribera, Murillo, Tiepolo, Gentileschi, Zurbáran and Veronese.

---

1 see for instance his *Diana and Her Nymphs Surprised by Fauns*, oil, 50 x 124in, Prado, Madrid

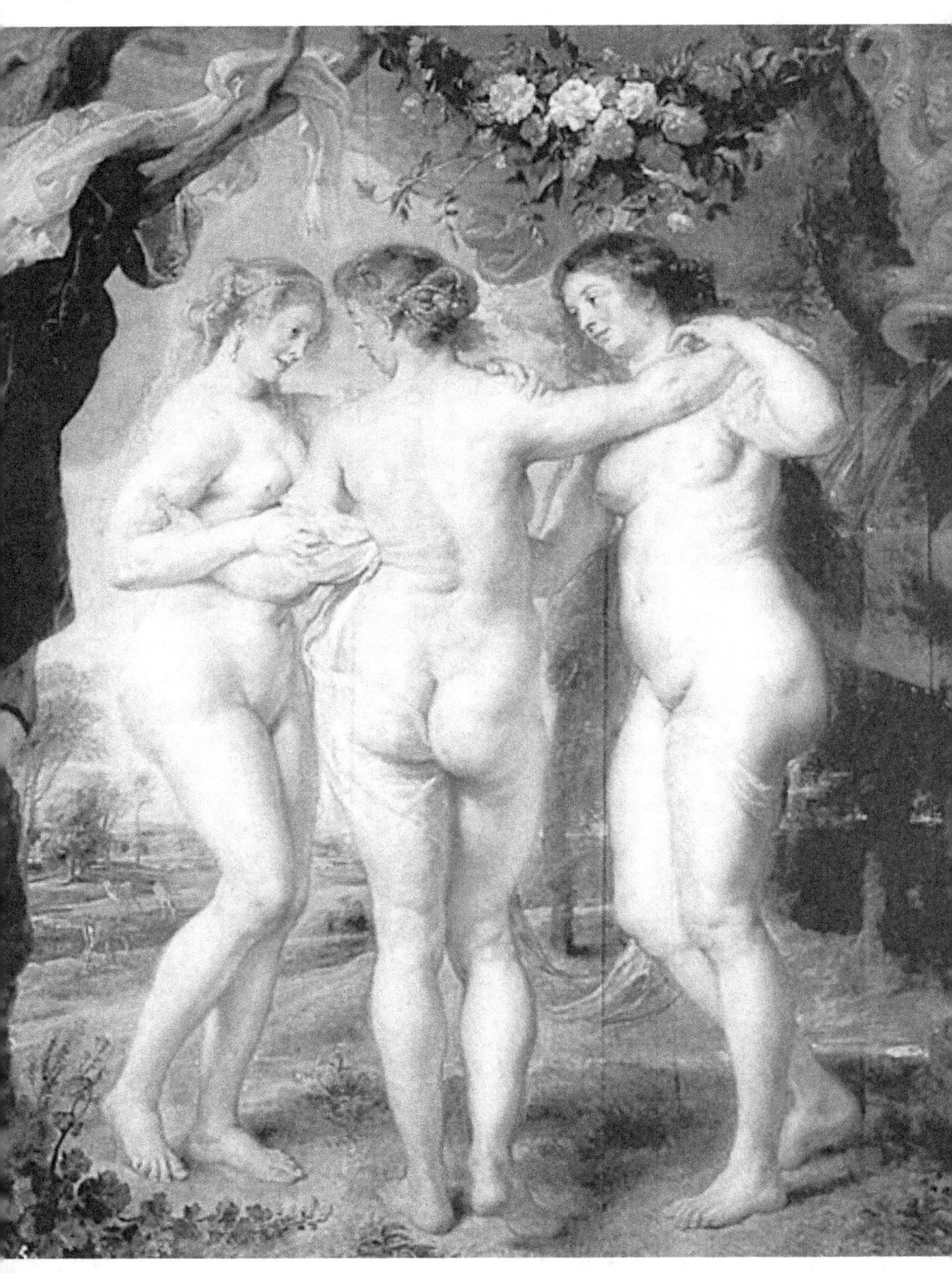

Peter Paul Rubens, The Three Graces, 1638-40, Prado, Madrid

JEAN FOUQET

An intriguing mix of the erotic and the spiritual, the sacred and the profane, occurs in Jean Fouquet's *The Melun Diptych*, where the Madonna bares her breast. This alone is not remarkable, although the breast is certainly more openly and erotically displayed, as spectacle, than in most Madonna art. The model for this voluptuous Mother of God, though, was Agnès Sorel, mistress of King Charles VII.[1]

---

1 See Marina Warner: *Alone of All Her Sex*, 203

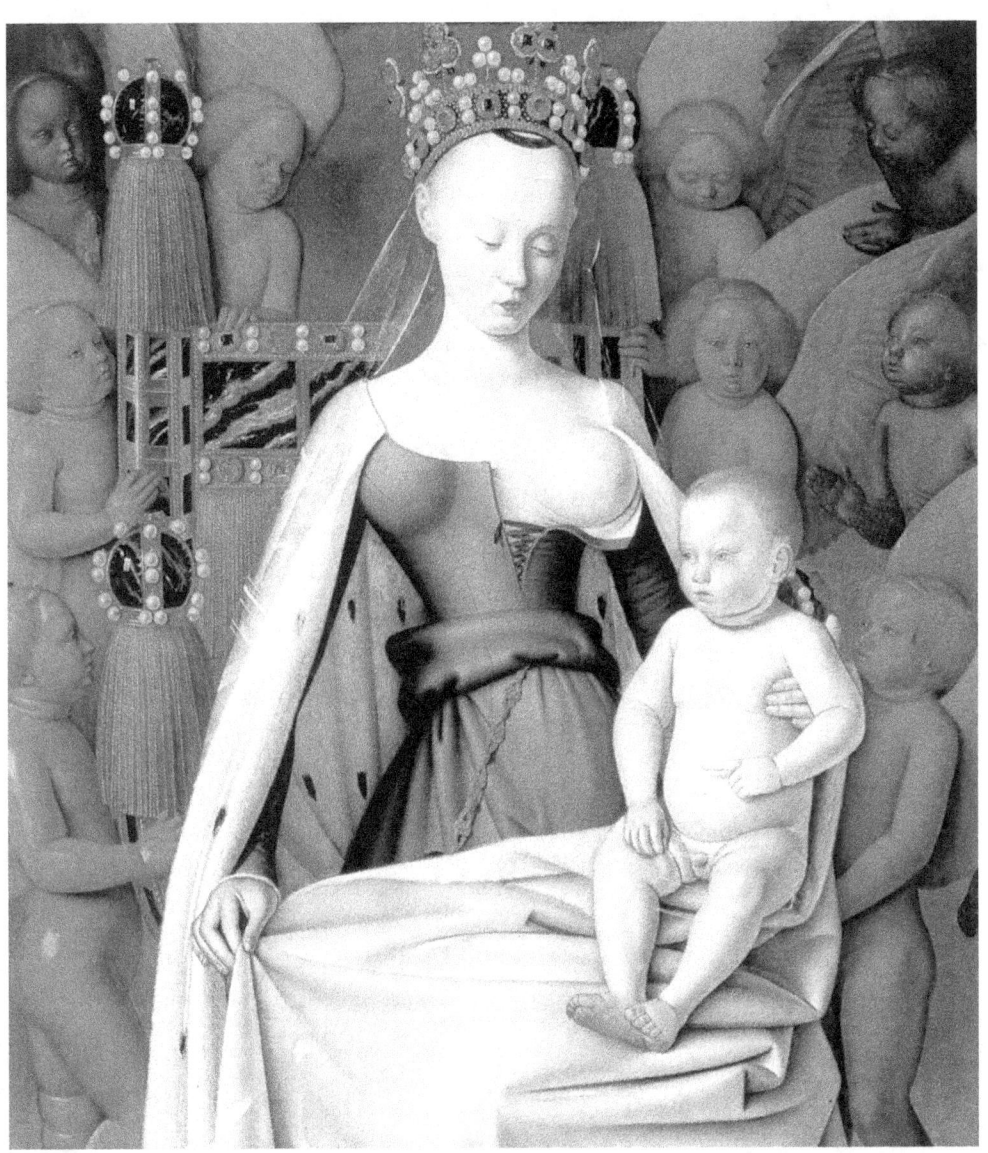

Jean Fouquet, The Melun Diptych, c. 1450

FRANCOIS BOUCHER

Erotic art may defined as simply 'æstheticized sexual representation' (L. Nead, 103), that is, erotic feelings processed through
the mechanisms of 'high culture'. For some feminists, there is no
doubt that the enjoyment of the female nude is pornographic, and
is largely inseparable from the lustful consumption of pornography. The boundaries between 'art' and 'pornography' are
being constantly blurred, constantly reset and rewritten. For
instance, Louise O'Murphy, the model for Boucher's famous nude
Mademoiselle O'Murphy, became King Louis XV's personal
prostitute (his 'mistress', as critics call them) after the King saw
Boucher's painting. The high art 'possession' or pleasure of the
female nude in Boucher's painting became the real 'possession' of
Louise O'Murphy's body. Clearly, kings can 'buy' what they
like: they can have the best art, and 'have' the best women.

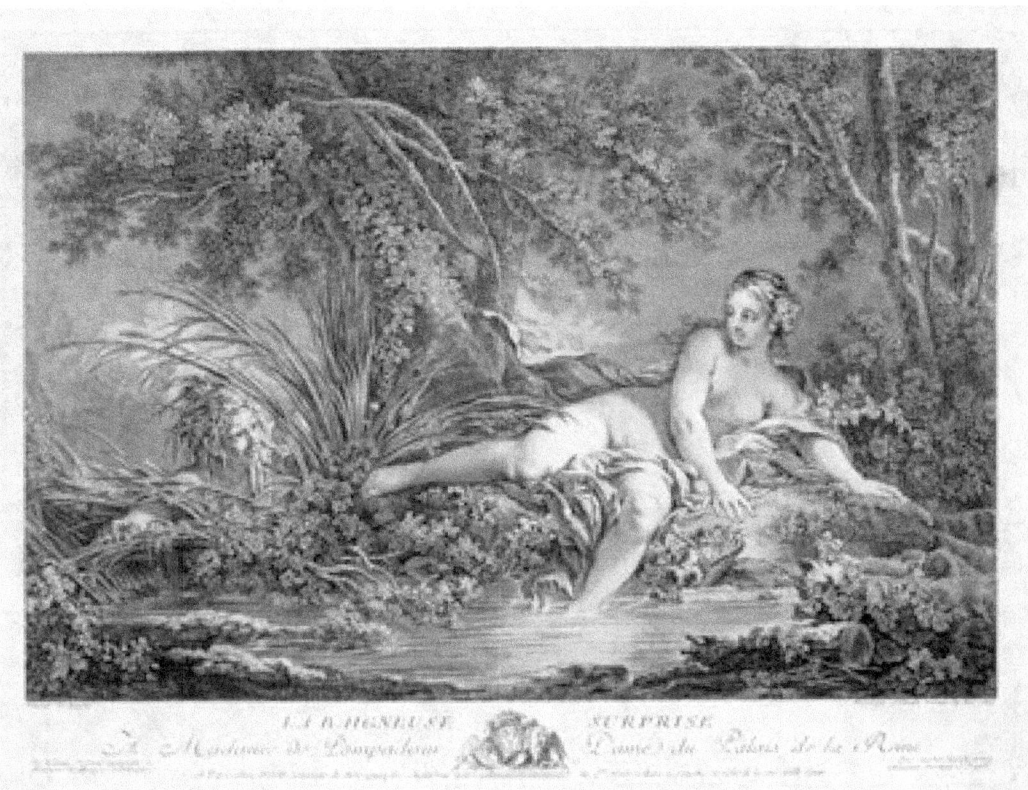

François Boucher, La Baigneuse Surprise

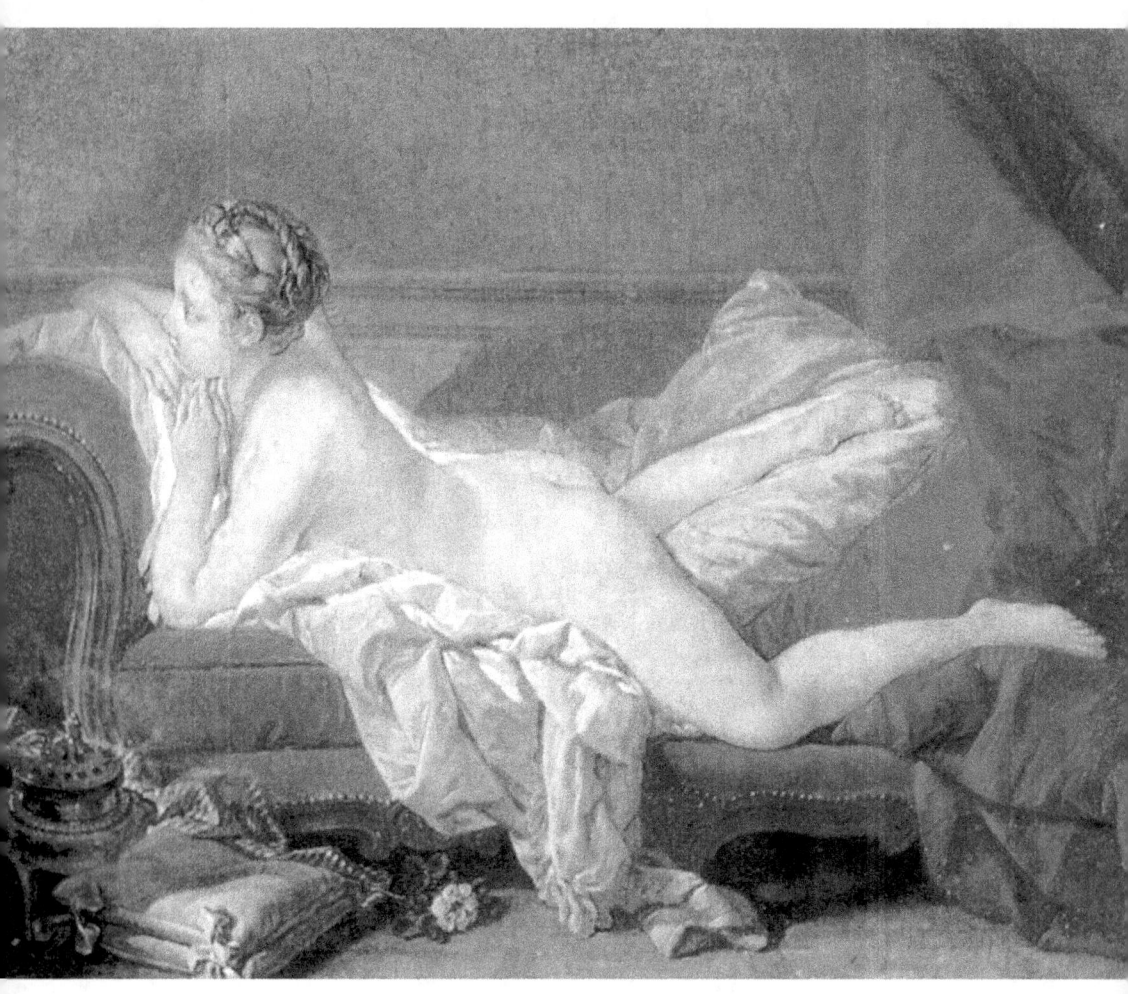

François Boucher, Madamoiselle O'Murphy, 1751

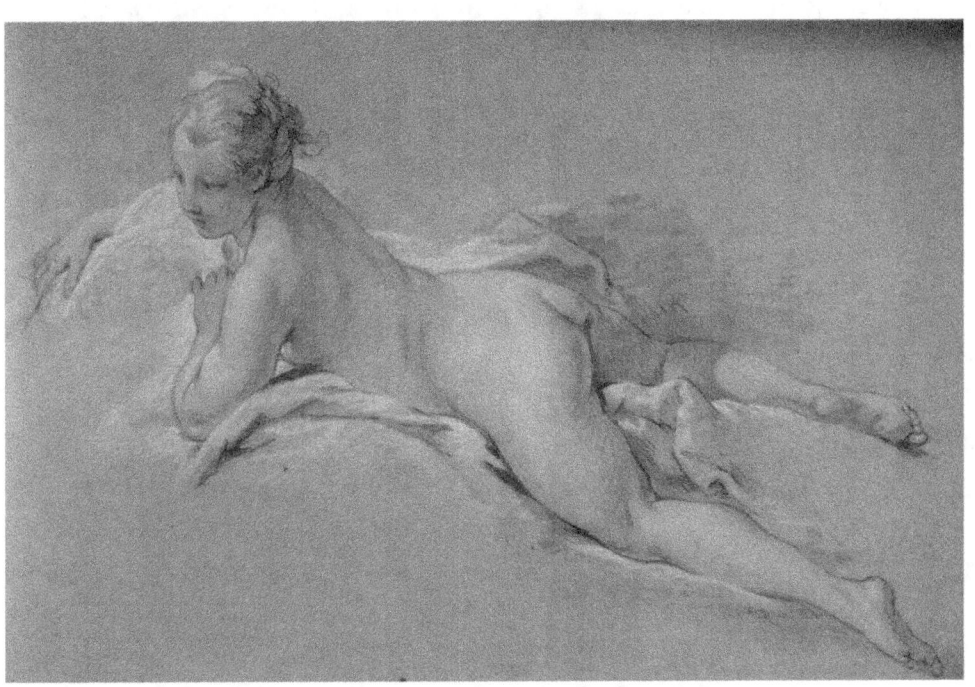

François Boucher, sketch

JOHN HENRY FUSELI

The Swiss artist John Henry Fuseli is a master of the macabre as well as the erotic. Fuseli's signature works include his *Nightmare* an influential slice of Romantic Gothic imagery. But *Sturm und Drang* art is only element in Fuseli's eccentric and individual work, which includes many erotic subjects, and nudes.

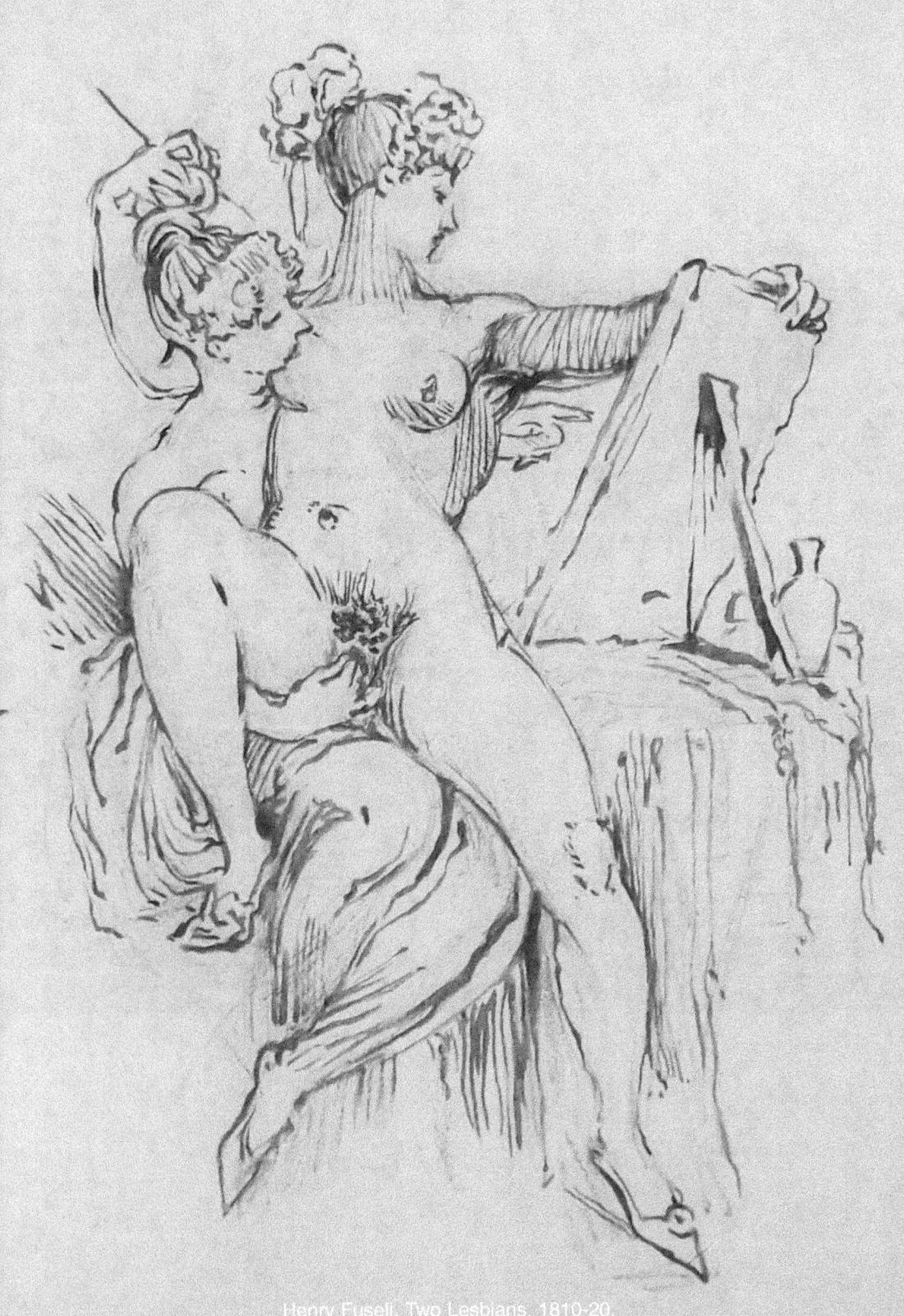

Henry Fuseli, Two Lesbians, 1810-20,
private collection

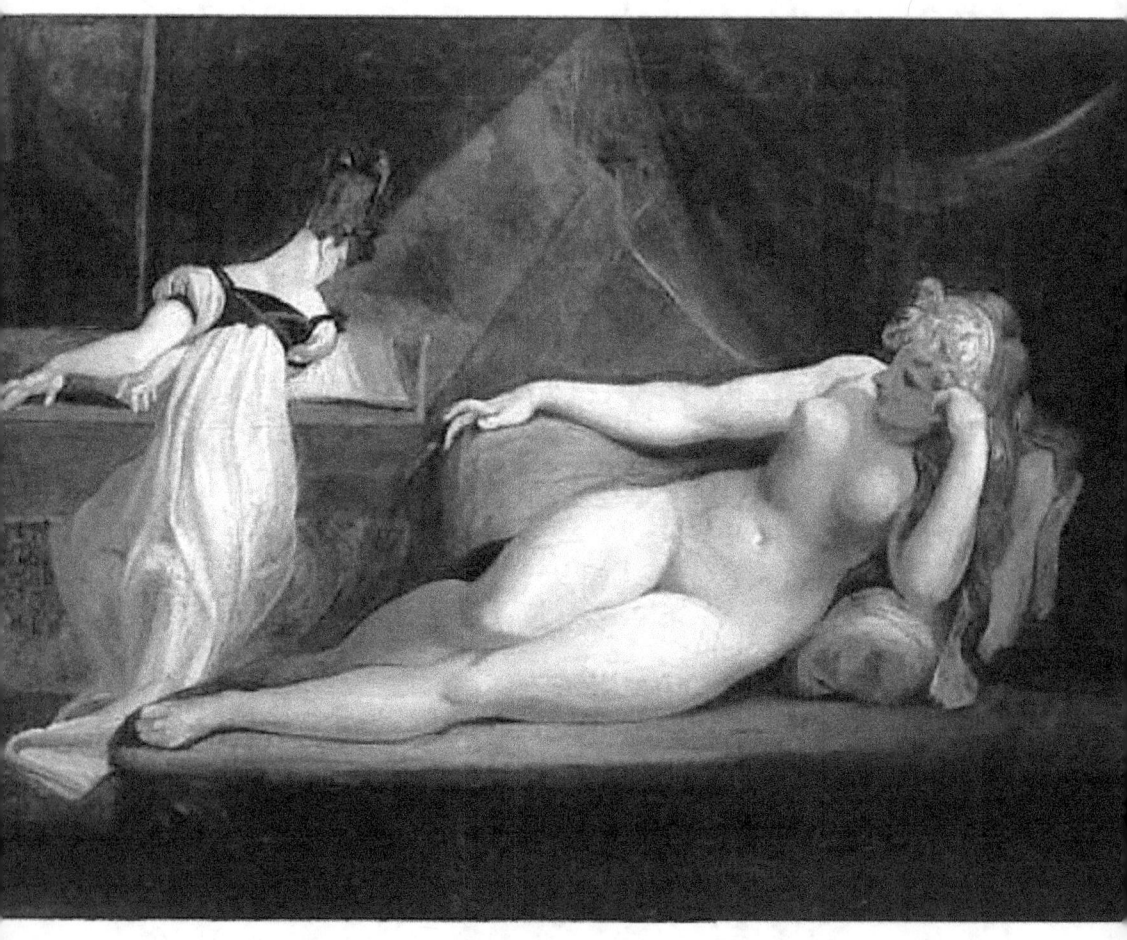

Henry Fuseli

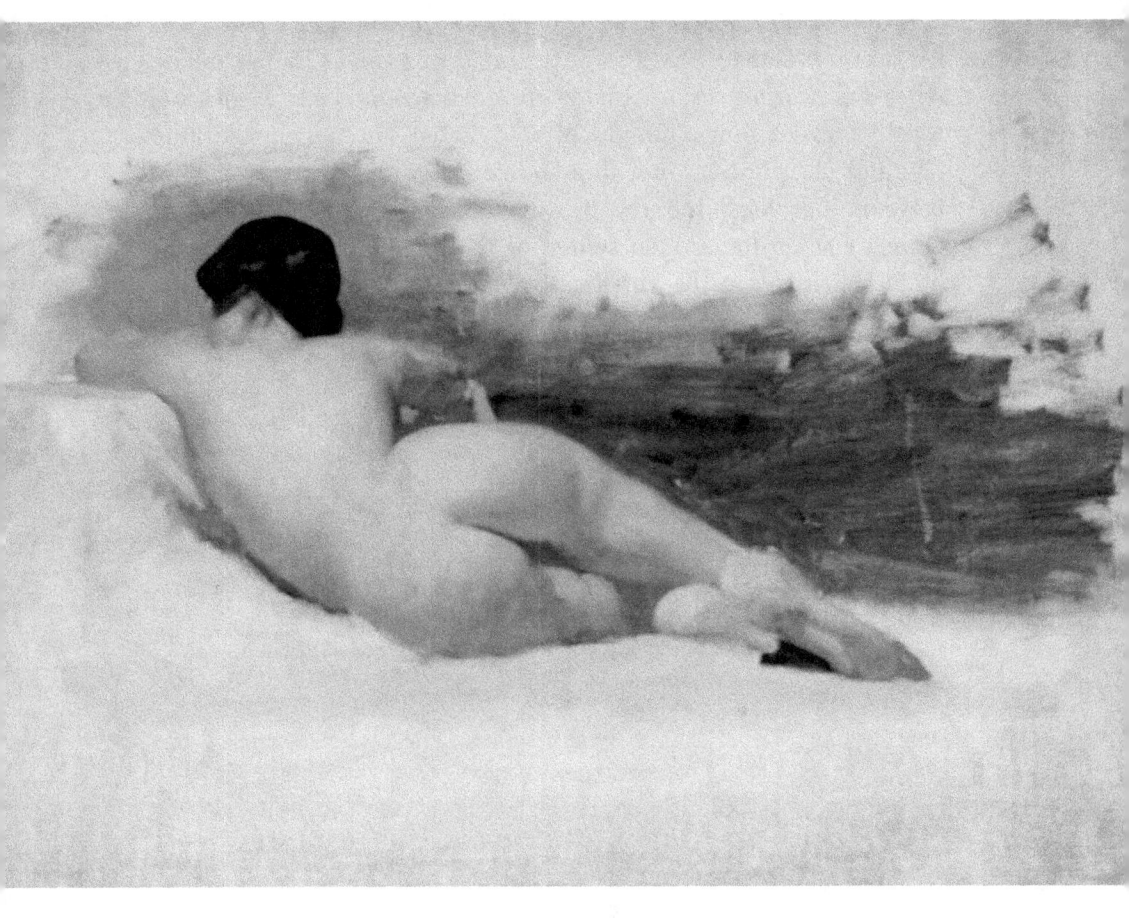

Henry Fuseli

REMBRANDT VAN RIJN

A mythic image that allowed for artists to paint a scene that
depicted nudity and eroticism, magic and heterosexual love, was
the myth of Danae. She was imprisoned in a tower by her father,
who was warned by an oracle that she would bear a son that
would murder him. The god Jupiter (Zeus) saw her, lusted after
her, and descended to her in a shower of gold, which she caught
between her legs; the result was Perseus. Painters depict the
moment when the golden semen of the phallic deity falls on the
nude Danae, as in the versions by Correggio, Titian, Rembrandt
and Mabuse.[1]

1 Rembrandt van Rijn: *The Danae*, 1636, oil on canvas, 186 x 201cm, Hermitage St Petersburg;
Titian: *Danae*, 1553-4, oil on canvas, 128 x 178cm, Prado, Madrid; Mabuse (Jan Gossaert:
Danaë, 1527, Alte Pinacothek, Munich; Correggio: *Danaë*, 1531/2, canvas, 161 x 193cm,
Borghese Gallery, Rome

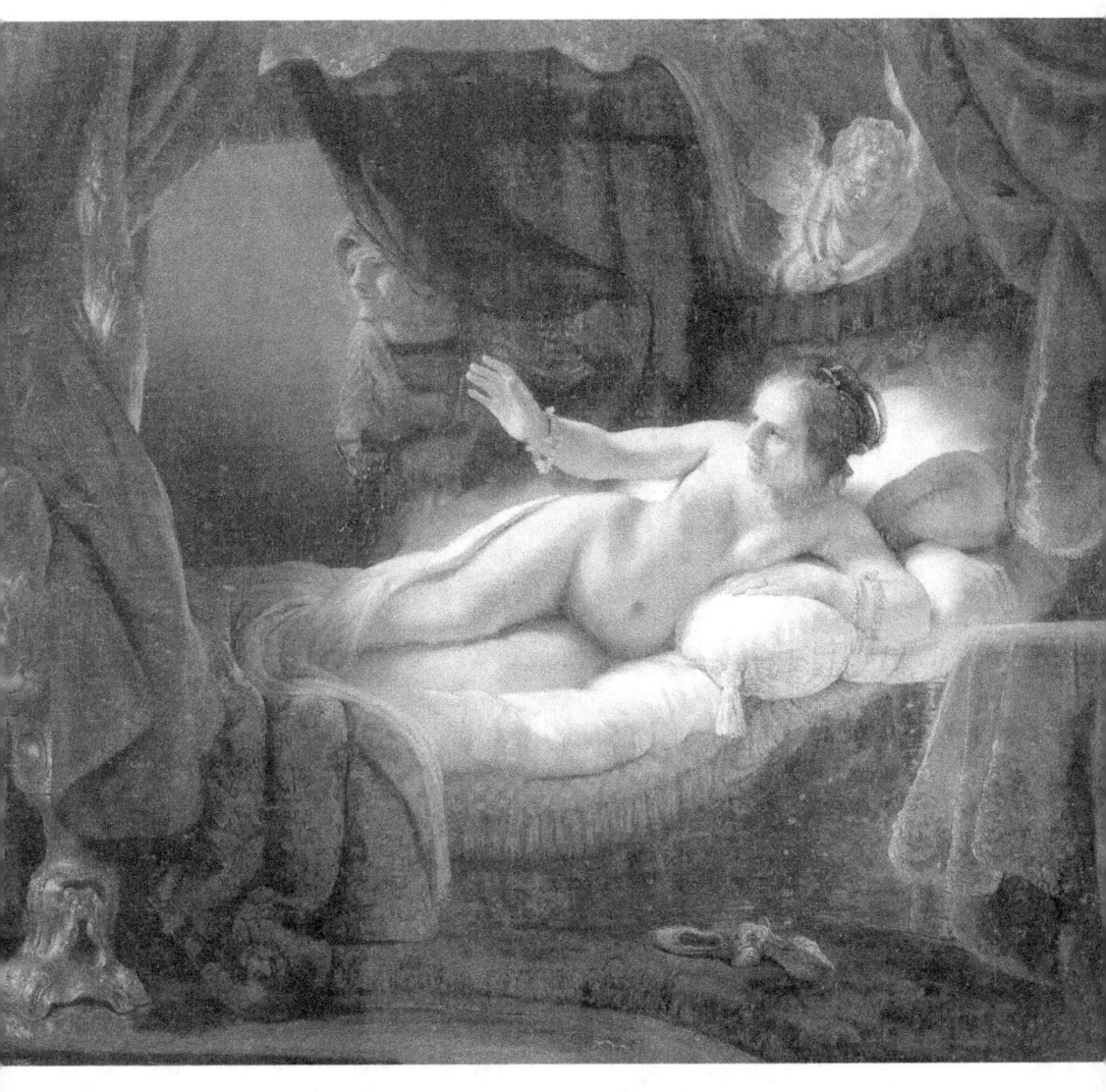

Rembrandt van Rijn, Danae, 1636, St Petersburg

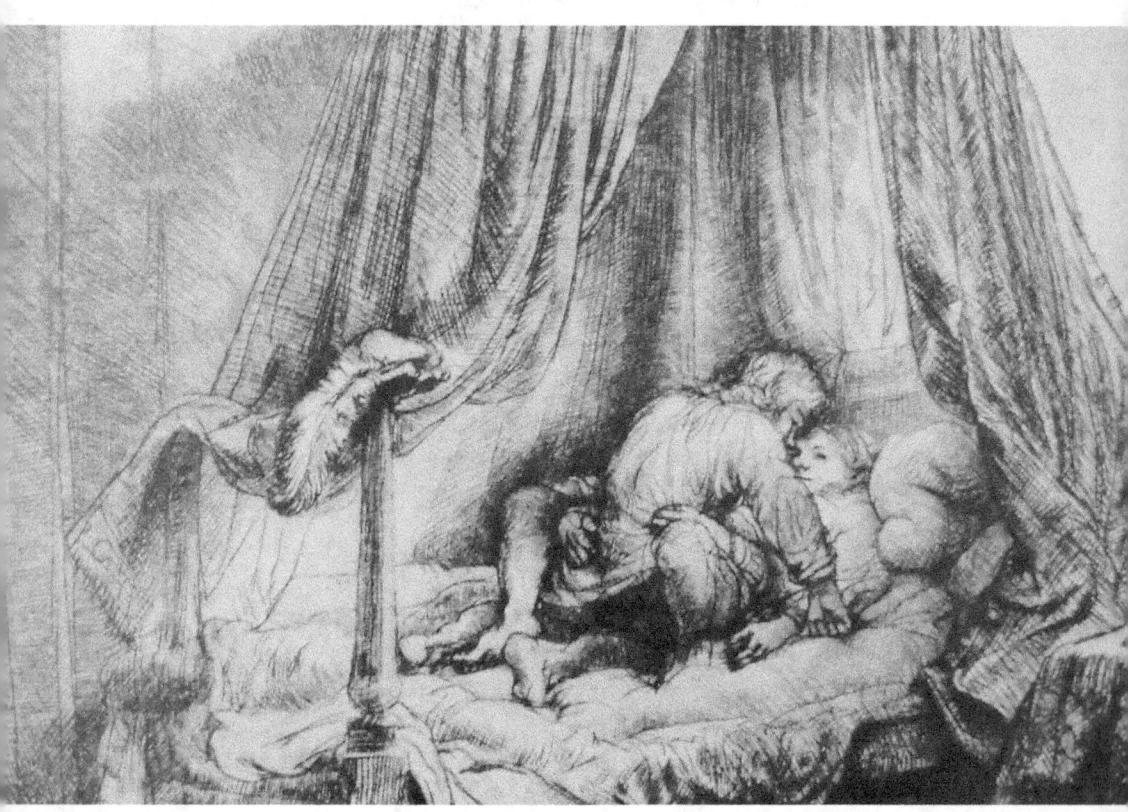

Rembrandt van Rijn, Ledakant, 1646

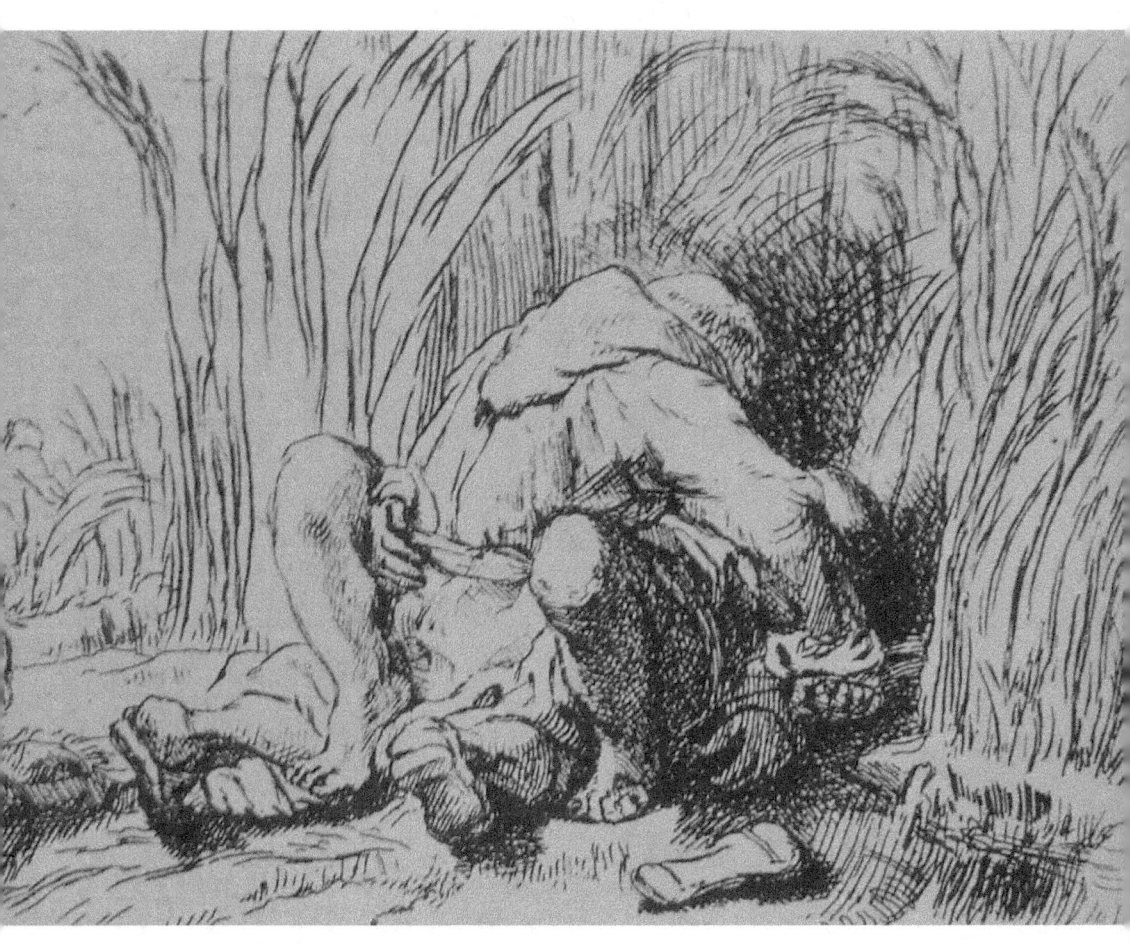

Rembrandt van Rijn, The Monk In the Cornfield

BIBLIOGRAPHY

E. de Antonio & M. Tuchman: *Painters Painting*, Abbeville Press, New York, NY, 1984

C.G. Argan: *The Renaissance*, Thames & Hudson, London, 1969

I. Armstrong, ed. *New Feminist Discourses: Critical Essays on Theories and Texts*, Routledge, London, 1992

J. Atkins: *Sex in Literature*, volume 2: *The Classical Experience of the Sexual Impulse*, Calder & Boyars, London, 1973

P. Bade: *Femme Fatale: Images of evil and fascinating women*, Ash & Grant 1979

M. Baxandall: *Painting and Experience in 15th Century Italy*, Oxford University Press 1988

—. *Patterns of Intention: On the Historical Explanation of Pictures*, Yale University Press 1985

G. Bazin: *A Concise History of World Sculpture*, David & Charles, Newton Abbot 1981

J. Beck: *Italian Renaissance Painting*, Harper & Row, New York, NY, 1981

B. Berenson: *The Italian Painters of the Renaissance*, Phaidon, London, 1952

—. *Looking at Pictures with Bernard Berenson*, selected by Hann Kiel, Abrahams, New York, NY, 1974

B. Bernard: *The Queen of Heaven: A Selection of Painting the Virgin from the Twelfth to the Eighteenth Centuries*, Macdonald/ Orbis, London, 1987

—. *The Bible and Its Painters*, Orbis, London, 1983

F. Bonner *et al*, eds. *Imagining Women Cultural Representations and Gender*, Polity Press, Cambridge 1992

S. Bramly: *Leonardo: The Artist and the Man*, Michael Joseph 1992

A. Brahama: *Italian Renaissance Painters of the Sixteenth Century*, National Gallery 1985

J. Burckhardt: *The Altarpiece in Renaissance Italy*, Phaidon, London, 1988

T. Burckhardt: *Sacred Art in East and West*, Perennial Book, Middlesex 1967

W. Chadwick: *Women, Art, and Society*, Thames & Hudson, London, 1990

—. *Women Artists and the Surrealist Movement*, Thames & Hudson, London, 1991

A. Chastel: *Art of the Italian Renaissance*, tr. P. & L. Murray, Alpine Fine Arts Collection, London, 1985

—. *The Studios and Styles of the Renaissance, Italy 1460-1500*, tr. Griffin, Thames & Hudson, London, 1966

G. Chester & J. Dickey, ed. *Feminism and Censorship: The Current Debate*, Prism Press, Bridport, Dorset 1988

H.B. Chipp, ed. *Theories of Modern Art,* University Press of California, Los Angeles, 1968

J.E. Cirlot: *A Dictionary of Symbols,* Routledge, London, 1981

Kenneth Clark. *The Nude,* Pantheon Books, 1957

B. Cole: *The Renaissance Artist at Work,* John Murray, London, 1983

J.C. Cooper: *An Illustrated Dictionary of Traditional Symbols,* Thames & Hudson, London, 1978

L. Dresen-Coenders, ed. *Saints and She-Devils: Images of Women in the 15th and 16th Centuries,* Rubicon Press 1987

W. Dube: *The Expressionists,* Thames & Hudson, London, 1972

S.C. Dubin: *Arresting Images: Impolitic Art and Uncivil Actions,* Routledge, London, 1992

G. Duby & M. Perrot: *Power and Beauty: Images of Women in Art,* Tauris Parke Books,

A. Dworkin. *Intercourse,* Arrow, London, 1988

— . *Pornography: Men Possessing Women,* Women's Press, London, 1984

C. Eisler: *Early Netherlandish Painting: The Thyssen-Bornemisza Collection,* Sotheby's Publications, London, 1989

A. Elsen: *Modern European Sculpture 1918-45,* New York, NY, 1979

J. Evans, ed. *The Flowering of the Middle Ages,* Thames & Hudson, London, 1966

J. Evola: *The Metaphysics of Sex,* East-West Publications, London, 1985

M. Foucault: *The History of Sexuality,* Penguin, London, 1981

— . *The Use of Pleasure: The History of Sexuality,* vol. 2, Penguin, London, 1987

S.J. Freedberg: *Painting of the High Renaissance in Rome and Florence,* Harper & Row, New York, NY, 1972

S. Freud: *Leonardo da Vinci,* tr. A. Tyson, Penguin, London, 1963

E. Gadon: *The Once and Future Goddess,* Aquarian Press 1990

Fred Gettings: *The Hidden Art: A Study of the Occult Symbolism in Art,* Studio Vista, London, 1978

P. Gibson & R. Gibson, ed. *Dirty Looks: Women, Pornography, Power,* British Film Institute, London, 1993

M. Gimbutas: *The Language of the Goddess,* Thames & Hudson, London, 1989

R. Goldwater & M. Treves, eds. *Artists on Art,* John Murray, London, 1975

E.H. Gombrich: *Norm and Form: Studies in the Renaissance I,* Phaidon, London, 1985

— . *Symbolic Images, Renaissance Studies II,* Phaidon, London, 1985

S. Griffin: *Pornography and Silence: Culture's Revenge Against Nature,* Women's Press, London, 1981

J. Hale: *Italian Renaissance Painting,* Phaidon, London, 1977

J. Hall: *A Dictionary of Subjects and Symbols in Art,* John Murray, London, 1984

M. Esther Harding: *Women's Mysteries,* Rider, London, 1989

F. Hartt: *History of Italian Renaissance Art: Painting, Sculpture, Architecture,* Thames & Hudson, London, 1987

N.G. Heller: *Women Artists: An Illustrated History,* Virago, London, 1987

J. Hobhouse: *The Bride Stripped Bare: The Artist and the Nude in the Twentieth Century,* Cape, London, 1988

271

A. Hollander: *Seeing Through Clothes,* Viking Press, New York, NY, 1980

M. Humm: *Feminisms: A Reader,* Harvester Wheatsheaf, 1992

—. ed. *The Dictionary of Feminist Theory,* Harvester Wheatsheaf 1989

M. Jacobs: *A Guide to European Painting,* David & Charles 1980

—. *Mythological Painting,* Phaidon 1979

P. Julian: *Dreamers of Decadence: Symbolist Painters of the 1890s,* tr. R. Baldick, Pall Mall Press, London, 1971

S. Kappeler: *The Pornography of Representation,* Polity Press, Cambridge 1986

D. Kelder: *Pageant of the Renaissance,* Pall Mall Press, London, 1969

J.A. Kestner: *Mythology and Misogyny: The Social Discourse of Nineteenth-Century British Classical-Subject Painting,* University of Wisconsin Press, Madison 1989

C. Kramarae & P.A. Treichler, eds. *A Feminist Dictionary,* Pandora Press, London, 1987

J. Kristeva: *The Kristeva Reader,* ed. Toril Moi, Blackwell 1986

—. *Desire in Language: A Semiotic Approach to Literature and Art,* ed. L. Roudiez, tr. T. Gora *et al,* Blackwell 1982

J. Lacan and the *Ecole Freudienne: Feminine Sexuality,* eds. J. Mitchell and J. Rose, Macmillan, London, 1982

A. Le Normand-Romain *et al. Sculpture: The Adventure of Modern Sculpture in the Nineteenth and Twentieth Centuries,* Skira, Geneva, 1986

L. da Vinci: *The Drawings of Leonardo da Vinci,* introduction A.E. Popham, Cape, London, 1964

M. Levey: *High Renaissance,* Penguin, London, 1975

—. *Early Renaissance,* Penguin, London, 1967

F. Licht: *Sculpture, 19th and 20th Centuries,* Michael Joseph, London, 1967

L. Lippard: *From the Center: feminist essays on women's art,* Dutton, New York, NY, 1976

—. *Six Years: The Dematerialization of the Art Object from 1966 to 1972,* Praeger, New York, NY, 1973

E. Lucie-Smith: *Symbolist Art,* Thames & Hudson, London, 1972

—. *Sexuality in Western Art,* Thames & Hudson, London, 1991

E. Marks & I. de Courtivron, eds. *New French Feminisms: an Anthology,* Harvester Wheatsheaf 1981

J.C.J. Metford: *Dictionary of Christian Lore and Legend,* Thames & Hudson, London, 1983

Michelangelo: *The Complete Paintings,* Granada, London, 1980

T. Moi: *Sexual/Textual Politics: Feminist Literary Theory,* Routledge, London, 1988

E. Mullins: *The Painted Witch: Female Body, Male Art,* Secker & Warburg, London, 1985

L. Mulvey: *Visual and Other Pleasures,* Macmillan, London, 1989

S. Munt, ed. *New Lesbian Criticism: Literary and Cultural Readings,* Harvester Wheatsheaf, London, 1992

P. & L. Murray: *The Penguin Dictionary of Art and Artists,* Penguin, London, 1976

L. Murray: *High Renaissance,* Thames & Hudson, London, 1977

L. Nead: *Female Nude: Art, Obscenity and Sexuality*, Routledge, London, 1992

E. Neumann: *The Great Mother*, Princeton University Press, NJ 1972

S. Nicholson, ed. *The Goddess Re-awakening: The Goddess Principle Today*, Theosophical Publishing House, New York, NY, 1989

J. Paladilhe. *Gustave Moreau*, Thames & Hudson, London,1972

E. Panofsky: *Studies in Iconology*, Harper & Row, New York, NY, 1972

—. *Early Netherlandish Painting*, Harvard University Press, Mass., 1953

R. Parker & G. Pollock. *Old Mistresses: Women, Art an Ideology*, Routledge & Kegan Paul, London, 1981

W. Pater: *The Renaissance*, Oxford University Press 1980

R. Payne: *Leonardo da Vinci*, Robert Hale, London, 1979

K. Petersen & J.J. Wilson: *Women Artists: Recognition and Reappraisal from the Early Middle Ages to the Twentieth Century* Women's Press, London, 1978

G. Pollock: *Vision and Difference: femininity, feminism and histories of art*, Routledge, London, 1988

M. Praz: *The Romantic Agony*, tr. Davidson, Oxford University Press 1933

Peter Redgrove. *The Black Goddess and the Sixth Sense, Bloomsbury, London, 1987*

F. Roh: *German Art in the Twentieth Century: Painting, Sculpture, Architecture*, Thames & Hudson, London, 1968

M. Roskill: *What is Art History?*, Thames & Hudson, London, 1976

G. Saunders. *The Nude: a new perspective*, Herbert Press, London, 1989

E. Showalter, ed. *The New Feminist Criticism*, Virago, London, 1986

Penelope Shuttle & Peter Redgrove. *The Wise Wound,* Paladin/ Grafton, 1978/86

M. Sjöo & B. Mor: *The Great Cosmic Mother*, Harper & Row, San Francisco 1987

F. Stella. *Working Space*, Harvard University Press, Cambridge, MA, 1986

—. *Frank Stella*, Madrid, 1995

K. Stiles & P. Selz, eds. *Theories & Documents of Contemporary Art: A Sourcebook of Artists' Writings*, University of California Press, Berkeley, CA, 1996

V.I. Stoichita: *Leonardo da Vinci*, Abbey Library, London, 1978

S. Rubin Suleiman, ed. *The Female Body in Western Culture: Contemporary Perspectives*, Harvard University Press, Cambridge, Mass., 1986

William Thompson. *The Time Falling Bodies Take to Light: Mythology, Sexuality and the Origins of Culture,* St Martin's Press, New York, NY, 1981

A. Tilly: *Erotic Drawings*, Phaidon 1986

P. Trevor-Roper: *The world blunted through sight: An inquiry into the influence of defective vision on art and character*, Thames & Hudson, London, 1970

W. Tucker. *The Language of Sculpture*, Thames & Hudson, London, 1974

L. Venturi: *Renaissance Painting, from Leonardo to Dürer,* Skira/ Macmillan 1979

—. *Italian Paintings,* Zwemmer, London, 1950

G. de Vries, ed. *On Art: Artists' Writings on the Changed Notion of Art After, 1965,* Cologne, 1974

B. Walker: *Body Magic*, Paladin, London, 1979

Marina Warner. *Alone Of All Her Sex: The Myth and Cult of the Virgin Mary*, Picador, London, 1985

—. *Monuments and Maidens*, Weidenfeld & Nicolson, London, 1985

Valerie Wayne, ed. *The Matter of Difference: Materialist Feminist Criticism of Shakespeare*, Harvester Wheatsheaf, Hemel Hempstead, 1991

P. Webb: *The Erotic Arts*, Secker & Warburg, London, 1983

D. Wheeler: *Art Since Mid-Century: 1945 to the Present*, Thames & Hudson, London, 1991

L. Williams: *Hard Core*: Power, *Pleasure, and the 'Frenzy of the Visible'*, Pandora, London, 1990

C. Wilson: *The Sexual Misfits: A Study of Sexual Outsiders*, Collins, London, 1989

H. Wolfflin: *Classic Art*, Phaidon 1952/80

M. Wudram: *Art of the Renaissance*, Weidenfeld & Nicolson, London, 1985

WEBSITES

eroticbibliophile.com
eroti-cart.com
deltaofvenus.com
erotomane.org

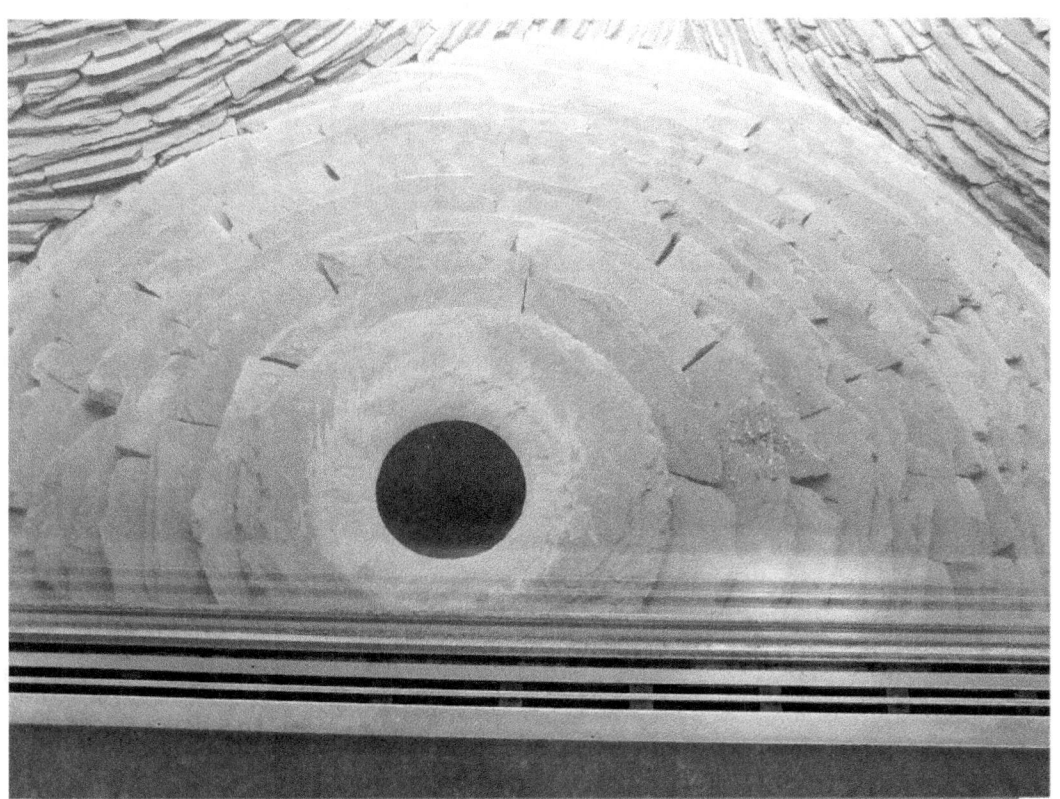

andy goldsworthy
touching nature

WILLIAM MALPAS

Contemporary British sculptor Andy Goldsworthy makes land and
environmental art, a sensitive, intuitive response to nature, light, time,
growth, change, the seasons and the earth. Goldsworthy's sculpture is
becoming ever more popular, appearing in TV documentaries, public works,
and Holocaust memorials. Goldsworthy has exhibited around the world, and
has become one of the foremost contemporary sculptors in Great Britain.

The book has been updated and revised for this new edition.

ISBN 9781861714122 Pbk   ISBN 9781861714138 Hbk
Fully illustrated   www.crmoon.com

MAURICE SENDAK

& the art of children's book illustration

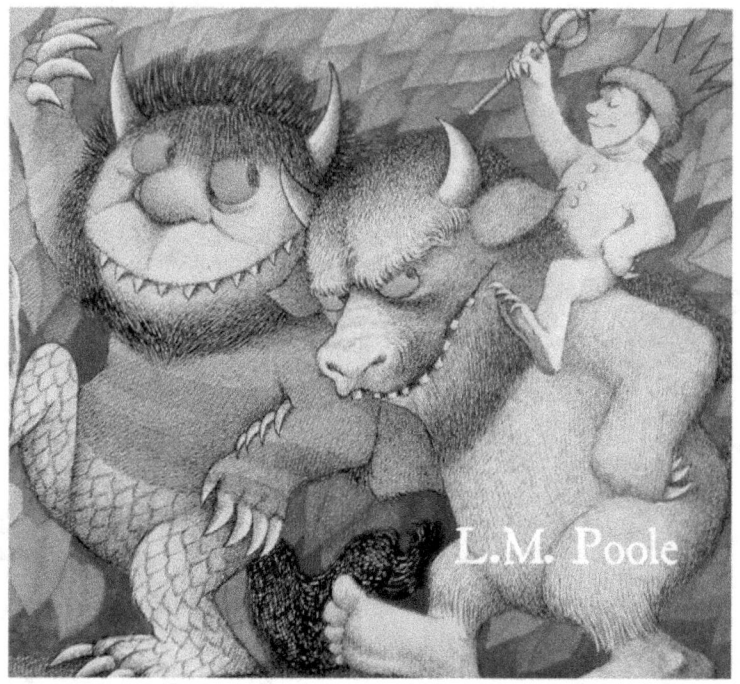

L.M. Poole

Maurice Sendak is the widely acclaimed American children's book author and illustrator. This critical study focuses on his famous trilogy, *Where the Wild Things Are, In the Night Kitchen* and *Outside Over There*, as well as the early works and Sendak's superb depictions of the Grimm Brothers' fairy tales in *The Juniper Tree*. L.M. Poole begins with a chapter on children's book illustration, in particular the treatment of fairy tales. Sendak's work is situated within the history of children's book illustration, and he is compared with many contemporary authors.

Fully illustrated. The book has been revised and updated for this edition.
ISBN 9781861714282 Pbk   ISBN 9781861713469 Hbk

Beauties, Beasts, and Enchantment

CLASSIC FRENCH FAIRY TALES

Translated and with an Introduction
by Jack Zipes

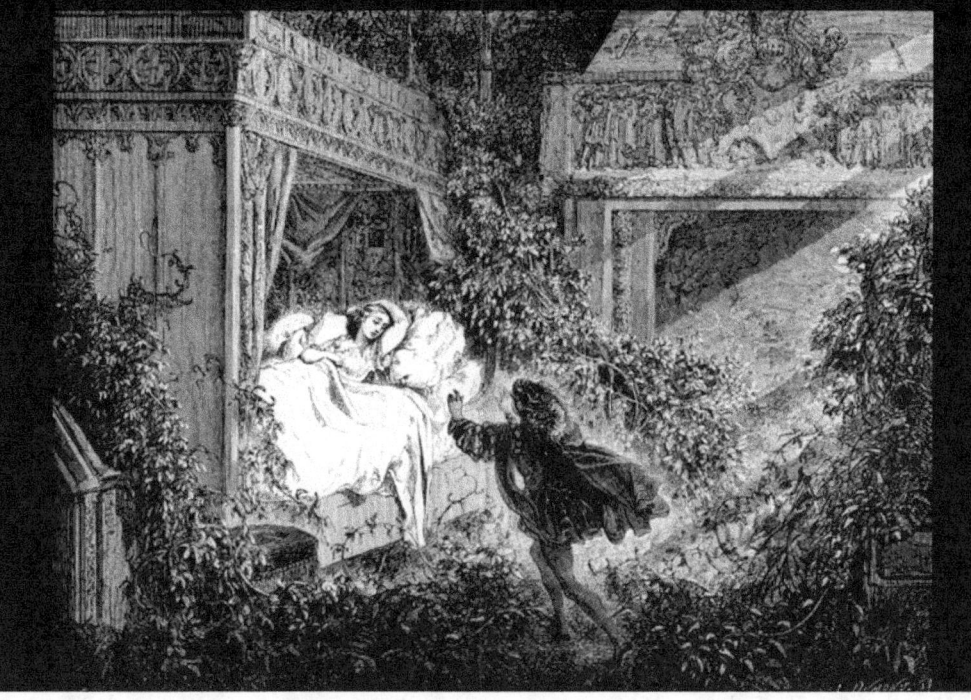

A collection of 36 classic French fairy tales translated by renowned writer Jack Zipes.
Cinderella, Beauty and the Beast, Sleeping Beauty and *Little Red Riding Hood* are among the
classic fairy tales in this amazing book.
Includes illustrations from fairy tale collections.
Jack Zipes has written and published widely on fairy tales.

'Terrific... a succulent array of 17th and 18th century 'salon' fairy tales'
- *The New York Times Book Review*

'These tales are adventurous, thrilling in a way fairy tales are meant to be... The translation
from the French is modern, happily free of archaic and hyperbolic language... a fine and
sophisticated collection' - *New York Tribune*

'Enjoyable to read... a unique collection of French regional folklore' - *Library Journal*

'Charming stories accompanied by attractive pen-and-ink drawings' - *Chattanooga Times*

Introduction and illustrations   612pp.   ISBN 9781861712510 Pbk   ISBN 9781861713193 Hbk

CRESCENT MOON PUBLISHING

web: www.crmoon.com e-mail: cresmopub@yahoo.co.uk

ARTS, PAINTING, SCULPTURE

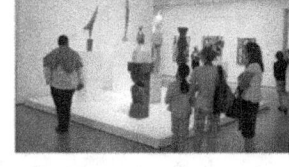
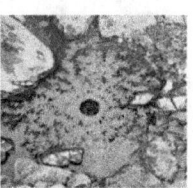
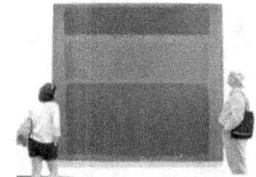

The Art of Andy Goldsworthy
Andy Goldsworthy: Touching Nature
Andy Goldsworthy in Close-Up
Andy Goldsworthy: Pocket Guide
Andy Goldsworthy In America
Land Art: A Complete Guide
The Art of Richard Long
Richard Long: Pocket Guide
Land Art In the UK
Land Art in Close-Up
Land Art In the U.S.A.
Land Art: Pocket Guide
Installation Art in Close-Up
Minimal Art and Artists In the 1960s and After
Colourfield Painting
Land Art DVD, TV documentary
Andy Goldsworthy DVD, TV documentary
The Erotic Object: Sexuality in Sculpture From Prehistory to the Present Day
Sex in Art: Pornography and Pleasure in Painting and Sculpture
Postwar Art
Sacred Gardens: The Garden in Myth, Religion and Art
Glorification: Religious Abstraction in Renaissance and 20th Century Art
Early Netherlandish Painting
Leonardo da Vinci
Piero della Francesca
Giovanni Bellini
Fra Angelico: Art and Religion in the Renaissance
Mark Rothko: The Art of Transcendence
Frank Stella: American Abstract Artist
Jasper Johns
Brice Marden
Alison Wilding: The Embrace of Sculpture
Vincent van Gogh: Visionary Landscapes
Eric Gill: Nuptials of God
Constantin Brancusi: Sculpting the Essence of Things
Max Beckmann
Caravaggio
Gustave Moreau
Egon Schiele: Sex and Death In Purple Stockings
Delizioso Fotografico Fervore: Works In Process I
Sacro Cuore: Works In Process 2
The Light Eternal: J.M.W. Turner
The Madonna Glorified: Karen Arthurs

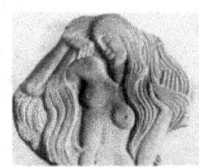
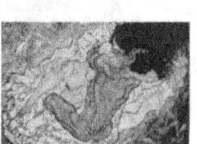
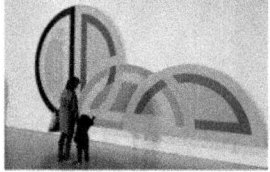
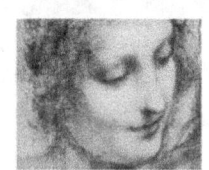
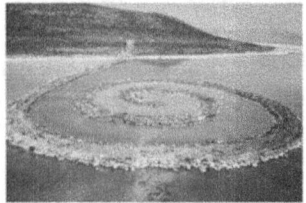

LITERATURE

J.R.R. Tolkien: The Books, The Films, The Whole Cultural Phenomenon
J.R.R. Tolkien: Pocket Guide
Tolkien's Heroic Quest
The *Earthsea* Books of Ursula Le Guin
Beauties, Beasts and Enchantment: Classic French Fairy Tales
German Popular Stories by the Brothers Grimm
Philip Pullman and *His Dark Materials*
Sexing Hardy: Thomas Hardy and Feminism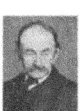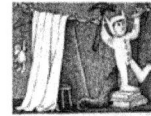
Thomas Hardy's *Tess of the d'Urbervilles*
Thomas Hardy's *Jude the Obscure*
Thomas Hardy: The Tragic Novels
Love and Tragedy: Thomas Hardy
The Poetry of Landscape in Hardy
Wessex Revisited: Thomas Hardy and John Cowper Powys
Wolfgang Iser: Essays and Interviews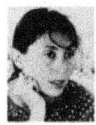
Petrarch, Dante and the Troubadours
Maurice Sendak and the Art of Children's Book Illustration
Andrea Dworkin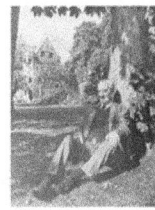
Cixous, Irigaray, Kristeva: The *Jouissance* of French Feminism
Julia Kristeva: Art, Love, Melancholy, Philosophy, Semiotics and Psychoanalysis
Hélène Cixous I Love You: The *Jouissance* of Writing
Luce Irigaray: Lips, Kissing, and the Politics of Sexual Difference
Peter Redgrove: Here Comes the Flood
Peter Redgrove: Sex-Magic-Poetry-Cornwall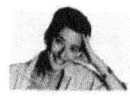
Lawrence Durrell: Between Love and Death, East and West
Love, Culture & Poetry: Lawrence Durrell
Cavafy: Anatomy of a Soul
German Romantic Poetry: Goethe, Novalis, Heine, Hölderlin
Feminism and Shakespeare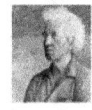
Shakespeare: Love, Poetry & Magic
The Passion of D.H. Lawrence
D.H. Lawrence: Symbolic Landscapes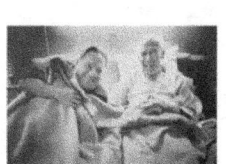
D.H. Lawrence: Infinite Sensual Violence
Rimbaud: Arthur Rimbaud and the Magic of Poetry
The Ecstasies of John Cowper Powys
Sensualism and Mythology: The Wessex Novels of John Cowper Powys
Amorous Life: John Cowper Powys and the Manifestation of Affectivity (H.W. Fawkner)
Postmodern Powys: New Essays on John Cowper Powys (Joe Boulter)
Rethinking Powys: Critical Essays on John Cowper Powys
Paul Bowles & Bernardo Bertolucci
Rainer Maria Rilke
Joseph Conrad: *Heart of Darkness*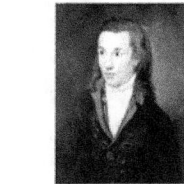
In the Dim Void: Samuel Beckett
Samuel Beckett Goes into the Silence
André Gide: Fiction and Fervour
Jackie Collins and the Blockbuster Novel
Blinded By Her Light: The Love-Poetry of Robert Graves
The Passion of Colours: Travels In Mediterranean Lands
Poetic Forms

POETRY

Ursula Le Guin: Walking In Cornwall
Peter Redgrove: Here Comes The Flood
Peter Redgrove: Sex-Magic-Poetry-Cornwall
Dante: Selections From the Vita Nuova
Petrarch, Dante and the Troubadours
William Shakespeare: Sonnets
William Shakespeare: Complete Poems
Blinded By Her Light: The Love-Poetry of Robert Graves
Emily Dickinson: Selected Poems
Emily Brontë: Poems
Thomas Hardy: Selected Poems
Percy Bysshe Shelley: Poems
John Keats: Selected Poems
Joh n Keats: Poems of 1820
D.H. Lawrence: Selected Poems
Edmund Spenser: Poems
Edmund Spenser: Amoretti
John Donne: Poems
Henry Vaughan: Poems
Sir Thomas Wyatt: Poems
Robert Herrick: Selected Poems
Rilke: Space, Essence and Angels in the Poetry of Rainer Maria Rilke
Rainer Maria Rilke: Selected Poems
Friedrich Hölderlin: Selected Poems
Arseny Tarkovsky: Selected Poems
Arthur Rimbaud: Selected Poems
Arthur Rimbaud: A Season in Hell
Arthur Rimbaud and the Magic of Poetry
Novalis: Hymns To the Night
German Romantic Poetry
Paul Verlaine: Selected Poems
Elizaethan Sonnet Cycles
D.J. Enright: By-Blows
Jeremy Reed: Brigitte's Blue Heart
Jeremy Reed: Claudia Schiffer's Red Shoes
Gorgeous Little Orpheus
Radiance: New Poems
Crescent Moon Book of Nature Poetry
Crescent Moon Book of Love Poetry
Crescent Moon Book of Mystical Poetry
Crescent Moon Book of Elizabethan Love Poetry
Crescent Moon Book of Metaphysical Poetry
Crescent Moon Book of Romantic Poetry
Pagan America: New American Poetry

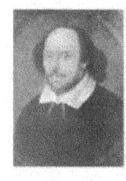
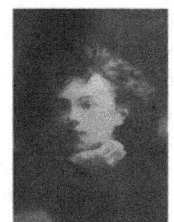
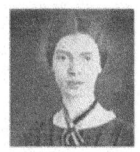
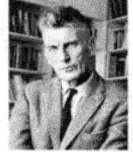
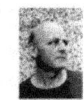
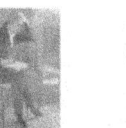
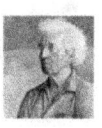
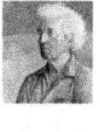
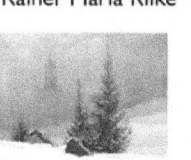
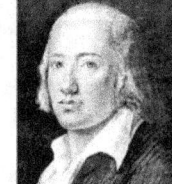
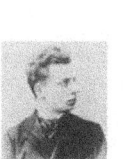
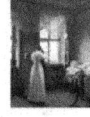
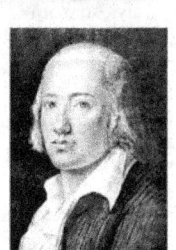

MEDIA, CINEMA, FEMINISM and CULTURAL STUDIES

J.R.R. Tolkien: The Books, The Films, The Whole Cultural Phenomenon
J.R.R. Tolkien: Pocket Guide
The *Lord of the Rings* Movies: Pocket Guide
The Cinema of Hayao Miyazaki
Hayao Miyazaki: *Princess Mononoke*: Pocket Movie Guide
Hayao Miyazaki: *Spirited Away*: Pocket Movie Guide
Tim Burton : Hallowe'en For Hollywood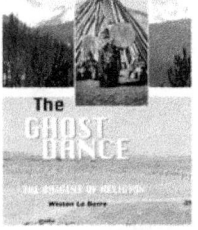
Ken Russell
Ken Russell: *Tommy*: Pocket Movie Guide
The Ghost Dance: The Origins of Religion
The Peyote Cult
Cixous, Irigaray, Kristeva: The *Jouissance* of French Feminism
Julia Kristeva: Art, Love, Melancholy, Philosophy, Semiotics and Psychoanalysis
Luce Irigaray: Lips, Kissing, and the Politics of Sexual Difference
Hélene Cixous I Love You: The *Jouissance* of Writing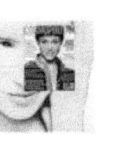
Andrea Dworkin
'Cosmo Woman': The World of Women's Magazines
Women in Pop Music
HomeGround: The Kate Bush Anthology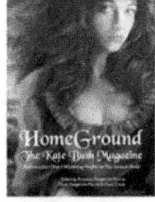
Discovering the Goddess (Geoffrey Ashe)
The Poetry of Cinema
The Sacred Cinema of Andrei Tarkovsky
Andrei Tarkovsky: Pocket Guide
Andrei Tarkovsky: *Mirror*: Pocket Movie Guide
Andrei Tarkovsky: *The Sacrifice*: Pocket Movie Guide
Walerian Borowczyk: Cinema of Erotic Dreams
Jean-Luc Godard: The Passion of Cinema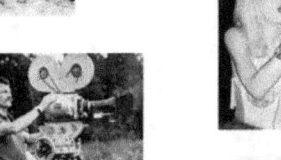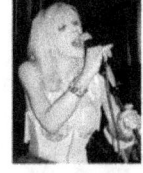
Jean-Luc Godard: *Hail Mary*: Pocket Movie Guide
Jean-Luc Godard: *Contempt*: Pocket Movie Guide
Jean-Luc Godard: *Pierrot le Fou*: Pocket Movie Guide
John Hughes and Eighties Cinema
Ferris Bueller's Day Off: Pocket Movie Guide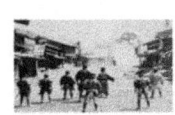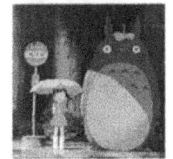
Jean-Luc Godard: Pocket Guide
The Cinema of Richard Linklater
Liv Tyler: Star In Ascendance
Blade Runner and the Films of Philip K. Dick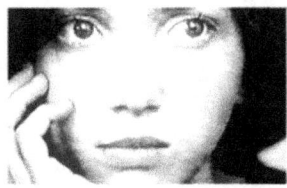
Paul Bowles and Bernardo Bertolucci
Media Hell: Radio, TV and the Press
An Open Letter to the BBC
Detonation Britain: Nuclear War in the UK
Feminism and Shakespeare
Wild Zones: Pornography, Art and Feminism
Sex in Art: Pornography and Pleasure in Painting and Sculpture
Sexing Hardy: Thomas Hardy and Feminism

The Light Eternal is a model monograph, an exemplary job. The subject matter of the book is beautifully organised and dead on beam. (Lawrence Durrell)
It is amazing for me to see my work treated with such passion and respect. (Andrea Dworkin)

CRESCENT MOON PUBLISHING
P.O. Box 1312, Maidstone, Kent, ME14 5XU, Great Britain. www.crmoon.com

cresmopub@yahoo.co.uk   www.crescentmoon.org.uk